To the Sea

Tony Meisel

To the Sea

SAGAS OF SURVIVAL AND
TALES OF EPIC CHALLENGE
ON THE SEVEN SEAS

BLACK DOG
& LEVENTHAL
PUBLISHERS
NEW YORK

Copyright © 2000 Black Dog & Leventhal Publishers, Inc.

Published by
Black Dog & Leventhal Publishers, Inc.
151 W 19th Street
New York, NY 10011

Distributed by
Workman Publishing Company
708 Broadway
New York, NY 10003

Designed by Dutton & Sherman
Book Manufactured in Hong Kong

ISBN: 1-57912-113-6
h g f e d c b a

Library of Congress CIP data is on file at the offices of Black Dog & Leventhal.

Contents

To Judi, who put up with countless sailing adventures, both real and imaginary; and to the men and women who brave the oceans.

I must go down to the sea again, to the lonely
  sea and the sky,
And all I ask is a tall ship and a star to steer
  her by,
And the wheel's kick and the wind's song
  and the white sails shaking,
And a gray mist on the sea's face and a gray
  dawn breaking.

—John Masefield

Acknowledgments

The writing, editing, and design of this book was a long voyage undertaken in a record-breaking passage. It would not have been possible without the involvement and aid of several extraordinary people. I should like to thank Jennifer Savage and Jenny Wierschem for expertise and speed in copyediting, Mark Blaine for his help in writing the biographies, Kim Mangun for photo research, Debbie Dutton and Joseph Sherman for flexibility and finesse in design.

I especially want to extend my appreciation to J.P. Leventhal for asking me to undertake this project and Jessica MacMurray for exquisite editorial guidance.

Introduction

As a child on Martha's Vineyard, my father taught me to sail the family catboat by the simple expedient of putting me aboard in the middle of Vineyard Haven harbor and unshipping the rudder, which he smilingly stowed in the skiff he was rowing. His command? Sail to shore. Since I was five years old at the time, I immediately solved the problem by bursting into tears. However, gentle coaxing from the old man taught me that you steer with the sails. Basic principles are rarely taught so simply.

Another principle is that the sea is vast and whimsical and dangerous. Prudence is the only course to take. To play dice with the weather gods is to court disaster, to tempt death.

And yet, from the earliest recorded history, men and women have been daunted and enthralled with the prospect of crossing water. The Bible is filled with references to the seas and we know from folktales and legend that the peoples of most of the coastlines of the world found ways and means to traverse their adjacent waters.

But these waters, whether a small bay or an endless ocean, were perceived to be filled with treacherous possibilities. Every cove, reef and obstacle held unseen and unpredictable dangers. Monster waves could appear from nowhere, currents were tricky, tidal races could crush boats and men. Yet, people persevered. The seas provided food, were a navigable roadway from point to point and became the source of legend and rich tradition.

Despite some archaeological finds, we know very little of the beginnings of seafaring. Wood, the principal boat building material of our ancestors, doesn't hold up forever and ancient pottery and bas relief, mosaics and wall paintings show highly metaphorical ships and boats. The answers, however, lie in the details, and the details are seldom available. We have to piece together the past from fragments, concrete and literary, and we always subject any distant historical past to the views and prejudices of our own era.

We know, for example, that the Greek triremes held three banks of rowers, but no practical explanation has ever shown how these rowers were able to function without clashing oars and descending into chaos. And every modern reconstruction of a trireme has been impractical, to say the least. We know the outlines, but not the particulars.

But slowly, mariners have brought new ideas and inventions to their vessels, and from hollow logs paddled with human hands evolved sleek, multi-hulled racing boats. The earliest mariners had no rudders. Paddles at first to propel a log. Then an early genius thought of hollowing and shaping the log so he could carry something other than himself from point to point. After a few thousand years or so, some bright soul came up with idea of a square or rectangular piece of cloth hung on a pole. A revolution! Suddenly a sailor could travel where ever the winds might blow.

Of course the winds were and are capricious, and it took thousands of years before the weather patterns over the surface of the seas were recognized. But whether in coastal waters or out of sight of land, the weather can and does play tricks; often fatal ones. Despite vast reserves of acquired knowledge, better ships, sophisticated navigation techniques, efficient propulsion machinery, a great storm can wreck havoc on any and all of man's creations. No ship is unsinkable—witness the *Titanic*—and none ever will be. Despite the rationalist notion that the human mind can overcome anything, it's doubtful that such a notion will ever again become accepted as a realistic promise.

We can build bigger ships, pollute the waters, poison the atmosphere, wreak havoc with our environment but the sea has the last word. It may change its patterns and its moods but it never loses its power.

A replica of Christopher
Columbus' ship *Nina* spreads all
plain sail running downwind in
the Tall Ships Columbus
celebration.

Discovering the Seas

What possesses people to sail into the unknown? What drives them to risk life and limb—and perhaps sanity as well—in a quest? From the very beginning of recorded history people have been intrigued, enamored, frightened and respectful of the seas. Over time, they have become more able to cope with the challenges of the sea—and lured to open water. The seas have become a place for transportation, recreation and an arena for humankind to test its courage and physical limits. Like most new things people confront, only through mistakes and disaster can we find a reasonably safe path to a destination. Many lives are sacrificed in that quest.

Left: Relief of a Phoenician ship. Note the steering oar at the stern and the rope staying for the mast, which carries a loose-footed squaresail.

Below: A 1595 Mercator projection of the world. This method of drawing a map allowed for representation of lines of longitude and gave a less distorted picture of the relationships between land and sea.

Exploration, Adventure and Commerce

Quite often the search is bound up in historical circumstances. The most important of these in the early age of exploration was the monopolies held by various cities and states in the spice trade. Rarity makes anything cost dearly, whether diamonds or rubies, nutmegs or vanilla beans. The East was a great draw in the Renaissance, an unknown land of immense and endless riches,

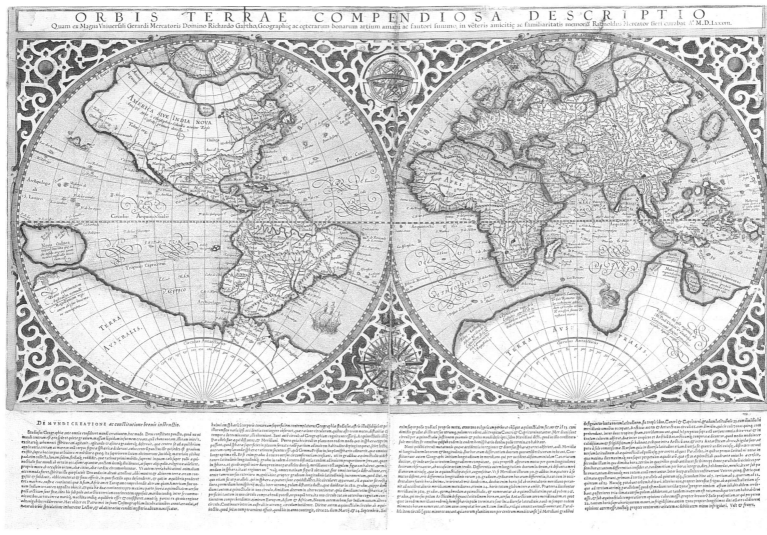

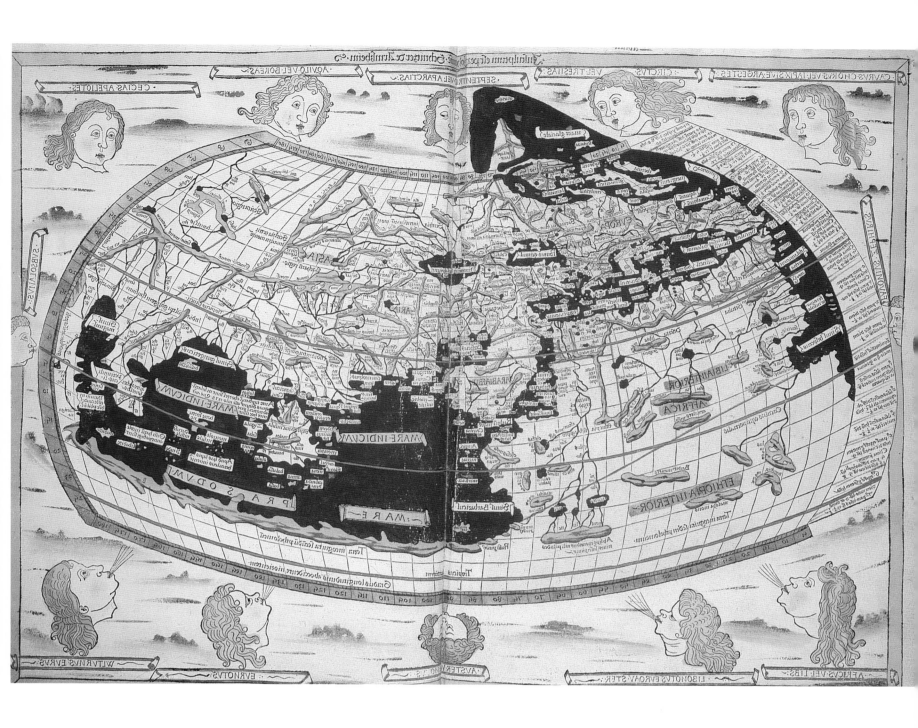

Above: A woodcut map of the
world (1482) based on the writings of Ptolemy, the Hellenistic
astronomer and geographer,
whose writings hindered the
course of exploration for
hundreds of years.

Beaching a Pink by E. W. Cooke

The Raft of the Medusa, painted in 1819 by Théodore Géricault.

spices, silks, and gems. As the seas became more traveled, commerce and history were intertwined for good. The Portuguese had rounded Africa's Cape of Good Hope. The Italians, particularly the Genoese and Venetians, controlled the overland routes to the East. Spain and England, the Netherlands and France felt left out. Anyone who could promise a safe route to the Orient was assured of great riches.

Today, when we go to the supermarket for a jar of spices, the value placed upon them five hundred years ago is unimaginable. Pepper, the most important spice in the world, was so precious that rents were paid in it, thus the term "peppercorn rent." Whoever laid claim to the lands of the East first was home free.

The dangers were great. No one knew the best routes, or even if there were navigable routes. 15th and 16th century ships were not particularly luxurious, or even comfortable; progress was slow. Being away from land for perhaps months at a time led to even greater fears of the unknown. When would land be sighted? Would it supply food and fresh water? Was it inhabited by savages? Was there even any land out there?

It took decades, even centuries, to answer all these questions.

Little by little sailors ventured farther into the oceans, to the coasts of the Americas, around the southern tip of South America and into the vast Pacific. The distances were inconceivable to European sailors, long accustomed to their own intimate coasts, or the confines of the Mediterranean. Storms, famine, losses of sails and equipment, death from disease, particularly scurvy, were constants. Since most of the oceans were uncharted, every tack or course correction could mean discovery or death.

Yet onward they pressed. Economic determinism was just as strong then as today and the chance for acquiring gold and precious goods was a driving force that knew few bounds. Greed can overcome an awful lot

of fear and discomfort, danger and privation. The age of exploration was very much a mercantile enterprise.

The Great Sailors: Vikings, the Imperial Chinese Flotilla and Commercial Fishermen
Heroic deeds generally demand heroes. These men are the ground breakers, the ones who take a chance and sail into the unknown. And despite the attendant myths, many of the journeys were certainly real. Odysseus may be the prime example from the era before Christ. The *Odyssey* is a seafaring story, interspersed with land adventures, and was destined to be the prototype for most of the tales that followed. Great man challenges sea, reaches land, has strange confrontation and

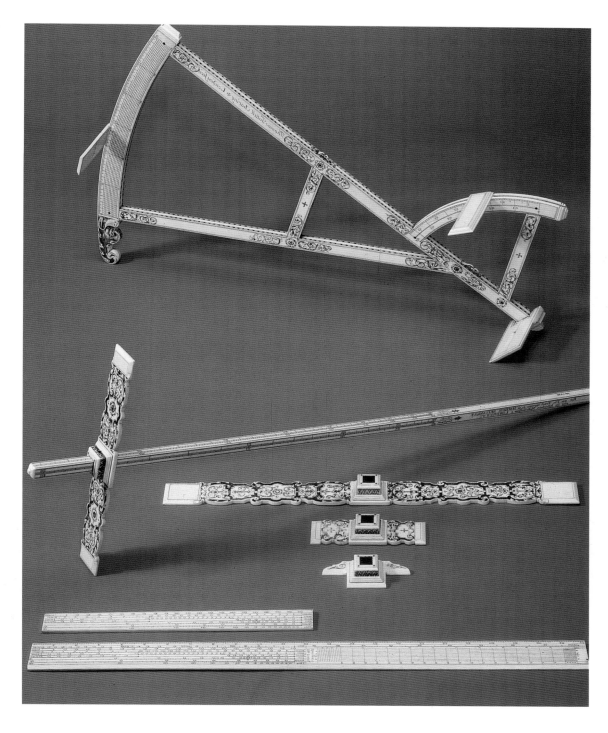

No man will be a sailor who has contrivance enough to get himself into a jail; for being in a ship is being in a jail, with the chance of being drowned.... A man in a jail has more room, better food and commonly better company.

— Samuel Johnson

resumes journey. Loyal companions aid his voyage of discovery, contrary winds blow him off course, battles and combat interrupt the land sorties. Beautiful women attempt to entrap him. But our hero, noble purpose engraved across his brow, perseveres through these various and grueling trials to finally achieve his end, bringing the voyage and the book to a close.

From what we know of ancient Europe, coastal shipping was well developed and ships were built of wood in fairly standardized forms, depending on region. But the world's oceans, if they were even known, were, by and large, an unknown and unexplored domain. It was rare that sailors themselves challenged the unknown, however. Sailors are notoriously conservative, or were until this century, and have always tended to do things as they have always been done. We know that

the Phoenicians traveled far and wide, but we have no records of their boats. Only literary and archaeological evidence has given us a glimpse of these heroic passages. In fact, little direct evidence has been found. But it has always been true that exceptional men make daring passages.

Until the Middle Ages, most voyages in the West were comparatively short, coast hopping from port to port, relying on accumulated knowledge and experience to guide the mariner. Compasses were unknown, charts likewise. Finding one's position was a matter of memorizing landmarks and guessing

the speed and time of a passage, a technique now known as dead reckoning. In the middle of the Mediterranean the waters were endless, and no aids to navigation were available except for the sun and stars. These ancient sailors learned to use nature's signs to guide their ships. Nevertheless, direction was defined by wind. Early charts from the Renaissance carried this habit on. Instead of the compass roses that we see on contemporary charts, four blowing heads appear, more or less defining north, south, east and west.

The Middle Ages provide more material, especially from

Ivory nautical instruments by Thomas Tuttell, England, ca. 1700; from top: octant, backstaff, rules.

Right: A full-rigged Viking ship. Though open, these ships were supremely seaworthy, designed to flex with the waves. The high prow and stern, though intended to appease the gods, also made for drier running in heavy seas.

the Vikings. In the 9th and 10th centuries, the Vikings started to make forays across the North Sea to England and mainland Europe. These were not pleasure trips, nor were they for trade. Viking marauders stormed ashore from their ships, raping, pillaging and spreading terror. And just as suddenly, they departed with their booty of goods and slaves. They were smart; their first targets were monasteries on the east coast of England. They were bold, and they were fearless. But most importantly, they came in beautiful ships of elegant and seaworthy design.

With their high and decorated prows and equally high sterns, their ships were capable of extended sea voyages, at least

for the brave and hearty. Viking ships were not decked, and in heavy weather there was always the chance of swamping. Nevertheless, in these ships, which reached up to 75 feet in length, Norsemen voyaged farther than and in more uncharted oceans than any documented people before. We know that they reached Iceland, Greenland and what is now Newfoundland but they were not colonizers. They reached these destinations essentially by island hopping. Admittedly, these passages were long and over open waters, and were accomplished without navigational tools, charts or any concept of latitude and longitude. Still, the heavens supplied some basic guidance and prevailing winds preordained destinations.

The rest of Europe, with the exception of minor coastal trade, was without desire for seagoing in the Middle Ages. But in China, great voyages were taking place, though not for any reasons that western mariners would understand.

In the years from 1405–33, seven major sea expeditions were sent out from China led by the Imperial Eunuch Chêng Ho. The voyages, initially sent out by the Emperor Yung Lo, were to proclaim the grandeur of China and the person of the emperor— an enormous undertaking and expense for the sake of ego.

Outfitted with equally grand ships, including the 444-foot Treasure Ship, the fleet, which was comprised of as many as 317 ships and 37,000 crew members, traversed an area from the China Sea throughout the Indian Ocean as far south as the coast of Zanzibar. It was by Western standards of the time—had the West but known—a breathtaking achievement.

Chêng Ho's flotilla rode in ships that were far better designed for ocean passages than anything the West had conceived. Bulkheads, compasses, multiple decks, charts were all in rudimentary forms or unknown in the West. But the cost of these regal passages was astounding, since the Chinese paid out in gifts and tribute to the states they visited. But by the end of the 15th century, the cost of these expeditions, coupled with the advancing Tartar and Mongol hordes, put an end to China's voyages.

But it was the commercial fisheries under sail that ultimately solidified humankind's relationship with the seas. At their height, in the 19th century, both Europe's and America's fishing fleets were immense, but the first commercial fishermen to voyage far from coastal waters were the Basques. They kept their discovery of the Grand Banks a close secret for decades, for here was an untold fortune in cod, the perfect fish for preservation before the advent of cold storage and freezing.

Cod, unlike herring and its relatives, including anchovies, sprats and sardines, is a very lean fish; therefore, it can be dried, or salted and dried, without fear of spoilage. Considering the number of meatless days on the Christian calendar up until recently, it was a godsend. Cod is a schooling fish and it gathered on the Grand Banks and outer banks in enormous quantity. One

observer claimed you could walk across the mass of cod there.

These fishermen sailed from Spain, and later France, England and Portugal, provisioned for an entire season. The boats were manned by crews who long-lined for cod, setting hundreds of hooks on seemingly endless lines and gathering them up the next morning. Salting could be done at sea, but drying couldn't, so these early merchants of the deep landed their catch on the shores of Newfoundland to set up their drying racks. These were very temporary settlements but racks of drying cod often extended for miles. When the fish were dried for the season, they were loaded aboard and the ships returned to their

home port, from whence the catch was sold.

The winter seas on the banks can be truly horrific. These are shoal areas of ocean. Waves break out of nowhere. Sudden snowstorms descend on the fleet. The seas can be whipped up into 50 foot waves in a matter of minutes. A ship had to be able to ride out these storms. Untold numbers of fishermen died in the process—the boats were too heavily loaded, they were swamped, they got lost in the heavy fogs that often descended on the banks. But on they fished. To our way of thinking this seems foolish, but the reliance on technology that developed in the 20th century was absent. Fishing was hard, dangerous and self-

Sorting cod on deck in a Gloucester fishing schooner in the 19th century. The fish were packed in layers of coarse salt, preserving them for drying once ashore.

The monument to Henry the
Navigator on the banks of the
Tagus River in Lisbon.

reliant. You succeeded or you perished.

Today, when we think of fish as an artfully arranged piece on a large plate, it's hard to imagine the hardships the fishermen had to endure: months at sea, primitive conditions, leaking ships, rats, bad food, constant repairs and little hygiene. Coupled with the invariable peculiarities of weather, this life attracted only the tough and hearty. And as time went on and fishing, especially for cod, developed into dory fishing, things did not exactly improve. Dory fishing was sort of like flotilla sailing today. Little boats, usually manned by two or three, were put out from the mother ship. All day they fished, using long lines. In the evening, the mother ship picked them up or they returned to the warmth of their

seagoing family. This was really dangerous stuff. A dory—flat bottomed, with removable thwarts and maybe 16 to 18 feet in length, totally open— was not a vessel in which to be caught in a storm. Hundreds disappeared over the course of the 19th century, yet fishermen continued to risk all.

Europe Looks to the Seas:
The Age of Discovery
When the Renaissance, with its exploration of ancient and Arab authors and scientists crept into the collective consciousness, the epoch to be known as the Age of Discovery dawned in Europe. Some of history's greatest sailors and boldest adventurers set out on journeys of remarkable distance and duration.

Exploration demands a combination of technical adequacy, courage and drive, and it is the rare man who combines all three to quest into the unknown. Sometimes vision is needed, along with the appropriate resources, to start the ball rolling. The man who got things going in the Western world was the Infante Don Henrique of Portugal, better known as Prince Henry the Navigator. He sent ships out to explore along the African coast, but much more was involved than ordering ships about. D. Henrique went about it with a rare combination of foresight, determination, organization and tact.

Setting up his headquarters in Sagres, at the very southeastern tip of Europe, he colllected charts and sailing directions from across Europe. He built an observatory and library, turning Portugal

Commercial fishing on Long Island Sound in 1949. Even as late as just after the war,   people were still fishing from longboats in protected waters, hauling nets by hand.

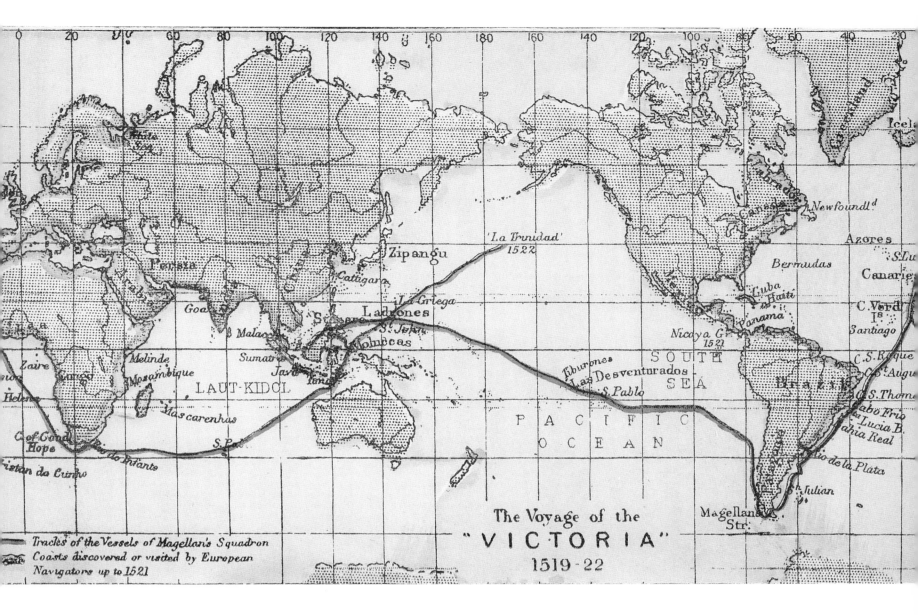

The Voyage of the
"VICTORIA"
1519-22

Tracks of the Vessels of Magellan's Squadron
Coasts discovered or visited by European
Navigators up to 1521

into the center of geographic knowledge in its time. He experimented to find the best types of ships and rigging for these voyages of exploration. And all this in the first half of the fifteenth century, at the very dawn of modern thought.

This is no place to discuss the history of geography, but it must be noted that the 15th century was enamored of the rediscovered work of Ptolemy. In the spirit of the age, anything derived from the ancients was sacrosanct, even when demonstrably wrong. D. Henrique was willing to test the ancients against the pragmatism of the sea. The desire for riches was always present; greed is a powerful motive. But Portuguese seamen slowly pierced further into the unknown of the Atlantic, despite Ptolemy's warnings of grave dangers, deadly

seas and inhospitable lands.

Of course the prime tenet of exploration is to go where no one has gone before. The explorers of the 15th and 16th centuries were doing this without any of the modern aids to navigation, such as rudimentary compasses, sextants, logs, ocean charts. Explorers had nothing but the stars and the dubious accuracy of their dead reckoning to estimate their position on the endless oceans.

When Columbus set sail, everyone knew the spherical nature of Earth. What they didn't know was the extent of landmass, the existence of North and South America and the vast distances between continents. Without such knowledge, planning and provisioning for voyages was a difficult and sometimes dangerous process. Fear of the unknown, unpredictable weather

and the primitive conditions of life aboard ship were not great enticements to the able-bodied seaman.

But old stories die hard, and the authority of the ancients, particularly Ptolemy, was hard to dismiss in these early centuries of exploration. Trade enticed the explorers with the promise of gold and spices. Thus constant tension was brought about on board ship by the conflicting emotions of greed and fear. It made for some interesting moments, such as the last few days before Columbus sighted land, when a mutiny was just avoided.

The explorers' routes generally followed trade wind patterns, though they didn't know it at the time because meteorology didn't exist. A good following breeze was the desire of all mariners. It was easier on the ship and the men, and was perfectly suited to

The voyage of the Victoria, 1519-1522. Magellan's great circumnavigation, as told in the journals of his shipmate, Antonio Pigafetta. Magellan did not survive the passage.

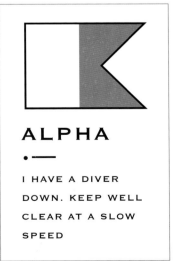

ALPHA

• ▬

I HAVE A DIVER
DOWN. KEEP WELL
CLEAR AT A SLOW
SPEED

The great explorer Vasco da Gama (1460-1524) as painted by Antonio Fonseca. Like so many of his compatriots, da Gama was a ruthless adventurer inspired by gold and riches.

the sail plan of Renaissance ships. Only when the explorers started to probe the far southern and northern oceans did they have to contend with contrary winds, and then in spades.

With exploration pushing farther, not only political frontiers expanded. Knowledge was accrued, in varying degrees of accuracy to be sure, but eventually the notion of sharing, or purloining, new information took hold. A race was on for possessions, colonies, raw materials, slaves, gold and spices. It was a contest that would encompass the world and make known the geography of the globe.

Means of Passage: From Hollow Logs to Schooners

If the earliest boats were hollowed logs, we can be sure that a great many people drowned in getting from place to place. For the prime requirement of a safe boat is stability and a log, being round in cross-section, is inherently unstable. Obviously something had to be done. Through trial and error it became apparent that by shaping the log, pointing the front end to cut through the water and flattening the bottom to keep the log from rolling and tipping out its occupants, a far more secure vessel could be created.

By the time of the earliest archaeological records, boats had developed into a recognizable form, including bow, stern, keel, planking and thwarts (cross

beams to hold the hull apart and in shape). Propulsion was still by paddle or oar. And as boats grew larger, the number of rowers, by necessity, had to become greater. Now, anyone who has ever rowed a flat-bottomed rowboat on a hot afternoon knows what a tiresome chore that can be.

Early sailors obviously tried different forms, always limited by the available technology. What seems to have developed, at least in the Middle East, was a long, narrow hull with high ends that followed the natural tendencies of the wood employed in building. Planks, usually of cedar, were bent around a series of forms with the ends coming together at bow and stern, where they were fastened to the more-or-less vertical timbers that, in turn, were attached to the keel (the long balk of wood running from stem to stern). Since all wood planks have a tendency to bend along their horizontal axes, the form depended on the thickness, length and width of the planks. Supporting frames seem to have been added after the hull was completed, to support the planking and prevent the hull from imploding. Since most of the joints were made with rope

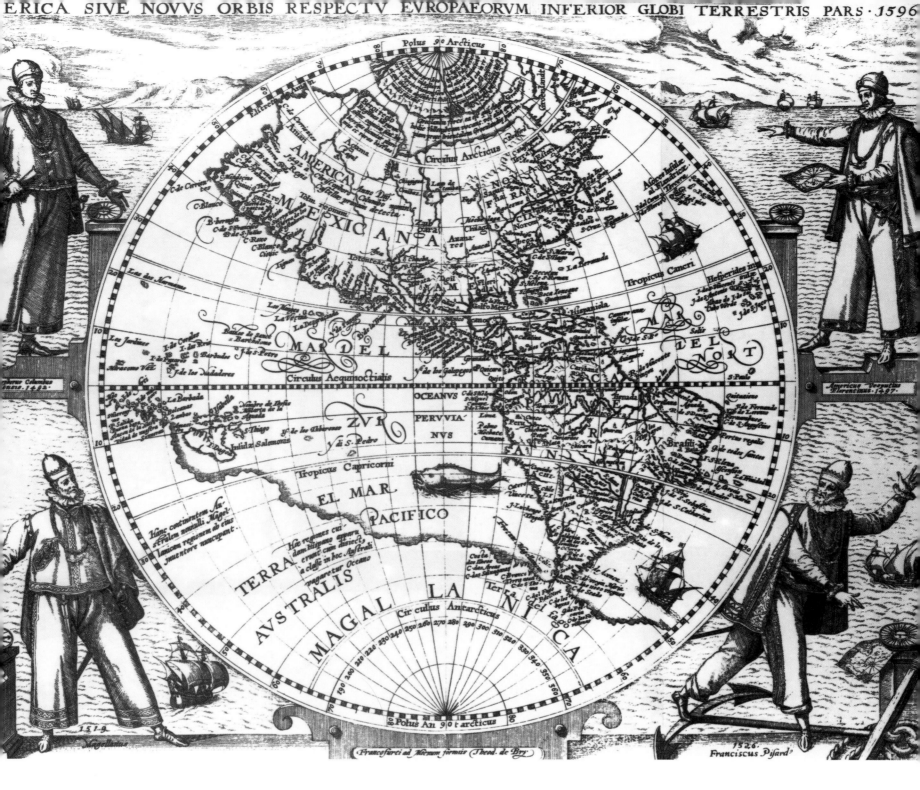

and peg fastenings, these boats were flexible to a degree and were certainly not meant for ocean voyaging.

Obviously, we have little other than wall paintings, pottery and vague descriptions to go on but it must have been several thousand years before the modern era that sails were developed. All that rowing needed a large number of people, and speed demanded that they all work in unison and very hard. That is fine for short bursts, but keeping it up for any length of time required enormous strength on the part of those at the oars. But, if the wind is coming from behind the ship, a sail could do the work of many oarsmen.

From what we know from the remaining evidence, the first sails were square or rectangular, made from flax and held aloft by a cross member to the mast, known as a yard. The sail was fastened to the yard with rope lashings, and the bottom corners were kept in place by ropes known as sheets that were led aft to stout wooden pillars. In this way the sail could be flattened or made fuller to match the wind conditions and even canted slightly to one side or the other to better catch the wind. The boat was steered by lashing an oar to the stern on the starboard side (from the English "steering board", though it appears that the Vikings were the first to use

such an arrangement as a matter of course.)

We are lucky in our knowledge of Viking ships. Archeologists have found burial ships in remarkably good condition, with the forms and construction techniques still clearly apparent. Viking ships were flexible; a single, long balk of wood was used as the keel. Planks were sprung from the stern and bow uprights, following their natural form. They were constructions of rare art, in as much the builder was guided by experience and eye alone.

Despite repeated telling, these early ships were probably far more seaworthy than we imagine. Anyone sailing in the

Map of the New World. In 1596, when this map was drawn, very little of the North and South American continents had actually been surveyed. The resulting, rather peculiar shapes were not the shapes of things to come. In each corner of the map, a different European explorer is featured: Christopher Columbus, Amerigo Vespucci, Ferdinand Magellan and Francisco Pizarro.

A Roman coastal vessel. The lack of rowing ports indicates this was not a warship, but the bow ram was for defensive purposes. The three tiers of oarsmen were displaced so as not to foul one another's oars.

Mediterranean or Aegean today well knows the seas built up by the north wind, known as the *meltemi* or *mistral*. The Mediterranean is known for sudden squalls and storms of great ferocity. Yet early sailors were able to crisscross these waters with some impunity, if not with efficiency.

Ships were still comparatively small and could be rowed in calms, but most traffic followed the wind. Over centuries, mariners slowly discovered seasonal wind patterns and were able to use them to their advantage when sailing to windward was mostly a dream. Voyages became seasonal, especially longer passages.

In the 15th century, Prince Henry the Navigator encouraged the use of caravels. The distin-

guishing feature of these ships was their lateen rigs, developed by Arabic sailors and much more efficient for sailing into the wind than the common square sails of the Mediterranean. Lateen sails were triangular and carried on a yard or spar held at an angle to the mast. With a much larger leading edge presented to the wind than a square sail, a lateen sail could sail at a more critical angle into the wind. Exploration ships had to sail out and *return* and the lateen rig helped enormously. Caravels were not large, measuring about 70 feet long and 20 to 25 feet wide, with a displacement of about 50 tons. They could carry a crew of about 20 and supplies for an extended voyage. Most were two- or three-masted. Being shallow, they could glide into small harbors for

landing and repairs. Columbus' three ships on his first voyage were all caravels ,though their rigs were changed during the course of the voyage.

During the Age of Exploration, ships became more efficient and sometimes even more seaworthy. There was no science of naval architecture. Ships were designed by reference to tradition. What had worked before was modified according to needs. Hulls remained beamy, rounded, with vestigial keels and heavy construction. Two types of hull construction, carvel and lap-strake, vied for acceptance. Both have survived, though for different purposes.

In carvel construction, a frame is erected on a backbone—the keel, stem and sternpost. This major structural member acts as the tie beam to hold the entire ship together. Thus, it must be extremely strong. Molds are erected at stations along the keel. These determine the shape of the hull, as the planking is sprung fore and aft with the molds acting as guides. But before the ship is planked, frames, or ribs, must be erected to hold the planks in place. These can be either steamed or sawn. Steamed frames are just that, lengths of timber cut to size that are steamed in an enclosed box to make them pliable and then forced into position and fastened to the ribbands, or temporary fore-and-aft timbers that delineate the hull shape. As they cool, they quickly take on the shape of the hull in skeletal form. Sawn frames are balks of timber that are cut and fastened together to make the shape frames necessary. Steamed frames make for a flexible hull, sawn for a rigid one. Both are satisfactory, but mixing the two can make for undue structural strains. Once the frames are in place, the planking can commence. Planks must be individually shaped and must match port and starboard. By themselves, they are not watertight, but with the addition of caulking, thin strands of cotton in smaller boats, oakum in larger ones, the hull will swell when immersed in water and close up, becoming tight.

Of course, much else has to be done. The construction of the hull accounts for perhaps 20 percent of a ship. Decks, interiors, rigging all account for thousands of hours of work.

In lapstrake construction, planks are "lapped" around molds and fastened on their overlapping edges, the frames are installed after the hull is complete. This is the original Viking method of construction and a quite lovely hull can be created using it. However, repairs are more difficult, and it works best with single lengths of planking running from stem to sternpost. Thus it became much more popular for smaller boats, especially as it was not as prone to drying out and opening up problems. A lapstrake hull makes wood-to-wood contact between the planks, thereby offering tighter joints between planks.

As ships got bigger and faster, new, generally empirical, methods of strengthening hulls were developed. After all, when voyaging far and long, ships had to be strong, easy to repair, and capable of carrying a very large amount of stores and equipment. As late as the 19th century, whaling ships might be gone from their home ports for as long as two or three years. But, of course, if successful, one could retire on the profits.

Eighteenth-century fisheries, had an enormous impact on design, not only on commercial ships but on later yacht design as well. Their ships were small, maybe 70 to 90 feet long, and they were burdensome, that is they were tubby and capable of holding a large tonnage of fish. They were also dangerous, not particularly stable and slow. These flaws were improved upon in time, but any ship designed to carry a large cargo will not be a graybeard. Sailing one of these ships was no easy task. Men were constantly

A tile depicting a Spanish caravel of the 15th century. Note the artist knew enough of seagoing ways to show the forward and aft balancing sails often seen on caravels.

The lateen rig survives in North Africa and in Arab coastal regions. In Houmt Souk Harbor, Tunisia, lateen-rigged fishing boats sail into harbor in 1998.

There is nothing—absolutely nothing—half so much worth doing as simply messing about in boats…or with boats… In or out of 'em, it doesn't matter.

— Kenneth Grahame

required to go aloft, clamber out on the bowsprit, and make repairs in all weathers. The chance of being washed overboard was great and many perished.

Despite the extraordinary danger aboard the fishing boats, the potential profits were so great that men longed to go on these voyages. Mariners are, by and large, conservative and superstitious. Being so, they do not take kindly to new developments in ship design. As the United States developed its coastal fisheries in the 18th century, fresh fish became the norm. Thus, so did the need to land the catch as soon as possible. Faster schooners were developed and allowed Americans to fish year round.

In the late 19th century Thomas McManus of Boston designed a new kind of schooner for the fisheries called the knockabout. Bowsprits, extending forward past the bow were a necessity to spread sail, but they were so dangerous, they were called "widowmakers." Sailors had to go out on the bowsprit to douse sail and in heavy weather this could be a death sentence. McManus' solution was a long, extended bow, spoon shaped, that allowed solid deck where once was angry ocean. However, the design cut down on cargo capacity and it cost much more to build. The one type of ship that could have saved lives was never widely adopted, partly because of economics and partly because this development came in at just about the time that steam power was taking over.

A Gloucester fishing schooner close-hauled. These ships had to be strong and self-sufficient for weeks at a time. Note the buried starboard rail and the crew lined up to port as live ballast.

A Canadian barque. These ships carried both square and fore-and-aft sails and were capable of swift downwind passages, while also having windward ability.

By the Sea

BY WILLIAM WORDSWORTH

It is a beauteous evening, calm and free;
The holy time is quiet as a nun
Breathless with adoration; the broad sun
Is sinking down in its tranquillity;

The gentleness of heaven is on the sea:
Listen! the mighty Being is awake,
And doth with his eternal motion make
A sound like thunder—everlastingly.

Dear child! dear girl! that walkest with me here,
If thou appear untouched by solemn thought
Thy nature is not therefore less divine:

Thou liest in Abraham's bosom all the year,
And worshipp'st at the Temple's inner shrine,
God being with thee when we know it not.

GEORGE VANCOUVER

1758–1798

HOME BASE ▪ *Norfolk, England*

ACHIEVEMENTS UNDER SAIL ▪ *Achievements under sail: Charted the coast of northwestern North America from San Francisco to Alaska; put to rest the notion of a navigable Northwest Passage.*

Captain George Vancouver spied the breaks and treacherous waters of what would come to be known as the Columbia Bar. River water turned the ocean a different color there, but the channel did not seem safely navigable. The bar would, when more ships arrived to the area following the young British explorer's maps, become the graveyard for many vessels. But this day in April 1792, Vancouver was not so much interested in rivers as in the Northwest Passage and he decided not to bother, passing on further exploration of the great northwestern river. It was a rare oversight.

Signing on with Captain James Cook when Vancouver was fourteen, he sailed on two of Cook's voyages and served as a midshipman on the voyage along the coast of North America. The British Admiralty drew on this experience, and in 1791, sent Vancouver to chart the coast of North America from San Francisco to Alaska, or specifically from 30 degrees to 60 degrees north latitude.

A precise and meticulous man, Vancouver spent four years picking northward among the inlets and islands of the coast of northern North America. When the expedition's main vessels, the *Discovery* and the *Chatham,* were too big to sail among narrow and rocky passages, Vancouver deployed smaller craft to chart the features of hard-to-reach coastline. The crews of these smaller boats often spent weeks away from the main ships, supplied with food, ammunition and goods to trade with the native people. On one outing, a crew rowed 800 miles to chart 60 miles of coastline. Taking compass bearings, marking position

by astronomical observations and sounding for depth, Vancouver was thorough—more thorough, perhaps, than his commission required. Over three summer surveying seasons, the explorers sailed 10,000 miles to chart 1,700 miles of coastline, including the network of islands that forms the Inside Passage to Alaska. But the effort was worth it to the sailors who would venture into these waters in later years: the maps Vancouver made of southeast Alaska remained in use for 100 years after his voyage.

Along the way, Vancouver put to rest the possiblility of a navigable Northwest Passage, exploring every break in the coastline north from California. He discounted Russian notions that Alaska was an island and refuted Spaniard Juan de Fuca's two-century-old claim that he sailed across the continent to the Atlantic. Bettering his former commander, Vancouver described the coastline in far more detail than Cook ever had. His only oversights came at the mouths of the Columbia and Fraser rivers, when he overlooked the waterways, discounting their significance and not including them in his charts. After completing his survey, Vancouver passed through Cabo San Lucas on his way home and using his newly made charts, he calculated the position of the port town and found his measurements deviated only a mile from the accepted coordinates.

Vancouver was a tempestuous man on the voyage, likely suffering from Graves' disease, a thyroid condition that caused his mood to swing severely from listless melancholy to fits of rage. But, despite his condition and his sometimes severe treatment of his crew, the *Discovery* and *Chatham* returned to port in 1795 having lost only six of 146 crew members over the four-year journey. At home however, the disease drove Vancouver to his sick bed. He pushed to complete the detailed charts and maps he was charged with making, the charts that would seal his place among the great British explorers, but he die before he could be paid for the work, and willed his family his pay for the voyage.

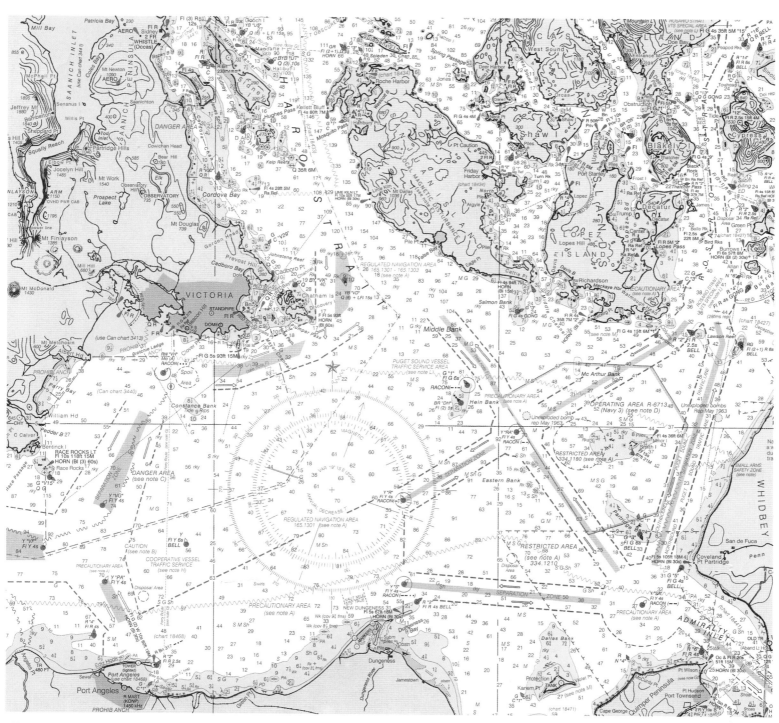

Chart showing the waters of northern Puget Sound and, in the west, the tip of Vancouver Island.

The Rime of the Ancyent Marinere, in Seven Parts

How a ship having passed the Line was driven by Storms to the cold Country towards the South Pole; and how from thence she made her course to the tropical Latitude of the Great Pacific Ocean; and of the strange things that befell; and in what manner the Ancyent Marinere came back to his own Country.

I.

It is an ancyent Marinere,
And he stoppeth one of three:
"By thy long grey beard and thy glittering eye
"Now wherefore stoppest me?

The bridegroom's doors are open'd wide
"And I am next of kin;
"The Guests are met, the Feast is set,—
"May'st hear the merry din.

But still he holds the wedding-guest—
There was a Ship, quoth he—
"Nay, if thou'st got a laughsome tale,
"Marinere! come with me."

He holds him with his skinny hand,
Quoth he, there was a Ship—
"Now get thee hence, thou grey-beard Loon!
"Or my Staff shall make thee skip.

He holds him with his glittering eye—
The wedding guest stood still
And listens like a three year's child;
The Marinere hath his will.

The wedding-guest sate on a stone,
He cannot chuse but hear:
And thus spake on that ancyent man,
The bright-eyed Marinere.

The Ship was cheer'd, the Harbour clear'd—
Merrily did we drop
Below the Kirk, below the Hill,
Below the Light-house top.

The Sun came up upon the left,
Out of the Sea came he:
And he shone bright, and on the right
Went down into the Sea.

Higher and Higher every day,
Till over the mast at noon—
The wedding-guest here beat his breast,
For he heard the loud bassoon.

The Bride hath pac'd into the Hall,
Red as a rose is she;
Nodding their heads before her goes
The merry Minstralsy.

The wedding-guest he beat his breast
Yet he cannot chuse but hear:
And thus spake on that ancyent Man,
The bright-eyed Marinere.

Listen, Stranger! Storm and Wind,
A Wind and Tempest strong!
For days and weeks it play'd us freaks—
Like Chaff we drove along.

Listen, Stranger! Mist and Snow,
And it grew wond'rous cauld:
And Ice mast-high came floating by
As green as Emerauld.

And thro' the drifts the snowy clifts
Did send a dismal sheen;
Ne shapes of men ne beasts we ken—
The Ice was all between.

The Ice was here, the Ice was there,
The Ice was all around:
It crack'd and growl'd, and roar'd and howl'd—
Like noises of a swound.

At length did cross an Albatross,
Thorough the Fog it came;
And an it were a Christian Soul,
We hail'd it in God's name.

The Marineres gave it biscuit-worms,
And round and round it flew:
The Ice did split with a thunder-fit;
The Helmsman steer'd us thro'.

And a good south wind sprung up behind,
The Albatross did follow;
And every day for food or play
Came to the Marinere's hollo!

In mist or cloud on mast or shroud
It perch'd for vespers nine,
Whiles all the night thro' [fog-smoke white]
Glimmer'd the white moon-shine.

"God save thee, ancyent Marinere!
"From the fiends that plague thee thus—
"Why look'st thou so?"—with my cross bow
I shot the Albatross.

II.

The Sun came up upon the right,
Out of the Sea came he;
And broad as a weft upon the left
Went down into the Sea.

And the good south wind still blew behind,
But no sweet Bird did follow
Ne any day for food or play
Came to the Marinere's hollo!

And I had done an hellish thing
And it would work 'em woe;
For all averr'd, I had kill'd the Bird
That made the Breeze to blow.

Ne dim ne red, like God's own head,
The glorious Sun uprist:
Then all averr'd, I had kill'd the Bird
That brought the fog and mist.
T'was right, said they, such birds to slay
That bring the fog and mist.

The breezes blew, the white foam flew,
The furrow follow'd free:
We were the first that ever burst
Into that silent Sea.

Down dropt the breeze, the Sails dropt down,
'Twas sad as sad could be
And we did speak only to break
The silence of the Sea.

All in a hot and copper sky
The bloody sun at noon,
Right up above the mast did stand,
No bigger than the moon.

Day after day, day after day,
We stuck, ne breath ne motion,
As idle as a painted Ship
Upon a painted Ocean.

Water, water every where
And all the boards did shrink;
Water, water every where,
Ne any drop to drink.

The very deeps did rot: O Christ!
That ever this should be!
Yea, slimy things did crawl with legs
Upon the slimy Sea.

About, about, in reel and rout
The Death-fires danc'd at night;
The water, like a witch's oils,
Burnt green and blue and white.

And some in dreams assured were
Of the Spirit that plagued us so:
Nine fathom deep he had follow'd us
From the Land of Mist and Snow.
And every tongue thro' utter drouth
Was wither'd at the root;
We could not speak no more than if
We had been choked with soot.

Ah wel-a-day! what evil looks
Had I from old and young;
Instead of the Cross the Albatross
About my neck was hung.

III.

I saw a something in the Sky
No bigger than my fist;
At first it seem'd a little speck
And then it seem'd a mist:
It mov'd and mov'd, and took at last
A certain shape, I wist.

A speck, a mist, a shape, I wist!
And still it ner'd and ner'd;
And, an it dodged a water-sprite,
It plung'd and tack'd and veer'd.

With throat unslack'd, with black lips bak'd
Ne could we laugh, ne wail:
Then while thro' drouth all dumb they stood
I bit my arm and suck'd the blood
And cry'd, A sail! A sail!

With throat unslack'd, with black lips bak'd
Agape they hear'd me call:
Gramercy! they for joy did grin
And all at once their breath drew in
As they were drinking all.

She doth not tack from side to side—
Hither to work us weal
Withouten wind, withouten tide
She steddies with upright keel.

The western wave was all a flame,
The day was well nigh done!
Almost upon the western wave
Rested the broad bright Sun;
When that strange shape drove suddenly
Betwixt us and the Sun.

And strait the Sun was fleck'd with bars
(Heaven's mother send us grace)
As if thro' a dungeon grate he peer'd
With broad and burning face.
Alas! (thought I, and my heart beat loud)
How fast she neres and neres!
Are those *her* sails that glance in the Sun
Like restless gossameres?

Are th[e]se *her* naked ribs, which fleck'd
The sun that did behind them peer?
And are th[e]se two all, all the crew,
That woman and her fleshless Pheere?

His bones were black with many a crack,
All black and bare, I ween;
Jet-black and bare, save where with rust
Of mouldy damps and charnel crust
They're patch'd with purple and green.

Her lips are red, *her* looks are free,
Her locks are yellow as gold:
Her skin is white as leprosy,
And she is far liker Death than he;
Her flesh makes the still air cold.

The naked Hulk alongside came
And the Twain were playing dice;
"The Game is done! I've won, I've won!"
Quoth she, and whistled thrice.

A gust of wind sterte up behind
And whistled thro' his bones;
Thro' the holes of his eyes and the hole of his mouth
Half-whistles and half-groans.

With never a whisper in the Sea
Oft darts the Spectre-ship;
While clombe above the Eastern bar
The Horned Moon, with one bright Star
Almost atween the tips.

One after one by the horned Moon
(Listen!, O Stranger! to me)
Each turn'd his face with a ghastly pang
And curs'd me with his ee.

Four times fifty living men,
With never a sigh or groan.
With heavy thump, a lifeless lump
They dropp'd down one by one.

Their souls did from their bodies fly,—
They fled to bliss or woe;
And every soul it pass'd me by,
Like the whiz of my Cross-bow.

IV.

I fear thee, ancyent Marinere!
"I fear thy skinny hand;
"And thou art long and lank and brown
"As is the ribb'd Sea-sand.

"I fear thee and thy glittering eye
"And thy skinny hand so brown—
Fear not, fear not, thou wedding guest!
This body dropt not down.

Alone, alone, all all alone
Alone on the wide wide Sea;
And Christ would take no pity on
My soul in agony.

The many men so beautiful
And they all dead did lie!
And a million million slimy things
Liv'd on—and so did I.

I look'd upon the rotting Sea,
And drew my eyes away;
I look'd upon the eldritch deck
And there the dead men lay.

I look'd to Heaven, and try'd to pray;
But or ever a prayer had gusht,
A wicked whisper came and made
My heart as dry as dust.

I clos'd my lids and kept them close,
Till the balls like pulses beat;
For the sky and the sea, and the sea and the sky
Lay like a load on my weary eye,
And the dead were at my feet.

The cold sweat melted from their limbs,
Ne rot, ne reek did they;
The look with which they look'd on me,
Had never pass'd away.

An orphan's curse would drag to Hell
A spirit from on high:
But O! more horrible than that
Is the curse in a dead man's eye!
Seven days, seven nights I saw that curse,
And yet I could not die.

The moving Moon went up the sky
And no where did abide:
Softly she was going up
And a star or two beside—

Her beams bemock'd the sultry main
Like morning frosts yspread;
But where the ship's huge shadow lay,
The charmed water burnt alway
A still and awful red.

Beyond the shadow of the ship
I watch'd the water-snakes:
They mov'd in tracks of shining white;
And when they rear'd, the elfish light
Fell off in hoary flakes.

Within the shadow of the ship
I watch'd their rich attire:
Blue, glossy green, and velvet black
They coil'd and swam; and every track
Was a flash of golden fire.

O happy living things! no tongue
Their beauty might declare:
A spring of love gusht from my heart,
And I bless'd them unaware!
Sure my kind saint took pity on me,
And I bless'd them unaware.

The self-same moment I could pray;
And from my neck so free
The Albatross fell off, and sank
Like lead into the sea.

V.
O sleep, it is a gentle thing
Belov'd from pole to pole!
To Mary-queen the praise be yeven
She sent the gentle sleep from heaven
That slid into my soul.

The silly buckets on the deck
That had so long remain'd,
I dreamt that they were fill'd with dew
And when I awoke it rain'd.

My lips were wet, my throat was cold,
My garments all were dank;
Sure I had drunken in my dreams
And still my body drank.

I mov'd and could not feel my limbs,
I was so light, almost
I thought that I had died in sleep,
And was a blessed Ghost.

The roaring wind! it roar'd far off,
It did not come anear;
But with its sound it shook the sails
That were so thin and sere.

The upper air bursts into life,
And a hundred fire-flags sheen
To and fro are hurried about;
And to and fro, and in and out
The stars dance on between.

The coming wind doth roar more loud;
The sails do sigh like sedge:
The rain pours down from one black cloud
And the Moon is at its edge.

Hark! hark! the thick black cloud is cleft,
And the Moon is at its side:
Like waters shot from some high crag,
The lightning falls with never a jag
A river steep and wide.

The strong wind reach'd the ship: it roar'd
And dropp'd down, like a stone!
Beneath the lightning and the moon
The dead men gave a groan.

They groan'd, they stirr'd, they all uprose,
Ne spake, ne mov'd their eyes:
It had been strange, even in a dream
To have seen those dead men rise.

The helmsman steer'd, the ship mov'd on;
Yet never a breeze up-blew;
The Marineres all 'gan work the ropes
Where they were wont to do:
They rais'd their limbs like lifeless tools—
We were a ghastly crew.

The body of my brother's son
Stood by me knee to knee:
The body and I pull'd at one rope,
But he said nought to me—
And I quak'd to think of my own voice
How frightful it would be!

The day-light dawn'd—they dropp'd their arms,
And cluster'd round the mast:
Sweet sounds rose slowly thro' their mouths
And from their bodies pass'd.

Around, around, flew each sweet sound,
Then darted to the sun:
Slowly the sounds came back again
Now mix'd, now one by one.

Sometimes a dropping from the sky
I heard the Lavrock sing;
Sometimes all little birds that are
How they seem'd to fill the sea and air
With their sweet jargoning,

And now 'twas like all instruments,
Now like a lonely flute;
And now it is like an angel's song
That makes the heavens be mute.

It ceas'd: yet still the sails made on
A pleasant noise till noon,
A noise like of a hidden brook
In the leafy month of June,
That to the sleeping woods all night
Singeth a quiet tune.

Listen, O listen, thou Wedding-guest!
"Marinere! thou hast thy will:
"For that, which comes out of thine eye, doth make
"My body and soul to be still."

Never sadder tale was told
To a man of woman born:
Sadder and wiser thou wedding-guest!
Thou'lt rise to morrow morn.

Never sadder tale was heard
By a man of woman born:
The Marineres all return'd to work
As silent as beforne.

The Marineres all 'gan pull the ropes,
But look at me they n'old:
Thought I, I am as thin as air—
They cannot me behold.

Till noon we silently sail'd on
Yet never a breeze did breathe:
Slowly and smoothly went the ship
Mov'd onward from beneath.

Under the keel nine fathom deep
From the land of mist and snow
The spirit slid: and it was He
That made the Ship to go.
The sails at noon left off their tune
And the Ship stood still also.

The sun right up above the mast
Had fix'd her to the ocean:
But in a minute she 'gan stir
With a short uneasy motion—
Backwards and forwards half her length
With a short uneasy motion.

The pilot, and the pilot's boy
I heard them coming fast:
Dear Lord in Heaven! it was a joy
The dead men could not blast.

I saw a third—I heard his voice:
It is the Hermit good!
He singeth loud his godly hymns
That he makes in the wood.
He'll shrieve my soul, he'll wash away
The Albatross's blood.

VII.

This Hermit good lives in that wood
Which slopes down to the Sea.
How loudly his sweet voice he rears!
He loves to talk with Marineres
That come from a far Contrée.

He kneels at morn and noon and eve—
He hath a cushion plump:
It is the moss, that wholly hides
The rotted old Oak-stump.

The Skiff-boat ne'rd: I heard them talk,
"Why, this is strange, I trow!
"Where are those lights so many and fair
"That signals made but now?

"Strange, by my faith! the Hermit said—
"And they answer'd not our cheer.
"The planks look warp'd, and see those sails
"How thin they are and sere!
"I never saw aught like to them
"Unless perchance it were

"The skeletons of leaves that lag
"My forest brook along:
"When the Ivy-tod is heavy with snow,
"And the Owlet whoops to the wolf below
"That eats the she-wolf's young.

"Dear Lord! it has a fiendish look—
(The Pilot made reply)
"I am afear'd.—"Push on, push on!
"Said the Hermit cheerily.

The Boat came closer to the Ship,
But I ne spake ne stirred!
The Boat came close beneath the Ship,
And strait a sound was heard!

Under the water it rumbled on,
Still louder and more dread:
It reach'd the Ship, it split the bay;
The Ship went down like lead.

Stunn'd by that loud and dreadful sound,
Which sky and ocean smote:
Like one that hath been seven days drown'd
My body lay afloat:
But, swift as dreams, myself I found
Within the Pilot's boat.
Upon the whirl, where sank the Ship,
The boat spun round and round:
And all was still, save that the hill
Was telling of the sound.

I mov'd my lips: the Pilot shriek'd
And fell down in a fit.
The Holy Hermit rais'd his eyes
And pray'd where he did sit.

I took the oars: the Pilot's boy,
Who now doth crazy go,
Laugh'd loud and long, and all the while
His eyes went to and fro,
"Ha! ha!" quoth he—"full plain I see,
"The devil knows how to row."

And now all in my own Countree
I stood on the firm land!
The Hermit stepp'd forth from the boat,
And scarcely he could stand.

"O shrieve me, shrieve me, holy Man!
The Hermit cross'd his brow—
"Say quick," quoth he, "I bid thee say
"What manner of man art thou?

Forthwith this frame of mine was wrench'd
With a woeful agony,
Which forc'd me to begin my tale
And then it left me free.

Since then at an uncertain hour
Now oftimes and now fewer,
That anguish comes and makes me tell
My ghastly aventure.

I pass, like night, from
I have strange power o
The moment that his fac
I know the man that mus
To him my tale I teach.

What loud uproar bursts
The Wedding-guests are t
But in the Garden-bower t
And Bride-maids singing ar
And hark the little Vesper-b
Which biddeth me to prayer

O Wedding-guest! this soul h
Alone on a wide wide sea:
So lonely 'twas, that God hims
Scarce seemed there to be.

O sweeter than the Marriage-fe
'Tis sweeter far to me
To walk together to the Kirk
With a goodly company.

To walk together to the Kirk
And all together pray,
While each to his great father bend
Old men, and babes, and loving frien
And Youths, and Maidens gay.

Farewell, farewell! but this I tell
To thee, thou wedding-guest!
He prayeth well who loveth well
Both man and bird and beast.

He prayeth best who loveth best,
All things both great and small:
For the dear God, who loveth us,
He made and loveth all.

The Marinere, whose eye is bright,
Whose beard with age is hoar,
Is gone; and now the wedding-guest
Turn'd from the bridegroom's door.

He went, like one that hath been stunn'd
And is of sense forlorn:
A sadder and a wiser man
He rose the morrow morn.

Then, like a pawing horse let go,
She made a sudden bound:
It flung the blood into my head,
And I fell into a swound.

How long in that same fit I lay,
I have not to declare;
But ere my living life return'd,
I heard and in my soul discern'd
Two voices in the air,

"Is it he? quoth one, "Is this the man?
"By him who died on cross,
"With his cruel bow he lay'd full low
"The harmless Albatross.

"The spirit who 'bideth by himself
"In the land of mist and snow,
"He lov'd the bird that lov'd the man
"Who shot him with his bow."

The other was a softer voice
As soft as honey-dew:
Quoth he the man hath penance done,
And penance more will do.

VI.
FIRST VOICE.
"But tell me, tell me! speak again,
"Thy soft response renewing—
"What makes that ship drive on so fast?
"What is the Ocean doing?

SECOND VOICE.
"Still as a Slave before his Lord,
"The Ocean hath no blast:
"His great bright eye most silently
"Up to the moon is cast—

"If he may know which way to go,
"For she guides him smooth or grim.
"See, brother, see! how graciously
"She looketh down on him.

FIRST VOICE.
"But why drives on that ship so fast
"Withouten wave or wind?
Second Voice.
"The air is cut away before,
And closes from behind.

"Fly, brother, fly! more high, more high,
"Or we shall be belated.
"For slow and slow that ship will go,
"When the Marinere's trance is abated.

I woke, and we were sailing on
As in a gentle weather:
Twas night, calm night, the moon was high;
The dead men stood together.

All stood together on the deck,
For a charnel-dungeon fitter:
All fix'd on me their stony eyes
That in the moon did glitter.

The pang, the curse with which they died,
Had never pass'd away:
I could not draw my een from theirs
Ne turn them up to pray.

And in its time the spell was snapt,
And I could move my een:
I look'd far-forth, but little saw
Of what might else be seen.

Like one, that on a lonely road
Doth walk in fear and dread,
And having once turn'd round, walks on
And turns no more his head:
Because he knows, a frightful fiend
Doth close behind him tread.

But soon there breath'd a wind on me,
Ne sound ne motion made:
Its path was not upon the sea
In ripple or in shade.

It rais'd my hair, it fann'd my cheek,
Like a meadow-gale of spring—
It mingled strangely with my fears,
Yet it felt like a welcoming.

Swiftly, swiftly flew the ship,
Yet she sail'd softly too:
Sweetly, sweetly, blew the breeze—
On me alone it blew.

O dream of joy! is this indeed
The light-house top I see?
Is this the Hill? Is this the Kirk?
Is this mine own countrée?

We drifted o'er the Harbour-bar,
And I with sobs did pray—
"O let me be awake, my God!
"Or let me sleep alway!"

The harbour-bay was clear as glass,
So smoothly it was strewn!
And on the bay the moon light lay,
And the shadow of the moon.

The moonlight bay was white all o'er,
Till rising from the same,
Full many shapes, that shadows were,
Like as of torches came.
A little distance from the prow
Those dark-red shadows were;
But soon I saw that my own flesh
Was red as in a glare.

I turn'd my head in fear and dread,
And by the holy rood,
The bodies had advanc'd, and now
Before the mast they stood.

They lifted up their stiff right arms,
They held them strait and tight;
And each right-arm burnt like a torch,
A torch that's borne upright.
Their stony eye-balls glitter'd on
In the red and smoky light.

I pray'd and turn'd my head away
Forth looking as before.
There was no breeze upon the bay,
No wave against the shore.

The rock shone bright, the kirk no less
That stands above the rock:
The moonlight steep'd in silentness
The steady weathercock.

And the bay was white with silent light,
Till rising from the same
Full many shapes, that shadows were,
In crimson colours came.

A little distance from the prow
Those crimson shadows were:
I turn'd my eyes upon the deck—
O Christ! what saw I there?

Each corse lay flat, lifeless and flat;
And by the Holy rood
A man all light, a seraph-man,
On every corse there stood.

This seraph-band, each waved his hand:
It was a heavenly sight:
They stood as signals to the land,
Each one a lovely light:

This seraph-band, each waved his hand,
No voice did they impart—
No voice; but O! the silence sank,
Like music on my heart.
Eftsones I heard the dash of oars,
I heard the pilot's cheer:
My head was turn'd perforce away
And I saw a boat appear.

Then vanish'd all the lovely lights;
The bodies rose anew:
With silent pace, each to his place,
Came back the ghastly crew.
The wind, that shade nor motion made,
On me alone it blew.

Sailors & Boats

A Falmouth oyster boat under her working rig. In their heyday, oystermen raced like fiends along the summer seas with much larger rigs. Despite her gaff rig and bowsprit, these were easily handled boats and were capable of hauling sizable cargoes with a very small crew.

CHARLIE
—·—·

YES.

A sailor today is at once very much the same and different from his or her ancestors. Everything changes, and today's sailor is in pursuit of pleasure (or glory or self-realization) while, until the decline of commercial sail just after World War I, sailors had only one goal in mind—profit.

The needs of sailors were different. Under commercial sail, boats had to be strong, commodious and economical to run. Depending on the route and the waters, crew size and speed were also factors. A Thames sailing barge was handled by a man and a boy, the massive winch on deck allowing them to sail these flat-bottomed, 100-foot long boxes with economy of movement and

effort. A full-rigged ship sailing around the Horn might have thirty or more crew with hundreds of lines, dozens of sails and the skill and ability to repair or replace these at sea. But the relationship between sailor and boat has remained a constant.

What a sailor needs most of all from a boat is a vessel he or she can trust, one that will take care of her crew in a blow. Not all ships or yachts will. Those machines designed for racing, whether today's hi-tech experiments or the skimming dishes (as very shallow centerboarders of the nineteenth century were called), invariable carry a risk, along with clouds of sail. Lightweight, meant above all for speed, they are yachts of a temperamental nature and do not

take kindly to being stressed beyond their designed capabilities.

But tradition has played an important role at sea—at least until recently. Boats were built in the past by practicing seamen who gradually shaped vessels to local conditions. They borrowed and paraphrased ideas from other successful boats, incorporating them into often novel and practical vessels.

In the film *Philadelphia Story* there's a scene in which Katherine Hepburn and Cary Grant talk about the yacht they owned when they were married, the *True Love*. "She was yar," says Miss Hepburn, and Grant explains that "yar" meant a balanced, beautiful boat, at peace with the waters on which she

Ha, ha, my ship! thou mightest well be taken now for the sea-chariot of the sun. Ho, ho! all ye nations before my prow, I bring the sun to ye! Yoke on the further billows … I drive the sea!

—*Herman Melville*

sailed. Achieving that balance is elusive. A proper yacht should move effortlessly through the water, bringing smiles of contentment and elation to the faces of captain and crew. In its special way, a yacht is the most perfect creation imaginable. She serves a purpose, she is beautiful, and she is utilitarian; everything fits together with seamless ease to propel her forward. In the end, it comes down to grace, an ineffable quality to be sure, but one necessary to the complete enjoyment of the waterborne experience.

A good boat, whether a sardine carrier of the Maine Coast or a Broads yacht, is beautiful: the lines are elegant, the shapes are pleasing to the eye and the bow parts the waters with determination and ease.

You love a boat because it pleases the senses, it protects and nurtures you and it provides a self-contained home, even for an afternoon's sail. It brings a sense of inner peace, a oneness with the world around you. There are few experiences to compare.

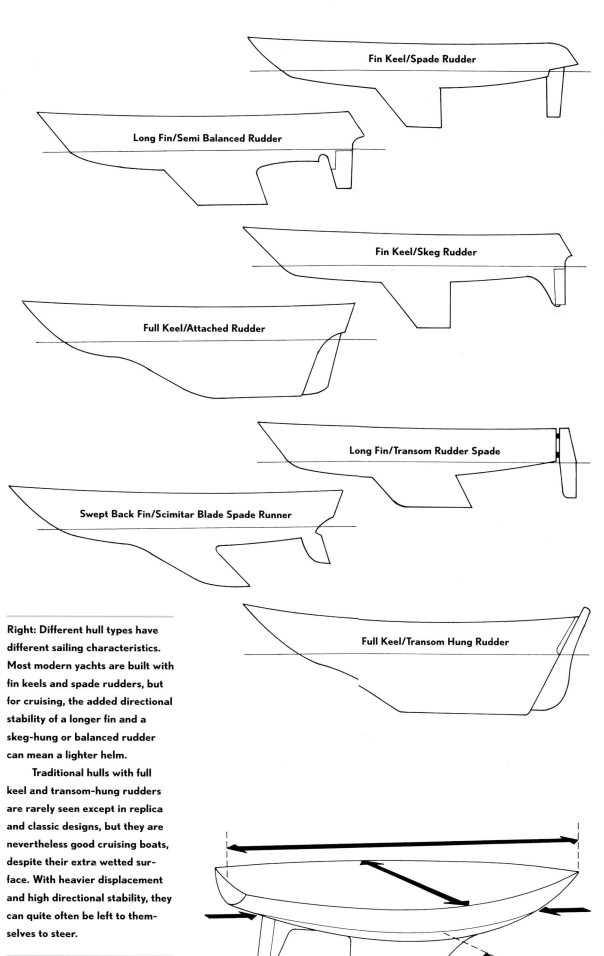

Fin Keel/Spade Rudder

Long Fin/Semi Balanced Rudder

Fin Keel/Skeg Rudder

Full Keel/Attached Rudder

Long Fin/Transom Rudder Spade

Swept Back Fin/Scimitar Blade Spade Runner

Full Keel/Transom Hung Rudder

Right: Different hull types have different sailing characteristics. Most modern yachts are built with fin keels and spade rudders, but for cruising, the added directional stability of a longer fin and a skeg-hung or balanced rudder can mean a lighter helm.

Traditional hulls with full keel and transom-hung rudders are rarely seen except in replica and classic designs, but they are nevertheless good cruising boats, despite their extra wetted surface. With heavier displacement and high directional stability, they can quite often be left to themselves to steer.

Right: The dimensions of a hull. The top rule represents the length over all (LOA); the lower horizontal at the waterplane represents the length waterline (LWL); the athwartships line is the beam and the bottom rule represent the draft of the yacht.

Sail-training ship *Marques* of Portugal.

They that go down to

the sea in ships, that do

business in great waters,

these see the works of

the Lord and his

wonders in the deep.

—*Hebrew Bible. Psalm 107*

The Evolution of Ship Design
Given the basics of a good vessel, a design that is appropriate for one set of conditions is not necessarily so for any other.

Yachts in England and Normandy are undercanvassed by American standards. Prevailing westerlies coming the full distance across the Atlantic account for this. The wind is generally much stronger on the eastern side of the pond. It is certainly something to take into account if one is planning on importing a yacht in either direction.

Over centuries, local boat types were developed for prevailing conditions. The East Coast of England is shoal, as is the Friesian coast of Germany. Working boats from these regions tended to be flatter in cross section and shallower in

draft. If a boat had to be launched from a shingle beach, a flat bottom with minimal keel was a necessity (not to mention beefed-up bottom planking). The Chesapeake Bay skipjack evolved from similar conditions—shoal waters and fluky winds. Skipjacks have shallow hulls, indeed, and large sail areas.

In Holland—the birthplace of yachting— the traditional bluff-bowed sailing boats are flat bottomed and are equipped with leeboards (pivoted boards port and starboard) that allow the yachts to sail in the thin waters of the Zuiderzee.

The debate over which is the best type of boat is pointless. Where one sails is what matters. In ocean sailing, complexities arise since the yacht will encounter many differing sets of weather, sea bottom, and land-

falls. And racing fashion plays a role. At the turn of the last century, America was devoted to comparatively beamy, shallow-draft hulls, while England was enamored of "plank-on-edge" (very narrow and deep) hulls. The beamy centerboarders were a dubious proposition in the ocean, and the cutter hulls were wet and difficult to control. Compromise was needed, but it took close to a century to achieve.

For hundreds of years, boats were designed by eyeballing existing hulls and making adjustments. It was an art, constrained by the use to which the ship would be put, the available materials and skills and the size of the crew. The ship would be constructed from wood chosen from hundreds of available species through trial and error.

The tall ships at Weymouth,
England, 1994. The great clipper
Cutty Sark sails in a gentle sea.

The sea has been called deceitful and treacherous, but there lies in this trait only the character of a great natural power, which renews its strength, and, without reference to joy or sorrow, follows eternal laws which are imposed by a higher power.

—*W. Humboldt*

Cutty Sark, a 4-masted schooner, originally rigged as a clipper ship. Built in 1869 by Scott and Linton, she was one of the very fastest of the tea and wool clippers. She survives in a permanent berth in Greenwich, England.

Some timbers were suitable for hulls, some for masts and spars, some for trim and joinery. The sea has lots of nasty little creatures—shipworms, teredos, barnacles, algae, and weeds—that either attach themselves to a hull or eat it. The attachments slow a vessel considerably; the worms and borers insinuate themselves into the ship's timbers and proceed to eat in tunnels, eventually making the ship dangerously unseaworthy.

With time and experience, shipwrights learned to carve models—half models actually—refining hull lines in the process

and learning to take off the lines. In this procedure, better known as lofting, the various dimensions and measurements are extrapolated from the model and blown up on a floor to full size. From these sections, frames can be constructed, and the ship's shape determined from them. In fact, ship and yacht builders of the nineteenth century generally worked in just such a manner. No theorizing for them: carve and build. Gradually, it became evident that there were basic concepts of ship design, hydrodynamic and aerodynamic that could be quantified mathe-

matically and represented visually. Of course, many of these early concepts proved to be wrong, but they were the glimmerings of a new approach to design, separating the builder from the naval architect.

Perhaps the greatest impetus for change was the desire for increased speed. The 19th century growth of world trade made speed a prerequisite for a successful mercantile economy. The traditional tradewind routes around the globe could be shortened with faster vessels, and those vessels came from America in the form of the clipper ship.

Clipper ships developed from coastal vessels used for local trade. Top-masted, with a fore-and-aft rig, they were and are known as schooners. And although similar rigs had been used before, Yankee ingenuity made some subtle improvements, fining the lines of the hull, giving the ship a leaner, more defined shape than the somewhat tubby merchant vessels that were traditional. Being slimmer and of less tonnage than similar length merchant vessels, clippers traded in valuable cargoes—coffee, tea, spices, silks and other luxury goods. They were the graybeards of the sea, sleek, elegant and fast. In fact, it was the record clipper ship passages that inspired Chichester to attempt his round-the-world voyage.

But these were still commercial ships, meant to carry cargo for a profit. And most yachts—that is, pleasure boats—were based on smaller fishing and inshore craft. Sailing them was hard work, and the notion of

sailing for pleasure was still new. Yachting as a sport didn't start until the seventeenth century, and then was limited to the aristocracy. The Dutch, in their increasingly protected waters,

Above: Olin Stephens, probably the most prolific and winning American yacht designer of the 20th century at the helm with Dennis Conner, America's Cup-winning helmsman.

Below: The sleek and elegant *Dorade*. Designed by Olin Stephens and campaigned by his brother Rod, *Dorade* was a revelation. She beat all comers in race after race, and set new standards for ocean-racing yachts. Seventy years later, she still sails in the Pacific Northwest.

1994

The great captain Charlie Barr. A tough sailor and a great commander of men, Barr held the transatlantic record for many years.

started it. The English picked it up when James II was given a sailing craft by the Dutch. Racing for large wagers was in keeping with the tenor of the times, and the care and maintenance of these "small" vessels (usually over 50 feet in length) was no small matter. Peter the Great, who worked in Holland, took back to Russia his love of sailing. One of the reasons St. Petersburg is where it is was to satisfy his desire to be on the water.

Legendary Shipwrights
Yachting was a sport for the rich until after World War II. The work of the great yacht designers started somewhat earlier, the most famous being Edward Steers, designer of *America,* the first challenger for what is now

known as the America's Cup. John Stevens, a wealthy merchant from New York and Hoboken, New Jersey, commissioned the boat. It was a two-masted schooner, based on the lines of fast coasting vessels. Once in England, where the races were to be held, *America* created a furor. She was vastly different than the current run of English yachts of the day with her rakish lines and clipper bow, and she cleaned up. Nothing could catch her, and she proceeded, in the Solent, to win the cup.

This win started the great racing rivalry between America and England. But this was not only a gentleman's sport; it was an inshore one. These large vessels, with their large crews, did not venture offshore. Rather, they raced in protected waters—

The sea, washing the

equator and the poles,

offers its perilous aid,

and the power and

empire that follow it....

"Beware of me," it

says, "but if you can

hold me, I am the key

to all the lands."

—*Ralph Waldo Emerson*

the Solent in England, New York Harbor in the United States. Despite their size, these were fragile yachts, for after *America*, seagoing ability was sacrificed for speed. The approaches varied on either side of the Atlantic, however. The English, with generally heavier weather opted for deep, narrow hulls. The Americans went for what became known as "skimming dishes," shallow-draft hulls with centerboards of immense size and dubious stability. Typical of the times, each thought the other's preposterous

and all designs were created more by instinct than through rational application of scientific principles. Design was in its infancy and many theories were propounded (most incorrect) to explain the behavior of a hull in water. Not until the latter part of the nineteenth century, with the advent of three great designers—Edward Burgess and Nathaniel Herreshoff in the United States and G.L. Watson in England—was yacht design able to move forward through rigorous thought and modern technology. Of the

three, Herreshoff was destined to become the giant of the profession. He may have been the greatest yacht designer of all time.

Trained at MIT as an engineer, Nathaniel Greene Herreshoff had designed and sailed boats since his childhood. His first work was as a designer of steam engines and powerboats, and his keen mind revolutionized both. He was the first designer to apply engineering principles to the design of ships with any consistency. But it was for his sailing yachts that Herreshoff

Nathaniel Herreshoff on the right in profile. Probably the greatest yacht designer of all time, Capt. Nat, as he was called, was responsible for the lightest, fastest wooden yachts ever conceived. He also designed a slew of America's Cup defenders and developed the modern sail, sail track, anchors, turnbuckles, fin keels, and catamarans. He was an artist and engineer without peer.

will be remembered. Using, at the end of the 19th century, state-of-the-art materials, he created lighter, stronger, faster yachts—yachts that won the America's Cup five times. His designs depended on meticulous craftsmanship in both wood and steel; the quality built into his boats has never been equaled. But it was more than care that brought him fame. He developed some of the truly revolutionary principles of yacht design: the cutaway underbody (reducing wetted surface), one of the first catamarans, fin keels and spade rudders, engineered steel rigging, engineered wood construction, improved sail cuts and metal fittings of elegant and novel design (including the best designed cleat of all time).

Burgess and Watson are not nearly as well known, but each designed beautiful, fast and seaworthy yachts and commercial ships. Edward Burgess, the father of Starling Burgess, the designer of *Nina, Christmas* and many other great yachts, was the great American designer prior to Nat Herreshoff. His best yachts were elegant schooners such as *Fleur de Lys*—86 tons, 87 feet waterline length, 108 feet on deck. *Fleur de Lys* was considered a small yacht in its day (1905) and hardly fit for ocean racing, but she handily won the transatlantic race that year in heavy going indeed. Burgess' America's Cup yachts, notably *Puritan* of 1885 and *Mayflower* of 1886 handily trounced the British challenger *Genesta* in

straight sets. His hulls were swift and sleek and he brought yacht design to its high point prior to the more scientific and engineered approach of Herreshoff, Stephens and Laurent Giles.

G.L. Watson, the great Scottish designer, was best known for the king's yacht, *Britannia*, in which George V sailed for 40 years, winning countless prizes and updating her as needed. The fact that she was still winning at the end of her career says something about the quality of the design. When the king died, *Britannia* was given a proper burial at sea, sunk off the Isle of Wight—no knacker's yard for her noble bones.

The first half of the 20th century, leading up to World War

Whoever commands the sea, commands the trade, whoever commands the trade of the world, commands the riches of the world, and consequently the world itself.

—*Sir Walter Raleigh*

II, was the golden age of yacht design. Philip Rhodes, Charles Nicholson, Clinton Crain, Robert Clark, Walter McInnes, Uffa Fox, Olin Stephens, Henry Gruber, Starling Burgess, William Atkin, Ray Hunt, L. Francis Herreshoff, Jack Laurent Giles—the list is endless. Of these, Olin Stephens is the most notable.

Dorade was the first ocean-going yacht designed by Olin Stephens. Looking at her today one sees an old-fashioned, sweet hull and a heavily-stayed yawl rig. She is narrow, deep and somewhat cramped by modern standards, but in her heyday—the 1930s—she was the wonder of the sailing world. Designed when Olin was still in his 20s, *Dorade* revolutionized ocean racing. She came in second in her class in the Bermuda race of 1931, but after that swept line honors on both sides of the Atlantic, winning the Transatlantic race of 1932 and then sweeping the Fastnet race the same year.

Built on City Island, New York in 1930, she was over-weight. Rod Stephens, Olin's brother and partner for the next 50 years, had specified construction scantlings to make her virtually unbreakable (she still sails on the West Coast). She was narrow, much like a then-popular meter boat, but had exceptionally smooth and clean lines. She could almost keep up with crack Twelve-Meter yachts (later used in the post-war America's Cup races) to windward. She carried a complexly-stayed yawl rig with double runners and a cutter-rigged foretriangle in the Bermudan style in an era when gaff rig was considered more appropriate for ocean passages. But in 1930, she was state-of-the-art.

In the Transatlantic Race of 1932, *Dorade* was pitted against a fleet of much larger yachts. Most serious yachtsmen of the day thought her far too small and fragile for ocean sailing. They were unaware that not only was she to prove herself a crack ship, but she was captained by the redoubtable Rod, one of the great sailors of the century. Rod chose the Great Circle route, giving him more favorable winds and shortening the distance considerably. When the fleet arrived in England at the finish, they were, to say the least, shocked to find that *Dorade* had beaten them by days, not even calling on her handicap time allowance. She was fast, weatherly, and had been expertly handled. A new era in ocean racing was born.

Sailing today in the Pacific Northwest in pristine condition, *Dorade* ushered in a new era in sailing, on both sides of the Atlantic. But, *Dorade* was far from Stephen's crowning

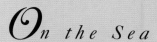

On the Sea

BY JOHN KEATS

It keeps eternal whisperings around
Desolate shores, and with its mighty swell
Gluts twice ten thousand caverns, till the spell
Of Hecate leaves them their old shadowy sound.
Often 'tis in such gentle temper found,
That scarcely will the very smallest shell
Be moved for days from whence it sometime fell,
When last the winds of heaven were unbound.
Oh ye! who have your eye-balls vexed and tired,
Feast them upon the wideness of the Sea;
Oh ye! whose ears are dinned with uproar rude,
Or fed too much with cloying melody,
Sit ye near some old cavern's mouth, and brood
Until ye start, as if the sea-nymphs choired!

achievement. *Stormy Weather, Yankee, Ranger, Columbia, Swans* and more poured forth from his drawing board. More boats were built from his designs than any other 20th century designer, and there was nary a dud among them.

Still, though Olin Stephens was often thought of in Europe as the only American designer, his compatriots, particularly Phil Rhodes and L. Francis Herreshoff, were designing yachts of supreme beauty and speed. Phil Rhodes has a long career and designed everything from day sailors to ocean liners. Francis Herreshoff was a true eccentric. Being the son of Captain Nat Herreshoff, he was in a position to command attention. His comparatively meager output is characterized by a very personal approach to yacht design. From his H-28 cruising ketch to his 71-foot, ocean-going ketch *Landfall,* all his boats were distinctive, though some engineering was dubious. But without question, he was a great

artist, the Leonardo of designers. His most famous design is *Ticonderoga,* one of the most impressive and beautiful yachts of all time. Winning races over 40 years, *Ti* (as she is affectionately known) is still sailing strong. Another design which must be mentioned is the *Marco Polo,* a 55-foot, very narrow (ten feet), double-ender with three masts and a cutaway underbody. It is an odd little ship, and not many have been built, but it is a fine example of radical thinking that works. Designed for speed with a minimum crew over long passages, she achieves just that.

Jack Laurent Giles brought new heights of engineering skill to design in England with boats like *Myth of Malham* and *Blue Leopard.* With his distinctive sheerline (the uppermost line of the hull), Laurent Giles boats made some extraordinary passages, especially the Vertue Class. Based on an early design, *Andrillot,* the Vertues were very small boats, slightly over 25 feet overall. Just after the war, they

Left: Ranger, perhaps the greatest of the "J" boats, designed by Starling Burgess and Olin Stephens for the 1937 America's Cup races. She was the most advanced pre-war yacht, and the last of the beautiful Js.

Above: *Dorade*, close-hauled. *Dorade* was a comparatively narrow and heavy boat, but, as can be seen here, she left a smooth wake, indicating a beautifully-shaped hull and great driving power.

He is the best sailor

who can steer within

fewest points of the

wind, and exact a

motive power out of

the greatest obstacles.

—*Henry David Thoreau*

became the ultimate pocket cruiser, capable of the most extraordinary feats. Humphrey Barton, Laurent Giles' partner, sailed the famous *Vertue XXXV* across the Atlantic, a feat almost unheard of for such a small boat. Bill Nance completed a circumnavigation via the southern capes. Even today, fiberglass Vertues are sailing the world's oceans, rounding Cape Horn, proving themselves again and again.

Other British designers of note include Morgan Giles, Robert Clark, Alan Buchanan, Uffa Fox, Tony Castro, Rob Humphries… the list goes on and on.

Multihulls, Titanium and Contemporary Design
In the last half of the century, designs split into pure racing machines and cruising boats, with, naturally enough, the racing machines garnering the most publicity. All racing design is governed by various racing rules. Once upon a time, these rules were devised to produce a seaworthy, all-around vessel—witness the Royal Ocean Racing Club and Cruising Club of America rules in the 1960s and 1970s.

But new rules, particularly the International Offshore Rule (IOR) in the 1970s and 1980s, paved the way for radical developments in design.

International Fisherman's Races
of 1938. The *Gertrude L.
Thebaud*, out Gloucester,
Massachusetts leading *Bluenose*
from Nova Scotia, Canada.

Any fool can carry

on but a wise man

knows how to shorten

sail in time.

—*Joseph Conrad*

Absolute speed through the water became less important than speed as judged by handicaps. Yachts became very oddly shaped indeed, all in an effort to take advantage of the rules. They also became less seaworthy, as witnessed in the 1979 Fastnet Race disaster. Light construction, unstable hull forms and drastic weather do not make for safe boating. But challenge is always present.

The great revolution in yacht design and construction came with introduction of GRP (glass-reinforced plastic) in the late 1950s. Suddenly it was possible to produce identical boats in series, not that this hadn't been done before with wooden hulls. Wood demanded a high level of crafts-

manship, however. Anyone could be trained to lay-up glass hulls.

It was the great solo and round-the-world races that most encouraged radical development. Water ballast, rotating masts, articulated keels, dual rudders, new sail fabrics, high-end metallurgy, rod rigging, exotic materials were all employed in attempts to stay at the top of the heap. Sometimes solo sailors were ensconced on sailing ships of over 200 feet. Sometimes, it led to loss of life.

The job of a good designer is to create a boat that will work effectively in a wide range of conditions. This dictates compromises in rig, appendages, hardware, rigging, weight, hull and deck shape, ballast, scant-

lings, materials and techniques. And, unless one is an out-and-out racer, aesthetics plays a part. A good boat is one that performs well the job for which it was designed. Thus taking a heavy double ender around the buoys for a Wednesday evening race is most likely a futile effort. Likewise an all-out racing machine would make an appalling platform for a family cruise.

Change is inevitable, and designers like Rob Humphreys, Bruce King, Bruce Farr, Chuck Paine, Ed Dubois, Doug Peterson and Tony Castro, have continued to forge new paths in yacht design. With new material at hand—titanium, kevlar, graphite and more— these designers have been able

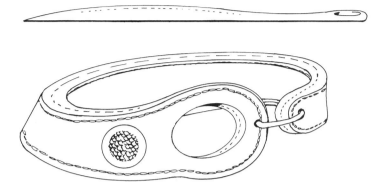

As usual I finish the day before the sea, sumptuous this evening beneath the moon, which writes Arab symbols with phosphorescent streaks on the slow swells. There is no end to the sky and the waters. How well they accompany sadness!

—*Albert Camus*

to produce lighter, stronger, faster boats, and a surprising number have been maxi yachts, ranging from 65 to 150 feet and more. Needless to say, these are boats for the new tycoons, and the same competitive spirit that drove them to succeed in business has been transferred to ocean racing.

These superyachts are nothing like the average sailboat. First, they are large—150 feet is

not unusual—and they are built using the latest techniques borrowed from aeronautic design. Exotic materials—titanium fittings, carbon fiber spars, engineered ropes made from combinations of kevlar, graphite and dacron, laminated hulls of veneers and carbon reinforcements—all combine to make for lightweight and slippery boats. It is not unknown for the behemoths to surf downwind at 20 knots or more. Other devices have been invented to make them even faster: water ballast tanks, hydraulic articulated keels, dual rudders, telescoping bowsprits for spinnaker flying, the list is endless.

Multihulls have also achieved a new respectability. Giant catamarans and trimarans have, in the past two decades, become the leading graybeards of the sea. These boats, unballasted as they are, are capable of blinding speed, often over 20 knots sustained on a reach. Multihulls are designed to sail over waves, not through them, cutting drag and resistance. But, as always, there are tradeoffs. Speed by itself is only viable if coupled with seaworthiness, and early multis were notoriously prone to breaking apart in heavy seas, or flipping over. Nowadays this has been

remedied, but there is still little comfort factor on a racing multihull yacht. At that speed one has to stay alert. Few of these boats steer themselves, and quite often they sail faster than the true wind speed. Self-steering vanes are useless in these conditions, and autopilots become a necessity.

Avoiding fatigue is also an important factor in obtaining optimum performance. Few sailors can maintain an accurate course for more than three or four hours at a stretch. This was the reason for the development of watch systems—so many hours on, so many off. In horrendous conditions, the watch may suddenly go to one hour on, especially in big following seas. In such conditions,

Left: Margaret Roth, intrepid admiral of the *Whisper* mending sails with a palm.

Right: A sail needle and palm. A palm fits over the hand and contains a hard insert which allows the need to be pushed through many layers of heavy sailcloth.

The eccentric and great English designer, Uffa Fox. A leading proponent of light-displacement yachts, Fox also experimented with molded plywood hulls and developed the famous flying boats which were dropped to RAF flyers who had ditched their planes near the English coast. His five books on yachts and design, written in the 1930s, are a priceless collection of perceptive commentary.

the slightest error can lead to a broach (slewing abeam to the wind and waves) or pitchpoling (flipping end over end), both with potentially disastrous results. Miles and Beryl Smeeton were pitchpoled on two occasions attempting to round Cape Horn in their 45-foot ketch, barely surviving. Dismasted, hatches torn off, half-filled with water, they were able—with the help of their crew John Guzzwell, a brilliant boatbuilder—to limp into a Chilean port.

In contemporary yachts, comfort is more easily obtained through the use of modern materials and techniques.

Watertightness is vital to a happy crew, not to mention heating and secure berths. If motion in a seaway can be kept reasonable,

then passages can be made without undue strain and fatigue. When one gets into the superyacht category, all the comforts of home can be had with no sacrifice to performance, accommodations taking up proportionally less displacement than on a smaller yacht.

Progress in yacht design and construction can't be stopped, nor should it. Certainly, some of the more radical yachts will turn out to be duds, but others will have their features adopted for production yachts in years to come. After all, 75 years ago, working boat derivatives were thought to be the only boats suitable for offshore racing. The great English designer Uffa Fox scoffed at this and pointed out that only from racing innovations do cruising yachts improve. So it still is.

The ocean's surf, slow, deep, mellow voice is full of mystery and awe, moaning over the dead it holds in its bosom, or lulling them to unbroken slumbers in the chambers of its vastly depths.

—*Haliburton*

ERIC TABARLY

1931–1998

"It was hard, but it was possible."

HOME BASE ▪ *Nantes, France*

ACHIEVEMENTS UNDER SAIL ▪ *Victories in the 1964 and 1976 OSTAR, the 1969 San Francisco-Tokyo solo race, two Sydney-Hobart races. Yachting innovator and instructor and inspiration to a current generation of world-class solo sailors.*

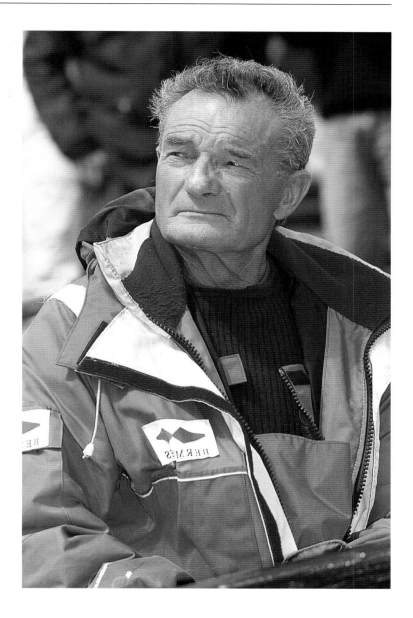

When Eric Tabarly was swept overboard from his century-old yacht, *Pen Duick*, off the coast of Wales in 1998, no less than French President Jacques Chirac spoke about the loss of the 66-year-old "iron man" of solo sailing. "Despite the last searches that seemed in vain, I didn't dare believe the demise of Eric Tabarly," Chirac said. "It is with great sadness and much emotion that I give in to the evidence."

Tabarly was a national hero in France and a mythic figure in the sailing community. He eschewed radios, life jackets and safety harnesses, preferring less contact from the outside world and more freedom of movement about the boat. A shy man, Tabarly pretended only to speak French, though his command of English was very good, so that he could limit intrusions upon his sailing adventures. He innovated the use of spent uranium for keels and water ballast in yachts. In the late '60s, when race officials required entrants to fit their boats with engines but didn't specify that the engines needed to work, Tabarly complied with the ruling but mounted the engine upside down, inoperable, so that it would lower his boat's center of gravity. It was a winning advantage, but one that left less margin for safety.

Tabarly was an unknown 32-year-old French Navy lieutenant when he won the 1964 Observer Singlehanded Trans-Atlantic Race (OSTAR) in his 44-foot ketch *Pen Duick II*, breaking Sir Francis Chichester's record for the 3,000-mile crossing by 13

days. The self-steering on his boat broke a third of the way into the race and Tabarly couldn't leave the helm. For two weeks, he stole naps while steering by hand. The victory earned him the Legion d'Honneur from President Charles de Gaulle and a ticker-tape parade down the Champs-Elysees.

In the 1976 OSTAR, Tabarly was pounded by storm after storm; patience spent, he nearly quit. His self-steering was broken again and he spent a day deciding whether to press on. In classic Tabarly fashion, he decided to stick it out. His rivals in the race fared worse, but having refused to listen to the radio, Tabarly didn't know their fates until he arrived in Newport the winner, seven hours ahead of the next boat.

Tabarly inherited the original yacht *Pen Duick* from his father and his boats bore the name in series. *Pen Duick II* won the 1964 OSTAR. *Pen Duick III*, with its upside-down-engine, won two Sydney-Hobart races and set a record for the Cowes Channel Race. *Pen Duick IV*, a 67-foot trimaran, did not finish the 1968 OSTAR, but *Pen Duick V* won the 1969 San Francisco-to-Tokyo solo transpacific race in 40 days. The 35-foot yacht was among the first to use water ballast. *Pen Duick VI*, with a keel of spent uranium, won the 1976 OSTAR but was dismasted twice in the 1973-1974 Whitbread Round the World race and disqualified in the 1977-1978 Whitbread, due to a mid-course rule change.

Tabarly flew jets in the French military in Vietnam to earn enough to keep the *Pen Duick* maintained. He retired from the navy in 1966, but he retained its sponsorship after winning the 1964 OSTAR and embarked on his storied 35-year sailing career.

In 1998, two weeks after celebrating the original *Pen Duick's* 100th birthday, Tabarly was heading for a regatta of Fife-designed yachts with four crew members when he faced his final storm. Around midnight, as *Pen Duick* was tossed in Force 6 winds and nine-foot swells, Tabarly was hit in the chest by the gaff while changing sails. The blow knocked him overboard. Without a radio, the crew was unable to call for help. They were able to flag down a passing yacht seven hours later, but by then, the sailing legend was lost.

Tabarly was heading for a regatta of Fife-designed yachts with four crew members when he faced his final storm. Around midnight, as Pen Duick was tossed in Force 6 winds and nine-foot swells, Tabarly was hit in the chest by the gaff while changing sails. The blow knocked him overboard.

$\mathcal{F}rom$ Two Years Before The Mast

BY RICHARD HENRY DANA, 1869

"We remained for the rest of the night, and throughout the next day, under the same close sail, for it continued to blow very fresh; and though we had no more hail, yet there was a soaking rain, and it was quite cold and uncomfortable; the more so because we were not prepared for cold weather"

Chapter IV

We met with nothing remarkable until we were in the latitude of the river La Plata. Here there are violent gales from the southwest, called Pamperos, which are very destructive to the shipping in the river, and are felt for many leagues at sea. They are usually preceded by lightning. The captain told the mates to keep a bright lookout, and if they saw lightning at the southwest, to take in sail at once. We got the first touch of one during my watch on deck. I was walking in the lee gangway, and thought that I saw lightning on the lee bow. I told the second mate, who came over and looked out for some time. It was very black in the southwest, and in about ten minutes we saw a distinct flash. The wind, which had been southeast, had now left us, and it was dead calm. We sprang aloft immediately and furled the royals and top-gallant sails, and took in the flying jib, hauled up the mainsail and trysail, squared the after yards, and awaited the attack. A huge mist capped with black clouds came driving towards us, extending over that quarter of the horizon, and covering the stars, which shone brightly in the other part of the heavens. It came upon us at once with a blast, and a shower of hail and rain, which almost took our breath from us. The hardiest was obliged to turn his back. We let the halyards run, and fortunately were not taken aback. The little vessel "paid off" from the wind, and ran for some time directly before it, tearing through the water with everything flying. Having called all hands, we close reefed the topsails and trysail, furled the courses and jib, set the fore-topmast staysail, and brought her up nearly to her course, with the weather braces hauled in a little, to ease her.

This was the first blow, that I had seen, which could really be called a gale. We had reefed our topsails in the Gulf Stream, and I thought it something serious, but an older sailor would have thought nothing of it. As I had now become used to the vessel and to my duty, I was of some service on a yard, and could knot my reef-point as well as anybody. I obeyed the order to lay* aloft with the rest, and found the reefing a very exciting scene; for one watch reefed the fore-topsail, and the other the main, and every one did his utmost to get his topsail hoisted first. We had a great advantage over the larboard watch, because the chief mate never goes aloft, while our new second mate used to jump into the rigging as soon as we began to haul out the reef-tackle, and have the weather earing passed before there was a man upon the yard. In this way we were almost always able to raise the cry of "Haul out to leeward" before them, and having knotted our points, would slide down the shrouds and back-stays, and sing out at the topsail halyards to let it be known that we were ahead of them. Reefing is the most exciting part of a sailor's duty. All hands are engaged upon it, and after the halyards are let go, there is no time to be lost—no "sogering" or hanging back, then. If one is not quick enough, another runs over him. The first on the yard goes to the weather earing, the second to the lee, and the next two to the "dog's ears:" while the others lay along into the bunt, just giving each other elbow-room. In reefing, the yard-arms (the extremes of the yards) are the posts of honor; but in furling, the strongest and most experienced stand in the slings, (or, middle of the yard,) to make up the bunt. If the second mate is a smart fellow, he will never let any one take either of these posts from him; but if he is wanting either in seamanship, strength, or activity, some better man will get the bunt and earings from him; which immediately brings him into disrepute.

We remained for the rest of the night, and throughout the next day, under the same close sail, for it continued to blow very fresh; and though we had no more hail, yet there was a soaking rain, and it was quite cold and uncomfortable; the more so because we were not prepared for cold weather, but had on our thin clothes. We were glad to get a watch below, and put on our thick clothing, boots, and southwesters. Towards sundown the gale moderated a little and it began to clear off in the southwest. We shook our reefs out, one by one, and before midnight had top-gallant sails upon her.

We had now made up our minds for Cape Horn and cold weather, and entered upon every necessary preparation.

---

* This word "lay," which is in such general use on board ship, being used in giving orders instead of "go;" as, "Lay forward!" "Lay aft!" "Lay aloft!" etc., I do not understand to be the neuter verb lie, mispronounced, but to be the active verb lay, with the objective case understood; as, "Lay yourselves forward!" "Lay yourselves aft!" etc.

CAPTAIN JAMES COOK

?–1779

HOME BASE ▪ *Yorkshire, England*

ACHIEVMENTS UNDER SAIL ▪ *Scientific exploration and charting of the Pacific for the British.*

When Captain James Cook landed at Kealakekua Bay in January 1779, some accounts suggest that the native Hawaiians welcomed him as a revered figure, perhaps even a god. It was Cook's third voyage to the Pacific Ocean—ostensibly to do scientific research and chart the unexplored reaches of the globe, but also to lay a foundation for British influence among far-flung territories. At first, the Hawaiians may have associated Cook with Lono, the god of peace, games and agricultural fertility. They presented him with gifts of pigs and red tapa cloth and prostrated themselves before him. That Cook was an alien figure cannot be disputed: his skin was white, he wore strange clothes and his men carried guns. This first contact with the West immediately set about tremendous changes for the native people of Hawaii as it had for many island cultures of the South Pacific when Cook arrived. The islands would soon appear on charts of the seafaring nations of the West.

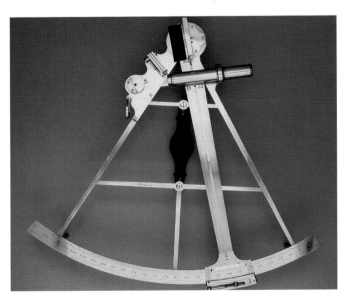

Captain Cook's sextant

Cook set out on the *Endeavour* for his first journey around the globe from 1768-1771. He returned to the Pacific Ocean in 1772, commanding the *Resolution* and *Adventure* on a three-year voyage. On his last voyage in 1776, he was persuaded to leave semiretirement to lead the *Resolution* and *Discovery* on another mission to the Pacific. It was three years into this trip that Cook met the native Hawaiians. Over the three journeys, he charted Australia, New Zealand, ranged north along the west coast of North America, stopped in Tahiti (where he developed a palate for dog) and ended up in the South China Sea. Along the way he saw the haka, the war dance of New Zealand's Maori people. In Australia, he described the kangaroo, a creature with a tail as long as its body that moved faster than a greyhound with giant two-legged leaps. His crew ate sauerkraut—7,860 pounds of it was carried on his first voyage—to combat scurvy. Among native people of the South Pacific islands, his power was assumed and he was treated with the respect given a chief.

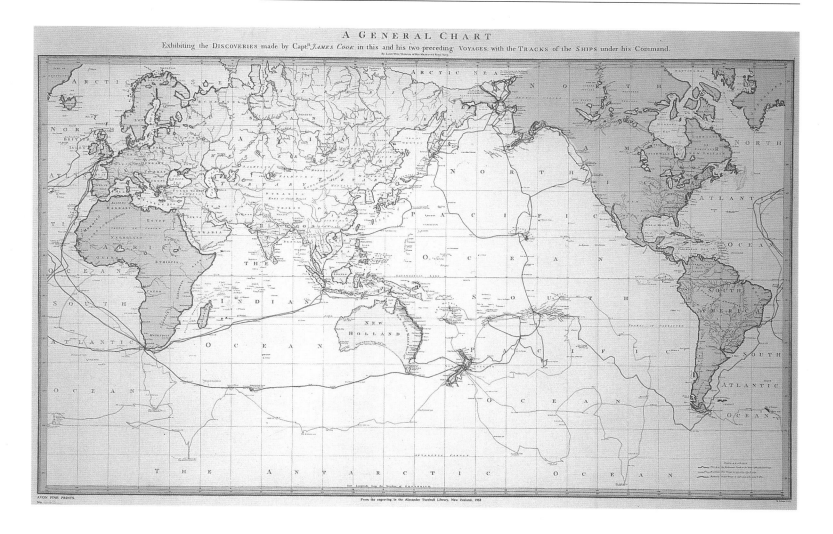

A GENERAL CHART

Exhibiting the DISCOVERIES made by Capt.n JAMES COOK in this and his two preceding VOYAGES, with the TRACKS of the SHIPS under his Command.

By Lieut.t Hen.y Roberts of His Majesty's Royal Navy.

From the engraving in the Alexander Turnbull Library, New Zealand, 1968

His name remains scattered about natural formations of the Pacific, but Cook's beginnings were humble. He was not considered a gentleman among the British aristocracy, having been born in Yorkshire to less than genteel stock, and the Admiralty refused to commission him as a naval officer. After fierce negotiations during the planning of the voyage, he was promoted to lieutenant before setting out to chart terra Australis, the southern continent. He would become Captain Cook later. Cook held high professional and moral standards, remaining chaste when confronted with the sexual advances of some native women, a temptation that others in his party didn't resist.

Cook sailed on his third voyage as a captain in the British Navy, and it was toward the end of this journey that he made contact with the Hawaiian people. Cook's arrival was celebrated with much ceremony, and he left Kealakekua Bay without incident. Upon his return 10 days later to fix a broken mast, his relations

Cook's beginnings were humble. He was not considered a gentleman among the British aristocracy, having been born in Yorkshire to less than genteel stock, and the Admiralty refused to commission him as a naval officer. After fierce negotiations during the planning of the voyage, he was promoted to lieutenant before setting out to chart terra Australis, the southern continent. He would become Captain Cook later.

with the Hawaiians had changed. Cook had taken a king hostage for the return of a stolen cutter, and the natives turned on him and killed him.

Lieutenant John Gore sailed the *Resolution* and *Discovery* home to England in 1780 to end Cook's third Pacific exploration journey. Many of the charts and documents from that voyage have only recently been published.

From Sailing Alone Around the World

BY CAPTAIN JOSHUA SLOCUM, 1900

Slocum was the first person to sail around the world alone. After having wrecked his sailing ship, he was finished as a commercial master. His solution was to rebuild an old wreck of a scalloping boat and set off on one of the great adventures of all times. He was also a wonderful writer, and this passage from his book—a best seller in its day—shows a man of great confidence and skill ploughing through some of the most treacherous seas in the world.

On January 26, 1896, the *Spray*, being refitted and well provisioned in every way, sailed from Buenos Aires. There was little wind at the start; the surface of the great river was like a silver disk, and I was glad of a tow from a harbor tug to clear the port entrance. But a gale came up soon after, and caused an ugly sea, and instead of being all silver, as before, the river was now all mud. The Plate is a treacherous place for storms. One sailing there should always be on the alert for squalls. I cast anchor before dark in the best lee I could find near the land, but was tossed miserably all night, heartsore of choppy seas. On the following morning I got the sloop under way, and with reefed sails worked her down the river against a head wind. Standing in that night to the place where pilot Howard joined me for the up-river sail, I took a departure, shaping my course to clear Point Indio on the one hand, and the English Bank on the other.

I had not for many years been south of these regions. I will not say that I expected all fine sailing on the course for Cape Horn direct, but while I worked at the sails and rigging I thought only of onward and forward. It was when I anchored in the lonely places that a feeling of awe crept over me. At the last anchorage on the monotonous and muddy

river, weak as it may seem, I gave way to my feelings. I resolved then that I would anchor no more north of the Strait of Magellan.

On the 28th of January the *Spray* was clear of Point Indio, English Bank, and all the other dangers of the River Plate. With a fair wind she then bore away for the Strait of Magellan, under all sail, pressing farther and farther toward the wonderland of the South, till I forgot the blessings of our milder North.

My ship passed in safety Bahia Blanca, also the Gulf of St. Matias and the mighty Gulf of St. George. Hoping that she might go clear of the destructive tide-races, the dread of big craft or little along this coast, I gave all the capes a berth of about fifty miles, for these dangers extend many miles from the land. But where the sloop avoided one danger she encountered another. For, one day, well off the Patagonian coast, while the sloop was reaching under short sail, a tremendous wave, the culmination, it seemed, of many waves, rolled down upon her in a storm, roaring as it came. I had only a moment to get all sail down and myself up on the peak halliards, out of danger, when I saw the mighty crest towering masthead-high above me. The mountain of water submerged my vessel. She shook in every timber and reeled under the weight of the sea, but rose quickly out of it, and rode grandly over the rollers that followed. It may have been a minute that from my hold in the rigging I could see no part of the *Spray*'s hull. Perhaps it was even less time than that, but it seemed a long while, for under great excitement one lives fast, and in a few seconds one may think a great deal of one's past life. Not only did the past, with electric speed, flash before me, but I had time while in my hazardous position for resolutions for the future that would take a

long time to fulfil. The first one was, I remember, that if the *Spray* came through this danger I would dedicate my best energies to building a larger ship on her lines, which I hope yet to do. Other promises, less easily kept, I should have made under protest. However, the incident, which filled me with fear, was only one more test of the *Spray*'s seaworthiness. It reassured me against rude Cape Horn.

From the time the great wave swept over the *Spray* until she reached Cape Virgins nothing occurred to move a pulse and set blood in motion. On the contrary, the weather became fine and the sea smooth and life tranquil. The phenomenon of mirage frequently occurred. An albatross sitting on the water one day loomed up like a large ship; two fur-seals asleep on the surface of the sea appeared like great whales, and a bank of haze I could have sworn was high land. The kaleidoscope then changed, and on the following day I sailed in a world peopled by dwarfs.

On February 11 the *Spray* rounded Cape Virgins and entered the Strait of Magellan. The scene was again real and gloomy; the wind, northeast, and blowing a gale, sent feather-white spume along the coast; such a sea ran as would swamp an ill-appointed ship. As the sloop neared the entrance to the strait I observed that two great tide-races made ahead, one very close to the point of the land and one farther offshore. Between the two, in a sort of channel, through combers, went the *Spray* with close-reefed sails. But a rolling sea followed her a long way in, and a fierce current swept around the cape against her; but this she stemmed, and was soon chirruping under the lee of Cape Virgins and running every minute into smoother water. However, long trailing kelp from sunken rocks waved forebodingly under her keel, and the wreck of a great steamship smashed on the beach abreast gave a gloomy aspect to the scene.

I was not to be let off easy. The Virgins would collect tribute even from the *Spray* passing their promontory. Fitful rain-squalls from the northwest followed the northeast gale. I reefed the sloop's sails, and sitting in the cabin to rest my eyes, I was so strongly impressed with what in all nature I might expect that as I dozed the very air I breathed seemed to warn me of danger. My senses heard "*Spray* ahoy!" shouted in warning. I sprang to the deck, wondering who could be there that knew the *Spray* so well as to call out her name passing in the dark; for it was now the blackest of nights all around, except away in the southwest, where the old familiar white arch, the terror of Cape Horn, rapidly pushed up by a southwest gale. I had only a moment to douse sail and lash all solid when it struck like a shot from a cannon, and for the first half-hour it was something to be remembered by way of a gale. For thirty hours it kept on blowing hard. The sloop could carry no more than a three-reefed mainsail and forestaysail; with these she held on stoutly and was not blown out of the strait. In the height of the squalls in this gale she doused all sail, and this occurred often enough.

After this gale followed only a smart breeze, and the *Spray*, passing through the narrows without mishap, cast anchor at Sandy Point on February 14, 1896. Sandy Point (Punta Arenas) is a Chilean coaling-station, and boasts about two thousand inhabitants, of mixed nationality, but mostly Chileans. What with sheep-farming, gold-mining, and hunting, the settlers in this dreary land seemed not the worst off in the world. But the natives, Patagonian and Fuegian, on the other hand, were as squalid as contact with unscrupulous traders could make them. A large percentage of the business there was traffic in "fire-water." If there was a law against selling the poisonous stuff to the natives, it was not enforced. Fine specimens of the Patagonian race, looking smart in the morning when they came into town, had repented before night of ever having seen a white man, so beastly drunk were

they, to say nothing about the peltry of which they had been robbed.

The port at that time was free, but a custom-house was in course of construction, and when it is finished, port and tariff dues are to be collected. A soldier police guarded the place, and a sort of vigilante force besides took down its guns now and then; but as a general thing, to my mind, whenever an execution was made they killed the wrong man. Just previous to my arrival the governor, himself of a jovial turn of mind, had sent a party of young bloods to foray a Fuegian settlement and wipe out what they could of it on account of the recent massacre of a schooner's crew somewhere else. Altogether the place was quite newsy and supported two papers—dailies, I think. The port captain, a Chilean naval officer, advised me to ship hands to fight Indians in the strait farther west, and spoke of my stopping until a gunboat should be going through, which would give me a tow. After canvassing the place, however, I found only one man willing to embark, and he on condition that I should ship another "mon and a doog." But as no one else was willing to come along, and as I drew the line at dogs, I said no more about the matter, but simply loaded my guns. At this point in my dilemma Captain Pedro Samblich, a good Austrian of large experience, coming along, gave me a bag of carpet-tacks, worth more than all the fighting men and dogs of Tierra del Fuego. I protested that I had no use for carpet-tacks on board. Samblich smiled at my want of experience, and maintained stoutly that I would have use for them. "You must use them with discretion," he said; "that is to say, don't step on them yourself." With this remote hint about the use of the tacks I got on all right, and saw the way to maintain clear decks at night without the care of watching.

Samblich was greatly interested in my voyage, and after giving me the tacks he put on board bags of biscuits and a large quantity of smoked venison. He declared that my bread, which was ordinary sea-biscuits and easily broken, was not nutritious as his, which was so hard that I could break it only with a stout blow from a maul. Then he gave me, from his own sloop, a compass which was cer-

tainly better than mine, and offered to unbend her mainsail for me if I would accept it. Last of all, this large-hearted man brought out a bottle of Fuegian gold-dust from a place where it had been cached and begged me to help myself from it, for use farther along on the

> "Fitful rain-squalls from the northwest followed the northeast gale. I reefed the sloop's sails, and sitting in the cabin to rest my eyes, I was so strongly impressed with what in all nature I might expect that as I dozed the very air I breathed seemed to warn me of danger."

voyage. But I felt sure of success without this draft on a friend, and I was right. Samblich's tacks, as it turned out, were of more value than gold.

The port captain finding that I was resolved to go, even alone since there was no help for it, set up no further objections, but advised me, in case the savages tried to surround me with their canoes, to shoot straight, and begin to do it in time, but to avoid killing them if possible, which I heartily agreed to do. With these simple injunctions the officer gave me my port clearance free of charge, and I sailed on the same day, February 19, 1896. It was not without thoughts of strange and stirring adventure beyond all I had yet encountered that I now sailed into the country and very core of the savage Fuegians.

A fair wind from Sandy Point brought me on the first day to St. Nicholas Bay, where, so I was told, I might expect to meet savages; but seeing no signs of life, I came to anchor in eight fathoms of water, where I lay all night under a high mountain. Here I had my first experience with the terrific squalls, called williwaws, which extended from this point on through the strait to the Pacific. They were compressed gales of wind that Boreas handed down over the hills in chunks. A full-blown williwaw will throw a ship, even without sail on, over on her beam ends; but, like other gales, they cease now and then, if only for a short time.

February 20 was my birthday, and I found myself alone, with hardly so much as a bird in sight, off Cape Froward, the southernmost point of the continent of America. By daylight in the morning I was getting my ship under way for the bout ahead.

The sloop held the wind fair while she ran thirty miles farther on her course, which brought her to Fortescue Bay, and at once among the natives' signal-fires, which blazed up now on all sides. Clouds flew over the mountain from the west all day; at night my good east wind failed, and in its stead a gale from the west soon came on. I gained anchorage at twelve o'clock that night, under the lee of a little island, and then prepared myself a cup of coffee, of which I was sorely in need; for, to tell the truth, hard beating in the heavy squalls and against the current had told on my strength. Finding that the anchor held, I drank my beverage, and named the place Coffee Island. It lies to the south of Charles Island, with only a narrow channel between.

By daylight the next morning the *Spray* was again under way, beating hard; but she came to in a cove in Charles Island, two and a half miles along on her course. Here she remained undisturbed two days, with both anchors down in a bed of kelp. Indeed, she might have remained undisturbed indefinitely had not the wind moderated; for during these two days it blew so hard that no boat could venture out on the strait, and the natives being away to other hunting-grounds, the island anchorage was safe. But at the end of the fierce wind-storm fair weather came; then I got my anchors, and again sailed out upon the strait.

Canoes manned by savages from Fortescue now came in pursuit. The wind falling light, they gained on me rapidly till coming within hail, when they ceased paddling, and a bow-legged savage stood up and

called to me, "Yammerschooner! yammerschooner!" which is their begging term. I said, "No!" Now, I was not for letting on that I was alone, and so I stepped into the cabin, and, passing through the hold, came out at the fore-scuttle, changing my clothes as I went along. That made two men. Then the piece of bowsprit which I had sawed off at Buenos Aires, and which I had still on board, I arranged forward on the lookout, dressed as a seaman, attaching a line by which I could pull it into motion. That made three of us, and we didn't want to "yammerschooner"; but for all that the savages came on faster than before. I saw that besides four at the paddles in the canoe nearest to me, there were others in the bottom, and that they were shifting hands often. At eighty yards I fired a shot across the bows of the nearest canoe, at which they all stopped, but only for a moment. Seeing that they persisted in coming nearer, I fired the second shot so close to the chap who wanted to "yammerschooner " that he changed his mind quickly enough and bellowed with fear, "Bueno jo via Isla," and sitting down in his canoe, he rubbed his starboard cat-head for some time. I was thinking of the good port captain's advice when I pulled the trigger, and must have aimed pretty straight; however, a miss was as good as a mile for Mr. "Black Pedro," as he it was, and no other, a leader in several bloody massacres. He made for the island now, and the others followed him. I knew by his Spanish lingo and by his full beard that he was the villain I have named, a renegade mongrel, and the worst murderer in Tierra del Fuego. The authorities had been in search of him for two years. The Fuegians are not bearded.

So much for the first day among the savages. I came to anchor at midnight in Three Island Cove, about twenty miles along from Fortescue Bay. I saw on the opposite side of the strait signal-fires, and heard the barking of dogs, but where I lay it was quite deserted by natives. I have always taken it as a sign that where I found birds sitting about, or seals on the rocks, I should not find savage Indians. Seals are never plentiful in these waters, but in Three Island Cove I saw one on the rocks, and other signs of the absence of savage men.

On the next day the wind was again blowing a gale, and although she was in the lee of the land, the sloop dragged her anchors, so that I had to get her under way and beat farther into the cove, where I came to in a land-locked pool. At another time or place this would have been a rash thing to do, and it was safe now only from the fact that the gale which drove me to shelter would keep the Indians from crossing the strait. Seeing this was the case, I went ashore with gun and ax on an island, where I could not in any event be surprised, and there felled trees and split about a cord of fire-wood, which loaded my small boat several times.

While I carried the wood, though I was morally sure there were no savages near, I never once went to or from the skiff without my gun. While I had that and a clear field of over eighty yards about me I felt safe.

The trees on the island, very scattering, were a sort of beech and a stunted cedar, both of which made good fuel. Even the green limbs of the beech, which seemed to possess a resinous quality, burned readily in my great drum-stove. I have described my method of wooding up in detail, that the reader who has kindly borne with me so far may see that in this, as in all other particulars of my voyage, I took great care against all kinds of surprises, whether by animals or by the elements. In the Strait of Magellan the greatest vigilance was necessary. In this instance I reasoned that I had all about me the greatest danger of the whole voyage & the treachery of cunning savages, for which I must be particularly on the alert.

The *Spray* sailed from Three Island Cove in the morning after the gale went down, but was glad to return for shelter from another sudden gale. Sailing again on the following day, she fetched Borgia Bay, a few miles on her course, where vessels had anchored from time to time and had nailed boards on the trees ashore with name and date of harboring carved or painted. Nothing else could I see to indicate that civilized man had ever been there. I had taken a survey of the gloomy place with my spy-glass, and was getting my boat out to land and take notes, when the Chilean gunboat *Huemel* came in, and officers, coming on board, advised me to leave the place at once, a thing that required little eloquence to persuade me to do. I accepted the captain's kind offer of a tow to the next anchorage, at the place called Notch Cove, eight miles farther along, where I should be clear of the worst of the Fuegians.

We made anchorage at the cove about dark that night, while the wind came down in fierce williwaws from the mountains. An instance of Magellan weather was afforded when the *Huemel*, a well-appointed gunboat of great power, after attempting on the following day to proceed on her voyage, was obliged by sheer force of the wind to return and take up anchorage again and remain till the gale abated; and lucky she was to get back! Meeting this vessel was a little godsend. She was commanded and officered by high-class sailors and educated gentlemen. An entertainment that was gotten up on her, impromptu, at the Notch would be hard to beat anywhere. One of her midshipmen sang popular songs in French, German, and Spanish, and one (so he said) in Russian. If the audience did not know the lingo of one song from another, it was no drawback to the merri-

ment. I was left alone the next day, for then the *Huemel* put out on her voyage the gale having abated. I spent a day taking in wood and water; by the end of that time the weather was fine. Then I sailed from the desolate place.

There is little more to be said concerning the *Spray's* first passage through the strait that would differ from what I have already recorded. She anchored and weighed many times, and beat many days against the current, with now and then a "slant" for a few miles, till finally she gained anchorage and shelter for the night at Port Tamar, with Cape Pillar in sight to the west. Here I felt the throb of the great ocean that lay before me. I knew now that I had put a world behind me, and that I was opening out another world ahead. I had passed the haunts of savages. Great piles of granite mountains of bleak and lifeless aspect were now astern; on some of them not even a speck of moss had ever grown. There was an unfinished newness all about the land. On the hill back of Port Tamar a small beacon had been thrown up, showing that some man had been there. But how could one tell but that he had died of loneliness and grief? In a bleak

land is not the place to enjoy solitude.

Throughout the whole of the strait west of Cape Froward I saw no animals except dogs owned by savages. These I saw often enough, and heard them yelping night and day. Birds were not plentiful. The scream of a wild fowl, which I took for a loon, sometimes startled me with its piercing cry. The steamboat duck, so called because it propels itself over the sea with its wings, and resembles a miniature side-wheel steamer in its motion, was sometimes seen scurrying on out of danger. It never flies, but, hitting the water instead of the air with its wings, it moves faster than a rowboat or a canoe. The few fur-seals I saw were very shy; and of fishes I saw next to none at all. I did not catch one; indeed, I seldom or never put a hook over during the whole voyage. Here in the strait I found great abundance of mussels of an excellent quality. I fared sumptuously on them. There was a sort of swan, smaller than a Muscovy duck, which might have been brought down with the gun, but in the loneliness of life about the dreary country I found myself in no mood to make one life less, except in self-defense.

Notable Marine painter James Mitchell's rendering of the Spray *off Juan Fernandez Island.*

ANATOMY OF A SAILBOAT

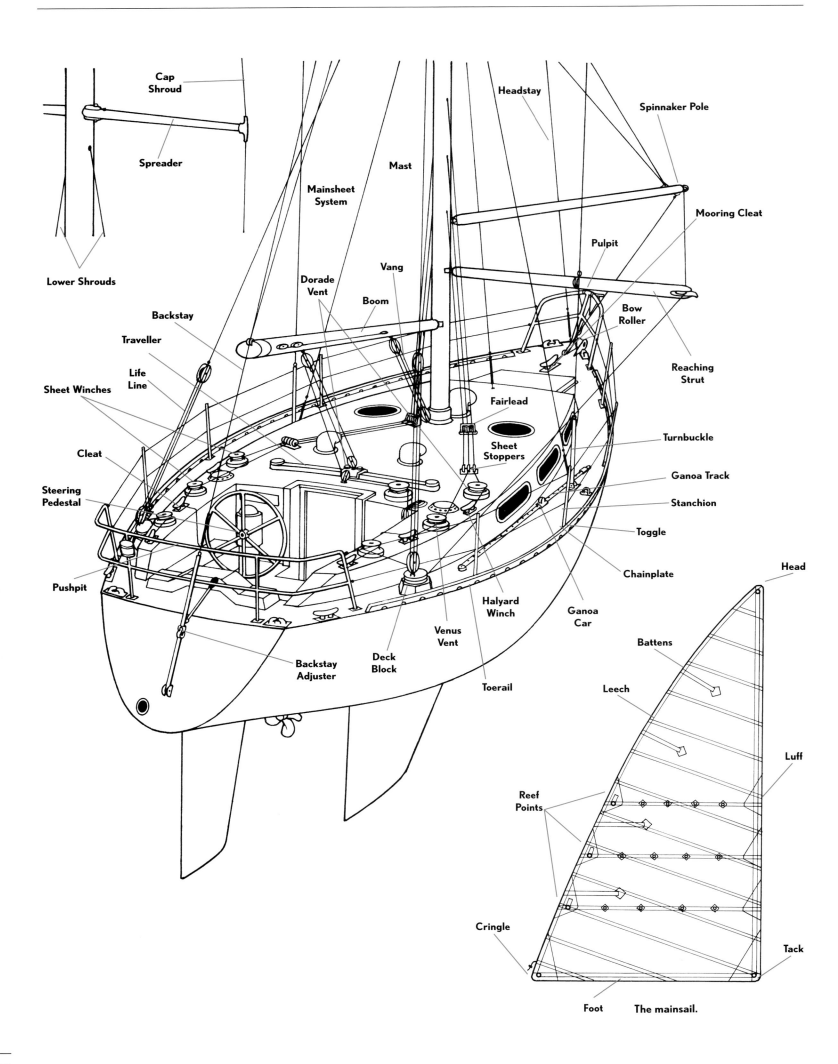

Cap
Shroud

Spreader

Lower Shrouds

Headstay

Spinnaker Pole

Mooring Cleat

Mainsheet
System

Mast

Pulpit

Bow
Roller

Vang

Dorade
Vent

Boom

Backstay

Traveller

Reaching
Strut

Life
Line

Sheet Winches

Fairlead

Turnbuckle

Sheet
Stoppers

Ganoa Track

Cleat

Stanchion

Steering
Pedestal

Toggle

Chainplate

Head

Pushpit

Halyard
Winch

Ganoa
Car

Backstay
Adjuster

Deck
Block

Venus
Vent

Battens

Toerail

Leech

Luff

Reef
Points

Cringle

Tack

Foot   The mainsail.

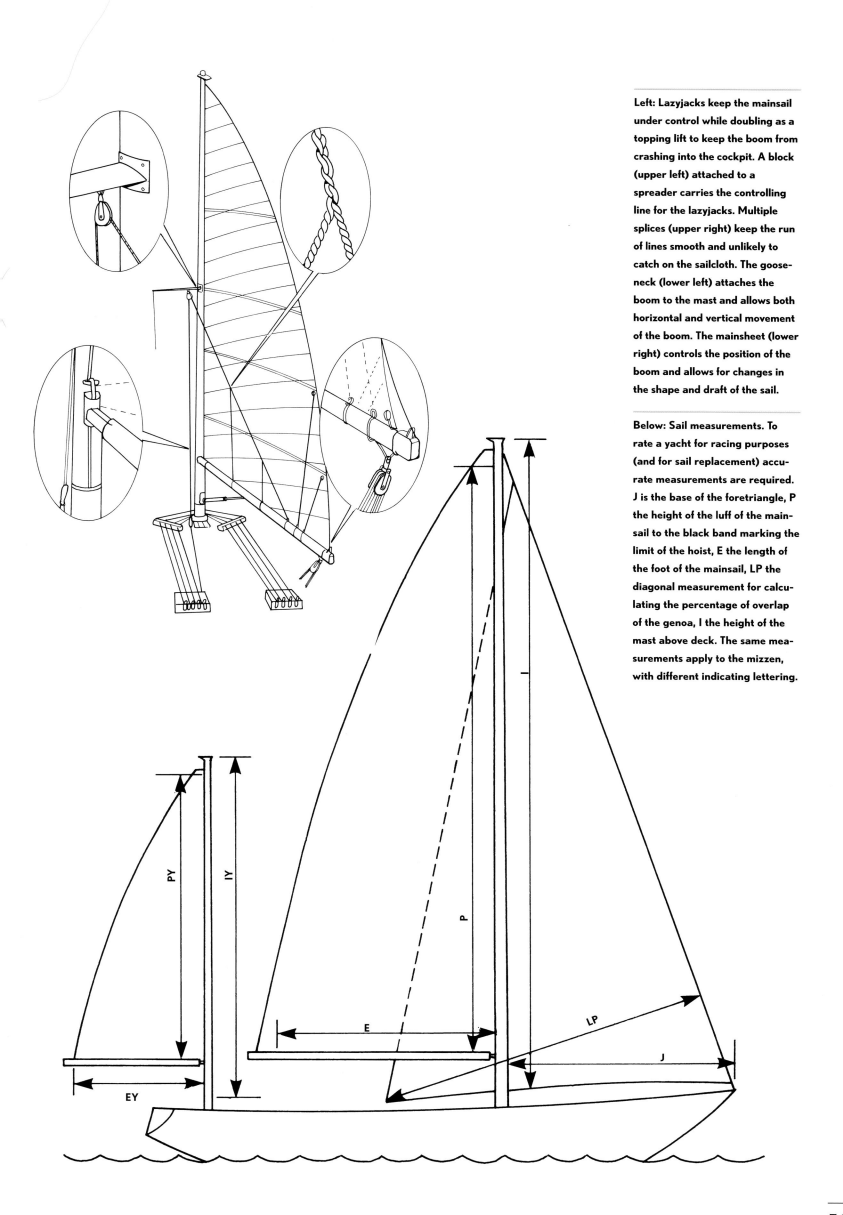

Left: Lazyjacks keep the mainsail under control while doubling as a topping lift to keep the boom from crashing into the cockpit. A block (upper left) attached to a spreader carries the controlling line for the lazyjacks. Multiple splices (upper right) keep the run of lines smooth and unlikely to catch on the sailcloth. The gooseneck (lower left) attaches the boom to the mast and allows both horizontal and vertical movement of the boom. The mainsheet (lower right) controls the position of the boom and allows for changes in the shape and draft of the sail.

Below: Sail measurements. To rate a yacht for racing purposes (and for sail replacement) accurate measurements are required. J is the base of the foretriangle, P the height of the luff of the mainsail to the black band marking the limit of the hoist, E the length of the foot of the mainsail, LP the diagonal measurement for calculating the percentage of overlap of the genoa, I the height of the mast above deck. The same measurements apply to the mizzen, with different indicating lettering.

WOODEN BOAT CONSTRUCTION

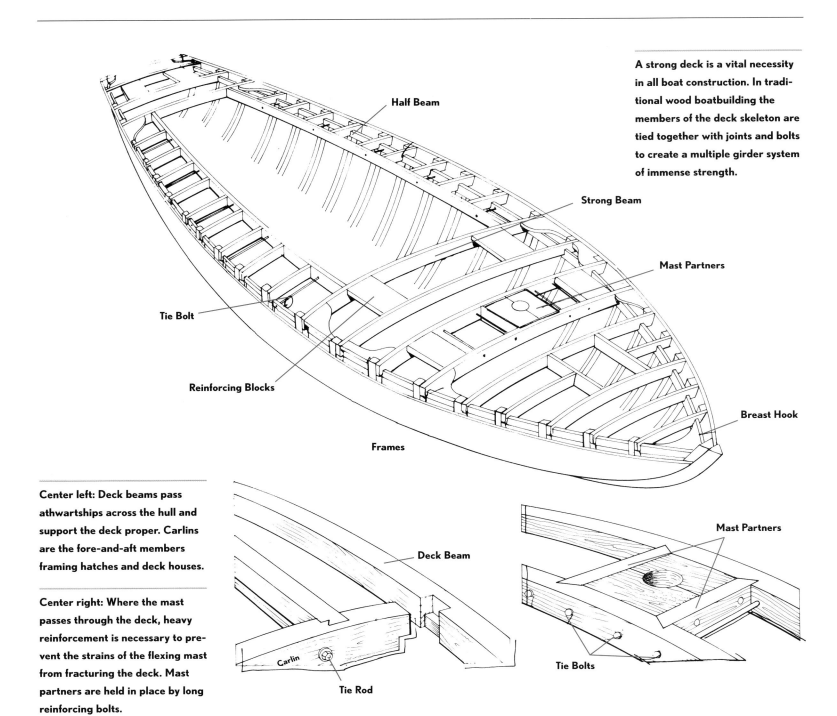

Half Beam

Strong Beam

Mast Partners

Tie Bolt

Reinforcing Blocks

Breast Hook

Frames

A strong deck is a vital necessity in all boat construction. In traditional wood boatbuilding the members of the deck skeleton are tied together with joints and bolts to create a multiple girder system of immense strength.

Center left: Deck beams pass athwartships across the hull and support the deck proper. Carlins are the fore-and-aft members framing hatches and deck houses.

Deck Beam

Mast Partners

Carlin

Tie Rod

Tie Bolts

Center right: Where the mast passes through the deck, heavy reinforcement is necessary to prevent the strains of the flexing mast from fracturing the deck. Mast partners are held in place by long reinforcing bolts.

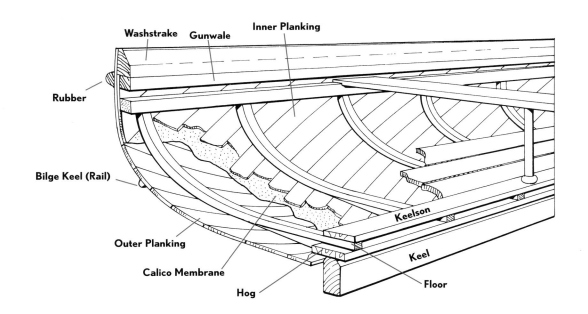

Washstrake   Gunwale   Inner Planking

Rubber

Bilge Keel (Rail)

Outer Planking

Calico Membrane

Hog

Keelson

Keel

Floor

Below: Double-planked hulls are strong and resistant to the ingress of the sea. Before cold molding became practicable, they were the construction method of choice for proper yachts. In this type of construction, the layers of planking were fastened at angles to one another, thus creating a sort of primitive, mechanically fastened, plywood.

Deck house or cabin top construction. Deck houses have to withstand great abuse by the sea. All parts must be mechanically locked into a single, strong unit. Using complex joinery and strategically-placed bolts, the shipwright can create a virtually indestructible unit.

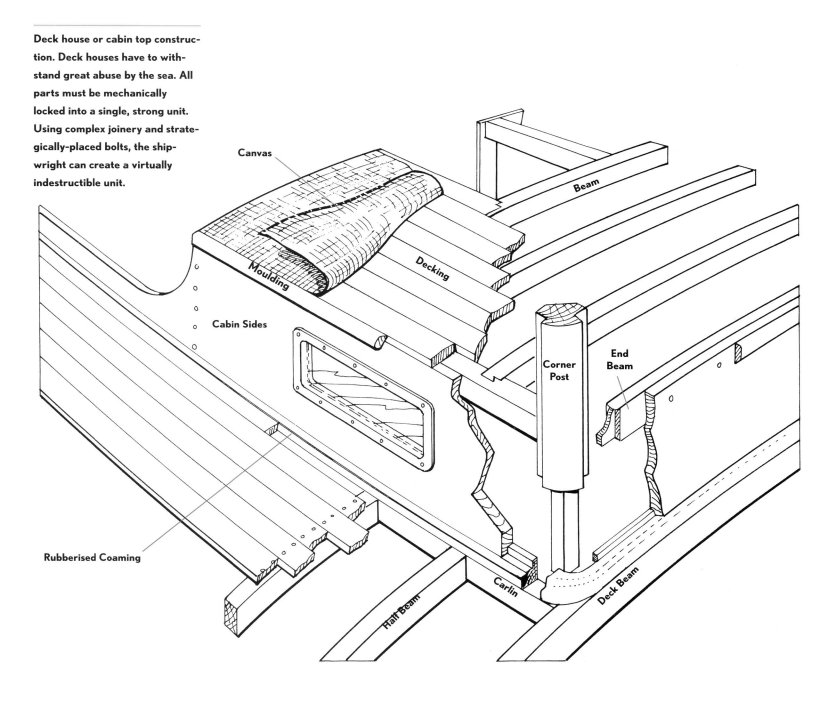

Canvas

Beam

Moulding

Decking

Cabin Sides

Corner Post

End Beam

Rubberised Coaming

Half Beam

Carlin

Deck Beam

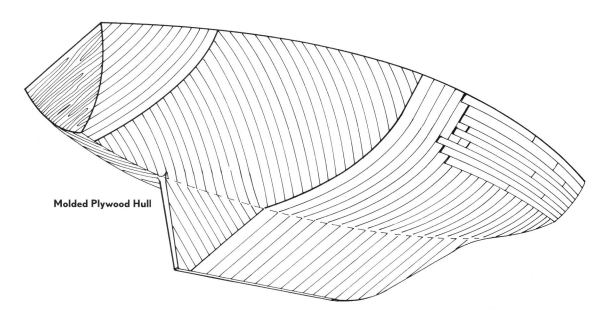

Molded Plywood Hull

In cold molded hulls, the planking (usually several layers of thin veneers) is layed at 45 degree angles to one another with the outer layer running fore-and-aft. Modern adhesives, such as epoxy, have made this form of construction totally impervious to the ingress of the sea.

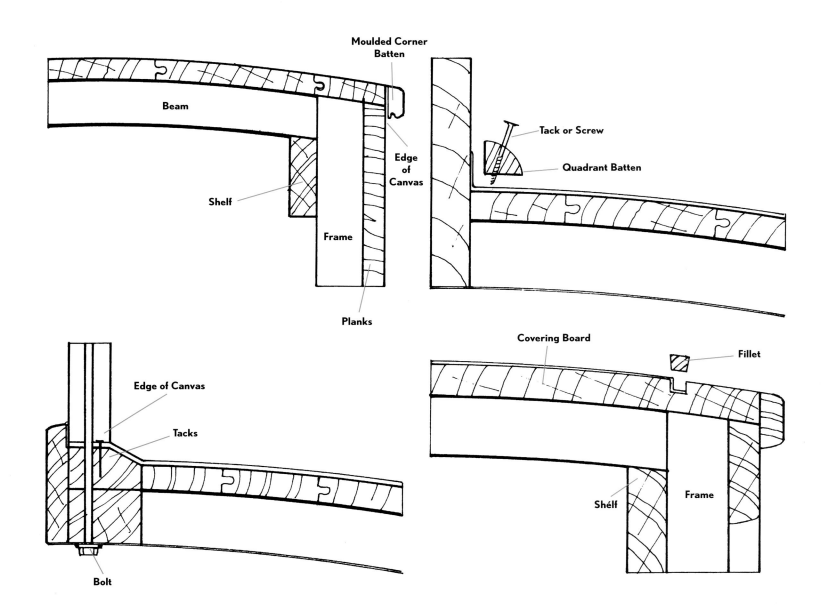

Beam

Moulded Corner Batten

Shelf

Frame

Edge of Canvas

Planks

Tack or Screw

Quadrant Batten

Edge of Canvas

Tacks

Bolt

Covering Board

Fillet

Shelf

Frame

Details of cabin top construction. Every possible precaution must be made for suppressing potential water damage. Battens and molding prevent covering canvas (or Dynel or fiberglass) from presenting a raw edge to incoming water.

Right: Stepping a mast using a crane in the famous yacht *Ranger*.

Solid Wood Partners

Heavy Room Beam

Half Beam

Wedges

Knees

Mast Step

Tie Bar

Tie Bolt

Right: Knees or tie bolts not only keep the mast in place, but also prevent the hull and deck from flexing under the enormous strains imparted by the downward thrust of the mast and the high tention of the standing rigging.

From The Sea-Wolf

BY JACK LONDON

"From out of the fog came the mournful tolling of a bell, and I could see the pilot turning the wheel with great rapidity. The bell, which had seemed straight ahead, was now sounding from the side. Our own whistle was blowing hoarsely, and from time to time the sound of other whistles came to us from out of the fog."

Chapter One

I scarcely know where to begin, though I sometimes facetiously place the cause of it all to Charley Furuseth's credit. He kept a summer cottage in Mill Valley, under the shadow of Mount Tamalpais, and never occupied it except when he loafed through the winter months and read Nietzsche and Schopenhauer to rest his brain. When summer came on, he elected to sweat out a hot and dusty existence in the city and to toil incessantly. Had it not been my custom to run up to see him every Saturday afternoon and to stop over till Monday morning, this particular January Monday morning would not have found me afloat on San Francisco Bay.

Not but that I was afloat in a safe craft, for the *Martinez* was a new ferry-steamer, making her fourth or fifth trip on the run between Sausalito and San Francisco. The danger lay in the heavy fog which blanketed the bay, and of which, as a landsman, I had little apprehension. In fact, I remember the placid exaltation with which I took up my position on the forward upper deck, directly beneath the pilot-house, and allowed the mystery of the fog to lay hold of my imagination. A fresh breeze was blowing, and for a time I was alone in the moist obscurity; yet not alone, for I was dimly conscious of the presence of the pilot, and of what I took to be the captain, in the glass house above my head.

I remember thinking how comfortable it was, this division of labor which made it unnecessary for me to study fogs, winds, tides, and navigation in order to visit my friend who lived across an arm of the sea. It was good that men should be specialists, I mused. The peculiar knowledge of the pilot and captain sufficed for many thousands of people who knew no more of the sea and navigation than I knew. On the other hand, instead of having to devote my energy to the learning of a multitude of things, I concentrated it upon a few particular things, such as, for instance, the analysis of Poe's place in American literature, an essay of mine, by the way, in the current 'Atlantic.' Coming aboard, as I passed through the cabin, I had noticed with greedy eyes a stout gentleman reading the 'Atlantic,' which was open at my very essay. And there it was again, the division of labor, the special knowledge of the pilot and captain which permitted the stout gentleman to read my special knowledge on Poe while they carried him safely from Sausalito to San Francisco.

A red-faced man, slamming the cabin door behind him and stumping out on the deck, interrupted my reflections, though I made a mental note of the topic for use in a projected essay which I had thought of calling 'The Necessity for Freedom: A Plea for the Artist.' The red-faced man shot a glance up at the pilot-house, gazed around at the fog, stumped across the deck and back (he evidently had artificial legs), and stood still by my side, legs wide apart and with an expression of keen enjoyment on his face. I was not wrong when I decided that his days had been spent on the sea.

'It's nasty weather like this here that turns heads gray before their time,' he said, with a nod toward the pilot-house.

'I had not thought there was any particular strain,' I answered. 'It seems as simple as a-b-c. They know the direction by compass, the distance, and the speed. I should not call it anything more than mathematical certainty.'

'Strain!' he snorted. 'Simple as a-b-c! Mathematical certainty!' He seemed to brace himself up and lean backward against the air as he stared at me.

'How about this here tide that's rushin' out through the Golden Gate?' he demanded, or bellowed, rather. 'How fast is she ebbin'? What's the drift, eh? Listen to that, will you! A bell-buoy, and we're atop of it! See 'em alterin' the course!'

From out of the fog came the mournful tolling of a bell, and I could see the pilot turning the wheel with great rapidity. The bell, which had seemed straight ahead, was now sounding from the side. Our own whistle was blowing hoarsely, and from time to time the sound of other whistles came to us from out of the fog.

'That's a ferryboat of some sort,' the newcomer said, indicating a whistle off to the right. 'And there! D'ye hear that? Blown by mouth. Some scow schooner, most likely. Better watch out, Mr. Schooner-man. Ah, I thought so.'

The unseen ferryboat was blowing blast after blast, and the mouth-blown horn was tooting in terror-stricken fashion.

'And now they're payin' their respects to each other and tryin' to get clear,' the red-faced man went on, as the hurried whistling ceased.

His face was shining, his eyes flashing with excitement, as he translated into articulate language the speech of the horns and sirens. 'That's a steam-siren a-goin' it over there to the left. And you hear that fellow with a frog in his throat- a steam-schooner, as near as I can judge, crawlin' in from the Heads against the tide.'

A shrill little whistle, piping as if gone mad, came from directly ahead and from very near at hand. Gongs sounded on the *Martinez*. Our paddlewheels stopped, their pulsing beat died away, and then they started again. The shrill little whistle, like the chirping of a cricket amid the cries of great beasts, shot through the fog from more to the side and swiftly grew faint and fainter. I looked to my companion for enlightenment.

'One of them daredevil launches,' he said. 'I almost wish we'd sunk him, the little rip! They're the cause of more trouble. And what good are they? Any jackass gets aboard one and thinks he can run it, blowin' his whistle to beat the band and tellin' the rest of the world to look out for him because he's comin' and can't look out for himself. Because he's comin'! And you've got to look out, too. Right of way! Common decency! They don't know the meanin' of it!'

I felt quite amused at his unwarranted choler, and while he stumped moodily up and down I fell to dwelling upon the romance of the fog. And romantic it certainly was—the fog, like the gray shadow of infinite mystery, brooding over the whirling speck of earth; and men, mere motes of light and sparkle, cursed with an insane relish for work, riding their steeds of wood and steel through the heart of the mystery, groping their way blindly through the unseen, and clamoring and clanging in confident speech the while their hearts are heavy with incertitude and fear.

The voice of my companion brought me back to myself with a laugh. I, too, had been groping and floundering, the while I thought I rode clear-eyed through the mystery.

'Hello! Somebody comin' our way,' he was saying. 'And d'ye hear that? He's comin' fast. Walkin' right along. Guess he don't hear us yet. Wind's in wrong direction.'

The fresh breeze was blowing right down upon us, and I could hear the whistle plainly, off to one side and a little ahead.

'Ferryboat?' I asked.

He nodded, then added: 'Or he wouldn't be keepin' up such a clip.' He gave a short chuckle. 'They're gettin' anxious up there.'

I glanced up. The captain had thrust his head and shoulders out of the pilot-house and was staring intently into the fog, as though by sheer force of will he could penetrate it. His face was anxious, as was the face of my companion, who had stumped over to the rail and was gazing with a like intentness in the direction of the invisible danger.

Then everything happened, and with inconceivable rapidity. The fog seemed to break away as though split by a wedge, and the bow of a steamboat emerged, trailing fog-wreaths on each side like seaweed on the snout of Leviathan. I could see the pilot-house and a white-bearded man leaning partly out of it, on his elbows. He was clad in a blue uniform, and I remember noting how trim and quiet he was. His quietness, under the circumstances, was terrible. He accepted Destiny, marched hand in hand with it, and coolly measured the stroke. As he leaned there, he ran a calm and speculative eye over us, as though to determine the precise point of the collision, and took no notice whatever when our pilot, white with rage, shouted, 'Now you've done it!'

'Grab hold of something and hang on!' the red-faced man said to me. All his bluster had gone, and he seemed to have caught the contagion of preternatural calm. 'And listen to the women scream,' he said grimly, almost bitterly, I thought, as though he had been through the experience before.

The vessels came together before I could follow his advice. We must have been struck squarely amidships, for I saw nothing, the strange steamboat having passed beyond my line of vision. The *Martinez* heeled over sharply, and there was a crashing and rending of timber. I was thrown flat on the wet deck, and before I could scramble to my feet I heard the screams of the women. This it was, I am certain,- the most indescribable of bloodcurdling sounds,- that threw me into a panic. I remembered the life-preservers stored in the cabin, but was met at the door and swept backward by a wild rush of men and women. What happened in the next few minutes I do not recollect, though I have a clear remembrance of pulling down life-preservers from the overhead racks while the red-faced man fastened them about the bodies of an hysterical group of women. This memory is as distinct and sharp as that of any picture I have seen. It is a picture, and I can see it now- the jagged edges of the hole in the side of the cabin, through which the gray fog swirled and eddied; the empty upholstered seats, littered with all the evidences of sudden flight, such as packages, hand-satchels, umbrellas, and wraps; the stout gentleman who had been reading my essay, incased in cork and canvas, the magazine still in his hand, and asking me with monotonous insistence if I thought there was any danger; the red-faced man stumping gallantly around on his artificial legs and buckling life-preservers on all comers; and, finally, the screaming bedlam of women.

This it was, the screaming of the women, that most tried my nerves. It must have tried, too, the nerves of the red-faced man, for I have another picture which will never fade from my mind. The stout gentleman is stuffing the magazine into his overcoat pocket and looking on curiously. A tangled mass of women, with drawn, white faces and open mouths, is shrieking like a chorus of lost souls; and the red-faced man, his face now purplish with wrath, and with arms extended overhead, as in the act of hurling thunderbolts, is shouting, 'Shut up! Oh, shut up!'

I remember the scene impelled me to sudden laughter, and in the next instant I realized that I was becoming hysterical myself; for these were women, of my own kind, like my mother and sisters, with the fear of death upon them and unwilling to die. And I remember that the sounds they made reminded me of the squealing of pigs under the knife of the butcher, and I was struck with horror at the vividness of the analogy. These women, capable of the most sublime emotions, of the tenderest sympathies, were open-mouthed and screaming. They wanted to live; they were helpless, like rats in a trap, and they screamed.

The horror of it drove me out on deck. I was feeling sick and squeamish, and sat down on a bench. In a hazy way I saw and heard men rushing and shouting as they strove to lower the boats. It was just as I had read descriptions of such scenes in books. The tackles jammed. Nothing worked. One boat lowered away with the plugs out, filled with women and children and then with water, and capsized. Another boat had been lowered by one end and still hung in the tackle by the other end where it had been abandoned. Nothing was to be seen of the strange steamboat which had caused the disaster, though I heard men saying that she would undoubtedly send boats to our assistance.

I descended to the lower deck. The *Martinez* was sinking fast, for the water was very near. Numbers of the passengers were leaping overboard. Others, in the water, were clamoring to be taken aboard again. No one heeded them. A cry arose that we were sinking. I was seized by the consequent panic, and went over the side in a surge of bodies. How I went over I do not know, though I did know, and instantly, why those in the water were so desirous of getting back on the steamer. The water was cold- so cold that it was painful. The pang, as I plunged into it, was as quick and sharp as that of fire. It bit to the marrow. It was like the grip of death. I gasped with the anguish and shock of it, filling my lungs before the life-preserver popped me to the surface. The taste of the salt was strong in my mouth, and I was strangling with the acrid stuff in my throat and lungs.

But it was the cold that was most distressing. I felt that I could survive but a few minutes. People were struggling and floundering in the water about me. I could hear them crying out to one another. And I heard, also, the sound of oars. Evidently the strange steamboat had lowered its boats. As the time went by I marveled that I was still alive. I had no sensation whatever in my lower limbs, while a chilling numbness was wrapping about my heart and

creeping into it. Small waves, with spiteful foaming crests, continually broke over me and into my mouth, sending me off into more strangling paroxysms.

The noises grew indistinct, though I heard a final and despairing chorus of screams in the distance and knew that the *Martinez* had gone down. Later, how much later I have no knowledge,- I came to myself with a start of fear.

I was alone, I could hear no calls or cries-only the sound of the waves, made weirdly hollow and reverberant by the fog. A panic in a crowd, which partakes of a sort of community of interest, is not so terrible as a panic when one is by oneself; and such a panic I now suffered. Whither was I drifting? The red-faced man had said that the tide was ebbing through the Golden Gate. Was I, then, being carried out to sea? And the life-preserver in which I floated? was it not liable to go to pieces at any moment? I had heard of such things being made of paper and hollow rushes, which quickly became saturated and lost all buoyancy. I could not swim a stroke, and I was alone, floating, apparently, in the midst of a gray primordial vastness. I confess that a madness seized me, that I shrieked aloud as the women had shrieked, and beat the water with my numb hands.

How long this lasted I have no conception, for a blankness intervened, of which I remember no more than one remembers of troubled and painful sleep. When I aroused, it was as after centuries of time, and I saw, almost above me and emerging from the fog, the bow of a vessel and three triangular sails, each shrewdly lapping the other and filled with wind. Where the bow cut the water there was a great foaming and gurgling, and I seemed directly in its path. I tried to cry out, but was too exhausted. The bow plunged down, just missing me and sending a swash of water clear over my head. Then the long black side of the vessel began slipping past, so near that I could have touched it with my hands. I tried to reach it, in a mad resolve to claw into the wood with my nails; but my arms were heavy and lifeless. Again I strove to call out, but made no sound.

The stern of the vessel shot by, dropping, as it did so, into a hollow between the waves; and I caught a glimpse of a man standing at a wheel, and of another man who seemed to be

doing little else than smoke a cigar. I saw the smoke issuing from his lips as he slowly turned his head and glanced out over the water in my direction. It was a careless, unpremeditated glance, one of those haphazard things men do when they have no immediate call to do anything in particular, but act because they are alive and must do something.

But life and death were in that glance. I could see the vessel being swallowed up in the fog; I saw the back of the man at the wheel, and the head of the other man turning, slowly turning, as his gaze struck the water and casually lifted along it toward me. His face wore an

"When I aroused, it was as after centuries of time, and I saw, almost above me and emerging from the fog, the bow of a vessel and three triangular sails, each shrewdly lapping the other and filled with wind."

absent expression, as of deep thought, and I became afraid that if his eyes did light upon me he would nevertheless not see me. But his eyes did light upon me, and looked squarely into mine; and he did see me, for he sprang to the wheel, thrusting the other man aside, and whirled it round and round, hand over hand, at the same time shouting orders of some sort. The vessel seemed to go off at a tangent to its former course and to leap almost instantly from view into the fog.

I felt myself slipping into unconsciousness, and tried with all the power of my will to fight above the suffocating blankness and darkness that was rising around me. A little later I heard the stroke of oars, growing nearer and nearer, and the calls of a man. When he was very near I heard him crying, in vexed fashion: 'Why in-don't you sing out?'

This meant me, I thought, and then the blankness and darkness rose over me.

Legendary sailor Hal Roth shoots a sight in heavy seas from the cockpit of *Whisper*.

Navigating the Oceans

Early Navigation: Instinct and Information

One of the salient characteristics of the world's oceans is that there are very few signposts in the endless expanse of sea. For thousands of miles, no land, no rock, no buoys appear. How does one find out where one is? And how can one keep track of where one is going?

For thousands of years this was a matter of guesswork. A person in a boat would do one of two things: follow intuition and paddle in the direction he or she *knew* was correct, or rig a panel of cloth and let the prevailing winds blow the boat where they would.

There were no compasses, no concept of magnetic poles. There was little need for sophisticated navigation instruments since people stayed close to land,

hugging the shores out of fear and respect for the waters.

In the Mediterranean, where western navigation began, prevailing winds are from the West or North and trade patterns developed from East to West and West to East. After all, in an enclosed sea sooner or later you will find a landfall, hopefully one where you can trade.

Over hundreds of years, sailors in the eastern Mediterranean learned the wind patterns, learned the seas and local conditions. Developed instinct became the norm for navigation. There were no charts in the modern sense, no surveying or mapping of shorelines, currents, tides or underwater obstacles. Gradually, however, the accumulated knowledge of generations of seafarers was put together in written form…not yet

a chart but more of a guidebook to landmarks, shoals, winds and tides in a given area.

These compilations were jealously guarded, for they could literally be worth their weight in gold. Now we know that the advancement of knowledge comes through openness and the free sharing of information. The people of the Renaissance knew this as well, but it took the vision of a determined and powerful person to organize the extant information on the seas— navigational, meteorological and seasonal—and create a center for its organization and eventual dissemination. This was Prince Henry of Portugal. He set up shop, so to speak, at the very southwestern tip of Europe, Sagres in Portugal. There he started to collect the data from merchants and seamen, applying

his passions to the realm of exploration. Portuguese ships went ever southward down the coast of Africa. After Henry's death, Portuguese seamen rounded the Cape of Good Hope, and proved that the world didn't end suddenly in a maelstrom of gigantic proportion, as sailors before them had thought. Thus were seamen inspired to a true exploratory zeal. All waters led somewhere and, were probably connected. A new era was open.

But, even with the accumulated knowledge that Prince Henry's ships gathered, a more nebulous problem loomed: sailors still had no way to find their position when out of sight of land. And even when sailing in proximity to land, if the coast had never been mapped one still had to deal with the unknown.

could be taken and the ship and crew were at the mercy of the navigator's correct interpretation of scant data. This was particularly a problem in the southern latitudes and in the North Atlantic, where overcast skies, winter storms and heavy fog all made life difficult, not to say treacherous. This was most evident in the approaches to New England and in rounding Cape Horn.

Sailing from Europe to America, ships usually headed west at the latitude of Newfoundland, dropping down the coast to reach the ports of New England. Unfortunately, these waters were, and are, littered with glacial rock formations, bound by fog (due to the warm Gulf Stream interacting with colder air and subject to severe winter storms, especially crossing the Grand Banks, which shelve up, causing heavy seas. Navigating a landfall in these waters was often a chancy operation and many ships were wrecked or sank without a trace.

When out of sight of land for more than a day, dead reckoning was pretty much a hit or miss

With two caravels in the distance, an early explorer shoots a sun sight from land.

The compass was just becoming accepted in a recognizable form with a needle suspended over a compass card, but magnetic variation was still a secret. Knowing what direction one was going was of little help unless one knew how far one was from an objective and how fast the ship was sailing.

But with confirmation that the earth was a revolving planet and spherical—more or less—it became obvious that the only way you could know where you were was to know the precise time at a given point on the planet. This became the greatest challenge of the early mariner.

Dead Reckoning
So, for centuries, sailors relied on dead reckoning, whereby the mariner estimated his course and speed through the water and calculated the distance run in a 24 hour period. No astronomical observations were involved and it wasn't very accurate. Columbus' dead reckoning was way off on his first voyage. Part of the problem is that we always guess our speed to be faster than it actually is. The speed of a sailing ship is a function of its waterline, the maximum being 1.34 times the square root of the waterline length. Rarely is that maximum reached, except in a strong gale. Thus a 70-foot caravel of the 15th century probably averaged about four to five knots…not exactly a thrilling rate.

Even after the invention of the compass, sextant, chronometer and the development of celestial navigation, dead reckoning remained the only way to plot one's position if the skies were cloudy. Without sun or stars visible, no sextant sights

A traditional, flat-card compass marked in points and set in gimbals to remain level in rough seas.

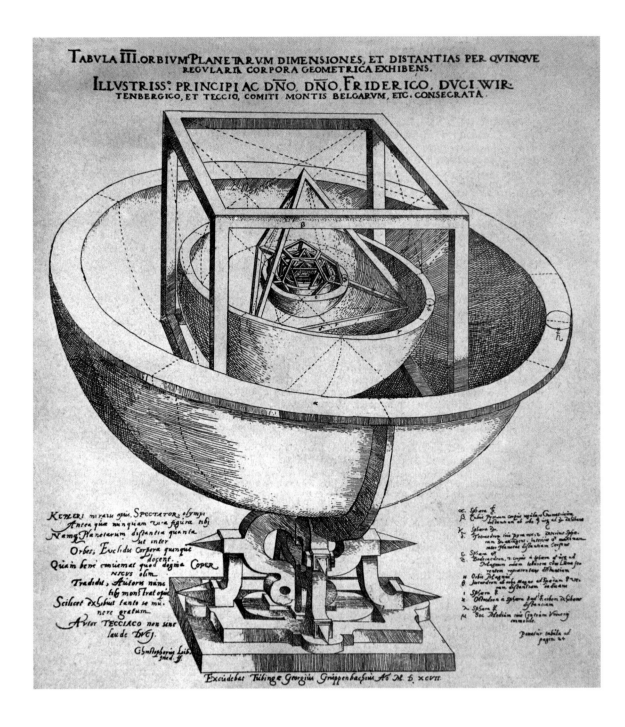

Kepleri miraru opis. Spectator olympi
Antea quã minquam via figura tibi
Namq Planetarum distantia quanta
et inter
Orbes, Euclidis Corpora quinque
docent.
Quãm bene conuenat quod dogma Coper
nicus olim
Tradidit, Autorem nunc
tibi monstrat opus.
Scilicet exibus tanto se mu-
nere gratum.
Auter Tecciaco non sine
laude Duci.
Christopherus Leib-
qued ff

Excudebat Tübingæ Georgius Grüppenbachius Aō M. D. xcvii.

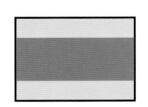

DELTA

— • •

KEEP WELL CLEAR OF ME, I AM MANEUVERING WITH DIFFICULTY.

proposition until the invention of the chip log. This rather simple device allowed the sailor to actually measure the real speed through the water. It wasn't a perfect solution, for a sailing ship's speed varies from minute to minute, depending on sea conditions, wind speed, sail trim and helmsmanship. But it was certainly better than looking over the side and guessing wrong.

Renaissance sailors had a reasonable way of judging latitude, using the cross-staff, or later the backstaff, a simple instrument that allowed the sailor to measure the altitude of the sun above the horizon, thus giving the position north or south of the equator.

Looking to the Skies: Celestial Navigation

But finding one's way east or west was more of a problem. Since longitude can be found accurately *at sea* only with knowledge of the precise time, solving the problem meant building a reliable, accurate clock: a chronometer. Before John Harrison was able to construct the first reliable chronometer (his fourth model) in 1761, the mechanical knowledge and material resources were not up to the task. The only way to find longitude was the lunar method, which required careful observations of the moon,

coupled with complex and frustrating mathematical calculations, a skill few sailors of the time possessed. The fact that early explorers actually accomplished what they did has to be understood as a remarkable feat of seamanship and navigation.

With time, technology and experience, things improved. From the 16th through the 19th centuries, the oceans and coastlines of the world were charted, currents were located and mapped, tides noted and seasonal wind patterns discovered and recorded.

But the fact is, the ocean is a very unpredictable place and human beings make errors. Through the centuries, captains still misjudged landfalls, ships were wrecked on rocks and outcroppings charted and uncharted, storms blew vessels off course and ashore and instruments were out of adjustment or compasses were not compensated for deviation. Anything could happen, and often did.

If a ship left the English Channel and headed toward the East Coast of America, over 3,000 miles of ocean had to be crossed and the margin for error was very

A Chart
of the Sea coasts of
NEW=ENGLAND
NEW-JARSEY VIRGINIA
MARYLAND and CAROLINA
From C.Cod to C.Hatteras
By John Seller Hydrogr.
to the King

Eng: and Fren: loagues
Dü̈ytsche Mylen
Leagueas de Spania

NEW YORKE

Long Island

Hudsons River

MARYLAND

UIRGINIA

HENRICO

NORTH PART OF CAROLINA

ALBEMARLE R

CAROLINÆ PARS

The Sound   Cape Hatteras

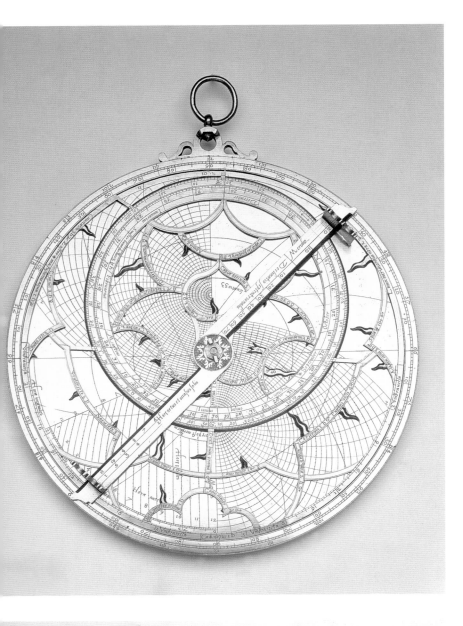

Above: Astrolabe. This rather beautiful example was used to measure the altitude of heavenly bodies, allowing the determination of longitude.

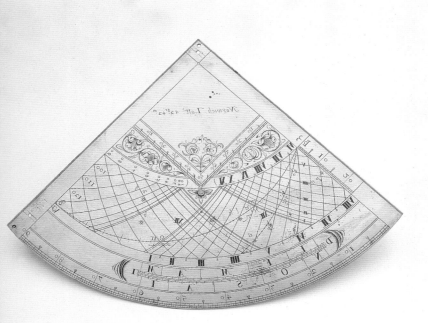

Below: The Quadrant. A reflecting astronomical instrument for measuring angles with a quarter circle graduated arc.

For the truth is that I already know as much about my fate as I need to know. The day will come when I will die. So the only matter of consequence before me is what I will do with my allotted time. I can remain on shore, paralyzed with fear, or I can raise my sails and dip and soar in the breeze.

—*Richard Bode*

slight indeed. Five seconds of lost time could mean a mistake of close to 30 miles in celestial navigation. If that ship were heading for Boston, chances are, the mistake could send her onto the shoals off Nantucket. The number of ships sunk on Nantucket Shoals over the centuries attests to this, even within the past decade.

In fog, reduced visibility or severe sea conditions, any mistake in calculating position can be fatal, especially in soundings—within the 100-fathom line or continental shelf.

Sailors in the Pacific faced the same problem, not only because of the enormous distances involved, but because the number of uncharted reefs (even today) and atolls made any

Opposite page: Even with GPS and satellite information systems, navigators use charts, like this one of the entrance to San Francisco Bay, to safely approach heavy traffic areas.

landfall both a hit-or-miss as well as a scarifying proposition. Hitting a reef usually meant the loss of the ship and all hands.

Before GPS and electronic navigation, all depended on sun sights, at least in ocean passages. On a ship this is comparatively easy, as the motion is dampened by sheer displacement of the vessel and two sailors traditionally took sights, one using the sextant, one noting angles and time. On a small yacht, multiple readings are usually necessary, meaning multiple computations as well.

Accuracy is usually not too great (within a mile or two) and in approaching any landfall, this can be a distinct disadvantage. Also, sextants can easily be damaged. Any misalignment or distortion in the frame (easy to occur in tropical climates) can throw a final position off by miles.

The Basics: Sextant, Compass, Chronometer

For many hundreds of years, sailors relied on sextants. A sextant is crucial in celestial navigation, as well as coastal navigation—and before GPS, was the most accurate way to find position.

A navigator looks through the horizon glass, and then moves the index bar along an arc on the frame of the sextant, until the sun (or star or moon) is visible in the horizon glass. The sextant is then set to display the angle at which the sight was taken, and after a few sights have been taken over time, position can be determined.

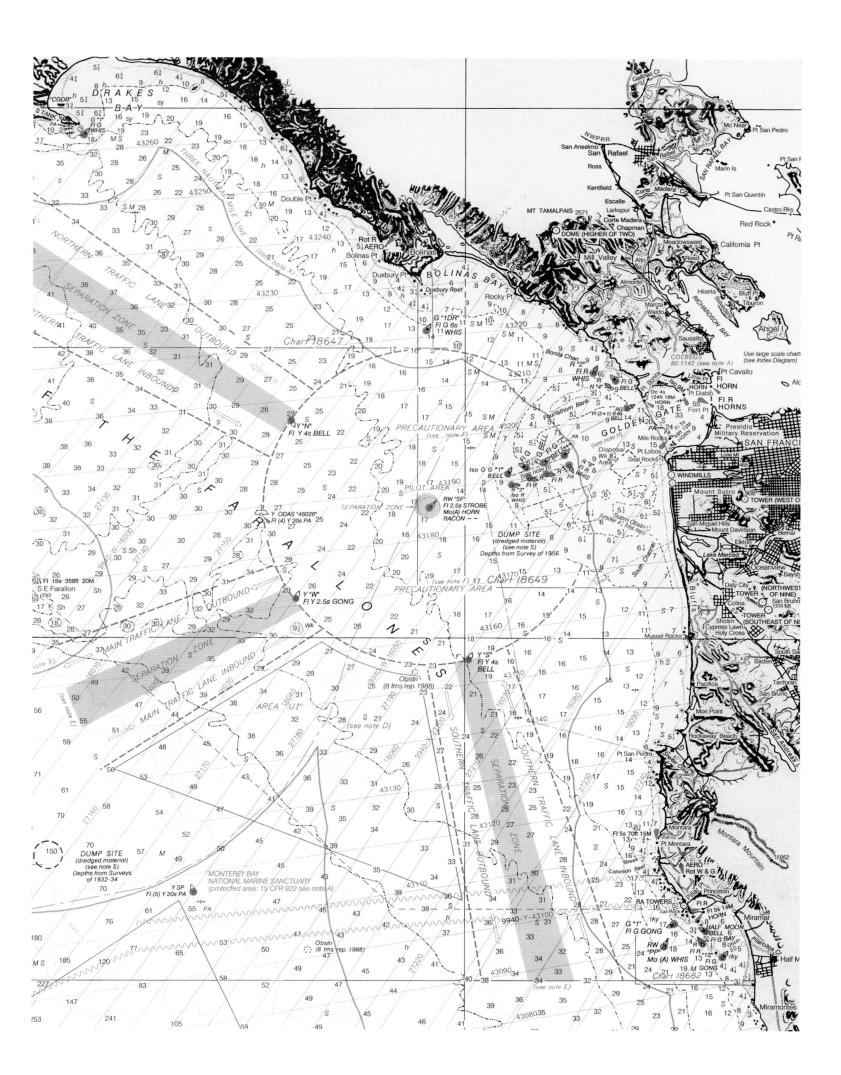

Above: The Ramsden Sextant. An early example of what was to become the standard ocean-going astronomical observation tool. By manipulating the images of sun and horizon and knowing the exact time, the user could calculate his position any place in the world.

Below: An ivory compass, ca. 1580, from Italy. Most early compasses were of the "box" type and were jealously guarded by sailing masters and captains.

The most basic navigational tool is the compass. A relatively simple device, the compass derives from the discovery of lodestone, a naturally occurring substance with inherent magnetic properties.

In the early days, when a sliver of metal or needle was rubbed with lodestone, it became magnetized and, mounted on a simple pivot, pointed to magnetic north. Columbus had a compass, and we know that the earliest application probably came about in the West in the 13th century, probably brought from China. The compass remains the basic tool of navigation, and we understand, unlike the earliest explorers, how the earth's magnetic fields vary from place to place on the globe. Interestingly, Columbus noted this variation as he sailed westward, but was unable to explain it.

Even after the development of the compass, mariners were hounded by lack of accurate timepieces. While early mariners had clocks, they couldn't rely on them when faced with motion, temperature changes and humidity. Creating a clock that would tick on unphased by these elements was one of the great mechanical challenges of the 18th century. John Harrison, after quite a struggle, solved the puzzle in 1761, and a chronometer became an essential part of the navigators equipage.

Finding the Way: Remarkable Feats in Navigation
The stories of pre-electronic navigation are remarkable tales of man against nature and of the ability of the human brain to find a landfall in the most unlikely spots. Bligh, Shackleton, Blyth and others had

to contend with conditions that would sorely test most men and women. But the sun and stars are a constant and with knowledge and luck, they survived.

The story of the mutiny on *H.M.S. Bounty* has been told countless times, most of it highly fictionalized and sensational. The book by Nordhoff and Hall was the basis for the film with Charles Laughton and the later one starring Marlon Brando, as well as Anthony Hopkins and others, but it was wrong.

Captain William Bligh was one of the most highly esteemed officers in the British Navy and had a long and distinguished career after the *Bounty* incident. Fletcher Christian was most probably a paranoid psychotic and hungry for power. By putting Bligh and his supporters in a small boat and setting them adrift, he left them in the middle of the Pacific with scant regard for their lives. That Bligh was able to pilot them safely to land makes for one of the most remarkable voyages in the history of seafaring.

In his diary, Bligh recounts the moment of mutiny on April 28, 1789:

Just before Sunrise Mr Christian and the Master at Arms... came into my cabin while I was fast asleep and seizing me tyed my hands with a Cord & threatened instant death if I made the least noise. I however called sufficiently loud to alarm the Officers, who found themselves equally secured by centinels at their doors... Mr Christian had a Cutlass & the others were armed with Musquets & bayonets. I was now carried on deck in my Shirt, in torture with a severe bandage round my wrists behind my back, where I found no man to rescue me...'

The Sea Limits

BY DANTE GABRIEL ROSSETTI

Consider the sea's listless chime;
Time's self it is, made audible—
The murmur of the earth's own shell.
Secret continuance sublime
Is the sea's end: our sight may pass
No furlong further. Since time was,
This sound hath told the lapse of time.

No quiet, which is death's—it hath
The mournfulness of ancient life,
Enduring always at dull strife.
As the world's heart of rest and wrath,
Its painful pulse is in the sands.
Last utterly, the whole sky stands
Grey and not known, along its path.

The infamous mutiny aboard the *HMS Bounty*. In this painting by R. Dodd, Captain Bligh and his men are cast adrift in the longboat. Their subsequent journey was one of the great feats of navigation and seamanship in the 18th century.

The mutineers then placed Bligh, along with his loyal officers in one of the ship's boats, probably about 20 feet long and open. Over the course of weeks of travail, in dead calms and gales, Bligh navigated the cockleshell for 3,618 nautical miles without loss of life to the safety of Coupang. And he did it with the most basic of navigational tools, without ocean charts and with remarkable sangfroid. It was a remarkable voyage and Bligh ended his career as a Vice Admiral in the British Navy. In fact, he was generally regarded as one of the most compassionate captains of his day, reluctant to resort to the lash and was highly regarded by his superiors. Bligh's journey was a highpoint in the history of seat-of-the-pants navigation.

For some cultures, nature held the key to successful navigation. Early Polynesians developed such a sophisticated understanding of natural patterns, they were able to navigate without the aid of Western instruments. By noting wave patterns, birds in flight, water temperature and marine life, it is possible to successfully navigate across large expanses of water. But, until the researches of the same David Lewis who attacked Antarctica, most of these heroic tales of epic passages without instruments were legends.

Certainly, others had tried. Thor Heyderdahl, first on the

Two seamen practice taking sun sights aboard the *Flying Clipper* in 1948. Until the development of GPS (Global Positioning System), this was the only reliable method of determining position at sea.

ECHO
•
I AM ALTERING MY COURSE TO STARBOARD.

Greenwich 00°00'00 W
Dublin 6

Meteosat - Image ATSR - 95/03/03

famous balsa raft *Kon Tiki*, later in a series of reed boats, attempted to show that migrations of people could be accomplished over long sea distances simply by following ocean currents and prevailing winds. And he did reach land on both occasions. But, and it's a big but, his journeys proved little, as they were designed from a false first premise. South American Indians did not drift west to Polynesia and Egyptians didn't cross the Atlantic. He and his crew underwent countless travails, especially in *Kon Tiki*, about which a popular film was

Left: Norwegian anthropologist Thor Hyerdahl believed (quite without scientific foundation) that ancient Mediterranean peoples were able to sail reed boats to the New World. His first attempt aboard Ra-1 failed, the reeds soaking up so much water that the boat foundered.

made in the 1950s. But the voyages were intuitive, rather than scientific, despite Heyerdahl's reputation as an anthropologist (he was a zoologist by training). They were "what if" voyages.

David Lewis' experiences in the 1970s were more germane. Lewis, an English doctor resident in Australia, set out to understand Polynesian navigation. In several articles in *National Geographic*, he showed that traditional navigators in the Pacific, through careful observation of natural phenomena and knowledge gained over generations and passed down, could accurately navigate the vast and empty expanses of the Pacific. To Western eyes, this was a remarkable feat, but what is miraculous to us, is merely ingrained in these skilled mariners.

The Information Age: From Loran to GPS

In the 1980s, a solo sailor embarked on a voyage from California to Hawaii, without sextant, chronometer or navigation tables. He was successful and arrived safely. When he landed in Hawaii, he was asked how he ever managed to find the islands. His response, "I followed the jet trails!" Whether this tale is rooted in urban legend or contains some kernel of truth, its lesson is well noted: the modern age has changed navigation on the open seas.

With GPS (global positioning system) and modern electronics, navigation has become much easier, with accuracy within a few feet. Nevertheless, electricity and water don't get along very well and back-up systems should be available and usable. With the increasing availability of satellite telephones and Internet access,

Currently, almost all navigation is done electronically. GPS, operated by the United States military has become the favorite. It works via a system of satellites in orbit above the earth. The GPS set receives a number of signals at precisely timed intervals, crunches the data and gives one a readout of latitude and longitude. For years, the US military has kept part of the data secret for national defense reasons. Just recently, this restriction has been lifted. Where before one got a reading within 50 meters, now position can be pinpointed within a couple of meters.

GPS makes celestial navigation extraneous and sets today can be had for as little as two hundred dollars, making it feasible for a cruising sailor to carry backups. There had been previous

navigation will soon become as easy as ordering a pair of pants over the Net.

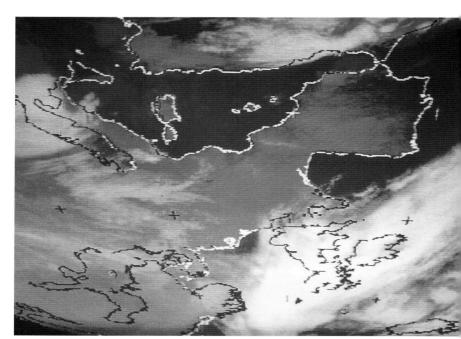

Above: World sailor Isabelle Autissier at the chart table. Though the term is still in use, navigation station might be more appropriate. The assortment of computers, telecommunications, weather, speed, depth, radar, and positioning devices is awesome.

Below: A satellite weather map of Europe. These maps can be received on board through weather faxes and wireless, e-mail.

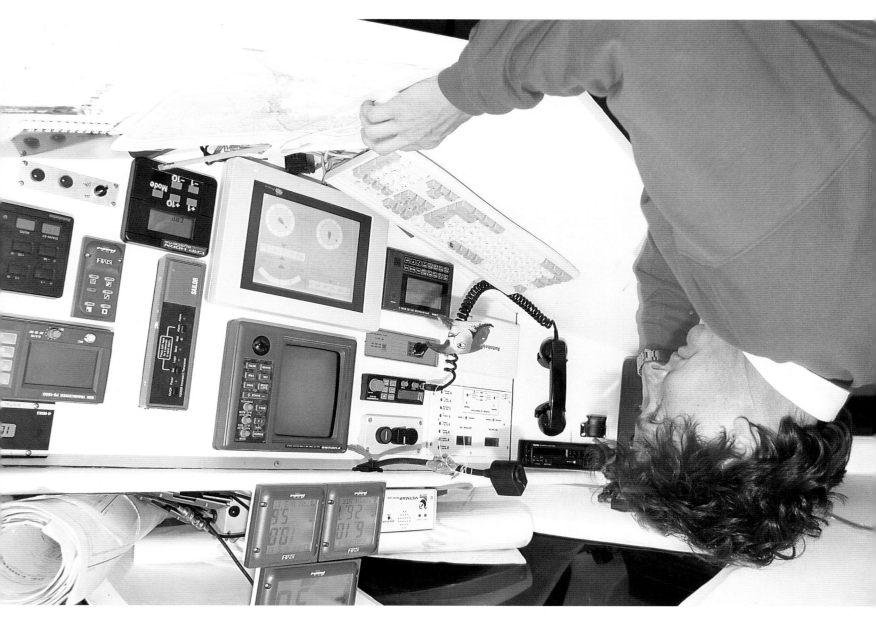

electronic navigation systems—Omega, Decca and Loran being the best known—but they were either variable in coverage, subject to error or localized. Since GPS has become an affordable and popular addition to navigator's tables, the other systems have virtually disappeared.

In fact, GPS has become so pervasive that few modern sailors know the traditional methods any longer. Fifty years ago soundings were taken with a weighted lead line. Now no self-respecting sailor would be without a depth sounder. GPS, depth sounders, radar, electronic logs have all made sailing safer and easier, but all traditional methods should not be so easily discarded. Sailing is, after all, a romantic sport. No one *needs* to sail to get somewhere. They do it because they want to. Keeping old skills alive can become very useful when all else—or all—fails.

Right: A modern spherical compass mounted on a steering binnacle. Though GPS has relieved many sailors of sextant use, the compass is still the primary tool of navigation.

Below: Weatherfax machines. Increasingly, these are being replaced by wireless e-mail and internet connections for more up-to-date and locale-specific weather reports.

$\mathcal{F}rom$ The Long Way

BY BERNARD MOITESSIER

TRANSLATED BY WILLIAM RODARMOR

"The clear night is gone. Day is breaking. I didn't see the dawn, I slept through it. I hurry to raise the main and shake out the reefs, except the staysail's, which is a bit hard to take in when things get rough. The whole sky is full of joy and sunshine. I missed the dawn, but I know the day is going to be a beauty."

One Day...and a Night

The wind drops a bit, so does the speed. I feel I am waking from a dream. Pity I took the mainsail off. You forget quickly...

The seas may soon start breaking dangerously, as often happens when a strong wind slackens after raising a heavy sea. At Good Hope the seas became nice and rounded as soon as the wind dropped a notch. Here, I do not know yet. Perhaps it will be the same, perhaps not. Three years ago, the sea here subsided as soon as the wind eased. But one would have to round the Horn a dozen times to know for sure, and even then...

I go below to tap on the barometer, and am surprised to see that it has fallen markedly during the gale, which was not a true one, since the wind did not shift after the clearing: it's still between NW and NNW. Odd, that 13 millibars drop.

I go on deck again to sniff the night after lighting the stove for coffee. The wind is down to force 6. No more teeth standing out against the sky, but beautiful silvery dunes instead. The mainsail looks at me, furled nice and tight. Raise it, or not? I wind up shaking a reef out of the mizzen. The simple, wise thing to do.

A glance at the log, with the flashlight between my teeth to keep my hands free. Thanks to the reef shaken out of the mizzen, the speed has gone from 6 to 6.6 knots. Just right; not too slow, not too fast either, and in case a big breaking sea hit for some reason, the mainsail will be safe and won't cause any damage to the rigging. I will set it again in two hours if no dirty trick occurs in the meantime.

No more porpoises, no more gulls, no more ghosts. The situation is well in hand. Moving around the deck without a harness is out of the question; just one bad one, and wham!...nobody on deck.

I go below to fix my coffee and drink it slowly, both hands gripping the hot mug. God, that's good. I did not realize my hands were that cold. They are all swollen from soaking such a long time in wet gloves.

I just can't keep still. I go back on deck to have a look. Moving around the deck without a harness is possible, only a complete moron would be caught unawares...Don't be a fool keep the harness!...I'll keep it on, but with just one snap, and only when I sit still in the cockpit, not when I walk on deck between the bowsprit and the mizzen. You can start dreaming and then lose attention when sitting still, but not if you keep on moving around with eyes and ears wide.

One more look at the log before I plot our dead reckoning position on the chart and take a little nap. We have made very good time

since yesterday noon, nearly 8 knots on average without counting the current which ought to give us another good knot. Nearly 2 a.m. and Cabo de Hornos is 130 miles away at the most. We will have to raise the mainsail again before long, to keep that nice average from dropping. If everything works out, the Horn should be right on the bow at sunset. I go below to sleep for a while.

The clear night is gone. Day is breaking. I didn't see the dawn, I slept through it. I hurry to raise the main and shake out the reefs, except the staysail's, which is a bit hard to take in when things get rough. The whole sky is full of joy and sunshine. I missed the dawn, but I know the day is going to be a beauty.

The entire sea is blue. It should be green, according to the *Sailing Directions*, because of a certain plankton which turns the Horn waters bottle green.

The sun climbs in the sky. The wind rises, and the mainsail is up close-reefed again. The wind rises further, backing gradually from NW to WSW. The mainsail has to be dropped, and the mizzen close-reefed.

The barometer has not fallen any more since last night's gale, and is not too low for the area. There is a terrific sun out. The noon sight is disappointing though, with only 171 miles covered in the last 24 hours. I had expected 20 miles more.

Diego Ramirez is still 47 miles away, so the Horn will not be rounded before night, which will come at 10 o'clock.

The sea becomes very heavy, very long, very high under a force 9 wind that has been blowing since the meridian sight. From the lower spreaders the scene is striking, with the tiny mizzen facing seas that look as if they are about to sweep over everything. Masses must have a hypnotic effect. You stare on and on...I am vaguely worried, but also feel there is no real danger thanks to the fairly strong current, 1.5 knots according to the chart, setting in the same direction as the wind, making the seas regular. Also, at 40 miles to port, the coast is too close for any secondary swell to come from here. Yet the sea is heavy, really heavy. It sweeps along in long, high, nearly horizontal crests, dotted with knolls and dips, but nothing like the sharp teeth and rough dunes of last night.

"I watch this fantastic sea, breathe in its spray, and feel blossoming here in the wind and space something that needs the immensity of the universe to come to fruition."

Occasionally a crest higher than the others becomes a wall of water, the sun slanting through its translucent peak giving it blue-green highlights. The sea then seems ready to change dress. But the rest remains deep blue, with hues melting every second into other shades of blue, like a great musical wave of endless vibrations. And the white streams down, iridescent with countless blues, green sparkling now and then. Once in a while part of the wall splits off, topples forward, and comes cascading down with a thunderous roar.

The wind is blowing as hard as before, still from the WSW. The sun slowly moves astern. The green highlights disappear, the blues turn almost violet. Heavy pink-lined clouds to the north tell me where land is, but I feel glad not to see it just now.

The sea continues to build. I drop the mizzen to keep the surfing within safe limits. One can never tell exactly what is going to happen while surfing in the high latitudes. The boat seems so happy, you're afraid she will try something new. I wonder how I dared go so far last night.

Standing on the pulpit, I search for Diego Ramirez, a bluish spot among the white patches sparkling on the horizon. I cannot see it yet. The storm jib boltrope caresses my gloved fist gripping the stay. It gives me a warm feeling. I so badgered the sailmaker about reinforcements that he gave me his competitor's address to get me off his back. I felt then that it was like something sacred; I took my storm jib back and reinforced the clew myself so that the thimble would never rip out, whatever wind it met. And here it is, gathering all the passing wind, and caressing my fist as it pulls with all its tiny might.

I ate nothing this morning, nothing at noon. Not from laziness or nerves; I just didn't feel like it. Penguins and seals go for long periods without food in the mating season, other animals do the same in the great migrations. And deep within himself man may carry the same instinct to leave food aside, as animals do in the solemn moments of their lives.

I watch this fantastic sea, breathe in its spray, and feel blossoming here in the wind and space something that needs the immensity of the universe to come to fruition.

At last Diego Ramirez comes out of the sea, a little dark blue speck of life on the blurred horizon. Each time *Joshua* rises on a crest, the little bit of life shows more clearly. And each time, it is like the flash of a beacon in my heart.

The sun is near the horizon and Diego Ramirez a tiny speck again, its neatly etched profile far astern. The wind has eased a lot, force 6 to 7. The sea became rounded and its rumbling gradually diminished. Only the sounds of the boat in the sea can be heard.

The Horn is very close, barely 30 miles off, out of sight under the mantle of big cumulus hiding the mountains of Tierra del Fuego. At times I seem to vaguely make something out a hand's breadth to the left of the bow. And Diego Ramirez, my whole life when I saw it appear a few hours ago, is now a memory of the southern route.

The sun has set. The sky readies itself for night. The first planets appear. The moon will be up within the hour; she will actually rise, because the horizon in that direction is clear as well. Clear ahead, clear astern, clear to the

right and clear above. The stars out, still almost invisible; later they will be bright. The clearness of the sky is exceptional; it has lasted all day long. And the barometer is as clear as the sky, with hardly a tremor.

It is night, a night full of stars. My exhausted body is resting in the berth, but I am in the rigging and sails, listening to the sea, feeling the air grow cooler with the stars, feeling the wind as it eases further, telling me the night will be truly fine.

Everything stretches and blends, the great wave is rocking me. A last lucid glance: alarm set for 1 a.m....the course will take us within 20 miles of the Horn...I will be on the deck well ahead just in case...but the wind will not increase, will not shift to SSW or even SW...*Sleep little brother, you've done all there is to do, now it's my turn to watch over you*...lightly, the great wave rolls over me, and I see the little islet my brothers and I found in the Gulf of Siam, with a tiny pebble beach facing the SW monsoon, its other beach facing the monsoon from the NW. There were neither water nor fruits, only crabs and periwinkles, so we brought water with us in our canoes and we ate the crabs and the periwinkles and it was the end of the earth, our little island, so pure, so green, with its Indochina trees, its black rocks, its pebbles on the one side and white sand on the other, and everywhere the sun of the sea and the forest, the sunshine of discovery. Many monsoons later, on a trip from Kampot to Rach Gia in my big junk loaded with sugar and a little contraband, I planted three sprouted coconuts and a mango pit, so the island of our childhood would also have water and fruits. A coconut tree for each of my brothers and the mango for me. They are 25 years old now, if nothing has happened to them...*Sleep quietly little brother, I just went to look...there is a junk from Kampot anchored close to the pebble beach, its lug sail well furled, and three fishermen under the coconut trees. There is also a young boy with a slingshot, shooting at the nests the yellow ants have woven with the leaves of your mango tree*...the wave envelopes and caresses me; I sleep without knowing.

I see a beacon in the night, it blinks between the waves, and I slowly awaken. The moon comes in through the porthole, brushes my lids, wanders down to my chin, comes back to my eyes for a second, goes over to see what is on the stove, returns to touch my eyes, lightly, insistently, goes away, comes back again.

I lie outstretched, not moving. I listen. The wind has dropped further. Before, it was whispering on the edge of the partly open hatch, talking in an undertone. Now too, but lower. The water sounds have also changed, and there is a slight rolling to starboard that was not there when I went to sleep. I try to guess whether the rolling is due to less pressure of wind against the sails, or a change of the course. But I don't understand, since the moon is to port, at the right place in the sky. She could not be coming through the porthole if the course had changed toward the coast. Rolling says it has changed, and Moon says no. I try to figure who is right, feeling with my senses. There is no danger, and plenty of time. If danger threatened, the fight of the swell with the coast would fill the cabin with its roaring. And I hear only the murmur of water on the hull, a sound from *Joshua* that says all is well despite the quarrel between the rolling and the moon. I do not want to shine a light on the compass to find out; it has to come by itself.

Yes, that's it, Moon is right, and rolling is right, and *Joshua*'s right. No need to look at my watch to understand that I did not hear the alarm at 1 a.m., or to need not to light the compass to know that the wind changed to SW and the boat has angled some 15° toward the Horn. And I know just where the Horn is: 15 miles away right under the moon, I can see it without getting out of my bunk. Not actually see it, because 15 miles is too far in this area, even on a clear night, and there are almost always clouds on the heights of this coast, no matter how good the weather. I also know that *Joshua* has been in the Atlantic for about an hour, as the moon has travelled some 10° or 15° to the west of her meridian and the Horn is right under the moon.

I stretch and get up, and glance forward out the porthole. I know it can't be there, but it is one of those things that are always possible at sea...Nothing, of course. And I feel that colossal thing 15 miles to port. Pity I didn't hear the alarm when it called me an hour ago:

I would have altered the course to pass close. Now the die is cast, the Horn is rounded, we are in the Atlantic and there is no time to waste. At the moment everything is perfect. In twelve hours it could become very bad; best to be far away then. I feel happy, joyful, moved; I want to laugh and joke and pray all at once.

Another long look ahead out the porthole, for possible icebergs. I had not really worried about them up to now. There are not supposed to be any so close to the Horn. I stick my head out the hatch to see better. I would sort of like an iceberg to be there, glowing in the moonlight...but then I wouldn't sleep for a week.

The air is cold, the wind only force 5. I look to port, toward the Horn. Nothing. In any case, it is too far away to be seen. A little cloud under the moon, and some big ones to the left. Pity...we might have glimpsed it, even at this distance, the air is so clear.

My ears start tingling. I close the hatch again, light the stove and put on the kettle. My motions are slow, as if nothing had happened. As if *Joshua* had not reached the Atlantic again with three capes in her wake. No...not quite three capes; the sea is still the sea, one must never forget. Good Hope was rounded once and for all 500 miles beyond its geographical location. Leeuwin was really astern when my two porpoises left us after the last dangers of New Zealand, 2500 miles later. And the Horn will be in the wake when the Falklands are too, not before.

A sailor's geography is not always that of the cartographer, for whom a cape is a cape, with a latitude and longitude. For the sailor, a great cape is both a very simple and an extremely complicated whole of rocks, currents, breaking seas and huge waves, fair winds and gales, joys and fears, fatigue, dreams, painful hands, empty stomachs, wonderful moments, and suffering at times.

A great cape, for us, can't be expressed in longitude and latitude alone. A great cape has a soul, with very soft, very violent shadows and colours. A soul as smooth as a child's, as hard as a criminal's. And that is why we go.

I pull on my boots to take a turn on deck. The usual routine. The routine, but also, above all, the religion of nights at sea.

The little cloud underneath the moon has moved to the right. I look...there it is, so close, less than 10 miles away and right under the moon. And nothing remains but the sky and the moon playing with the Horn.

I look. I can hardly believe it. So small and so huge. A hillock, pale and tender in the moonlight; a colossal rock, hard as diamond. The Horn stretches a long way, from 50° Pacific latitude to 50° Atlantic. Yet it is that rock, set alone on the sea, alone under the moon, with all the glaciers, the mountains, the icebergs, the gales and the beauty of Tierra del Fuego, the smell of seaweed, the colours in the sky and the serenity of the great albatrosses gliding above the sea, not moving a feather of their immense wings, over troughs and crest, for whom all things are alike.

"For the sailor, a great cape is both a very simple and an extremely complicated whole of rocks, currents, breaking seas and huge waves, fair winds and gales, joys and fears, fatigue, dreams, painful hands, empty stomachs, wonderful moments, and suffering at times."

The whistling of the kettle calls me. I go below, dry off my hands, roll myself a cigarette and smoke it in light puffs with a mug of hot coffee. Thousands of little warm things stir throughout my being. I turn the oil lamp up a bit, and the shadows come to life; I turn the wick up some more, and my little world glows softly.

I wonder. Plymouth so close, barely 10,000 miles to the north...but leaving from Plymouth and returning to Plymouth now seems like leaving from nowhere to go nowhere.

From Survive the Savage Sea

BY DOUGAL ROBERTSON

"He fought with alternate periods of listless acquiescence and galvanic action, twisting and plunging savagely to rid himself of the hook. I was afraid of the line breaking but I feared more the arrival of a larger shark which would attack the hooked one. Slowly, foot by foot, he came to the surface, the line cutting deep into the heel of my hand."

Twenty-ninth day

We made good headway in the gentle westerly breeze throughout the night, with the sea anchor tripped and *Ednamair* making over a knot to the east-north-east. The rising sun guided our daylight progress and the business of survival resumed its daily routine. I had barely started work on my gaff when, looking down into the sea past the flashing blue, green and gold of the dorado, I spotted the brown shape of a shark, but it was the first small one I had seen since my short-lived love affair with the one on the raft. This one was catchable too. We had caught a flying fish in the night, a very small one, so I put it on the large hook and weighting the line heavily I cast well out to clear the scavenger fish. My baited hook drifted down past the shark and at first I

thought he was going to ignore it but after it came to rest he turned and nosed towards it. Douglas, stretched across the dinghy in my usual place beside the thwart, called: 'What're you doing Dad?' 'Catching a shark,' I said calmly, watching the shark nose a little closer. 'You're bloody mad,' Douglas said, sitting up quickly; Robin, too, was sitting up apprehensively and Lyn said 'You musn't.' 'Good old Dad,' said Neil and Sandy from the bows. 'I'm having him," I said watching tensely now, as the shark reached the bait; the moment I felt him touch I would have to strike, for if he got the nylon line between his teeth he would bite through it like butter. I was going to try to get the steel shank of the hook between his jaws. He was over it now, I felt the contact with tingling fingers and struck swiftly, the line exploded into action, he was hooked!

He fought with alternate periods of listless acquiescence and galvanic action, twisting and plunging savagely to rid himself of the hook. I was afraid of the line breaking but I feared more the arrival of a larger shark which would attack the hooked one. Slowly, foot by foot, he came to the surface, the line cutting deep into the heel of my hand. Lyn sat ready in the stern, paddle in hand. The shark broke surface, struggled savagely and plunged deeply. I had to let him go, he was still too strong, but he was a nice five-footer. A Mako shark, Douglas said (he was our shark expert) and I'd hooked him in the eye! Back up he came. 'We'll have him this time,' I grunted, my hands aching. 'Be ready to take the line, Robin...I'm going to grab his tail and pull him in that way.' Excitement rose high in the dinghy; Robin and Lyn looked a bit uncomfortable at being given the biting end to look after, but were determined to do their best. (I knew he

would break free if I tried to haul him in head first by the line.)

The shark surfaced again; gingerly Robin took the line from my hand as I quickly leaned over and grabbed the shark's tail. 'Trim!' I shouted and Douglas leaned out on the other side of the dinghy. The harsh skin gave me a good grip, and with a quick pull the shark lay over the gunwhale. 'Lift its head in now!' I kept a firm grip on the tail as Robin lifted the struggling fish inboard with the line. Lyn rammed the paddle into the gaping jaws and they clamped shut on it. Knife in hand I leaned forward and stabbed it through the other eye; the shark struggled then lay still. Giving Douglas the tail to hold, I stabbed the knife into the slits of the gills behind the head, sawing away at the tough skin until finally the head was severed. 'Right, you can let go now!' I felt like Bruce after Bannockburn. We had turned the tables on our most feared enemy; sharks would not eat Robertsons, Robertsons would eat sharks! Quickly I gutted out the liver and heart: a solid thirty-five to forty pounds of fish with very little waste apart from the head. We breakfasted on the liver and heart, then Robin chewed the head, watching carefully for the razor-sharp teeth while I cut strips of white flesh from the almost boneless carcase. It was tougher than the dorado but juicier and we chewed the moist strips of shark meat with great relish.

Our larder now began to look good; long strips of shark swung from the forestay while the remains of the turtle meat had dried nicely. I cut out the jaw bone from the shark's head while Lyn and the twins cleaned the spinal column. We had lost all our Indian necklaces from the San Blas Islands, the most valued of which were the shark's teeth and backbone necklaces. Now we had the raw materials to hand and time spare to make our own!

Our noon position of 7° 50' North and 160 miles west of Espinosa showed our better progress and though the weather had become overcast and unsuitable for drying the shark meat, at least it afforded us a little shade from the hot sun.

I set to work on the gaff again and Douglas steered while Lyn and Robin tended the hanging fish and meat. Robin had

> "As we watched the pieces of shark swinging against the clearing sky in the evening we felt some satisfaction that with the turtle meat already in store we had enough food to last us for a week…"

become rather edgy these last two days and now, under Lyn's exacting instructions, he became petulant and stupid, leaving jobs unfinished and making little attempt to put things right when the fault was brought to his notice. I had to speak sharply to him and to check his work to make sure it was done as he had been told.

During the afternoon we had noticed that the water which had been decanted from one of the tins was foul so that we now checked and found that, of the remaining cans, four of which were unopened, one more was unpalatable, being full of black sediment, and one was brackish where salt water had trickled in from the waves washing in on the stern seat. There was still a gallon and a half of water in a plastic bag, so that we were not unduly worried, but I decided to test it to make sure it was fresh. It was good water and we settled down to our various chores again. Lyn had found a foot of stout copper wire in her sewing basket and I was getting the germ of an idea about con-

structing a more efficient gaff than the model I was working on.

Lyn had given the twins a small turtle oil enema in the early afternoon to try to ease their blocked systems and now Sandy was responding. Our nickname for the bailer, which we still used for urinating to save trimming the boat when its use was necessary, up to now had been 'pissoir,' for there had been no need for a receptacle of any sort in our constipated condition, but now, after a short conference in the bow, Neil shouted, 'Pass the shittoir, Sandy wants to go!' Sandy's experience was not nearly so exhausting as Douglas's or mine, and Lyn thought that the turtle oil had helped in this respect.

As we watched the pieces of shark swinging against the clearing sky in the evening we felt some satisfaction that with the turtle meat already in store we had enough food to last us for a week, plus some of the emergency rations which were reserved for the children's 'little supper' before they went to rest.

Hurricane Dennis tosses the yacht Seven Bells *in May 1982, in a paintig by James Mitchell*

From The Armada

BY GARRETT MATTINGLY

XXVII
The Order Broken

Calais Roads to Gravelines,
August 8, 1588

When he saw that his screen had lost the fireships, Medina Sidonia fired a gun, slipped his cables, and stood out to sea, close-hauled. This time, however, the fleet did not conform. Instead something like a panic swept the crowded anchorage. Perhaps there had been too many lurid stories of hellburners spread by too many veterans of the Flanders wars. Perhaps, though this is less likely, Medina Sidonia's orders had got twisted in oral transmission. Whatever the reason, most captains simply cut their cables and ran before the wind, scattering, some here, some there, as if they were as much afraid of one another as they were of the fireships. The strong set of the current and the rising gale swept the whole disorderly mob out through the straits and on towards the sands of the Flemish coast. The formidable Spanish order was broken at last.

The *San Martín* made one short leg out to sea and another back again, and dropped her sheet anchor a mile or so north of her first anchorage. Just beyond her, four of her closest companions of the night also anchored: Recalde's *San Juan*, the *San Marcos*, and two more, perhaps the *San Felipe* and the *San Mateo*, all royal galleons of Portugal, anyway, as usual in the post of danger and of honor. When the blustery dawn came these five were all of the great Armada in sight, except Don Hugo de Moncada's *San Lorenzo*, the *capitana* of the galleasses, rudderless and with something wrong with her mainmast, crawling along inshore like a wounded beetle. She had fouled her unlucky rudder ("Frail ships for these rough seas!") on a neighbor's cable, and got involved in some complicated collision in the night's panic. Nearer Calais jetty, the ribs of six fireships smoldered. After the last loaded gun had gone off, there had been no more explosions. They were not hellburners after all.

Southward, the English still lay at their last night's anchorage, but a gun was fired from Howard's *Ark* and trumpets called across the water. Anchors were coming up, sails being shaken out, banners hoisted. The whole naval force of England, a hundred and fifty sail, all the queen's galleons, as many more tall, heavy armed merchant ships and private men-of-war, and some five-score smaller craft, the Grand Fleet, in fact if not in name, was moving to the attack.

Medina Sidonia had to decide at once what to do, but fortunately it was the kind of decision which came easily to him. He was the commander. It was his duty to face the enemy, alone if need be, until his scattered command could be rallied. He weighed anchor and stood out defiantly into the straits. Behind him came Recalde's *San Juan* and the other three royal galleons, close-hauled under light canvas. As they made the open strait, their pinnaces scudded away from them before the wind, sent to rally the scattered ships and order them back to support their admiral.

Until day broke, Howard was not sure of the success of his fireships. Obviously two had been towed ashore, and perhaps all the rest had been similarly diverted, for except for their dying glow there was no sign of any conflagration. The Spaniards might have moved out and then returned to reanchor or they might not have shifted at all. In either case, there would be nothing for it but to try to dislodge them by gunfire, and Howard himself meant to lead the first assault. This time there would be no cautious long-range bombardment. The emphasis all the English accounts put on shortening the range in this Monday's battle shows that everyone realized they had been keeping too far off.

The scene at dawn changed Howard's plans. The Spaniard had scattered. Howard sent his other four squadrons to deal with the only Spanish galleons in sight, yielding the honor of giving the first charge to Sir Francis Drake, and led his own squadron to capture or destroy the great galleass. That crippled monster, seeing the English line bearing down, scrambled desperately towards the shelter of Calais harbor. A fast ebbing tide, a heavy surf, no rudder, and no knowledge of the contour of the beach made escape unlikely, and at the last moment the straining exertions of the galley slaves tugging at the great sweeps only drove the galleass that much more firmly aground. There she lay, quickly heeling over more and more towards her beam ends as the water ebbed from beneath her, her deck canting inshore and her port batteries pointing foolishly skyward, stuck fast under the walls of Calais Castle.

For the English there was one exasperating circumstance about this incident. English galleons drew, on the whole, more water than Spanish ones, and galleasses far less than any galleon. The *San Lorenzo* had grounded too far inshore to be smashed by gunfire. Howard ordered off a flotilla of ships' boats to carry her by boarding, and these, for a while, had hot work. The *San Lorenzo* was canted over so far that none of her guns could be brought to bear, but that very fact helped shelter her crew and made her sides harder to climb. For a time the boats wheeled warily past the galleass to seaward—it was too shoal for them to get round to the more vulnerable landward rail—keeping up a brisk fire of small arms and being briskly answered. Such indecisive attempts at boarding as they made were beaten back, and there began to be wounded and some dead in the boats. Then Don Hugo de Moncada was shot through the head by a musket ball, and the defenders he had been holding at their posts, seeing very little future, probably, in this kind of fighting, broke, and, jumping from the low landward rail, waded and scrambled ashore. Already, the English sailors were clambering over the seaward rail and through the gunports beneath it.

"The crew of one of the urcas saw Bertendona's great carrack drive past, her decks a shambles, her battery guns silent, and blood spilling out of her scuppers as she heeled to the wind, but musketeers still ready in tops and on her quarterdeck as she came back stubbornly to take her place in the line."

By conquest and the laws of war the loot of the galleass was theirs, as M. Gourdan the governor of Calais acknowledged, and they soon stripped her clean of everything of value a man could lift and carry, but the governor reminded them that the vessel, with her guns and rigging, was his, and when it looked to him as if they were going not only to disregard his warning but to plunder, as well, the burghers of Calais who had gathered on the beach to watch the fight, he opened fire from the castle on their boats. It needed that to persuade the boats' crews to pull back to their ships where Howard was impatient to join the now distant battle.

The looting of one stranded ship seems a strange reason for keeping a powerful squadron for hours out of a major battle. But it is to be remembered that the *San Lorenzo* was the strongest ship of a formidable class which had given a lot of trouble in the Channel, and it was worth some delay, in Howard's cautious but sensible view of his mission, to make sure, before leaving her unwatched, that she was permanently out of action. His returning boats were able to assure him that she was, that no one would ever get her afloat again. That proved so; the *San Lorenzo* rotted to pieces under Calais Castle. Meanwhile Howard steered for the sound of the guns.

Of the last fight of the Armada off Gravelines, as of the battles coming up the Channel, we can catch only partial glimpses. Nobody on either side left a satisfactory record of the movements of even a single ship. The ordinary fog of war at sea, the noise, the smoke, the danger, the confusion, the too many things to do in too little time, and the difficulty of making out what anybody else is doing, was compounded, as before, by the fact that in this campaign nobody understood the new weapons employed or the tactics they required, and compounded afresh by Monday's fight having been the first in heavy weather, high winds, rough seas, and limited visibility.

Some things seem clear. The wind must have been about south-southwest, perhaps no more than a strong breeze in the morning, perhaps a moderate gale. The *San Martín* and her consorts must have moved before it, though under small canvas, through the straits and into the North Sea, with the *San Martín* the rearmost, and the *San Juan* with one or two of the others getting well to leeward. Even at this point Medina Sidonia was concerned to lead his straggling fleet away from the dangerous Dunkirk banks and into deep water. Perhaps he meant the more leeward of the scattered ships to form on Recalde's *San Juan* and the nearer ones on the *San Martín*. Nobody says. At any rate, his northern movement gave the English something of a stern chase and delayed the beginning of the action.

Sir Francis Drake in the *Revenge* gave the first charge, as the Lord Admiral had appointed him to do. The Spanish flagship, as the English approached, wore round further to present her broadside to the enemy and lay to, and for some time, while the distance between the *Revenge* and the *San Martín* lessened, both ships held their fire. This time the English were determined to make every shot tell and the Spanish, since they had so few left, were obliged to. Not until the ships were at about "half-musket shot" (a hundred yards?) did the *Revenge* fire first her bow guns, then her broadside, to be answered in thunder from the *San Martín*. It may have been in this exchange that the *Revenge* was "pierced through by cannon balls of all sizes," as Ubaldini says. Fenner in the *Nonpareil* came close after Drake, followed by the rest of Drake's squadron, each ship as she came up loosing off her broadside and risking the *San Martín's* reply. Then the whole squadron followed its commander on a course to the northeast, out of the ken, for a while, of any of the surviving narratives.

That is not to say they may not have been doing good work somewhere. Corbett's guess that Drake saw that the proper tactical target was farther to leeward, where the stronger galleons were hauling off the shoals and reforming in deep water, is very plausible. That does seem to have been the critical point, and to have prevented and broken up this rally would have been a tremendous gain, far more decisive than the capture or sinking of the *San Martín*. It is no reflection on Drake's tactical insight that Sir Martin Frobisher, who came up next, did not appreciate it. Later on, at Harwich, in the presence of Lord Sheffield and others, Frobisher was to say of this action, "He [Drake] came bragging up at the first indeed, and gave them his prow and his broadside; and then kept his luff, and was glad that he was gone again like a cowardly knave or traitor—I rest doubtful, but the one I will swear." Frobisher was angry at Drake over another matter, and he was always a hotheaded man, likely to say more than he meant. But certainly he did not fathom the purpose of Drake's movement or try to support it. If he had, it might have succeeded.

Instead, Frobisher stayed and fought the *San Martín*. The *Triumph's* castles were higher, and its bulk greater, and Frobisher lay close to the Spanish flagship, though he did not offer to board, beating her with his great guns, while the rest of his squadron swarmed across her bow and stern and under her lee, riddling her upper works with shot. When Hawkins came up in the *Victory* and way was made for him, it almost seemed that Medina Sidonia was fighting alone against the whole English fleet. Or nearly alone. The *San Marcos de Portugal* in which the marquis of Peñafiel and a number of other persons of illustrious lineage served as gentlemen adventurers, had never been far off from the admiral. She had been able to close some of Drake's squadron, and since had stood by, taking her share of the fighting and, like the *San Martín*, replying to the fire of the enemy, not just with her woefully stinted great guns, but, the range was so close, with muskets and arquebuses.

By the time all Hawkins's squadron had come up, other Spanish ships were beginning to join the fight. They were the familiar names, the same ships that had borne the brunt all the way up the Channel, the galleons of Portugal, the galleons of Castile, de Leiva's carrack and Bertendona's, the Florentine galleon, Oquendo's flagship, two or three of the biggest and best-armed Biscayans like the *Grangrin*. At first there were only seven or eight of them, then fifteen, then twenty-five, not the familiar crescent but its tough outer rim, a shield behind which the slower and weaker ships could form. Seymour and Wynter, when they joined the battle, found the Spaniards back in something like regular formation. "They went," says Wynter, "into the proportion of a half moon, their admiral and vice-admiral in the midst and the greatest number of them; and there went on each side, in the wings, their galleasses, armados of Portugal and other good ships, in the whole to the number of sixteen in a wing which did seem to be out of their principal shipping." The recovery of that formidable but tricky order in the first blustery hours of Monday morning was one of the more remarkable feats of Spanish discipline and seamanship. It was

made possible, of course, by the leadership of the duke of Medina Sidonia and the stubborn courage of his rear-guard action.

With high courage and bold leadership on both sides, the victory goes to the best ships and the best guns. The superiority of English ships had been demonstrated already, time and again. They could outflank and worry the enemy at will, keep the weather gauge, choose their own range, and always be sure of disengaging when they liked. The superiority of English guns and gunnery the Spanish were inclined to concede, but the chief superiority of the English off Gravelines lay in the fact that they still had ammunition. When they decided to close the range, as must have been agreed Sunday morning, they cannot have known how short the Spanish were, but in the second phase of Monday's battle, when all five English squadrons were harrying and jostling the Spanish crescent and trying to worry it into bits, they found they could close to easy hailing distance and not take too much punishment.

The English were still overestimating the most effective range. "How much nearer, so much the better," said Sir Richard Hawkins later. He had commanded the *Swallow* in his father's squadron, and learned by the campaign's experience. But at Monday's usual range, the English guns could do real damage. The tough layers of Spanish oak guarding the lower hulls of the galleons were not smashed, but they were pierced repeatedly. Before the battle was over, most of the Armada's first line ships were leaking, and some were mortally hurt. Their upper works were only musket-proof at best, and by evening they had been beaten to bloody flinders. The slaughter on the upper decks must have been terrible.

The Spanish fought gallantly. Again and again one galleon or another struggled desperately to board. It was, after all, the only chance of fighting on even terms. Badly mangled as the *San Martín* had been in the first phase of the action, afterwards, twice at least, she thrust herself into the midst of the melee to rescue a ship in trouble. The crew of one of the *urcas* saw Bertendona's great carrack drive past, her decks a shambles, her battery guns silent, and blood spilling out of

her scuppers as she heeled to the wind, but musketeers still ready in tops and on her quarterdeck as she came back stubbornly to take her place in the line. The *San Mateo*, which twice had found herself surrounded and fighting a ring of enemies, was in even worse case. More than half her men, soldiers and sailors, were killed or disabled, her great guns were useless, she was leaking like a sieve and wallowing low in the water, but when the *San Mart_n* bore up to cover her and the admiral offered to take off her officers and crew, Don Diego de Pimentel proudly refused to abandon ship. Later an English galleon, probably Seymour's *Rainbow*, impressed by such heroic and useless sacrifice, steered close enough for an officer to hail, offering good terms. For answer a musketeer shot him through the body, and the *San Mateo* went on suffering broadside after broadside, and replying with a futile sputter of small arms.

By this time Medina Sidonia could see his painfully re-established formation breaking up again before his eyes, ships being isolated, group being cut off from group, and the whole increasingly helpless mob of shipping being crowded inexorably onto the Flanders sands. The Lord Admiral had long since come up and, whether following Drake's example or not, the main pressure of the English attack was on the Armada's weather wing. It was four o'clock. The battle had gone on since an hour or two after sunrise and there looked like being time enough before sunset to finish off the Spanish fleet.

Then, just when it seemed that, in another hour, the Armada would be broken up and most of its ships driven on the sands, there came a violent squall with blinding torrents of rain. For fifteen minutes or so the English were too busy keeping out of each other's way to pay much attention to the enemy. When they had time to look, they saw the Spaniards standing away northward, already out of range, and re-forming, even as the English watched, their old, tough half-moon. Presently the *San Martín* defiantly shortened sail, and the reordered fleet conformed. The battered Spaniards were offering to renew the battle.

DECK GEAR & SAFETY EQUIPMENT

Right: A turnbuckle or rigging screw. Used to attach and tension the wire stays and shrouds that hold up the mast to the hull. A toggle is placed between the bottom fork of the turnbuckle and the chainplate to allow movement both fore-and-aft and athwartships.

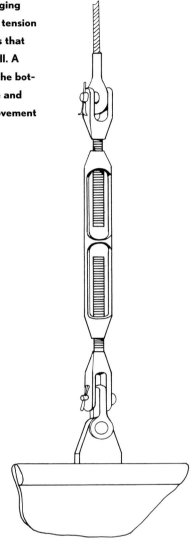

Parts of a winch.

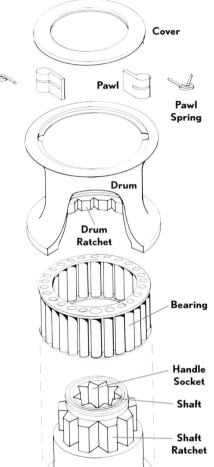

Snap Ring

Cover

Pawl

Pawl Spring

Drum

Drum Ratchet

Bearing

Handle Socket

Shaft

Shaft Ratchet

Base

Pawl

Anchoring at the end of a journey is dependant on the holding power of a particular anchor. The Danforth is most popular in America, the plow and Bruce in Europe. The old reliable fisherman is still the best choice for rocky bottoms and, in certain configurations, a perfect storm anchor. The best anchors are forged, not cast.

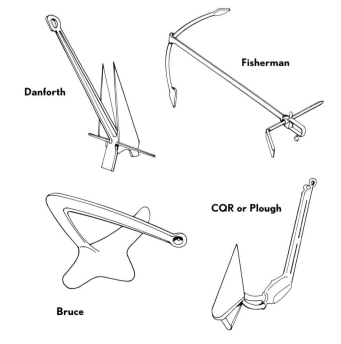

Danforth

Fisherman

Bruce

CQR or Plough

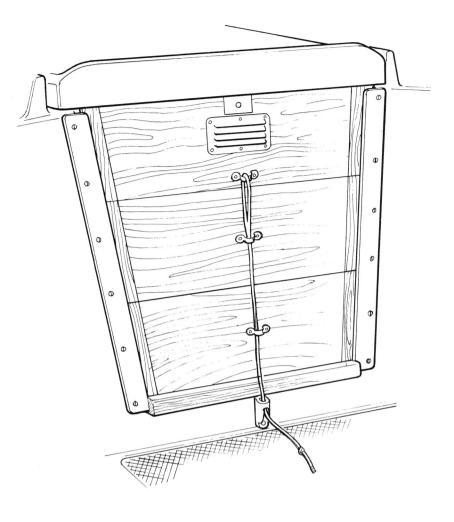

Left: Keeping hatchboards in place with devices like these is crucial, especially when trying to avoid a flooded cabin in a storm.

Seacocks are the only sure method of closing off thru-hulls from the ingress of the sea. Constructed of bronze alloy or reinforced plastics, seacocks can be opened or closed at the quarter-turn of a lever.

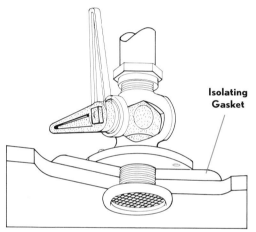

Isolating Gasket

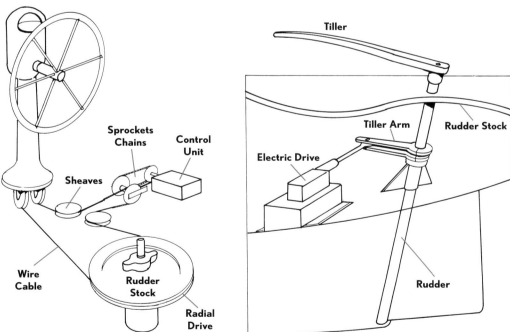

Tiller

Sprockets
Chains

Control
Unit

Sheaves

Wire
Cable

Rudder
Stock

Radial
Drive

Tiller Arm

Rudder Stock

Electric Drive

Rudder

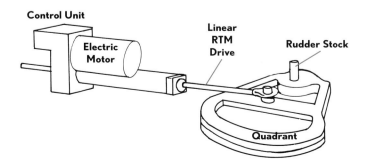

Control Unit

Electric
Motor

Linear
RTM
Drive

Rudder Stock

Quadrant

Electric autopilots are a necessity on long-range powerboats, and a nice convenience on sailing yachts with sufficient battery and generating power. Three different methods of connecting these devices are shown here, tailored to various steering systems.

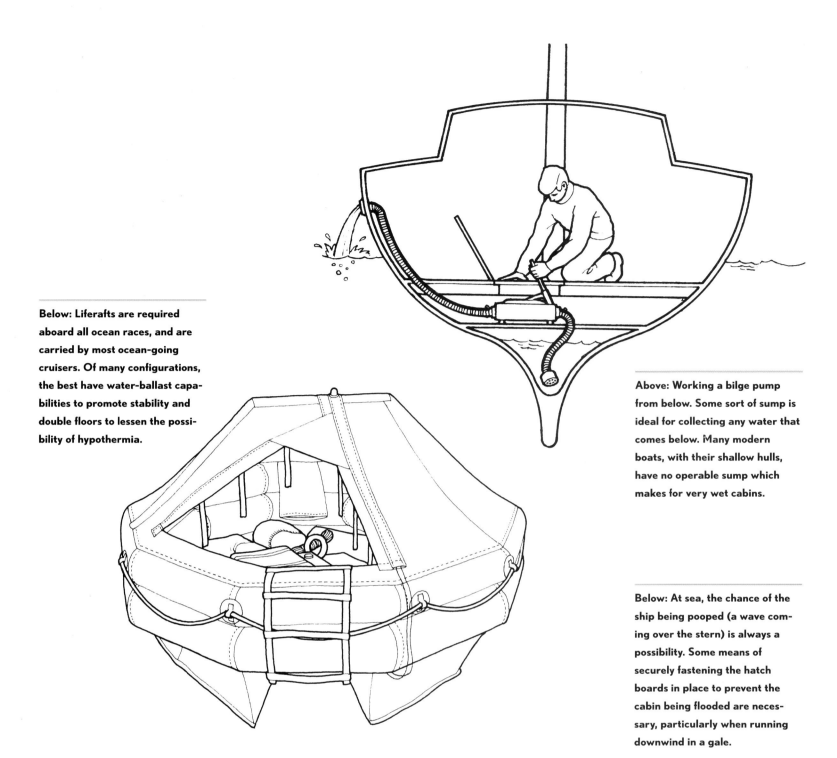

Above: Working a bilge pump from below. Some sort of sump is ideal for collecting any water that comes below. Many modern boats, with their shallow hulls, have no operable sump which makes for very wet cabins.

Below: Liferafts are required aboard all ocean races, and are carried by most ocean-going cruisers. Of many configurations, the best have water-ballast capabilities to promote stability and double floors to lessen the possibility of hypothermia.

Below: At sea, the chance of the ship being pooped (a wave coming over the stern) is always a possibility. Some means of securely fastening the hatch boards in place to prevent the cabin being flooded are necessary, particularly when running downwind in a gale.

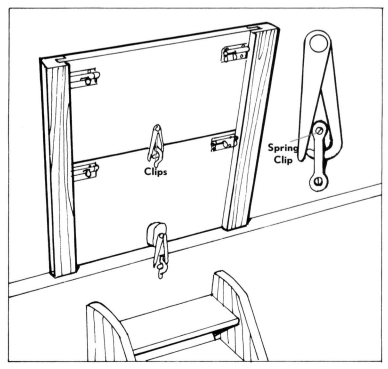

Clips

Spring Clip

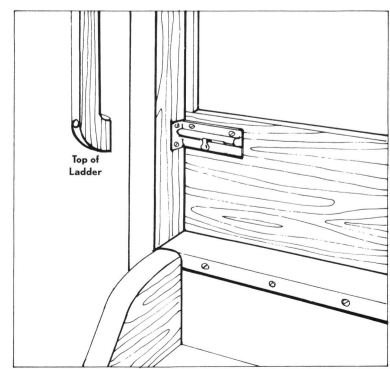

Top of Ladder

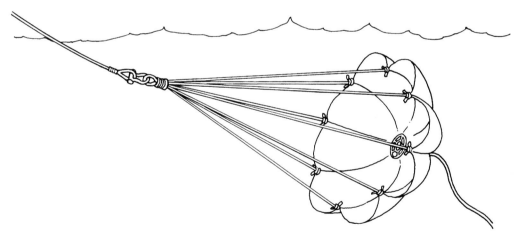

Above: The world-girdling sailor Thierry Dubois after he lost his yacht, waiting to rescued from his liferaft.

Left A sea anchor or drogue. Deployed from the bows of a yacht in heavy weather, it can keep the bows pointed into the wind and dampen motion.

Right: Cleats. Aboard any vessel, a reliable fastening point for lines is a necessity. From top, and moving clockwise: the so-called "sailboat" cleat, a bollard, a rope clutch (for quick fastening of a line), a clam-cleat, a swivelling cam cleat, the Herreshoff cleat. Of all the modern developments, probably no cleat is as perfect in form and function as the Herreshoff.

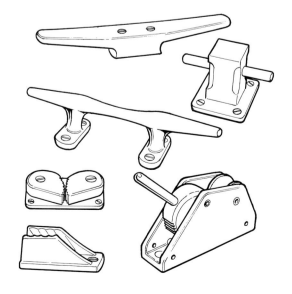

Far right: Free access to bilge pumps is needed in every boat. Though electric pumps are popular, they can short out, and a manual back-up of serious capacity is needed.

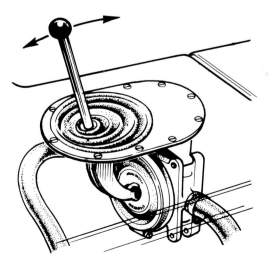

Cannister liferaft mounted on deck. A liferaft is of little or no use unless it can be instantly deployed. At the pull of a cord, the cannister breaks open and CO2 cylinders inflate the raft.

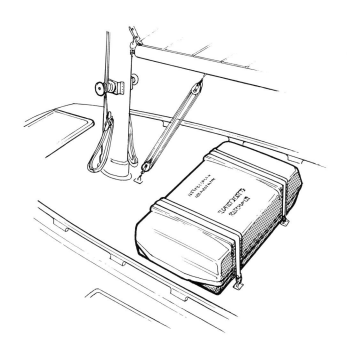

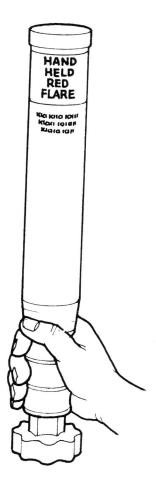

HAND HELD RED FLARE

BOUYANT ORANGE SMOKE

INSTRUCTIONS

AUG. 88

Smoke signals and flares are amongst the best methods of signaling distress. However, depending on conditions, the distance at which they are visible is not great.

Below: Davy Martin and Mike Brewer on Citius in the Transpac Race. Safety harnesses are perhaps the surest method to avoid being thrown overboard. On any ocean passage they should be de rigeur for all crew on deck.

From Gulliver's Travels: "A Voyage to Brobdingnag"

BY JONATHAN SWIFT

During this storm...we were carried by my computation about five hundred leagues to the east, so that the oldest sailor on board could not tell in what part of the world we were....

On the 16th day of June 1703, a boy on the top-mast discovered land. On the 17th we came in full view of a great island or continent...[with] a creek too shallow to hold a ship of above one hundred tuns. We cast anchor within a league of this creek, and our captain sent a dozen of his men well armed in the long boat, with vessels for water, if any could be found. I desired his leave to go with them, that I might see the country, and make what discoveries I could. When we came to land we saw no river or spring, nor any sign of inhabitants....I returned gently down towards the creek; and the sea being in full view, I saw our men already got into the boat, and rowing for life to the ship....I observed a huge creature walking after them in the sea, as fast as he could: he waded not much deeper than his knees, and took prodigious strides: but our men had the start of him half a league, and...the monster was not able to overtake the boat....[I] then climbed up a steep hill, which gave me some prospect of the country.

I found it fully cultivated; but that which first surprised me was the length of the grass, which in those grounds seemed to be kept for hay, was above twenty foot high....I was an hour walking to the end of this field; which was fenced in with a hedge of at least one hundred and twenty foot high, and the trees so lofty that I could make no computation of their altitude....I discovered one of the inhabitants in the next field advancing towards the stile, of the same size with him whom I saw in the sea pursuing our boat. He appeared as tall as an ordinary spire-steeple; and took about ten yards at every stride, as near as I could guess. I was struck with the utmost fear and astonishment, and ran to hide myself in the corn...I came to a part of the filed where the corn had been laid by the rain and wind: here it was impossible for me to advance a step....Being quite dispirited with toil, and wholly overcome by grief and despair, I lay down between two ridges, and heartily wished I might there end my days....In this terrible agitation of mind I could not forbear thinking of Lilliput, whose inhabitants looked upon me as the greatest prodigy that ever appeared in the world; where I was able to draw an imperial fleet in my hand, and perform those other actions which will be recorded for ever in the chronicles of that empire, while posterity shall hardly believe them, although attested by millions.

I reflected what a mortification it must prove to me to appear as inconsiderable in this nation, as one single Lillipution would be among us. But, this I conceived was to be the least of my misfortunes: for, as human creatures are observed to be more savage and cruel in proportion to their bulk; what could I expect but to be a morsel in the mouth of the first among these enormous barbarians, who should happen to seize me? Undoubtedly philosophers are in the right when they tell us,

> "We cast anchor within a league of this creek, and our captain sent a dozen of his men well armed in the long boat, with vessels for water, if any could be found. I desired his leave to go with them, that I might see the country, and make what discoveries I could."

that nothing is great or little, otherwise than by comparison: it might have pleased fortune to let the Lilliputions to find some nation, where the people were as diminutive with respect to them as they were to me. And who knows but that even this prodigious race of mortals might be equally overmatched in some distant part of the world, whereof we have yet no discovery?

The wreck of the *Maria Sumpter* off the coast of Cornwall in 1995. This celebrated catastrophe was, according to the offical report, due to a piloting error. The captain was held legally responsible.

Sea &
Land

Storm wave crashing against a jetty. Though many harbors are protected by jetties, in truly great storms, they may be a hindrance, protecting one part of the shore while allowing severe erosion on the other side.

FOXTROT

·· — ·

I AM DISABLED, COMMUNICATE WITH ME.

The scariest part of sailing or any ocean travel is actually making a landfall. In the middle of the ocean, the only threatening thing the mariner needs watch out for is wind and waves, as bad as they may be. As he or she approaches the shore, all sorts of new hazards appear.

Wind, Tide and Breakers
If the wind is onshore, blowing toward shore, it is very difficult to judge the size and ferocity of the seas. This is one reason why, when approaching a bar at the entrance to an inlet, it is imperative to do so at slack water with as little sea running as possible. Many boats have flipped in these conditions because a wave always looks smaller from its rear. If the

wind is blowing offshore approaching a bar, the waves can break and overwhelm a boat. All bars should be approached with extreme caution except in a calm.

The same holds true for narrow harbor entrances, especially those in areas of high tidal range. Tides sweeping in and out of these pinched openings can accelerate to remarkable speeds, throwing a vessel to either side of the center channel and creating eddies that make steering touch and go. This is especially true of some of the harbors in the Bay of Fundy and along the coast of Brittany where tides can reach more than 40 feet high, and sweep in with speed and apparent suddenness that can catch the unwary in a swirling maelstrom of death.

When a ship or yacht is pushed by a wave with its beam to the seas, several things can happen none of which is pleasant to contemplate. Waves breaking against the side of a ship will cause it to roll. Hull form and ballast will cause the ship to counteract the roll. However, if the breaker is large enough or if two breakers hit in quick succession, the dynamic stability of the ship will very likely be lost and the vessel can capsize or be roll 360 degrees. Either is a recipe for disaster. If any hatches or ports are open, chances are the ship will fill with water and start to sink. The rig in a sailing yacht, with some rare exceptions, is liable to be carried away. The spars can possibly puncture the hull and cause the yacht to founder.

Safe harbor is a relative term. A ship is only safe once it is tied to the dock or at anchor. Many shores are fiendishly dangerous, littered with rocky outcroppings and reefs, swept by fierce tides and currents, scoured by contrary winds. Approaching an unknown shore is the ultimate test of seamanship, short of a survival storm.

I wish to have no connection with any ship that does not sail fast for I intend to go in harm's way.

—John Paul Jones

Hidden Danger: Brittany's Lee Shore

Brittany, on the Atlantic Coast of France, is one of the most dramatic and beautiful places on earth. Granite cliffs and jutting rocks, green pastures and bleating sheep charm tourists. But those same cliffs and roiling waters have spelled doom to mariners over the centuries. Not only do these shores end the sweep of Atlantic weather, they are the home to some of the fiercest tides and currents in the world.

Ships crossing from England to Spain and the Mediterranean must cross these waters, most particularly the Bay of Biscay. The entire coast is a lee shore. Everything passing along its length is in a position of danger, with the possibility of being driven ashore, foundering against the boulders strewn haphazardly along this shore.

With frequent storms, tricky currents and constant, vicious tidal ranges, even fair weather sailing is a challenge here. Despite numerous lighthouses standing lonely guard against the jagged outcroppings of rock, small boats can be helpless. With the wind sweeping across the entire reach of the Atlantic, and with the sea bottom shoaling quite rapidly within the bay, the seas can fetch up steep and wicked. These coasts have been a graveyard of ships for centuries and once caught up in a ferocious storm with a lee shore looming, prayer may be the best solution. Waves more than 40 feet tall have been known to engulf boats, and even if the waves don't overcome a sailor, the shore is a ragged bed of rock and rubble, ready to smash or pierce a hull to a thousand bits.

The number of wrecks along these coasts is legion. As the water shoals from the depths of the ocean, seas can build very quickly. For all the sailors who journey from England and Northern Europe to the sunnier precincts of the Mediterranean, crossing Biscay—unless they travel by the far slower and lock-infested canals of France—is a to-be-feared necessity. And despite the large number of lighthouses and beacons along this shore, it is most inhospitable. Few harbors and one of the world's largest collections of glacial rocks and outcroppings make it a particularly-feared lee shore.

Perilous River: The Columbia River Bar

Not only coastlines present dangers to mariners. One of the most frightening landfalls is crossing a bar, that silted entranceway to a river or inlet

that in the wrong conditions, becomes a hidden minefield for even the most experienced sailor.

The Columbia River bar is at the seaward entranceway to one of the great rivers of America's West Coast. It is also a monumental destroyer of boats and slayer of men. Whenever prevailing winds have a long reach across oceans, the lee shores in their path suffer. A bar is a build-up of sand underwater and usually appears at the entranceway to a river or inlet. When water depths offshore are radically greater than the depths of the bar and the bay or river bottom beyond, waves pile up much as the breakers on a beach. One problem with bars is waves break over the bar, which creates a menace to mariners. And, since the Columbia River is flowing outward and the seas in an onshore gale are pounding inward, the resultant crash can easily become a deadly explosion of tons of water.

The Columbia drains most of the northwest river basins of the United States. It is large and powerful. It has supported people for thousands of years, especially with salmon. And it is a major

Rowing ashore through surf is a dangerous undertaking. The oarsman's strokes must be timed to allow passage of the seas under the boats, not into it.

thoroughfare for commercial and pleasure boats.

The West Coast is peculiar because very few harbors exist on such a long stretch of coast. The harbors that do exist suffer from a certain amount of swell and breakers in heavy weather. Man has improved upon nature whenever possible, witness, for example, the breakwaters and harbor enclosures of San Pedro in Southern California. But some natural phenomena man cannot readily change and the Columbia River bar is one.

In anything approaching a gale, the bar becomes a massive line of towering breakers, easily capable of swamping or grounding a ship. In fact, this is where the United States Coast Guard teaches heavy weather lifeboat handling. In these waters, under the right conditions, a sizable ship can be sloughed around and capsized by a single wave. Once these seas catch a vessel broad-

side, there's little even the most experienced mariner can do to forestall disaster.

The sea conditions at the Columbia River bar can build, creating life-threatening breakers. The United States Coast Guard uses these waters for heavy weather training. If someone were to be thrown overboard by the pitching motion or the impact after coming off a wave, there is little chance he or she could ever be recovered.

In fact, most bars around the world are dangerous places to be in any sort of onshore breeze. And for the unwary mariner, arriving in port can be a frightening experience. Seas always look much calmer than they are. Since the sea bottom shelves,

Opposite: the French Coast

often quite abruptly, what looks like gentle swells from offshore can become following seas very quickly, causing a boat to broach, be turned sideways to the breakers or be somersaulted end-over-end. A major bar, in heavy weather, is Russian roulette.

Breakwaters and Harbors

Almost every harbor has had some improvements made over the centuries by man. Very few natural harbors are protected from all directions, and a sudden wind shift or rolling swell can disturb the peace of boats at anchor, as well as wreck havoc in truly wild conditions. Some coasts and islands have no practicable harbor, and this makes for very dangerous landings. For example, Pitcairn is a volcanic rock ascending steeply from the sea Pitcairn

Island in the Pacific. In calm weather, boats can anchor offshore, and the inhabitants come out in longboats, launched off a rock ledge on shore. With any swell running, bringing a boat into shore is an act of faith.

In the 18th and 19th centuries, harbors were improved. Military and commercial considerations demanded safe havens along coasts. In England, much of the commercial development was speculative. A landed nobleman might well enclose a cove with stout rock breakwaters to create a port for coal, steel, or wheat shipments. On the more exposed coasts, particularly the North Sea ports and the Channel Islands, these breakwaters served to halt the destruction of local fleets of fishing and trading boats. In winter storms, waves

Fierce storm off the coast of Brittany. The jagged rocks and many reefs make the Breton coast one of the principal ships' graveyards in the world. The full force of the Atlantic waves, travelling over 3,000 miles, crashes with unpitying force on these coasts.

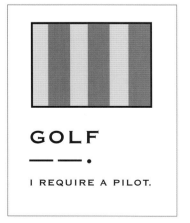

GOLF

I REQUIRE A PILOT.

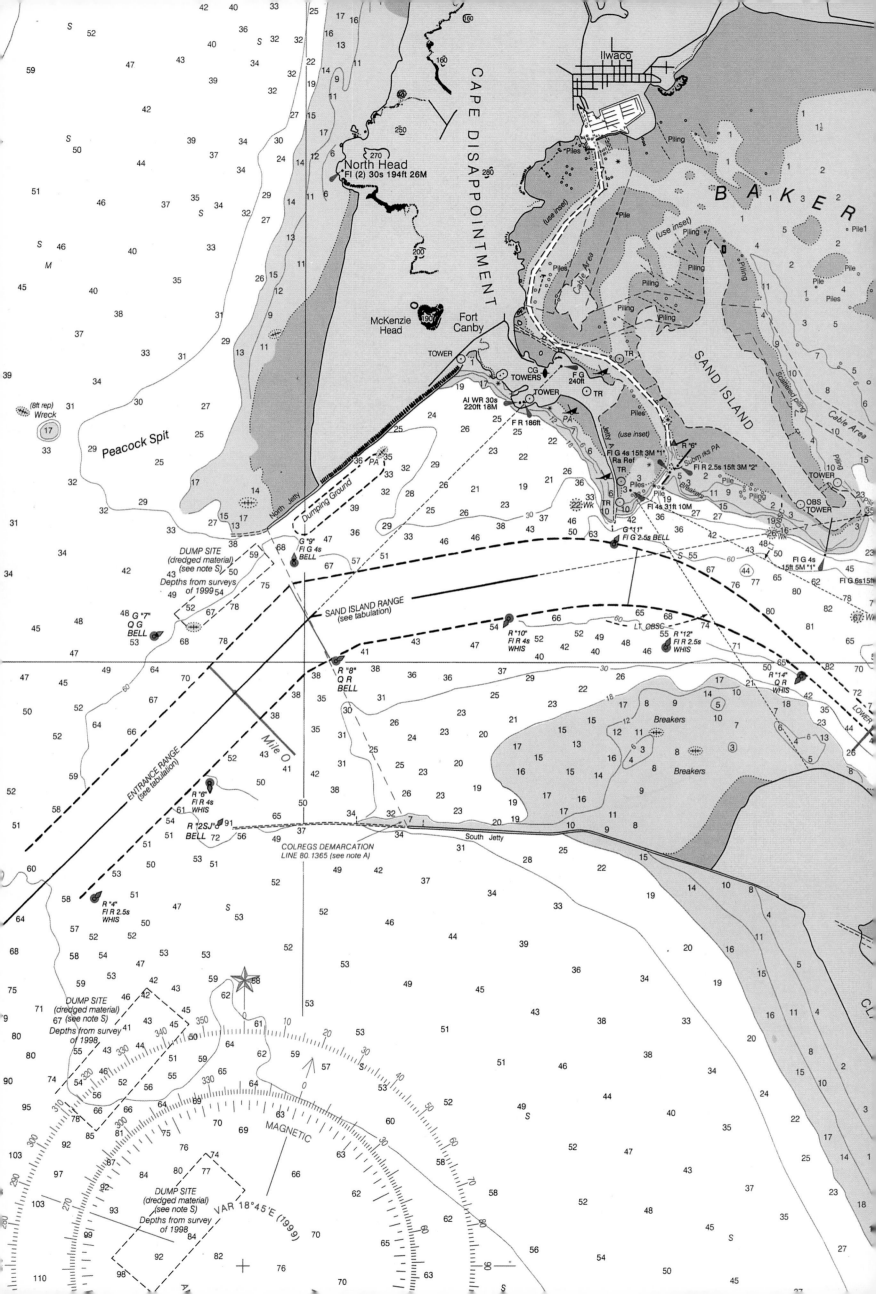

would often crash over the protecting battlements, but the swell
and wind were lessened and relative safety was achieved.

If nature could be improved
upon, the early Victorians did
their utmost. They set to this
civil engineering task with a
vengeance. In the same spirit
that built the Suez and Panama
Canals, these men created a
network of terminals for the
primarily seaborn trade of the
times. What these engineering
marvels did to the seabed is
another story. Most of the
coastal ecology of the world
was permanently altered. Our
forefathers had no idea of con-
servation in the modern sense
and they dug and rearranged
with abandon. Without these
developments, trade would have

Opposite: the Columbia Bar

been stifled, the improvement
of diet and housing would have
been slowed, hygiene lessened
and economies choked.

Even today, these harbors
serve their original purpose.
Atlantic and Pacific ports keep
the world humming. Hong Kong
harbor is one of the busiest in the
world. The British occupied it
originally with the purpose of
trading opium, which made a lot
of merchants rich. But no single
commodity can support a harbor
for long and Hong Kong developed into the greatest commercial
port in the Far East. It is a large
harbor and thereby hangs its
occasional misfortune. Typhoons
can and have blasted through,
causing death and destruction on
a massive scale. No man-made
constructions can withstand these
storms forever and ships are the
most likely to go down.

In the Northern Hemisphere,
harbors are subject to the ravages
of winter. In the great blizzard of
1888, Boston Harbor was frozen
solid and ships crushed in the
grip of the ice. In the still waters
of an enclosed harbor, ice can
form much faster than in open
sea and prolonged periods of
severe cold can not only shut
down shipping, the resulting pack
ice and floes can crush a ship's
hull. Ice is sharp and constant
motion around a hull is enough to
splinter timbers, open seams, and
damage even steelhulls.

The Ultimate Challenge:
Cape Horn

The Southern Ocean is perhaps
the most fearsome on earth.
Skirting the undersides of Africa
and South America, and with little land mass to break the winds
that circle the globe, the seas

**Entrance to the Columbia River.
This engraving of the ship *Tonquin*
crossing the bar on March 25,
1811 gives a good idea of the
steep waves and fierce conditions.
The Columbia River bar is, in fact,
used by the United States Coast
Guard for heavy weather training
in ship handling.**

There is nothing so

desperately monotonous

as the sea, and I no

longer wonder at the

cruelty of pirates.

—*James Russell Lowell*

Harbor Entrance. The jetties to either side protect the dredged entrance from silting, while the breakwater to seaward helps keep the entrance proper free from excessive swell and breaking waves.

below the 40ᵗʰ parallel south build to a crescendo of fury and, sometimes, violence. Blowing from west to east, these winds run free and storms increase their velocity many fold. Shelter is nonexistent. Waves build to monstrous proportions, sometimes exceeding 100 feet in height.

In the days of the clipper ships, fighting around Cape Horn at the bottom of South America was the most feared prospect of a voyage to the West Coast of the Americas. When the ships reached the Horn, they had not only to contend with the weather patterns established by nature in those regions, they had the added obstacle of the proximity of the two land masses of Antarctica and South America. Coming together like the spout of a giant funnel, the shores of these two continents forced the wind and waves into a maelstrom of spume and shrieking air. Unpredictable currents, confused seas, freak waves and howling winds do not make for a pleasant journey.

Cape Horn was discovered by Isaac LeMaire, a Dutch merc-ahnt, and Willem Schouten, his navigator, on a hunch. LeMaire, was granted trading privileges in the Pacific providing he didn't use the Straits of Magellan or the Cape of Good Hope routes to the East Indies. These routes were a trading monopoly, granted by the Dutch crown, and held by the Dutch East India Company. In the manner of the times, and as a holdover from guild practices in medieval times, monopolies were granted by governments—purely out of greed

The protected and bustling harbor at Bonifacio, Corsica.

and the expectation of monetary gain—to companies formed for the express purpose of exploring colonial possessions, or what were soon to become colonial possessions. LeMaire knew that Magellan suspected the land south of his namesake passage was not a continent, and Sir Francis Drake had been driven south of the Magellan Passage by a fierce storm, experiencing only open water. Sailing from England in May 1615 in two

A lighthouse at the end of a breakwater warns incoming ships of the obvious dangers as well as providing a beacon and mark for navigation.

ships, the *Eendracht* and the *Hoorn*, they reached the shores of Patagonia, where the *Hoorn* was accidently burned to a hulk. Continuing in the *Eendracht*, they passed south of the Straits of Magellan in January 1616, noting the tip of visible land (Staten Landt) and naming it Cape Horn. In fact, the intrepid mariners were imprisoned after they arrived in Batavia on the charge they had violated the Dutch East India Company's monopoly. Not until after LeMaire's death, two years later, was his father able to sue the Company, with data supplied bu LeMaire's logbooks, and estab-lish the legal existence of the passage south of Cape Horn.

Things haven't changed since the days of the great sailing ships. Cape Horn was, and is, the ultimate challenge to sailors brave or foolhardy enough to risk its precincts. From LeMaire's first passage to the exploits of Francis Chichester and Chay Blyth, the Horn had held an unholy fascination.

Actually, the Horn is the southernmost tip of an island, but it is the southernmost land of the South American continent. A craggy, rocky cliff, 1,400 feet high, often obscured by spray, rain, fog and overcast skies, it pokes through the sea as a warn-ing to all who range within sight. Yet despite the storms and huge seas, the fear and hardships, for

hundreds of years—until the opening of the Panama Canal—it was the only sea route from the Atlantic to the Pacific.

It was a long, tedious, perilous voyage since—depending on the season—it was either terrifying or horribly terrifying. No mod-ern cruise ship passenger can even begin to appreciate the con-ditions: cramped quarters, little if any fresh food, brackish water, days spent bracing oneself against the heel and roll of the ship. And it could take weeks to pass the Horn going from east to west.

The biggest problem, of course, was the limited ability of square-rigged ships to sail into the wind...to windward.

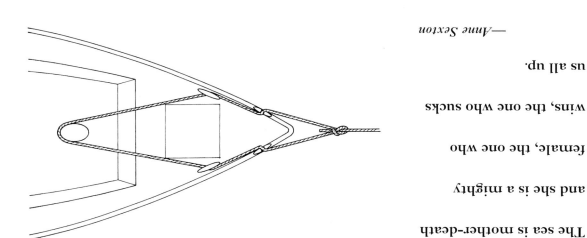

Commercial sailing ships destined for the open ocean, with the exception of the much later clipper ships, were rigged with the sails "square" to the length of the hull. In other words, they were meant to be pushed by the wind, not sail at an angle into the wind. And going from east to west, that is exactly what the ship was required to do. Also, the aerodynamics and hydrodynamics of efficient sailing were not understood until this century. But, still, well-designed sailing ships could sail into the wind at an angle, rarely closer than 60 degrees.

Stories abound of the oft times weeks necessary to break through past the Horn. Shelter was almost nonexistent unless the ship turned and ran hundreds of miles east to the Falkland Islands, and the chances of being blown off course always existed, perhaps to perish in the ice of Antarctica. If the ship were to be dismasted or somehow incapacitated during this battering journey, chances of survival were—not impossible

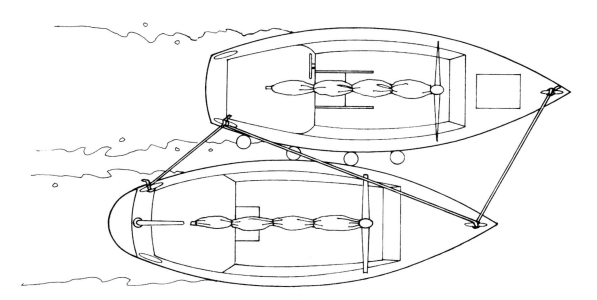

> The sea is mother-death
>
> and she is a mighty
>
> female, the one who
>
> wins, the one who sucks
>
> us all up.
>
> —*Anne Sexton*

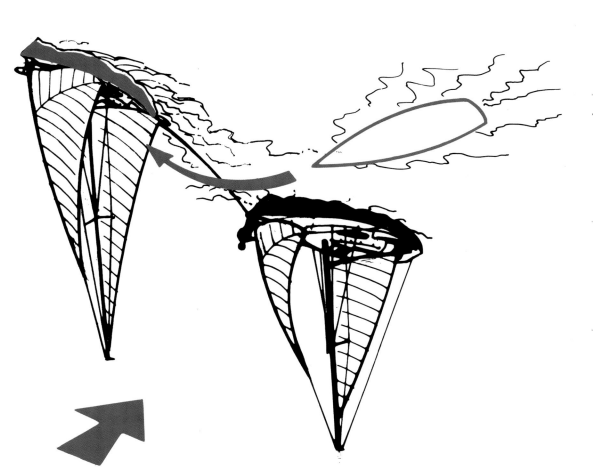

Right: Towing a disabled ship under sail demands care and attention, especially in executing turns. A spotter should always be at the bows of the towed boat.

Center: One of the safer methods of towing is to lash the ships together. Care must be taken to protect the topsides and to run spring lines to absorb the inevitable shocks of a tandem tow.

Below: Snubbing strains imparted on the towed boat can be severe. If the towline is run around the mast and then through cleats and fairleads there is a lesser chance of deck fittings being distorted or ripping out.

but—remote.

Nevertheless, the Horn has been a magnet for amateur sailors in the past century, an ultimate challenge. With the death of commercial sail and the opening of the Panama Canal, the *need* to sail south and west and the return voyage was made redundant. And to round the Horn from west to east is to face the ultimate in wind and waves.

One ship in the vicinity of the Horn recorded a wave 112 feet higher: the equivalent of an eleven story building waiting to crash down on a small craft. Of course, no one can be sure of exact wave heights in such conditions, but no one can survive that kind of brute force.

Of course, the waters of the Southern Atlantic and Pacific are not always that treacherous. David and Daniel Hays, on their voyage in a 25-foot Vertue sloop, had conditions at the Horn approaching an afternoon sail in the Solent. But bad weather is the norm, with gales occurring for two-thirds of the year. From aerial photographs it's always difficult to judge the size of seas. In the Sidney-Hobart Race of 1998, where a monstrous storm devastated the fleet, pictures taken from rescue craft give little indication of the 80- to 100-foot waves crashing around the yachts.

Francis Chichester, in his book *Gypsy Moth Circles the World*, records a Reuter reporter, Michael Hayes, aboard the Royal Navy ice patrol ship, HMS *Protector*, noting in awe the size of the waves and the violent motion of the seas. Yet aboard *Gypsy Moth*, Chichester thought that *Protector* appeared to be steady as a rock. Perceptions are very relative.

But in such conditions, any

small boat will be in danger. Only the soundness of ship and the unerring seamanship of the sailor can prevent foundering.

Beacons and Lighthouses

In fog and storm, in waters treacherous with shoals and bars, before the advent of modern electronics, only beacons could insure a safe passage past jutting headlands and isolated islands. The first lighthouses, built by people of the ancient Mediterranean, were usually no more than fires on shore to warn

boats of nearby dangers. Though records survive of lighthouses from the 7th century before Christ, there are no surviving remains. However, by the 3rd century B.C., the Pharos, the great lighthouse at Alexandria in Egypt was built, towering over the port at perhaps 350 feet. Built by Sostratos of Cnidus during the reign of Ptolemy II, it was considered one of the seven wonders of the ancient world and survived, surprisingly enough, until destroyed by an earthquake in the 14th century

Ships at a distance

have every man's wish

on board.

—Zora Neale Hurston

Ghosts of Cape Horn

Fal deral da riddle de rum
With a rim dim diddy
And a rum dum dum
Sailing away at the break of morn
They are the ghosts of Cape Horn

Come all you old sea dogs from Devon
Southampton, Penzance, and Kinsale
You were caught by the chance
Of a sailor's last dance
It was not meant to be
And ya read all yer letters
Cried anchor aweigh
Then ya took them to the bottom of the sea
All around old Cape Horn
Ships of the line, ships of the morn
Those who wish they'd never been born
They are the ghosts of Cape Horn

Fal deral da riddle de rum
With a rim dim diddy
And a rum dum dum
Sailing away at the break of morn
They are the ghosts of Cape Horn

All around old Cape Horn
Ships of the line, ships of the morn
Some who wish they'd never been born
They are the ghosts of Cape Horn

Fal deral da riddle de rum
With a rim dim diddy
Sailing away at the break of morn
They are the ghosts of Cape Horn

Demons dance everywhere
See them all in sad repair
Southern gales, tattered sails
And none to tell the tales
Come all of you rustic old sea dogs
Who follow the great Southern Cross
You we're rounding the Horn
In the eye of a storm
When ya lost 'er one day
And you read all yer letters
From oceans away
Then you took them to the bottom of the sea
All around old Cape Horn
Ships of the line, ships of the morn
Those who wish they'd never been born
They are the ghosts of Cape Horn

Cape Horn seen from the deck of
Hal Roth's sloop, *Whisper.*

Cape Hatteras Light shows a beacon from one of the most dangerous areas of coastal America.

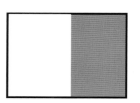

HOTEL

· · · ·

I HAVE A PILOT
ON BOARD.

of the modern era.

Despite the fact that the Romans built numerous lighthouses around the Mediterranean, with the fall of the Roman Empire and the virtual cessation of seaborne trade, the need for beacons disappeared. In fact, until the 17th century, the best a mariner in the Western world, beset by night, fog or stormy weather could only hope for was a fire lit ashore for guidance. Town lighting was nonexistent, shorelines were tar black at night and, with the exception of a brilliant moon, no ship was safe as it approached an unknown shore. But too often that fire ashore was a decoy, a malevolent construct to lure the ship's master into a reef or jagged rock pile and into the grips of scavengers

and wreckers. Many seaside towns made their livelihood from the booty of wrecked ships.

The need for recognizable structures to be built along treacherous shores was long understood. By the 17th century, shipping had become far more complex. Boats were crossing oceans, coastal trade was increasing and the toll taken by the sea of lives and goods was frightening. It became increasingly apparent that some means of

guiding ships past and away from nautical hazards was necessary.

The problem with all premodern lighthouses was their source of light. Wood fires were not dependable and were difficult to keep going in adverse conditions. Oil lamps were neither bright nor cheap to operate before the introduction of kerosene in the 19th century.

Furthermore, early European lighthouses were built of wood

and were invariably damaged or washed away in storms. Not until John Smeaton built the Eddystone Light on the infamous reef of the same name off the coast of England in 1759, were sound engineering principles used, including interlocking stone. Eddystone was also the first light to use the curved, hyperbolic tower, which was to become the standard for the next 200 years.

The light source continued to be a problem for hundreds of years. Even with the introduction of kerosene, the lights needed some means to amplify the feeble flame provided by even the largest wick. Not until the Fresnel brothers of Paris developed their lenses in the 19th century could lighthouse beams be clearly seen far out at sea. The fresnel lens uses a series of prisms, usually molded into the glass, to focus a beam of light,

thereby increasing its intensity many. Refined by the Stevensons over a period of years, these lenses made lighthouses true beacons in the night by allowing even a comparatively weak oil lamp flame to be directed and made far more brilliant than the original source could supply.

Of all the many lighthouse engineers and builders, the most interesting and influential was the Stevenson family of Scotland.

Cape Disappointment Light on the coast of Washington. This stretch of the Northwest coast has few harbors and the sweep of the Pacific makes for sometimes frightening conditions.

The famous Nantucket lightship. Lightships have been used for centuries to warn ships off outlying reefs where a permanent lighthouse is not feasible.

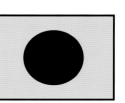

INDIA

• •

I AM ALTERING
MY COURSE TO PORT.

This was the same family that produced Robert Louis Stevenson, author of *Treasure Island* and *Kidnapped*. For more than 100 years, the Stevensons were the official builders of the many lighthouses scattered along the coast of Scotland. Some were built on rock ledges that were underwater at high. The most famous of these were the lighthouses on the Bell Rock and Muckle Flugga, the northernmost lighthouse in Europe at the time.

Some of their structures, such as Muckle Flugga, at the northernmost tip of Scotland are monuments to engineering. Others, such as the pioneering Bell Rock Light completed in 1811, are a tribute to the sheer endurance of man over the elements. It was built on a rock ledge that was covered by tides, allowing only eight or so hours of work per day in the vilest conditions. All materials had to be carried from shore out into the Firth of Forth on the east coast of Scotland. Previous attempts to establish a beacon on the ledge had been quickly destroyed by winter storms, the longest lasting only five months. But Robert Stevenson was a man of deep convictions and his design, based on a parabolic curve built with interlocking granite blocks, has withstood the test of time. In the four years it took to construct Bell Rock, more than 100 men were ferried to the site, along with materials, tools, forges, rations and supplies. It was grueling and dangerous work. For most of the winters, this coast is battered by ferocious storms.

Workers had to be strong. Often a single wave could destroy a day's work and seasickness was constant. On one occasion, the dormitory ship, the *Smeaton*, broke loose from its mooring. Only Robert Stevenson saw it and in horror he realized that they would be doomed to drown when the tide came in. Luckily, just as the water was rising, the supply ship hove into view, carrying, of all things, letters. Never has the mail been more welcome.

The men spent the first year digging foundations by chiseling a round crate in the rock. Though it was backbreaking labor, it was nonetheless necessary to receive the first courses of stone. These were designed with precisely cut dovetails so that no stone could move on its own. Each block weighed tons. Slowly the tower was raised, course by course. When the tower was finished, but the light was not yet in place, an enormous storm descended on Bell Rock, lasting four days with 110-foot waves crashing over the top of the tower. The tower survived and the light was lit for the first time February 1, 1811. Truly a work of engineering genius, Bell Rock has stood as a sentinel to the Firth of Forth ever since.

With all the structures the Stevensons built, it was courage, ingenuity and hand labor that erected beacons that have stood the test of time. Just getting materials to these distant locations was almost impossible. Everything, including complex stonemasonry, had to be prefabricated ashore and sailed out to the location. Once there, all work had to be done by hand during brief hours of low tide. It was daunting work, lives were lost, impossible-to-imagine hardships were endured.

But Stevenson's example was only one among hundreds, for lighthouses are dotted along all the dangerous shores around the world. From Tierra del Fuego to the Great Lakes, from Hong Kong to the Gulf of Finland, these beacons of hope and promise continue to shine.

Not until the 20th century was electricity used to power the beacons, first with arc lamps, then with modern high-intensity bulbs. But during this time, shipping changed, navigational aids improved and the lives of lighthouse keepers became more and more foreign. Today, almost all lighthouses are automated, though many have been abandoned or are kept alive by nonprofit groups and historical preservationists.

With development of GPS, an electronic satellite positioning method developed by the U.S. military, the need for expensive lighthouses has diminished almost to the point of no return.

But the romance of lighthouses remains. The lives saved, the devotion to duty of the keepers, the ships spared for yet another voyage have all become part of the lore and heroism of the sea.

Lightships

Lightships, though now almost extinct, were an alternative to lighthouses. In waters that were without the rock ledges necessary to anchor a lighthouse, a lightship could be heavily anchored, to warn ships of impending danger. However, since a lightship had only a mast on which to perch a light, the altitude and therefore the visible reach of the light was never equal to that of a lighthouse. A crew was aboard, unlike the solitary confinement of a lighthouse keeper. These ships could initiate search and rescue missions more easily and with greater dispatch than land-based facilities.

It was a cramped and uncomfortable life and in storms, it could be downright dangerous, especially if the ground tackle broke loose. Yet even in the foulest weather, these ships held to their posts. Some sank and some achieved wide fame like the Nantucket lightship. Nantucket Island is surrounded on all sides by treacherous reefs for miles out into the ocean. The currents are variable and fierce and the litany of wrecks in these environs is legendary. Hundreds of ships over the years went down here, and though the Island is close to Cape Cod, it is suprisingly isolated. Even today, the fogs which often envelop it and many other coastal islands in the Northeast, make flying in and out impossible. Despite its current sophistication, you can be marooned on the island for days at a time. When ships were wrecked on the shoals, little help could be expected from the people on Nantucket Island. Sailors had to take to the boats or drown. The Nantucket lightship was stationed 40 miles from the nearest land and guided ships not only by

Probable northeast to southwest winds, varying to the northward and westward and eastward and points between. High and low barometer swapping around from place to place, probable areas of rain, snow, hail, and drought, proceeded or preceded by earthquakes with thunder and lightning.

—*Mark Twain*

means of its light, but also via a radio beacon in the days of radio direction finding. In May 1934, the British ocean liner *Olympic* sliced through *Nantucket 117* at 16 knots in heavy fog. She sank in minutes and lost more than half of her crew. The British replaced the lost lightship, and a new one was launched in 1936.

Life aboard a lightship was one of the most dangerous duties in the coastal service. Constant motion, frequent storms and limited accommodations were all trying. But those who braved the storms and could tolerate the lifestyle saved countless ships and lives.

ANN DAVISON

HOME BASE ▪ *Plymouth, England*

ACHIEVEMENTS UNDER SAIL ▪ *First woman to cross the Atlantic alone*

When World War II ended, Ann Davison and her husband Frank were living on an island in a Scottish loch, farming. Peace in Europe revitalized Frank and Ann's adventurous spirits (before farming, the two worked through the 1930s as flight instructors) and they decided to buy a boat and attempt a circumnavigation. And so, for the following two years, they sunk every penny they had, and then some, into buying and outfitting a 70-foot ketch. But in postwar Britain, resources were scarce and this major undertaking propelled them deep into debt. To escape their creditors, they simply slipped out of port and sailed into the ocean, toward the Caribbean.

Unfortunately, they encountered truly ferocious weather, and handling a yacht of such size was more than they could manage. After 19 days at sea, the boat was driven ashore on the south coast of England and wrecked. Their liferaft was repeatedly capsized and Frank died of hypothermia.

Ann survived and began to rebuild a life. She got a job in a boatyard, and wrote two books—the story of her tragic adventure at sea, and another about the war years in Scotland. After the success of her books, she finally had the wherewithal to follow her dream—sailing across the Atlantic.

But Davison faced some serious hurdles; she didn't really know how to sail. So she took lessons from a retured naval commander and went hunting for an affordable boat. And she found it, named with amazing propriety *Felicity Ann*. At 23 feet in length, it was small, but was stoutly built by the famous Cremyll Boatyard in Plymouth by the Mashford Brothers.

But, it was 1952. Transocean voyaging was the pursuit of very few people indeed. It was considered a man's job, too rough and strenuous for women. Certainly a few eccentric women had sailed as skippers, but that was mostly for family cruises and inshore racing. But the end of the war had changed everything and conditions in England were drab and depressing. Ann Davison was determined.

Overburdened with supplies and riding very low in the water, *Felicity Ann* and Ann Davison set off from Plymouth, England. Her goal was the sunny Caribbean, but it was to be a slow and tedious voyage. Coast hopping first to Douarnenez, France, then southward to Vigo, Spain, Gibraltar, Casablanca, the Canary Islands, she finally headed across the Atlantic. The winds were fickle, the Trades were not blowing as usual. She was in a small, slow boat made even slower by a reduction in sail area (recommended by the great sailor Humphrey Barton and, to a great degree, the cause of her slow passage) and too much weight, *Felicity Ann* inched acrosss the ocean.

Perhaps Davison's greatest problem was her inexperience. Sailing across an ocean is difficult enough, but sailing singlehanded is a psychological challenge as well as a physical one. Enduring endless days and nights, constant repairs, tedium interspersed with the violence of squalls, little sound sleep and hurried meals is not condusive to a well-ordered life.

But she persevered and only had to really fight when she was within sight of land. Hoping to make landfall at Barbados (then a British possession), she arrived without time to enter the harbor at Bridgetown before darkness. Heaving-to, she awoke in the morning to discover that she had been driven west of the island and had to beat to windward. With few supplies left, no sleep and eye problems caused by salt and sun, she was unable to raise help by means of flares or flag signals. Days of frustrating headwinds slowed her even more. The boat was swamped. She was beyond exhaustion. But she finally made landfall on January 24, 1953 in Dominica, over 60 days after setting off. It was an abysmally slow passage, but it was the very first transatalantic crossing by a woman, and it set the stage for more and more as the decades passed.

From My Ship is So Small

BY ANN DAVISON

When Ann Davison crossed the Atlantic from Plymouth, England, to Antigua, in the West Indies, in 1952, she became the first woman ever to sail across an ocean alone. Her accomplishment was made even more extraordinary by the size of her boat Felicity Ann—23 feet long, 7 1/2 feet wide—and by the fact that a previous attempt, in a 70-foot ketch, had ended in a shipwreck that had claimed the life of her husband. Her journal of the leg from Casablanca to the Canary Islands captures many of the elements of solo sailing; the courage, the endurance, the loneliness, the peace, the serenity, the need for constant vigilance, the sense of connection with the living sea. And always, just over the horizon, the unknown dangers and the unexpected pleasures—not only wind and weather but also passing ships.

Conditions had a delicious dreamy Southern feel about them, calm and unhurried. There were lovely soft pearl-grey nights of a peculiar luminosity and soothing restfulness that were the physical manifestation of contentment. There were sunrises of such crystalline clarity and pristine glory that one could forgive any amount of travail for the joy of beholding those few golden moments when the world was born anew. There were sunsets so lurid, when an orange sun crept down a black and blood-red sky into a smooth lead-coloured sea, that one was convinced there was nothing less than a hurricane in the offing. I would shorten sail and batten down and prepare for the worst, only to discover that all the fuss in the heavens was for a few drops of rain. The weather eye I had acquired through years of flying and farming in England was sadly out in the lower latitudes, where the familiar signs and portents meant nothing at all. The

weather could, and did, change with extraordinary rapidity, and the minutest rise or fall in barometric pressure might mean a severe blow, or nothing.... I soon gave up trying to forecast and took the weather as it came. After all, there is very little else you can do in the ocean, with no convenient ports to run to for shelter there, so I gave up reefing until it was necessary, and it was hardly ever necessary on this trip, as most of the time there was either a glass calm or a very light breeze, and our average day's progress was twenty miles.

The snail-like advance was a straight invitation to barnacles to grow on the log line, and they were surprisingly tenacious and difficult to remove. The water was so still and clear that sometimes it was almost as if you could see straight down to the bottom of the sea. Fascinating little striped fish, black and bright blue, swam about in the shade of the ship. A few flying fish skittered across the surface like flat stones thrown on a pond. They were very small flying fish, no bigger than minnows. There were times when rubbish thrown over the side in the morning would still be alongside at nightfall. Then the air was breathless and there would not be the smallest sound from the ship, not even a creak, and the silence was primeval. One might have been alone on the planet where even a cloud spelt companionship.

Most of the time, however, there was a huge swell in which FA rolled abominably and flung her boom from side to side with a viciousness that threatened to wrench it clean out of its fastenings. She rattled her blocks and everything not immovably fast below with an aggravating irregularity, so that I was driven to a frenzy of restowing and rigging preventers in an effort to restore peace. An

intermittent blop—rattle—crash on a small boat at sea is the nautical version of the Chinese water torture.

Calms permit a little basking, but not much for a single-handed sailor. They provide an opportunity to overhaul gear and repair or renew anything that might give way under more embarrassing circumstances,

"The snail-like advance was a straight invitation to barnacles to grow on the log line, and they were surprisingly tenacious and difficult to remove. The water was so still and clear that sometimes it was almost as if you could see straight down to the bottom of the sea."

for if there is one thing the sea will not forgive it is a lost opportunity. I made up and reeved new jib sheets, mended slide-seizings on the mainsail, patched the sails where they showed signs of chafe, and recovered the fenders whose canvas covers had been ruined by oil in the dock at Gibraltar, and felt no end salty at my work, deriving a deep satisfaction in the doing of it, even though the patches on the sails were by no means the finest examples of a sailmaker's art.

For the first nine days out of Casablanca

there was not a ship to be seen, and I missed them, grizzling quietly to myself at the loneliness; then we joined the north- and south-bound shipping lane and two steamers appeared on the horizon at the same time, whereon, embarrassed by riches perhaps, I perversely resented their presence. "What are you doing on my ocean?"

Being in the shipping lane again meant

"Calms permit a little basking, but not much for a single-handed sailor. They provide an opportunity to overhaul gear and repair or renew anything that might give way under more embarrassing circumstances, for if there is one thing the sea will not forgive it is a lost opportunity."

the resumption of restless, sleepless nights. I figured out it took twenty minutes for a ship invisible over the horizon to reach us, and as a big ship was extremely unlikely to see me I had to see her, so any rest below was broken every twenty minutes throughout the hours of darkness. Enough practice since leaving England had endowed me with a personal alarm system which rang me out of a comatose condition at the appropriate intervals. Occasionally it let me oversleep, and once I awoke to find a south-bound steamer twenty-five yards astern of us.... A miss is as good as a mile maybe, but twenty-five yards is a narrow enough margin in the ocean, and it gave the required jolt to the personal alarm clock. On these ship-watching nights I used to get two hours of genuine sleep at dawn, when it could be assumed that FA was reasonably visible, and I couldn't care less by then anyway, but the overall lack of sleep did not improve the general physical condition, already much lowered by dysentery. The thought process, never on Einstein levels, were reduced to a positively moronic grasp, and I had some rare hassels with navigational problems. However, the balance of nature was somewhat restored in that I was eating better on this trip than on any of the previous ones—the voyage from Douarnenez to Vigo was made almost exclusively on oranges—and there are several references to cooked meals in the log book.... I had an uncomplicated yearning for plain boiled potatoes and cabbage. As these do not represent a normal taste on my part, I concluded it was a deficiency desire, and stepped up the daily dose of vitamin tablets: a strict necessity for ocean voyagers, as I discovered on the nineteen-day Vigo to Gibraltar run, when I tired to do without them and broke out into reluctant-to-heal sores. The only canned goods whose vitamin content survives the canning process are tomatoes, which probably explains why canned foods lost all appeal for me as soon as I went to sea. Very practically I was learning what stores would be required for the long passage.

One supper was especially memorable, though not for the menu. At 1750 hours, Sunday, October 5th to be exact, I was fixing some cheese nonsense on the stove, for it was a flat calm and I was in an experimental mood, and whilst stirring the goo in the pan I happened to glance through the porthole over the galley and spied a steamer way over on the horizon, the merest speck to eastward of us, going south. A few minutes later I looked out again and to my surprise saw she had altered course and was making towards us. Coming out of her way specially to look at a little ship. Thrilled to the quick, I abandoned supper, brushed my hair, and made up my face, noting with detached amazement that my hands were trembling and my heart was beating, and I was as excited as if I was preparing for a longed-for assignation.

She was a tall, white-grey Italian liner, the Genale of Rome, and she swept round astern of us, the officers on her bridge inspecting FA keenly through their binoculars. As she had so kindly come many miles out of her way, I had no wish to delay her needlessly, for minutes are valuable to a ship on schedule, so I made no signals, but waved, and the whole ship seemed to come alive with upraised arms waving in reply. She went on her way satisfied that all was well with her midget counterpart, and the night was a little less lonely from the knowledge of her consideration.

"Being in the shipping lane again meant the resumption of restless, sleepless nights. I figured out it took twenty minutes for a ship invisible over the horizon to r each us, and as a big ship was extremely unlikely to see me I had to see her, so any rest below was broken every twenty minutes throughout the hours of darkness."

From My Old Man and the Sea
A Father and Son Sail Around Cape Horn

By David Hays and Daniel Hays

"Now my navigation is critical, and I cannot afford the arrogance and luxury of having a thousand miles on all sides. A landsman might think a five-mile error big, but actually that's not bad—it's usually good enough for a landfall. "

David

...On January 6, we cut to The Horn. At 1145 we passed due south of (and half a world away from) our Manhattan home, and by noon we were south of the East 80s where our friends the Bicks and Lorin families lived. Distances in reference to north are shortened: the lines of longitude gather in, ready to meet at the pole. Soon we'd be south of Montauk Point, the tip of Long Island, and farther east than *Sparrow* had ever gone. We were coming to it. I couldn't write or read. I was stupefied by excitement.

Dan

DAY 176. Dawn—Force 6 following wind, first reef and no jib. The barometer is falling fast. Bow foam roars six feet on either side—*Sparrow's* soft feathers. A few birds. Nervous. We should sight the little southernmost island of Diego Ramirez tonight. The clouds have left a little gap and I can see the sunrise, an awful red. "Red in the morning, sailors take warning..."

Now my navigation is critical, and I cannot afford the arrogance and luxury of having a thousand miles on all sides. A landsman might think a five-mile error big, but actually that's not bad—it's usually good enough for a landfall. Yet after twenty-two days of vast ocean I wonder if I've made some tiny error compounded twenty-two times. Then who knows where we'd fetch up? I'm hoping for a couple of good days now—I want to see Horn Island and throw the plaque I made in the Galápagos toward it. How territorial—man and his desire to leave his mark. Maybe I should just empty the trash! If I were to climb Horn Island, what would I do at the top? The same thing any animal would do—pee.

I love the hissing and the chewing cold. I like burning calories just to stay heated. I feel awake and alive.

0600. Seas eight to ten feet, rolling but generally smooth. Trouble with the steering gear with wind building to Force 8. It's a real gale, but pleasant below. Brief galley fire. Pâté, artichoke hearts, crackers, peanut butter, and chicken spread by Dad, à la floor of the cabin, for brunch.

0800-1200. Lively tiller steering—the good old days! Visibility, one-quarter mile; seas, sixteen feet, not so bad. Moving fast under triple-reefed main and full dodger.

DAY 177. Barometer easing its angle of dive. Alter course to stay north of Diego Ramirez—can't risk approaching that rock in this visibility. Will go down Drake Passage between it and The Horn, angling up to The Horn. I'm disappointed—Cape Horn is the last land mass of South America, and Diego Ramirez is just a rock, covered by cold waves and the ultimate lonely place before Antarctica. Even so, it's land.

DAY 178. On January 6, just after I got our noon position and wrote the above, a gale clomped down on us—with Force 8 winds and gusts to Force 9. In the afternoon I came on deck and besides seeing that Dad was working hard at the tiller, the seas and sky looked furious. White streaks were smeared along the waves, the wind almost visible! Seas built and grew until it was necessary for us to look aft and steer down each wave, keeping the stern toward the following seas. Some waves were bigger than others—foaming and looking really mean. Graybeards. The automatic steering wouldn't work—the paddle was spending too much time out of the water. (The whole boat seemed to be spending too much time out of the water.) We took two-hour watches.

It's hard to see a wave (in photos, impossible). You see the mass of it—not much height—then you rise slowly as the water floods beneath you and you're on top. I was at the helm watching this really big one and suddenly I knew *Sparrow* hadn't risen and twenty feet of wave was straight up over us.

We surfed for a moment and fell off it to starboard, flat into the water. The boat didn't seem to tip over but the port rail rose up suddenly above me as I slid down. What I'd been standing on was above my shoulder level. I was in the ocean! The foaming waves I'd been looking at were at my chin. My tether was yanked tight as *Sparrow* came up level, surfed again, and fell over to port, the starboard deck and rail shooting up over my head. I kicked my legs and paddled for a moment in free water, then *Sparrow* righted and I was scooped on deck.

By the time all this happened, it had been thirty-six hours since I'd had a fix on the sun to establish our position. My dead reckoning put us near Diego Ramirez (fifty miles southwest of Cape Horn). But you can't steer accurately

The Cape Enrage Lighthouse looks out over a stormy Chignecto Bay, the northern arm of Canada's Bay of Fundy. The lighthouse was built in 1848 and stands on a promontory surroun ded by water on three sides.

in a gale, so I was jumpy.

The gale broke up by 0100 and, with the moon full, there it was: a frozen wave at the end of the continent. A fearless gray hump. The Horn.

David

My Horn passage started at 0700 on January 7. The sunrise had been ominous. The paddle that goes down into the water to work the self-steerer was jumping out as the stern lifted high. I jibed and the main sheet looped under the paddle, threatening to snap it off. I called for Dan and he held me by the heel like Achille's mother as I went in headfirst for the line and cleared it. Dan was angry because I unclipped my tether, but it didn't stretch that far and I didn't want to take time to reclip it. "But we're not moving, Dan," I said weakly. I was glad he was angry because that meant he'd use the tether himself. We dismantled the Navik and steered by hand for the first time on this passage. Seas and wind built and it was a proper gale, going with us. We took in the jib, she flew with only a spot of mainsail exposed. Slocum's phrase repeated in my head: "Even while the storm raged at its worst, my ship was wholesome and noble." And *Sparrow* was magnificent: delicate but steady, swift and airy on the foam crest, strong and driving through the great valleys. She seemed born for this day.

At noon, Dan shifted course, visibility was down to a few hundred yards. Forget Diego Ramirez. If we didn't hit it we wouldn't see it. And in the slop of this gale we wouldn't see The Horn either. The Horn is three things: the rock itself, Drake Passage (the water in which you sail around it), and the whole idea of the passage. We were in the Passage, and surely we'd survive for the third. I settled for two out of three. At one that afternoon I asked Dan when we'd be off (if not crashed onto) The Horn and he said, "0100 tomorrow morning." The gale picked up and Dan steered, howling "Aaayippeeeeeee!" as we surfed down the long gray waves with their tops torn off and the spray racing us. It was quiet and dry below. I realized that Dan had hardly ever steered by tiller, but his skill was marvelous, undoubtedly honed by hours of handling the joystick in video-game parlors. He looked possessed.

Horsemen have their centaurs, why don't we sailors have a name for the half-man, half-boat that Dan was at that moment?

Because we were hand-steering we changed to two-hour stints. During my early-evening watch, the gale started to fly apart, moderating. This is the most dangerous time of a gale, because the puffs can be fierce after random lulls, and the wind can shoot at you suddenly from a different direction. At eight-thirty at night I was below making tea and lighting the evening lamp when *Sparrow* went down hard to starboard. Then bam! down to port. Without a horizon below, hanging on and standing not upright but with the angle of the boat, I only knew that we were down because the water covering the porthole was not wave froth but solid green—I was looking straight down into the ocean. A felt bootliner that was drying knocked the lamp out of my hand and onto the bunk. The water roared, lie a train running over us.

"OK, Dan?"

"I'm fine, Dad." His voice sounded subdued.

My eye was taken during this by the blue plastic cat pan, which was secured by cord on two sides. It jumped up, did a 180° turn and landed upside down, then leaped again and did a full 360° flip and landed face down again. It looked like a little girl in a blue dress, skipping rope. I thought of that calmly. The binoculars were in my berth with the oil lamp; their teak box had broken. It was the only thing we hadn't built ourselves. Everything else was in place. I didn't learn until he told me the next day that Dan had gone overboard.

The gale broke on my ten-to midnight watch, and the moon, almost full, showed through the racing clouds as they tore apart: a slow film flicker. After my watch I was below, again making tea, and Dan called, "Dad, I think I see The Horn," and I was up on deck at ejection speed and there it was.

"How did you see it, Dan?"

"One wave didn't go down."

I'd never seen it but of course it was The Horn; its form must have been in my genes. The great rock sphinx, the crouching lion at the bottom of the world. The sea and the sky and the faintly outlined huge rock were all the same color—indigo, graded like the first three pulls of the same ink on a Japanese woodblock print.

We embraced, then stood entranced. I went below and poured a finger of Kahlua for each of us (I oddly remembered a guest saying, "No, Leonora, the finger is held sideways, not straight down"). We toasted. I was about to say, "To the men who died here," when Dan said, "To the people who died here." It was the only possible thing to say. There was the rock, after 2,500 miles of ocean, our first sighting, the rock itself.

"You said 0100, Dan, and here we are."

"I'd never seen it but of course it was The Horn; its form must have been in my genes. The great rock sphinx, the crouching lion at the bottom of the world. The sea and the sky and the faintly outlined huge rock were all the same color—indigo, graded like the first three pulls of the same ink on a Japanese woodblock print."

"Yes, but I was aiming for ten miles off."

"You can't be less than eight..." I was staggered by that. Two hundred and thirty miles in thirty-six hours without sky for sights, only our eyes on the compass and on our wake to judge speed, in full gale, in strong current, and with a course change in the middle, and his error was two miles. The Horn bore north and I stepped behind him. Few had rounded The Horn in a boat this small, and he was ahead of me.

We were in the Atlantic. I had a sudden craving for simple food, and made a plain omelette for us. Three eggs in the pan, one on the floor. Perfectly moist in the middle. Just a sprinkle of dill. It was getting light. Between us and The Horn, thousands of small petrels fluttered and dipped, like a vast spread of brown-and-white lace undulating a foot about the surface. `

HAL ROTH

1927–

QUOTATION ▪ *"The essence of adventure is a little danger. If you didn't scare yourself to death once in a while, life would have no zest."*

HOME BASE ▪ *Born in Cleveland, Ohio. Now lives in Maine.*

ACHIEVEMENTS UNDER SAIL ▪ *1986-87, 1990-1991 BOC Challenge; with wife Margaret has sailed every ocean.*

With all his might, Hal Roth could budge the tiller only a little. The rudder groaned and squeaked and the wind relentlessly pushed him where it would. Unable to steer in the conventional way, nearly 1,000 miles downwind from Cape Town on the second leg of the 27,000 mile 1991 BOC Challenge, Roth had few options. The rudder was fouled with lines that had come loose a few days before in a heavy squall, but the seas were calmer now. With the autopilot useless, Roth wouldn't be able to manage the boat 24 hours a day. Alone, asleep, he would be at the mercy of the wind. So Roth tied a lifeline to his chest, held a bread knife in his jaws and jumped over the side of his 49-foot cutter *Sebago*.

The December water was not as cold as he expected. Anticipation was worse than action, he wrote in his diary. He freed the lines from the rudder and crawled back into the boat. He needed to go again to make sure that the rudder was free. Going over the side, it seems, was easier than getting back in the boat, especially on a deck iced over from his first foray. He barely made it back in the *Sebago* on his second swim, but the rudder was clear. After donning some dry clothes and taking a brandy, he radioed in that he was on his way.

"The story of long distance sailing is fix, fix, fix all day long," Roth wrote in his diary from the race. He returned to Cape Town a few days after the fouled rudder incident with further repairs, set out again and was capsized in a storm. The boat slowly righted itself and he pushed on to Sydney.

Roth discovered sailing in 1962 when he and his wife Margaret sailed on a friend's ketch in San Francisco Bay. Their passion for sailing grew from that first experience and soon they were crossing oceans. They have since sailed every ocean, together circumnavigating the globe on a four-year trip, and Roth has documented many of the voyages in books and on film. He tried his first solo circumnavigation in the 1986-87 BOC Challenge and followed that with the 1990-1991 race. Roth recently retraced the sailing adventures of Odysseus in the Mediterranean for his ninth book, *We Followed Odysseus*.

ROPES & RIGGING

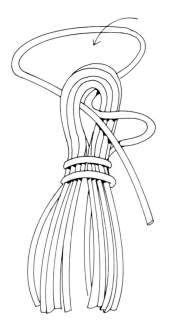

Above far left: Flaking a line down so it runs out smoothly. Above right: A coil of rope fastened in a timely manner with a looped half-hitch.

Heavy Warp Stropped

A   B

A coil of rope fastened in a timely manner with a looped half-hitch.

1

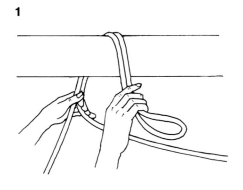

2

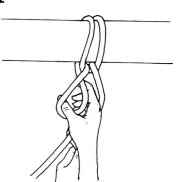

3

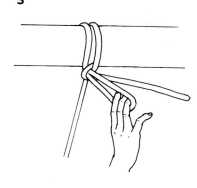

Below: Clove hitch with loop.

Above: A slip hitch.

1

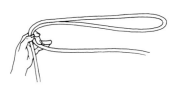

2

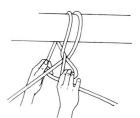

3

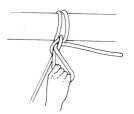

4

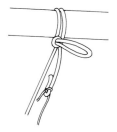

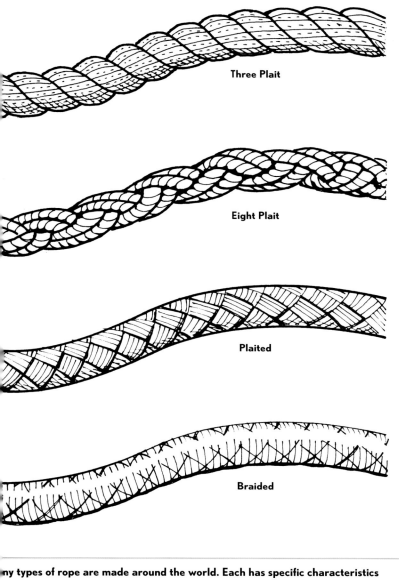

Three Plait

Eight Plait

Plaited

Braided

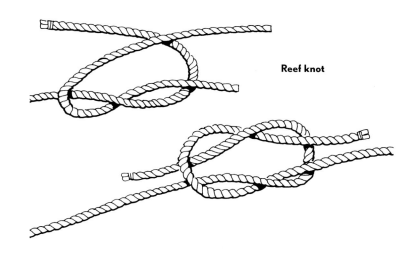

Reef knot

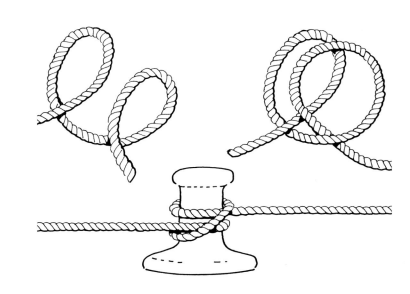

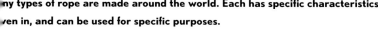

ny types of rope are made around the world. Each has specific characteristics
ven in, and can be used for specific purposes.

Overriding turn on a winch. Only
by lessening the tension of the sail
end of the sheet can this be
undone.

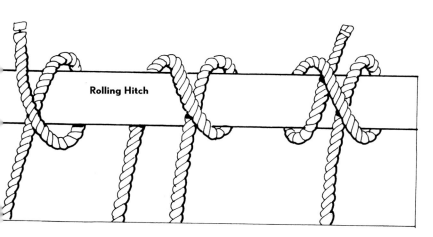

Rolling Hitch

Two lines joined by two bowlines

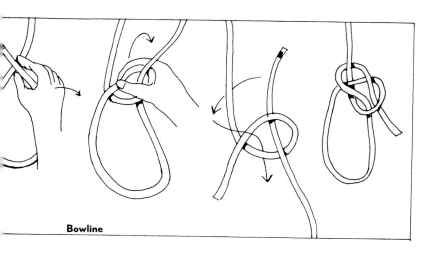

Bowline

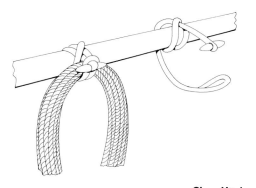

Clove Hitch

Attaching line to bollard

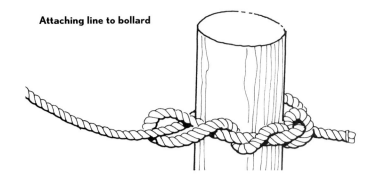

Snug Hitch

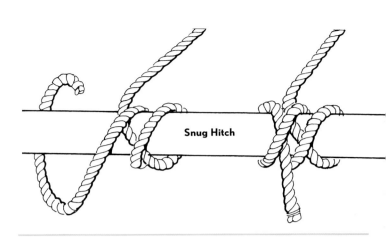

Attaching a rope to a spar using a snug hitch. This knot is easy to undo, but extremely secure.

Mooring with a rolling hitch

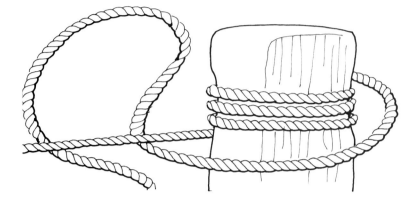

Round turn and half hitches

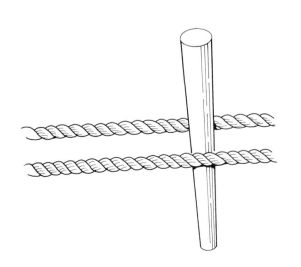

A Spanish windlass. This primitive device, basically a dowel, can be used to tension two lines.

Long Splice

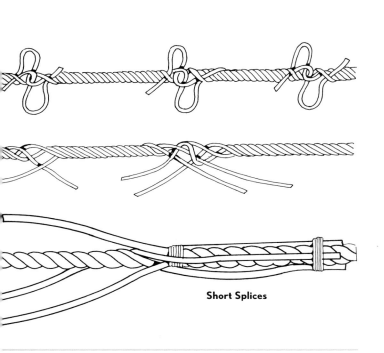

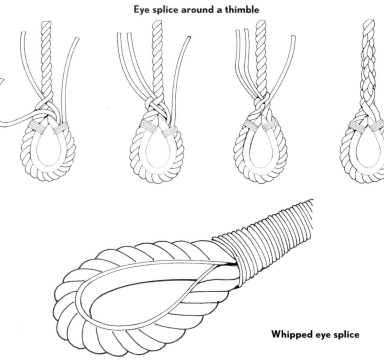

Eye splice around a thimble

Short Splices

Whipped eye splice

...licing is an art. Short splices are best for joining two lines or wires when ...e resulting connection does not need to pass through a block. Long ...ices are both smoother and more secure.

Above: Caption Caption goes heregoes Caption goes Caption goes here here here Capti.

Above: Caption Caption goes heregoes Caption goes Caption goes here here here Capti.

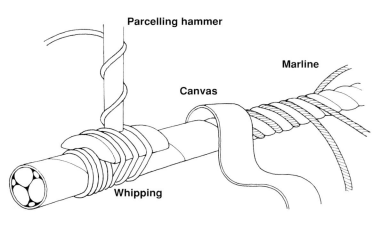

Parcelling hammer

Marline

Canvas

Whipping

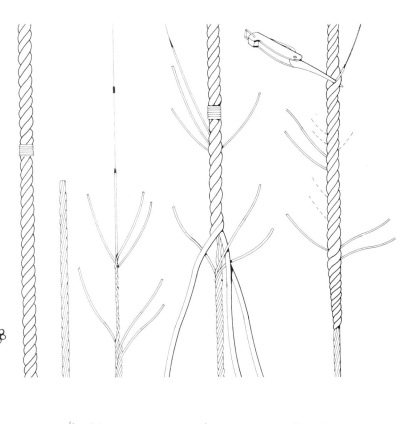

...celling a rope or especially a wire rope protects its from the ingress of moisture ...creates a smoother surface. First the marline is coiled into the rope to fill in gaps ...ween strands, then strips of canvas are tightly wrapped around the rope, then ...lly the rope is whipped, using a parcelling hammer to ensure a tight, even fit.

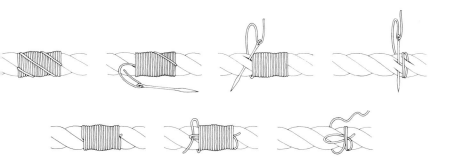

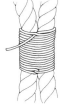

Whipping prevents the ends of ropes from unravelling.

Seizing is a method of joining two lines or fastening a loop or eye in a line.

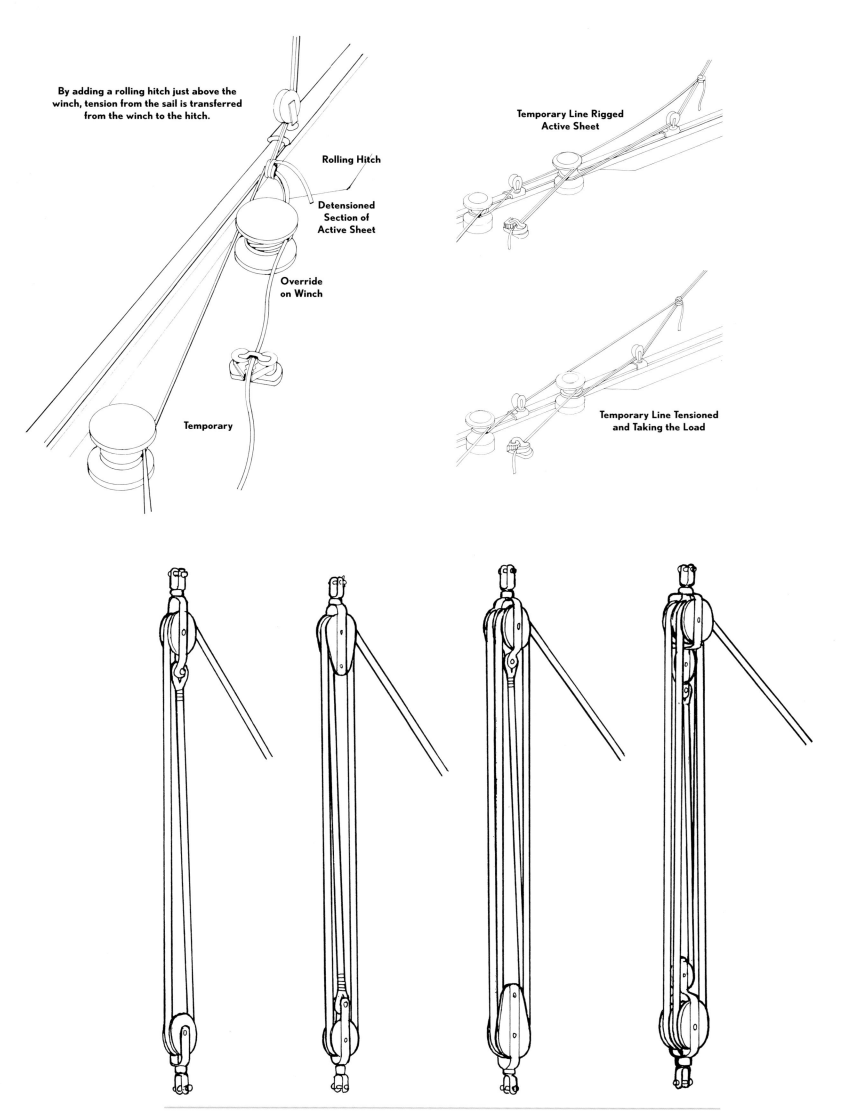

By adding a rolling hitch just above the winch, tension from the sail is transferred from the winch to the hitch.

Rolling Hitch

Detensioned Section of Active Sheet

Override on Winch

Temporary

Temporary Line Rigged Active Sheet

Temporary Line Tensioned and Taking the Load

Purchases, from right to left: 2 part, 3 part, 4 part, 5 part. As the number of turns around the pulleys increase, pulleying power increases.

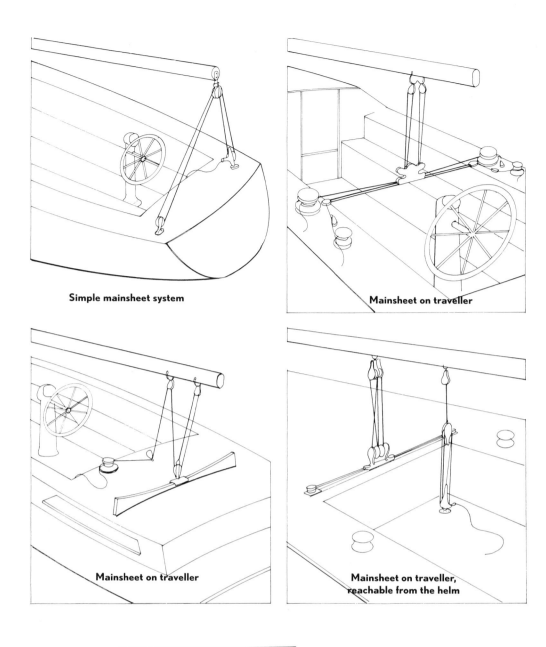

Simple mainsheet system

Mainsheet on traveller

Mainsheet on traveller

Mainsheet on traveller, reachable from the helm

Left: Four systems to control the mainsheet. The travellers allow the mainsheet to be adjusted laterally and flattened, while the simple system raises and lowers the boom.

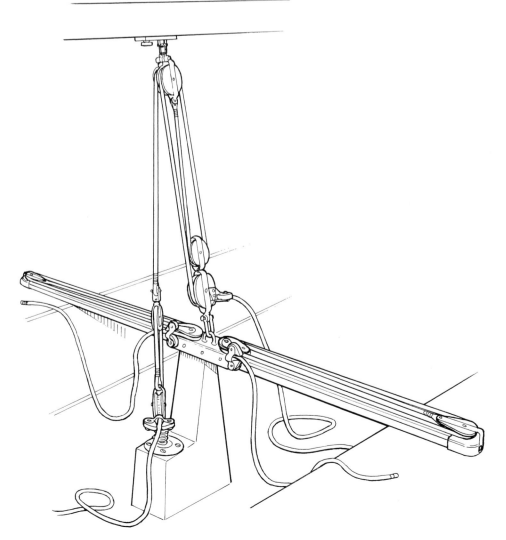

Fine adjustment with cam cleats along the traveller allow the sail trimmer to move the mainsheet to port and starboard against heavy winds.

Whisper sailing south from a point approximately 10 nautical miles north of Cape Horn. Hal and Margaret Roth, one of the most successful ocean cruising couples, have accomplished a number of impeccably planned and executed voyages.

Voyages

Voyaging across oceans
is not for everyone. It
is slow, dirty, uncom-
fortable, hard work and sometimes
deadly. Why spend days, even
months getting somewhere when
a plane can whisk you across
thousands of miles in mere hours?

Sailing from point A to point
B on a chart or along a coast is a
passage; you and your ship are
traveling to get somewhere for a
purpose, be it commercial or for
pleasure. But a voyage is something more. Columbus "voyaged," the Smeetons, in their
disastrous attempts to round

Cape Horn, did the same.
Charles Darwin's scientific journey on *The Beagle* qualifies as a
voyage. These were all passages
as well, but they were passages of
discovery, trips of wonder.

We are so used to driving or
flying somewhere quickly, that
we forget that few people traveled until comparatively recently.
Any trip away from home was a
voyage of discovery, a bout of
personal learning and enlightenment. To see what you have
never seen before, to experience
new places, people, creations is a
wondrous thing. So voyages,

whether filled with pleasure or
beset by catastrophe, are periods
in one's life when eyes are
opened anew, brains are turned
inside-out and refreshed, ears
hear new and strange sounds and
fingers touch plants and animals,
water and soil that they have
never experienced.

One voyages, then, because
one cannot cease to experience
the world. It is a compulsion that
propels people to know more.
More and more people are able
to occasionally break away from
the strictures of job and home
and see and experience some of
the world for themselves. Even
two weeks holiday can become a
voyage.

The Origins of Voyaging

For the years prior to the development of steam-powered vessels,
people sailed, usually to trade,
fish, or start a new life. No one
sailed transatlantic for fun. As
far as we know, the Vikings went
farthest first, though they
hopped from island to island,
with present-day Iceland as their
base. By the 15th century, exploration began in earnest and a
century later, fishing spread
westward with the discovery of
the rich fishing grounds of the
banks off North America. None
of these adventures were particularly pleasant and involved hard

Looking at the back side of a
wave is the most accurate way to
judge its height—even so, it is
almost impossible to really know
how big a wave or swell is until
you drop to other side.

Left: Dame Naomi James checks her rigging prior to setting sail. The oscillating strains imposed on any sailing rig are astounding, and metal fatigue is a major source of concern for ocean sailors. Every part of the rig must be inspected with care.

Right: Robin Knox-Johnston won the first round-the-world non-stop race in an inappropriate vessel under appalling conditions. His apprenticeship in the British Merchant Marines had prepared him for the worst.

work and appalling conditions in stinking tubs infested with vermin. In the beginning, people voyaged because they had to.

But, the difficult conditions were expected. For thousands of years, seafarers were notoriously tough and passages of any length demanded iron men. No weekend sailor today can begin to comprehend the discomforts and difficulties encountered: no bunks, no toilets, no galley, no refrigeration, no fresh water, no safety devices, nothing except wood, iron and rope. For a thousand years oceans were crossed in much the same way, under the same conditions. From our somewhat jaded point of view, these boats were technologically primitive, clumsy and forlorn.

These sailors had experience gained through apprenticeships and drudgery. Boys went to sea at age twelve or thirteen on a coastal trading vessel. They learned the ropes, literally. For long voyages, crews were recruited from the ranks of the best and most experienced sailors.

The early Victorians were not particularly interested in outdoor leisure endeavors. As the century progressed, the bluff and hearty Englishman took to the water. First in small boats, men like R.T. McMullan went sailing—around the coasts, across the English Channel, and they went alone. This was waterborne camping and was accompanied by pride and unalloyed bravery. Some remarkable voyages were made in the name of expanding and defending the British Empire.

Besides McMullen, whose book *Down Channel* is now a classic, Albert Strange, marine artist and yacht designer, created

Four things shalt

thou not see aboard a

yacht for its comfort:

A cow, a wheelbarrow,

an umbrella, and a

naval officer.

-Anonymous

JULIET

· ▬ ▬ ▬

I AM ON FIRE, AND HAVE DANGEROUS CARGO ON BOARD. KEEP WELL CLEAR OF ME.

a whole slew of pretty and seaworthy small boats which ranged far and wide. One, *Saiorse,* made an epic adventure in the 1920s. But even then, most experienced sailors shuddered at the thought of putting to sea in these little "cockleshells." In fact, it wasn't until the 1950s that small boat voyaging became more than an occasional stunt. The designer Laurent Giles' partner, Humphrey Barton, crossed the Atlantic with a mate in *Vertue XXXV.* Ann Davison became the first woman to solo across the pond in a 23-foot sloop. Suddenly, despite the hardship, sailing was becoming a reality for dreamers. By the 1960s, with the development of GRP yachts, voyaging suddenly became a possibility for thousands.

Singlehanding

What possesses anyone to sail alone across vast expanses of ocean? Sailing a yacht by oneself is an exercise in boredom, excitement, frustration, exhilaration and futility. And yet, since the nineteenth century, men and women have set out to prove they can conquer alone what entire crewed ships have feared.

People have sailed by themselves when they had to—when crew was incapacitated, when standing watch alone or when on short voyages. To cross the oceans alone, without hope of assistance, takes a special kind of person, one who is supremely confident *and* competent. These days solo sailing is almost commonplace, but a century ago, the idea of going to sea alone in a small boat was looked on with a combination of awe, admiration and horror. As a result, many early solo voyages were undertaken without the fanfare that would surely accompany them today.

The most famous of these early trips was Joshua Slocum's voyage around the world in the 1890s. Slocum was a commercial sea captain who was "beached," unable to garner another command in the fading days of sail. As something of a joke, a friend offered him a ship, which turned out to be the hulk of an old oyster boat, sitting on the Massachusetts foreshore. Patiently, Slocum rebuilt the boat, launched it, laid in a supply of food and spares and set off from Boston. Of all the possible boats to circumnavigate in, *Spray,* his rebuilt oyster sloop had to be one of the most inappropriate. She was beamy, shallow, blunt bowed, but she did have one important ability—she could steer herself on almost any point of sail for hours on end.

Slocum was a consummate seaman with vast ocean experience. Setting off in 1895, he spent three years sailing through appalling weather and monstrous seas, dealing with unfriendly natives, coping with the vagaries of supplies and repairs, but never wavering in his determination. When he sailed back into Newport, RI harbor in 1898, he

Joshua Slocum and Spray. Slocum, out of work and unable to find a berth, rebuilt an old oyster smack and proceeded to be the first man to circumnavigate the globe in the last decade of the 19th century.

had not only accomplished a great feat, he opened the floodgates to the solo sailors of the twentieth century.

The story of his adventures became a bestseller and Slocum himself was turned into a literary lion at the turn of the century. He presented himself as a sly, clever sailor, but his accomplishments were no less heroic.

Singlehanding is more than the sum of its parts. Sailing alone demands much greater preparation and stamina than sailing with crew. And it needs a yacht that will sail itself—something that modern yachts will not, by and large, do—or that can be fitted with a self-steering device. Prior to the 1960s and the development of the auxiliary self-steering vane by Colonel

Slocum's boat, *Spray*, in Boston Harbor.

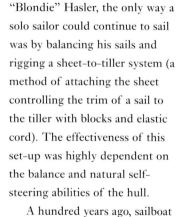

KILO

— • —

I WISH TO
COMMUNICATE
WITH YOU.

"Blondie" Hasler, the only way a solo sailor could continue to sail was by balancing his sails and rigging a sheet-to-tiller system (a method of attaching the sheet controlling the trim of a sail to the tiller with blocks and elastic cord). The effectiveness of this set-up was highly dependent on the balance and natural self-steering abilities of the hull.

A hundred years ago, sailboat hulls were based on working craft with long keels. These boats were designed to look after their often undermanned crew and could handle being put out to sea in all sorts of weather. Thus they were ideal for the impecunious solo sailor. They were stout, cheap, heavily built and weatherly. Of course most were also slow, ponderous, waterlogged, wet and leaky, but they did get one across oceans with a minimum of fuss. Witness the exploits of the late Frank Mulville, who was sailing an ancient gaff cutter across oceans in the 1990s.

After Slocum's voyage, oddly enough, very few sailors set off alone. Harry Pigeon, Fred Rebell, Edward Allcard and John Guzzwell were among the pioneers, but it was not until after World War II that sailing fever became widespread. Some of the early sailors were real loners—impecunious, patient, willing to take chances and undoubtedly brave. But the dangers were real enough. One might get run down by a ship, capsize, fall overboard, run out of victuals or water, or be dismasted, the list is endless. These men were pioneers. They sailed because they wanted to or, particularly in the case of Fred Rebell, had to.

Rebell was in deep trouble when he left Australia aboard an 18-foot open sloop in 1939. A Latvian refugee who had wandered across Europe and stowed away aboard a freighter to reach Australia, his life became a series of operatic disasters: failed marriage, lost jobs and finally the

onset of the Depression. Unable to find work, Rebell decided to emigrate to America. But he was dead broke. He spent his last £100 on a boat and supplies.

He didn't know how to sail. He bought a couple of books and taught himself, practicing in Sydney harbor. Moreover, he made his own passport which was actually accepted and stamped by authorities along the way. Rebell was nothing if not ingenious and resourceful. His passage was a collection of island-hopping trips across the Pacific, lasting over two years and beset by hardships. The major problem was that his boat was so small and fragile. Storms, adverse currents, lack of knowledge (his charts were traced from out-of-date maps in an old atlas) all conspired to make his trip herculean by anyone's standards. And, after all the travails, immigration authorities dragged him through hell when he arrived in Los Angeles. But he had done what no one else before had even considered and he had survived.

Rebell sailed because he had no other options. Others went on solo passages for the challenge of it. One of the most remarkable journeys was undertaken by the nineteenth century sailor Howard Blackburn. Blackburn, a seaman aboard the fishing schooner *Grace L Fears,* was three days out of Nova Scotia in January 1883, fishing in a dory with his partner Tom Welch. As they hauled their final catch, a snowstorm blew in. They were separated from their ship and when the storm subsided discovered they were alone on the sea in bitter cold. Blackburn's mittens were washed overboard. Knowing that if his hands froze in an open position, he wouldn't be able to row, Blackburn grasped the oars and waited until his hands froze around them, then released the oars and continued to bail out the dory. Welch died and Blackburn, after three days of bailing, watched the storm subside. He proceeded to row, with frozen hands, for four days. His rescue came from a group of fishermen on shore, who took him to the house of the Lishmans. These kindly people tended him for almost two months, during which time he lost all his fingers, some of his toes and one heel. But he survived. And, moreover, he proceeded to challenge the oceans again.

In 1899, he designed his own boat, the sloop *Great Western,* thirty feet in length and gaff-rigged and proceeded to set off across the Atlantic to Gloucester in England. With his lack of fingers, he had been careful to make things easier for him to sail, such as oversize reef points and larger than normal lines. Carrying a vast amount of stores, Blackburn headed out and proceeded to suffer from rheumatism. He made only 250 miles of easting in the first week. He battled contrary winds, calms, the need for sleep, but despite a slow passage, sailed into Gloucester on August 14, 1899 after 62 days at sea. Perhaps the most amusing aspect of his reception in England was the reaction of his hosts to the large supply of "Old Crow" whiskey he had aboard. It was agreed that it could raise the dead.

Blackburn again sailed transatlantic in 1901 in another sloop, the *Great Republic,* arriving in Lisbon, Portugal in a record 39 days. This boat is now restored and in the Cape Ann Historical Museum in Gloucester, Massachusetts. Howard Blackburn retired from the sea and ran a successful saloon in Gloucester until his death in 1932 at the age of 73.

All these early singlehanders were dependent on sheet-to-tiller rigs or the ability of their yachts to sail themselves on certain points of the wind. Most heaved-to (stopped the yacht with the foresail aback) at night or in heavy weather.

Steering a sailboat is a question of balance. If the boat can be made to balance herself, all the better, and a number of yachts can sail to windward fairly well without a hand on the tiller. But steering is tiring, demanding fierce concentration and exposure in all weathers. The classic four-hour watch represented the near-maximum a helmsman could stay alert in heavy weather. And, though it may be difficult to imagine, keeping a small sailboat "in the groove" is more difficult than with a large sailing ship. It's mostly a question of inertia. A heavy, large boat is less likely to be bullied by the sea than a small one, though there are limits. In the realm of steering, though, a yacht is more likely to be buffeted about by wind and sea.

A sheet-to-tiller rig uses blocks and elastic cord to keep pressure on the tiller. Thus, when the boat veers off course, the sail, the controlling sheet of which is led through a block, attached to the tiller and balanced on the opposite side by a length of elastic, pulls the tiller and causes the boat to regain its original course in relation to the wind. No self-steering device dependent on the wind will steer a compass course, but most offshore passages are made in steady trade winds. However, for a sheet-to-tiller rig to work effectively, the boat must be balanced both in hull shape and sail plan. Modern yachts tend to be designed for speed with a lot of crew and need a more powerful and reliable means of steering.

Staying the Course: Steering on a Solo Voyage

Hence the development of the self-steering vane. Blondie Hasler realized that the wind could be harnessed efficiently to control the boat. His vane gear consisted of a wind sail or panel attached to the rudder by means of a linkage. When the yacht wandered off course the vane would be activated, moving the rudder and correcting the ship's course. In principle, this was a highly attractive method of helming. However, many modifications were necessary, depending on boat type, rudder location, rig and stern design.

Yet, in a few short years (from the early 1960s), vanes were commonplace on ocean

Liberty is being free from the things we don't like in order to be slaves of the things we do like.

—*Ernest Benn*

cruising sailboats. Variations appeared. More efficient and stronger construction, better materials, and lighter weight all improved the performance of vane gears.

The first real test of vane steering was in the 1960 Transatlantic Race. Passage times were drastically reduced. Suddenly, it was possible for a solo voyager to approximate passage times of fully-crewed yachts. Now sailors, even with crews, could leave the most intense chore of helmsmanship to a mechanical device independent of the ship's batteries.

For someone who has never helmed a sailboat, the concentration needed to steer a reasonably accurate course is astounding. One must take into account the ever changing wind, the condition of the waves, the point of sailing (with the wind ahead, on the beam or abaft the boat), the set of the sails, the angle of heel, any currents running and the natural balance or lack thereof of the hull. And, one must do this constantly, as well as keep a lookout for other ships, obstructions, rocks and floating debris. It's a tall order and the time of a traditional watch at the helm—four hours—can test the limits of anyone's concentration, especially in heavy weather, when the boat is being buffeted by extraordinary forces. Self-steering vanes banished a good deal of that. Of course a

Starting in the 1960s and 70s, it became more and more common for sailors to make long passages, even circumnavigations, alone. The most famous were Sir Francis Chichester, Sir Robin Knox-Johnston, Sir Alec Rose. Chichester had gained fame first as an aviator in the 1920s and 30s, Knox-Johnston was a merchant seaman on leave. Rose was a reticent, quiet English grocer. He made his circumnavigation in 1967-68. He did it in an old, wooden yawl, with nothing special in the way of technology and succeeded by sheer perseverance. His yacht, *Lively Lady*, was built in 1948 to the designs of Fred Shepard, best known for his solid cruising boats. Though it was rerigged for the voyage, it was the family cruising boat. Rose set off shortly after Chichester and despite a slow passage completed his voyage to much acclaim. Interestingly enough. Both Rose and Chichester were past middle age. Planning a long ocean passage for singlehanding is an exacting exercise. Everything must be anticipated. David Lewis' attempted circumnavigation of Antarctica was stymied by his lack of proper clothing for the bitter Southern winter and by shortage of funds for proper fitting out.

watch must still be kept and deck work has to proceed, but a good vane gear will steer a better course than most helmsmen.

A crew member checking the spreaders from a bosun's chair. This is dangerous work in a seaway, and care must be taken to have a spotter on deck. The chair holds the sailor firmly in place and provides pouches for tools.

10 M

30 M

Catenary

All boats snub their anchors. With a chain between the boat and anchor, a scope of 3:1 is usually sufficient in settled conditions. With a rope line, the scope must be increased to 5:1. The weight of the chain is highly useful in increasing the catenary and preventing the anchor from breaking out.

Tidal range must be allowed for when anchoring, especially in close quarters. Anchors set from both bow and stern will keep the yacht in position, a useful device in tidal streams to prevent the anchor from breaking out.

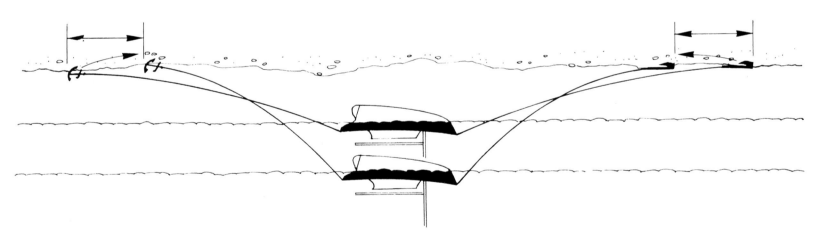

Anchoring to a single anchor allows the boat to swing widely to either side. With two anchors set at angles the boat will be kept in a relatively short arc.

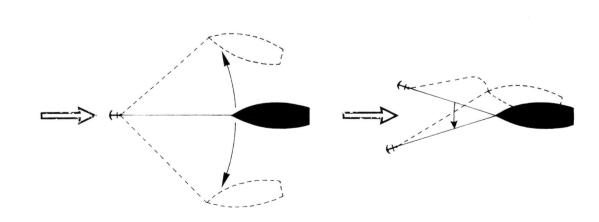

The Great Lakes sailor is wild-ocean nurtured; as much of an auda-cious mariner as any.

—Herman Melville

Epic Challenges: Circumnavigation, First Crossings, Small Craft

Not all great voyages are under-taken solo. That is a fairly new phenomenon. Magellan's circum-navigation was epic, especially as he had no reliable charts or navi-gation aids. There is a difference between sailing into the known or the unknown. Known waters can be approached with a bit more abandon than new seas. As the earth was mapped and charted in the seventeenth, eigh-teenth and nineteenth centuries, sailors posed more and more difficult challenges for them-selves. Many sought knowledge, but the element of glory was never far from the surface. And one must also differentiate between those voyages made for the sake of the passage such as Chay Blyth's solo circumnaviga-tion the "wrong way" around the world (against the prevailing winds) and the more inadvertent ones, such as Shackleton's heroic voyage to save his men.

Then there were those like the late Bill Tilman who bought old pilot cutters and embarked from England with pick-up crews to climb mountains in the remotest corners of the earth accessible by water. This is cer-tainly a strange amusement and that Tilman and his men sur-vived years of this rough and hearty torture is either a testa-ment to their skill or luck. The boats were in a constant state of repair, provisions were of the lowest order, the trips were beset by storms, fog, calms. Yet they trooped on. In the end nature got the better of him, and in his seventies he sailed off never to return. All hands lost at sea.

While many challenges had been met, some still remained. Who could find a passage from the Atlantic to the Pacific? Who could be the first to sail alone around the globe? Who could do it nonstop? Who could do it in the fastest? Who could sail in the smallest boat? Who could find the Northwest Passage? Who could circumnavigate Antarctica? Who would be the first woman to do these things? The list is endless. All these sailors had one thing in common: they were all dissatisfied with life on land.

The challenge to cross the oceans in the smallest possible boat is one of the more dangerous of the lot. The most famous of these voyages, at least in popular imagination, was Robert Manry, who sailed across the Atlantic in 1965 in a 13.5 foot centerboarder, *Tinkerbelle*, with an ungainly cabin perched on top in a mind-boggling 78 days.

Another, more contemporary member of this breed is the Swede Sven Lundin who, in a series of boats named *Bris* (Swedish for breeze,) attempted to sail around the world. *Bris* was, in its most advanced configuration, an aluminum boat, almost totally enclosed, roughly 18-feet in length and controlled from inside. Lundin, poor and resourceful, built most of it himself and bat-tled half-way around the world,

LIMA

YOU SHOULD STOP YOUR VESSEL INSTANTLY.

A drawing of *Spray* showing the two cabins and mizzen sail at the very aft end of the boat. The mizzen is an excellent sail for maintaining directional stability and for dampening the motion of the boat while at anchor.

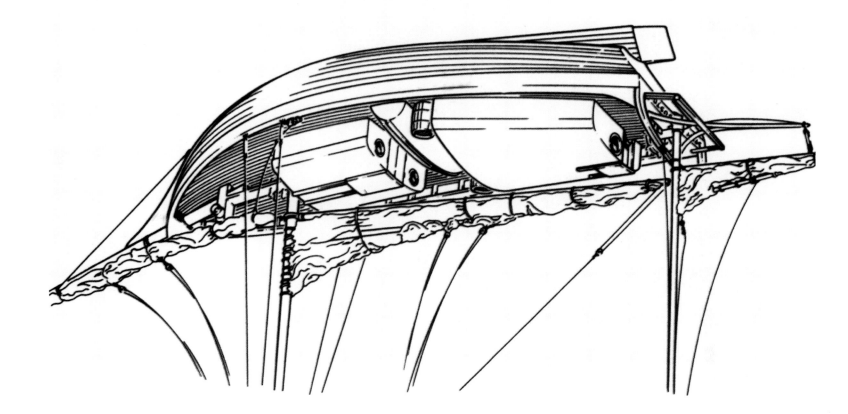

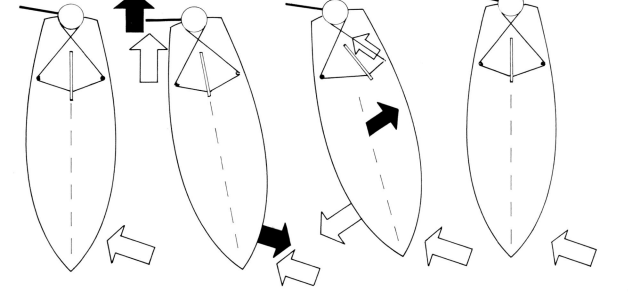

Right: All vanes work on the same basic principle. They do not steer compass courses, but rather steer the boat on a course in relation to the wind. As the wind changes, the vane is pushed causing the rudder or auxiliary rudder to move and adjust the course.

Above left: Self steering can take many forms. This is an auxiliary rudder vertical vane.

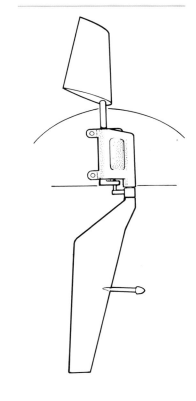

Increasingly, modern yachts have the generating power to use electric autopilots.

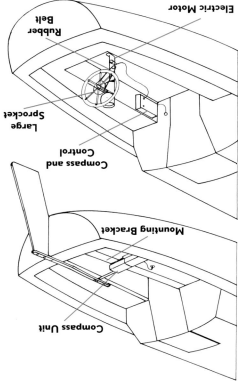

Electric Motor

Rubber Belt

Large Sprocket

Compass and Control

Mounting Bracket

Compass Unit

A servo-pendulum horizontal wind vane.

A singlehander must have some-way of stopping his boat should he or she go overboard. This simple device allows for a trailing line to be pulled from the water, releasing the control lines

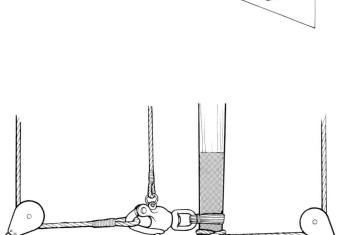

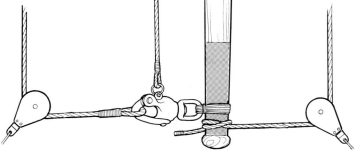

Pull to Disengage Self-Steering Gear

Steering Gear

The sea never changes

The winds and waves

are always on the side of

the ablest navigators.

—*Edward Gibbon*

despite countless knockdowns, pitchpoling and assorted unforeseen tragedies. Because of the immense strength of his boat, he survived. In fact, he has recently developed the world's smallest sextant (not to mention the cheapest) which will allow one to take sun sights for around $65.00.

Of late, circumnavigation has been attempted in vessels of about five feet in length. This is a challenge to compression, not seamanship. The speed obtainable by a boat this long is so slow that the volume of provisions needed to cross, say the Atlantic, is beyond the displacement of the vessel. But sailors persist in challenging the limits of possibility.

Of interest are the voyages of Frank and Margaret Dye, a British couple who crisscrossed the North Sea and North Atlantic in a 16-foot Wayfarer Class sailing dinghy. Their modest craft was partly a result of economy, but the Dyes were consummate sailors, preparing carefully for each passage and bringing them off with superb seamanship. In a boat that size, personal fortitude is more important than anything else. One tires from exposure before the seas get you, and a small boat can be more seaworthy than a large one. If one considers a yacht longitudinally as a girder, the longer the girder, the less supported it will be in large seas. A small boat will give more to the onslaught of the sea. The Dyes survived and retired happily. If nothing else, this proves that care and prudence can prolong one's life on and off the water.

Most challenges take place in somewhat larger yachts. After all, one hopes to stay reasonably dry and well fed. Probably the great exponents of this are the French who, in various very large multihulls, have beaten everyone. Sailing, in France, is a national sport, heavily subsidized and attracting media stars. In fact the current solo sailing champions are almost always French, especially since hi-tech industry there sponsors many of

A three-masted barque under full sail.

MIKE

MY VESSEL IS
STOPPED, AND
MAKING NO WAY
THROUGH THE WATER.

foot boat in the 1930s to Vito Dumas' wartime southern circumnavigation to the current crop of world-girdling voyagers, doing it is the whole point. Admittedly, one can make a good living out of sailing these days from prize winnings and sponsorship, but one still has to want to go. This type of sailing is not for the faint-hearted. It is rugged, dangerous and without pity.

There are two basic types of sailors: those who cruise to relax and those who compete. All the glory goes to the competitors. That is the nature of our culture.

gadgets and materials. When Chichester circled the globe he relied on a sextant and sight-reduction tables. Now GPS, Sarnav, total radio communications, wireless internet and Argos positioning equipment mean that a sailor can read out his or her position from a screen and jot it down on the chart. No, record breaking is not a sport for most—at least not without sponsorship. Every great sailing feat has commenced with a challenge, whether personal or organized. From Commander Graham's solo voyage across the Atlantic in a 30-

the record-breaking attempts. Isabelle Autissier, Mark Pajot, the late great Eric Tabarly and many others have fed a legend of invincibility. Where Americans look for baseball news or the British for cricket scores, the Gallic passion (after soccer, of course) is the exploits of their world-girdling sailors.

Challenges can be personal, corporate, or national but they are all expensive. Gone are the days, even 40 years ago, when a sailor could set out in an old small boat. Now sailors are faced with increasingly expensive hi-tech

The crew of a nineteenth century whaling ship attacks the tongue of a whale. Whaling was a major industry before the discovery of petroleum, and its refining into kerosene. Whale oil provided the best illumination in lamps and was used as high-grade machinery oil.

Roll on, thou deep and dark blue ocean—roll,

ten thousand fleets sweep over thee in vain;

man marks the earth with ruin—his control stops

with the shore;

upon the watery plain the wrecks are all thy deed,

nor doth remain a shadow of man's ravage, save his

own, when,

for a moment like a drop of rain,

he sinks into thy depths with bubbling groan,

without a grave, unknell'd, uncoffin'd, and unknown.

—*Lord Byron*

The strength of a whale is extra-ordinary. Even forged harpoons were no match for an infuriated whale, as this picture shows; this harpoon was reportedly mangled into this twisted state as the angry whale thrashed and writhed.

Hermann Melville's *Moby Dick* is the ultimate whaling novel, but it was based on an actual incident. On November 20, 1820, the whaling ship *Essex*, out of Nantucket, Massachusetts (then the premier whaling port in the world), was rammed and sunk in the middle of nowhere by a very large sperm whale. The story of the survivors in whaleboats, crazed and reduced to cannibal-ism, is one of the more grisly episodes in the history of American fisheries. A month spent struggling to reach land with no provisions is not a pretty thought. The crew of the *Essex* was gone for three years.

Why would whalers risk so much? Before the discovery of petroleum and its refining into kerosene, whale oil was the prime means of illumination. Pure and odorless, it burned bright and clean, and one whale could supply an enormous amount of oil. Sailors could make a pretty profit from a single voyage—witness the mansions along Nantucket town's main street. The Civil War effectively killed off whaling as a viable commercial enterprise, partly due to changing economic conditions, partly due to the discovery of oil in Pennsylvania.

Voyages of a Different Sort: Whalers

Not every voyage has at its core the completion of a difficult course, a solo adventure on open water or a long trip in a small craft. Up until the Civil War, sailors embarked on extraordi-nary voyages in both the Atlantic and Pacific with one goal in mind: hunting whales. Now, eco-logical concerns and a lack of demand have ended the hunts for these magnificent creatures, but for some, it was a consuming passion that pitted sailors against

extremes of wind and waves for years at a time.

Whaling was not merely a case of riding out the weather. It also meant riding out the whale.

But the cruising sailors are not without their own honor. Eric and Susan Hiscock spent four decades cruising the world in an efficient, safe and seamanlike manner. They had no catastrophes, they avoided horror storms, they died peace-fully in their beds. From the 1930s until the 1980s, they traveled the globe in a series of yachts all named *Wanderer*. It was literally a simpler time, when the ability to handle a yacht under sail was not sacrificed to an engine or electron-ics. You left port and you were on your own.

Another, contemporary example of the cruising couple is Lin and Larry Pardey. For over a quarter century they have made exemplary passages in their wood Lyle Hess-designed cut-ters, all under 30 feet. They work along the way—Lin writes and Larry is an expert ship-wright—and they have shown the way for thousands of sailors who have followed.

None of these men and women are bums. They work and create along the way. They are seeking a different view of the world, an unfettered way of life. They are the last true wan-derers across the oceans.

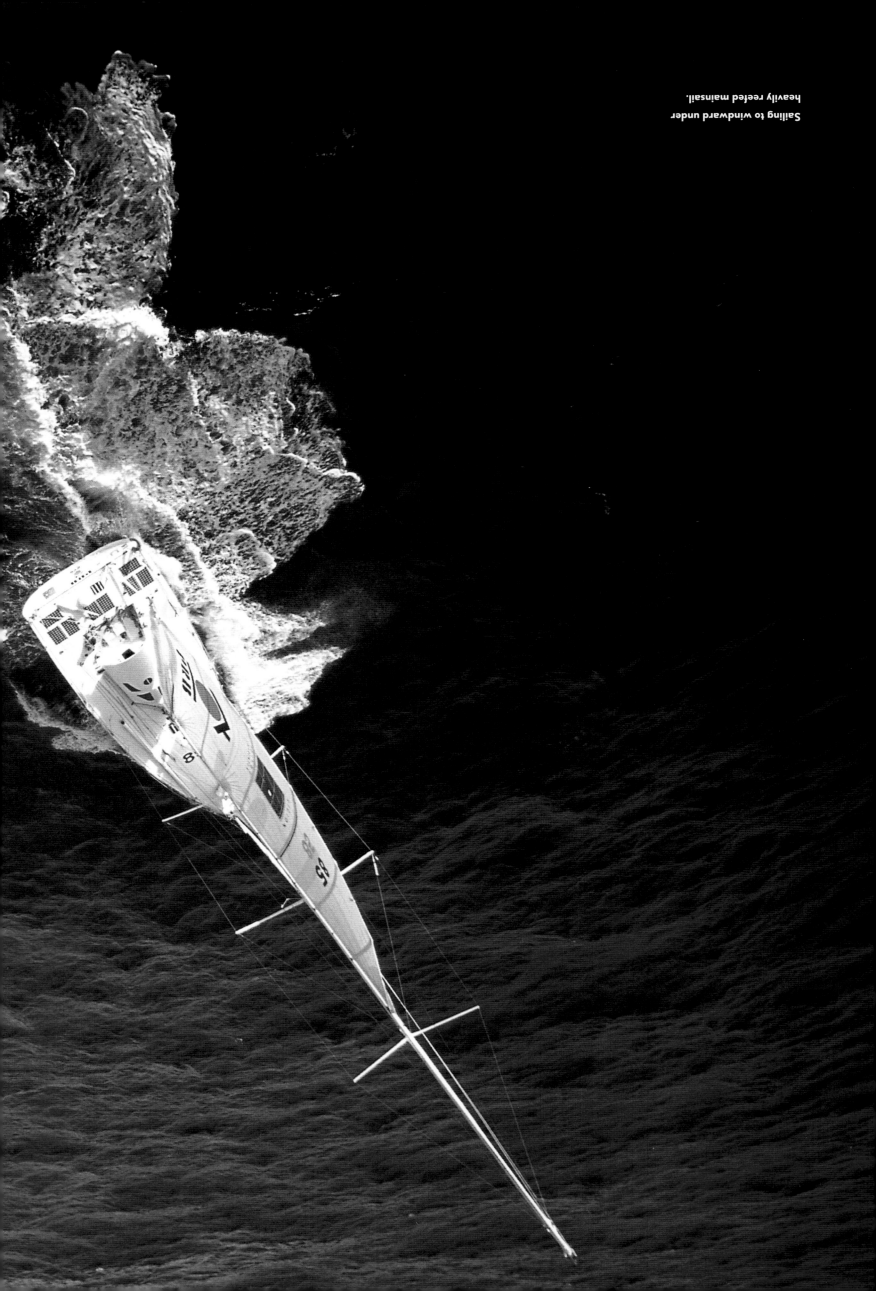

Sailing to windward under
heavily reefed mainsail.

TANIA AEBI

1967–

HOME BASE ▪ *East Corinth, Vermont*

ACHIEVEMENTS UNDER SAIL ▪ *Youngest person to circumnavigate the globe, first American woman to sail around the world alone.*

Tania Aebi was an 18-year-old dropout. During the day she worked as a bicycle messenger in New York. At night she bar hopped around the trendy, avant garde Lower East Side. It was an empty existence, and her father, knowing she needed a challenge, offered her a choice: either go to college or take a gift of a 26-foot sloop, provided she sailed around the world alone, and earned enough money along the way to support herself.

Tania had grown up sailing with her family—her father was an artist from Europe, and they lived an urban life. Tania decided, when faced with her father's challenge, to take her life in a new direction. On May 30, 1985, Tania boarded her little boat, *Varuna*, and embarked on her remarkable voyage. She was excited to escape her parents and the structure of her city life, but underestimated the challenges ahead. Every day became a challenge for survival and progress—especially in navigation. Using her radio direction finder, she made her way around the world, picking up the knowledge she needed along the way.

Two and a half years and 27,000 miles later, on November 6, 1987, she returned to New York Harbor, cruising into the South Street Seaport decked in rain gear and a new sense of herself.

She was greeted with a showering of love and flowers from her family and friends, as well as world-wide media attention. She was hailed as the first American woman to sail around the world and the youngest person ever to circumnavigate the globe. Although it turned out that technically, she couldn't claim the records because a friend had joined her for 80 miles in the South Pacific, her voyage was a historic one, and she is widely regarded as the record holder.

Now in her thirties, Aebi lives in Vermont. Her life has moved beyond her historic voyage, and into motherhood and life with her husband Olivier Beucher (a fellow sailor who she met on her journey) and their two children. But her voyage transformed her life, and she still gives lectures, interviews and slide shows centering around the trip. She is revered by circumnavigators all over the world, young and old, male and female, a heroine for those who embark on the ultimate challenge of the mind, body and sea. Her book, *Maiden Voyage*, which began as a series of articles for *Cruising World* magazine has become a classic, still widely read—and acclaimed—in many languages.

From Maiden Voyage

BY TANIA AEBI • WITH BERNADETTE BRENNAN

"October 20. Time is crawling by. I hear things on the radio that stun me. A commentator might say, 'Mr. So and So made a statement on the proposition that was made two weeks ago.' I shake my head and look again at the dates in the Nautical Almanac. *I can remember the proposition being made, but was it really two weeks ago? As far as my time frame goes, it could have been yesterday, or this morning, or even five minutes ago."*

VOA and the BBC were running continuous bulletins on the stock-market crash and I listened for updates on the Black Monday debacle as the Dow Jones average slowly began to climb again. Not that I had any stocks or bonds to worry about, but world news had become my fix, my private soap opera, the connection to a home that was getting closer and more real with every passing mile. Wall Street was New York, New York was my singular objective, and I listened more hungrily for news as the weather worsened.

My energies were continually refocused on small calamities aboard—a spilled container of sugar, the solar-panel wiring that corroded through, needing to be respliced and retaped, and the loss of the Swiss Army knife's tweezers. One day something that resembled horrible foot odor permeated the cabin, and after checking my own feet, I was unable to identify it source.

I checked all the lockers, and finally found the culprit behind the sliding panels of the locker next to my bed. A UHT carton of milk that had survived since Malta had exploded, spewing forth a vile lumpy white mixture that covered the bottles of oil and vinegar, wood splints, cans and the rest of its neighbors. As a result, I killed two good hours lugging buckets of water into the cabin, keeping them balanced with *Varuna's* motions, shoving a curious Tarzoon out of the way and scrubbing and drying all the contaminated objects and the locker itself. Two days later, with the first inkling of the malodorous scent, I knew where to look when my last carton of milk expired in yet another glorious ascent to milk heaven.

The next system to hit, a stationary cold front, started as something comparable to steady trade winds from astern on the twenty-second, and by the next morning, we had three reefs in the main and a poled-out storm jib. The puffy clouds stacked up into an ugly black canopy that covered our skies from horizon to horizon.

Unlike the eastbound depressions of days gone by, the wind howled from the southeast, pushing us up and dropping us down the monster waves like a roller coaster gone berserk for thirty-six sleepless hours, whereupon it stopped and poured down rain as we thrashed on beam ends over the bumpy swell. During the four hours of torrential rain that followed, I climbed out into the cockpit and managed to collect several buckets of fresh water as it streamed down the face of the mainsail and channeled along the groove of the boom.

Then, out of nowhere, the wind rushed in from the northeast, picking up at a furious clip until the next day, when the mainsail became too much for the conditions and had to come down. The only foresail that could handle the spasmodic weather was the tiny storm jib, whose miniature size had earlier convinced me that we would never find a use for it. Now it was to be our salvation, as any other piece of canvas aboard would have been too much.

"October 23, and I'm really scared. I can't relax, sleep, eat or think about anything other than staying alive. The waves around us now are the biggest I've ever seen—probably 25 feet high. The weather says that we have a cold front passing overhead. My heart is thumping so hard in my chest and I can't stop the tears of fear. Varuna *is carried and thrown with each breaking wave, breaking over us, on our sides, in front and behind. The sky is black. There is very little sail up, we're going practically downwind, and we're going fast. I am wedged into my bed with Tarzoon as we listen to the noise and pray. I haven't been able to get a sight, but according to my DR*

we're about 880 miles from home. It's not like Med, where after a storm there is a calm. Here it's just one giant, non-stop storm."

The waves steadily grew into the size of alps, and in terror I watched through the Plexiglas slats as they caught up to us from astern, dwarfing *Varuna* and picking her up and throwing her down the slope to wait for the next. The heaving swells crashed everywhere around the boat and hissed and pawed menacingly underneath us as they carried us along on a boiling froth. *Varuna* was continuously swamped, and the type of knockdowns that she had endured near Sri Lanka and in the Mediterranean became an hourly occurrence, except this time we were prepared for the worst, and that made all the difference.

The jerry cans, sails and cat-litter sacks in the cockpit were lashed down, the cubbyholes were stripped bare, and inside everything was securely lodged. As the thundering waterfalls flooded the cockpit, the water slowly funneled out by the way of the drains until it was empty and ready to swallow the next deluge. Unable to take a sight for days, I prayed that I was grossly underestimating our progress and hoped for a wonderful surprise if and when the sun ever shone again.

"October 24. It's the next day, the waves are even bigger and my DR says we're still 780 miles away from the mark. The sun hasn't been out in days. My heart is working overtime and I can't stop the trembling. The looming outlines of the waves are humongous, and we are so small and insignificant. This day feels like it will never end."

Continuing to stare out the hatch, and hypnotized by the towering seas overtaking us, I lived on the edge of existence through that gloomy day and pitch-dark night. For forty-eight hours, I feverishly dealt out game after game of solitaire on the bunk beside me; if anything would get me through this, other than the taffrail log ticking away the miles, it would be my cards of fate.

From Ice Bird
The First Single-Handed Voyage to Antarctica

BY DAVID LEWIS

"Navigation was far from easy. A quick sight of the sun emerging from cloud cover; a dubious horizon as the sloop, rolling her gunwales under, lifted on a crest; numb fingers feverishly manipulating the sextant."

Capsize

Ice Bird continued to make steady, if unspectacular, progress eastward, keeping generally about 61°S. A progression of gales—northwest with heavy snow and falling glass, as the warm front of the depression rolled over us—would be succeeded abruptly after eight to twelve hours by the cold front, with its falling temperatures, clearing sky and rising glass—and intensified southwest gale. The resulting jumble of cross seas kept the ocean's face in a state of furious confusion even without the rogue seas which, every now and then, reared up and dashed right across the line of the prevailing swells. I kept the yacht running with the wind on one or other quarter, nearly downwind. Usually she carried only the storm jib, sometimes the storm tri-sail as well. The mainsail had been put to bed somewhere in the mid-fifties and had remained furled ever since.

One of the most awkward operations that had to be carried out in the brief intervals

between gales was filling the petrol tank. Balancing a four-gallon plastic can on a deck rolling at a 30° angle was not easy, but at least it had the advantage that the considerable spillage was soon washed overboard. This was more than could be said when I performed the chore of topping up lamps and stove with kerosene. Inevitably a good deal of kerosene spilled over as the yacht lurched and wallowed and this made of the cabin floor a skating rink on which I slithered helplessly.

The fresh water in the tank let into the keel froze. Fortunately I had a supply of plastic cans to fall back upon. The drop in sea temperature was because we were now south of the Antarctic Convergence. Fogs, due to relatively warm north-west winds blowing over a colder sea, became more frequent and persistent than ever. Heavy snow showers became the norm.

Navigation was far from easy. A quick sight of the sun emerging from cloud cover; a dubious horizon as the sloop, rolling her gunwales under, lifted on a crest; numb fingers feverishly manipulating the sextant. To balance things a little, radio time signals were being received very clearly. Not so radio transmissions. An attempt to keep a schedule with Sydney on the 22nd, not unexpectedly, failed.

Evening, 26 November, the worst gale so far, a raging 50 knot, force ten north-wester that drove long lines of foam scudding down the faces of enormous waves and literally whipped away their crests. Each time a breaker burst against *Ice Bird* everything loose in the cabin went flying and I was forever thankful for the steel plates protecting her

windows. The bilge water appeared to defy gravity by distributing itself everywhere. It surged violently uphill and whizzed round the hull.

I kept *Ice Bird*, under snow-plastered storm jib, running off before the seas at about 20(from a dead down-wind run, so that she moved diagonally across the faces of those huge waves at a slight angle. During the night the gale backed to the south-west and the glass began to rise. It must eventually blow itself out, but when? I was shocked with the scene that full daylight revealed; scared, then gradually fascinated; though still terrified on looking out through the dome. It seemed as if the yacht's stern could never lift to each wave that reared up behind us. But rise it did; each time with a sensation like being whisked up in a lift. The yacht was being steered by the wind vane, assisted from inside the cabin by occasional tugs at the tiller lines. 'She's bloody near airborne,' I wrote, and added that she was running incredibly smoothly. But was this in spite of, or because of, my tactics? Were they the right ones?

This last is a perennial query in storms. Vito Dumas, the heroic Argentine farmer who in 1944 circumnavigated alone through the roaring forties in a yacht the same size as *Ice Bird*, never took in his jib. He did the same as I was doing now. Bernard Moitessier, after his memorable non-stop voyage from Tahiti to Spain, had also suggested the tactics I was adopting—running before gales at an angle under headsail, the sail being necessary to give control and manoeuvrability.

Dumas and Moitessier had been two of the successful ones, but so many had come to grief in the Southern Ocean. I recalled reading in Captain W.H.S. Jones's book, *The Cape Horn Breed*, that out of 130 commercial sailing vessels leaving European ports for the Pacific coast of America in May, June and July 1905, four were known to have been wrecked and *fifty-three* were still missing in Cape Horn waters in November—four to six months later.

The 37-foot Australian ketch *Pandora*, the very first yacht ever to round Cape Horn—this was 1911—was capsized and dismasted off the Falkland Islands. She was towed into port by a whaler. The Smeaton's big British *Tzsu Hang* was pitchpoled and dismasted on her first attempt to round the formidable Cape; on her second gallant try she was rolled and lost both masts. She succeeded the third time. Only the previous year the 34-foot *Damien*, crewed by two young Frenchmen, was thrice capsized off South Georgia, the first time righting herself only after a considerable interval. Again the mast was a casualty.

Yet here I was, traversing even stormier waters than they. No wonder I was scared. The gale seemed to be bearing out what I had somewhat wryly termed Lewis's law—for every point the wind increases your boat shrinks and becomes one foot shorter. This great truth has been my own discovery. I was brought back from my musings about other voyagers by bilge water surging up over the 'permafrost' that coated the inside of the hull these days, as an exploding crest threw the yacht over on her beam ends. She righted herself, water streaming off her decks. So far there had been no damage. But there was very little respite. This 26-27 November gale was barely over before, on the night of the 27th, the barometer started dropping again.

These repeated gales were at last seriously beginning to get me down. Gradually my morale was being sapped and increasing physical exhaustion was taking its toll. My whole body was battered and bruised and I was suffering from lack of sleep. Increasingly I dwelt on my in many ways disastrous personal life; what a mess I had made of things. I could hardly remember when my storm clothes had last been removed; standing in

squelching boots had become habitual but was hardly comfortable. To make matters worse, my left hip, damaged in a skiing accident the previous winter, ached intolerably. I no longer day-dreamed about the voyage and its outcome—I had already dreamed and was now living it.

Instead, present reality became illusory. In my exhausted state the wild irregular seas that were tossing us around like a cork were only half apprehended. I jotted down in the log that everything was an effort; there were constant mistakes of every kind in my sight workings; I could no longer grasp simple concepts. Twice, I recorded with scientific detachment that I heard ill-defined imaginary shouts. I drifted out of reality altogether...

A girl companion and I are ploughing through the long fragrant grass of autumn towards the Ginandera Falls. Green scarlet lorikeets flash by in streaks of vivid colour. We push our way through some heavy scrub, then go stumbling thigh-deep over slippery stones across the icy Murimbidgee. A tangle of deadfall, tall gums and casuarinas, then a grassy glade under lichen-covered rock walls and ahead the leaping cascade. Imperceptibly the scene changes to the coast. A water-lily covered secret lake behind the sandhills. The same girl, Susie and Vicky, naked and laughing in the hot sunshine, splashing up into the shallows.

Such are my memories, false and nostalgic though they be, of 27 November, the last day of my great adventure; such was my mental condition on the eve of disaster.

On the 28th the bottom fell out of the glass. How true, even if unintended, were the words of the poet MacNiece.

The glass is falling hour by hour, the glass will fall for ever,

But if you break the bloody glass you won't hold up the weather.

Nothing I or any other man might do could control the barometer. The pointer moved right off the scale and continued downwards to about twenty-eight inches during the night. This time it was for real. Long before the

barometer had reached this point it was apparent that something altogether new had burst upon us—a storm of hurricane intensity. This was the home of the unthinkable 105-foot waves the Russians had recorded, I recalled with dread. A breaker half as tall, falling upon *Ice Bird*, would pound her flat and burst her asunder.

"I was brought back from my musings about other voyagers by bilge water surging up over the 'permafrost' that coated the inside of the hull these days, as an exploding crest threw the yacht over on her beam ends. She righted herself, water streaming off her decks."

The waves increased in height with unbelievable rapidity. Nothing in my previous experience had prepared me for this. Yet I had known the full fury of North Atlantic autumn gales when homeward bound in 25-foot *Cardinal Vertue* from Newfoundland to the Shetlands in 1960 (coincidentally, the Shetlands straddle the 60th *north* parallel).

Barry and I had weathered Coral Sea cyclone 'Becky' in *Isbjorn*, only partially sheltered by an inadequate island. Severe gales off Iceland, Magellan Strait and the Cape of Good Hope had been ridden out by *Rehu Moana*—the most seaworthy catamaran built so far—in the course of her Iceland voyage and her circumnavigation.

But this storm was something altogether new. By evening the estimated wind speed was over sixty knots; the seas were conservatively forty feet high and growing taller—great hollow rollers, whose wind-torn crests thundered over and broke with awful violence. The air was thick with driving spray.

Ice Bird was running down wind on the starboard gybe (the wind on the starboard quarter), with storm jib sheeted flat as before. Once again I adjusted the wind-vane to hold the yacht steering at a small angle to a dead run, and laid out the tiller lines where they could be grasped instantaneously to assist the vane. The strategy had served me well in the gale just past, as it had Dumas and Moitessier. But would it be effective against this fearful storm? Had any other precautions been

> "Came a roar, as of an approaching express train. Higher yet tilted the stern; Ice Bird picked up speed and hurtled forward surfing on her nose, then slewed violently to starboard, totally unresponsive to my hauling at the tiller lines with all my strength. A moment later the tottering breaker exploded right over us, smashing the yacht down on to her port side."

neglected? The Beaufort inflatable life raft's retaining strops had been reinforced by a crisscross of extra lashings across the cockpit. Everything movable, I thought, was securely battened down; the washboards were snugly in place in the companionway; the hatches were all secured. No, I could not think of anything else that could usefully be done.

Came a roar, as of an approaching express train. Higher yet tilted the stern; *Ice Bird* picked up speed and hurtled forward surfing on her nose, then slewed violently to starboard, totally unresponsive to my hauling at the tiller lines with all my strength. A moment later the tottering breaker exploded right over us, smashing the yacht down on to her port side. The galley shelves tore loose from their fastenings and crashed down in a cascade of jars, mugs, frying pan and splintered wood. I have no recollection of where I myself was flung – presumably backwards on to the port bunk. I only recall clawing my way up the companionway and staring aft through the dome.

The invaluable self-steering vane had disappeared and I found, when I scrambled out on deck, that its vital gearing was shattered beyond repair – stainless steel shafts twisted and cog wheels and worm gear gone altogether. The stout canvas dodger round the cockpit was hanging in tatters. The jib was torn, though I am not sure whether it had split right across the luff to clew then or later. My recollections are too confused and most of that day's log entries were subsequently destroyed.

I do not know that I lowered the sail, slackening the halyard hauling down the jib and securing it, repeatedly unseated from the jerking foredeck, half blinded by stinging spray and sleet, having to turn away my head to gulp for the air being sucked past me by the screaming wind. Then lying on my stomach and grasping handholds like a rock climber, I inched my way back to the companionway and thankfully pulled the hatch to after me.

I crouched forward on the edge of the starboard bunk doing my best to persuade *Ice Bird* to run off before the wind under bare poles. She answered the helm, at best erratically, possibly because she was virtually becalmed in the deep canyons between the waves; so that more often than not the little yacht wallowed broadside on, port beam to the sea, while I struggled with the tiller lines, trying vainly to achieve steerage way and control.

And still the wind kept on increasing. It rose until, for the first time in all my years of seagoing, I heard the awful high scream of force thirteen hurricane winds rising beyond 70 knots.

The remains of the already-shredded-canvas dodger streamed out horizontally, flogging with so intense a vibration that the outlines blurred. Then the two stainless steel wires supporting the dodger parted and in a flash it was gone. The whole sea was white now. Sheets of foam, acres in extent, were continually being churned anew by fresh cataracts. These are not seas, I thought: they are the Snowy Mountains of Australia – and they are rolling right over me. I was very much afraid.

Some time later – I had no idea how long – my terror receded into some remote corner of my mind. I must have shrunk from a reality I could no longer face into a world of happier memories, for I began living in the past again, just as I had in my exhaustion in the gale two days earlier. It is hard to explain the sensation. I did not move over from a present world into an illusory one but temporarily inhabited both at once and was fully aware of doing so, without feeling this to be in any way strange or alarming. My handling of the tiller was quite automatic.

Mounts Kosciusko, Townsend, the broken crest of Jagungal; sculptured summits, sweep-

> "The whole sea was white now. Sheets of foam, acres in extent, were continually being churned anew by fresh cataracts. These are not seas, I thought: they are the Snowy Mountains of Australia – and they are rolling right over me. I was very much afraid."

ing snow slopes streaked with naked rock; all this mighty snow panorama rolled past like a cinema film. It was moving because those snow mountains were simultaneously the too-fearful-to contemplate watery mountains of paralysing reality.

I am watching, as from afar, four of us gliding down off the snow-plumed divide, four dots in a vast whiteness. Then I am striving for balance under the weight of my pack, skis rattling a bone-shaking tattoo over a serration of ice ridges. We ski to a rest under a snow cornice overlooking the headwaters of the Snowy River, where we tunnel a snow cave to shelter us for the night – a survival exercise in preparation for my present venture.

But why are those snow mountains rolling onward? Where are they going? I have drifted away even further from the present and my tired brain baulks at the effort of solving the conundrum.

The picture blurs. I am leading a party up this same Kosciusko during the winter lately past, something like three months ago, amid the same rounded shoulders and rolling summits— literally rolling. My little Susie, refusing help with her pack, plods gamely up the endless snow slope, eyes suffused with tears of tired-ness. We halt to rest. Almost at once, with the resilience of childhood, Susie is away— laugh-ing, her tears forgotten, the swish of her skis answering the song of the keen mountain wind.

The intolerable present became too intru-sive to be ignored; the past faded into the background. Veritable cascades of white water were now thundering past on either side, more like breakers monstrously enlarged to perhaps forty-five feet, crashing down on a surf beach. Sooner or later one must burst fairly over us. What then?

I wedged myself more securely on the lee bunk, clutching the tiller lines, my stomach hollow with fear. The short sub-Antarctic night was over; it was now about 2 a.m.

My heart stopped. My whole world reared up, plucked by an irresistible force, to spin through giddy darkness, then to smash down

into daylight again. Daylight, I saw with horror, as I pushed aside the cabin table that had come down on my head (the ceiling insulation was scored deeply where it had struck the deck head)...daylight was streaming through the now gaping opening where the forehatch had been! Water slopped about my knees. The remains of the Tilley lamp hung askew above my head. The stove remained upside down, wedged in its twisted gymballs.

Ice Bird had been rolled completely over to starboard through a full 360° and had righted herself thanks to her heavy lead keel— all in about a second. In that one second the snug cabin had become a shambles. What of the really vital structures? Above all, what of the mast?

I splashed forward, the first thought in my mind to close that yawning fore hatchway. My second—oh, God—the mast. I stumbled over rolling cans, felt the parallel rules crunch underfoot and pushed aside the flot-sam of clothes, mattresses, sleeping bag, splintered wood fragments and charts (British charts floated better than Chilean, I noted—one up to the Admiralty). Sure enough the lower seven feet of the mast, broken free of the mast step, leaned drunk-enly over the starboard bow and the top twenty-nine feet tilted steeply across the ruptured guard wires and far down into the water, pounding and screeching as the hulk wallowed.

The forehatch had been wrenched open by a shroud as the mast fell. Its hinges had sprung, though they were not broken off and its wooden securing batten had snapped. I forced it as nearly closed as I could with the bent hinges and bowsed it down with the block and tackle from the bosun's chair.

Then I stumbled back aft to observe, incredulously, for the first time that eight feet of the starboard side of the raised cabin trunk had been dented in, longitudinally, as if by a steam hammer. A six-inch vertical split between the windows spurted water at every roll (it was noteworthy, and in keeping with the experience of others, that it had been

the lee or down-wind side, the side under-neath as the boat capsized, that had sus-tained damage, not the weather side where the wave had struck.

What unimaginable force could have done that to eighth-inch steel? The answer was plain. Water. The breaking crest, which had picked up the seven-ton yacht like a match-box, would have been hurtling forward at something like fifty miles an hour. When it slammed her over, the impact would have been equivalent to dumping her on to con-crete. The underside had given way.

Everything had changed in that moment

"The intolerable present became too intrusive to be ignored; the past faded into the background. Veritable cascades of white water were now thundering past on either side, more like breakers monstrously enlarged to perhaps forty-five feet, crashing down on a surf beach. Sooner or later one must burst fairly over us. What then?"

of capsize on 29 November at 60°04'S., 135° 35'W., six weeks and 3,600 miles out from Sydney, 2,500 miles from the Antarctic Peninsula. Not only were things changed; everything was probably coming to an end. The proud yacht of a moment before had become a wreck: high adventure had given place to an apparently foredoomed struggle to survive.

FRANCIS CHICHESTER

1901–1972

"To a man of imagination, a map is a window of adventure—life is an adventure or nothing at all."

HOME BASE ▪ *London, England*

ACHIEVEMENTS UNDER SAIL ▪ *Solo circumnavigation of the world, 1966*

Chichester was 65 when he made his solo circumnavigation under sail. He did it after a long and distinguished career as a flyer and navigator, and proprietor of his own map making business; and he did it in an unsuitable boat. He sailed alone around the world with only one stop. Today, that's impressive; but not inconceivable for a committed sailor. When Chichester sailed, in 1966, such a feat was almost unthinkable and certainly a challenge.

Chichester, born in England, emigrated to New Zealand as an adolescent. Logger, miner, gold digger, real estate agent—he did what he must to live. But he also discovered flying, and in 1929 made the second solo flight from England to Australia, naming his plane *Gypsy Moth*. He crashed, recovered and continued to make daring flights.

In the process, he developed streamlined methods of air navigation, and during World War II taught navigation to the Royal Air Force.

After the war, Chichester established a map making business in London, which did well enough to allow him to undertake his new passion, sailing, christening his boat *Gypsy Moth II*. In it he ranged the coasts and ocean races of England until diagnosed with lung cancer in 1956. Refusing an operation, he went to the south of France and, remarkably, went into remission.

His sailing, however, continued, and he first came to prominence in the first Singlehanded Transatlantic Race, in 1960, thought up by his friend "Blondie" Hasler, the inventor of the self-steering vane gear for yachts. But this merely whetted his appetite for more. A man of unlimited grit and determination Chichester decided that a solo voyage, following the route of the 19th century wool clippers, would be an appropriate way to test his mettle. And test he did.

Chichester had two problems to overcome. The press promply decided he was too old and infirm. In England, and especially in the tabloids, this campaign reached a screaming pitch, with experienced Cape Horners—there were still a few alive—like Alan Villiers warning of dire consequences. Also his yacht, built specially for this endeavor and designed by the noted British racing yacht designer, John Illingworth, turned out to be a most inappropriate vessel for this particular journey. When launched, it was discovered that it was improperly ballasted, had very little form stability and was difficult to handle. Some work was carried out in England by the builders, but Illingworth's assurances were wildly misplaced.

However, he was in superb physical and mental shape. He had a wonderfully supportive wife and son, and a staff to help him prepare for his ordeal. The yacht was another problem, and one that wasn't fully solved. Reballasted, reworked and rerigged in Australia, it never was the potent machine it should have been, and Chichester's achievement is all the more impressive, considering the flaws of his vessel.

Leaving Plymouth, England on August 27, 1966, his passage, as is the case with most long voyages, was beset by problems—but Chichester had the disadvantage of being alone. The greatest danger to the singlehanded sailor is fatigue. With it comes lack of judgment and then mistakes, some of which can prove fatal. Additionally, the sea plays no favorites. Rogue waves can appear anywhere, but especially in the Southern ocean.

Neverthless, Chichester got to Australia by way of the Cape of Good Hope without grave difficulties. After extensive modifications of the yacht, he set off again, and almost immediately got into serious trouble. His yacht was capsized in the notorious Tasman Sea between Australia and New Zealand. The man's determination was extraordinary. Remember, he was 65 years old. He sorted the mess out on deck and below, though it took several days, and continued. By this time, the entire world was following his exploits. His passage to the Horn, which took three months, was frustrating, dangerous and filled with breakdowns. But pass it he did, and continued home to Plymouth, where he was greeted as a national hero and knighted by the Queen at Greenwich (with Francis Drake's sword, no less).

Chichester had accomplished the seemingly impossible. Nowadays, this voyage has been repeated many times, but thirty-five years ago to sail around the world with but a single stop was without precedent. A new era had been born on the seas.

His passage to the Horn, which took three months, was frustrating, dangerous and filled with breakdowns. But pass it he did, and continued home to Plymouth, where he was greeted as a national hero and knighted by the Queen at Greenwich

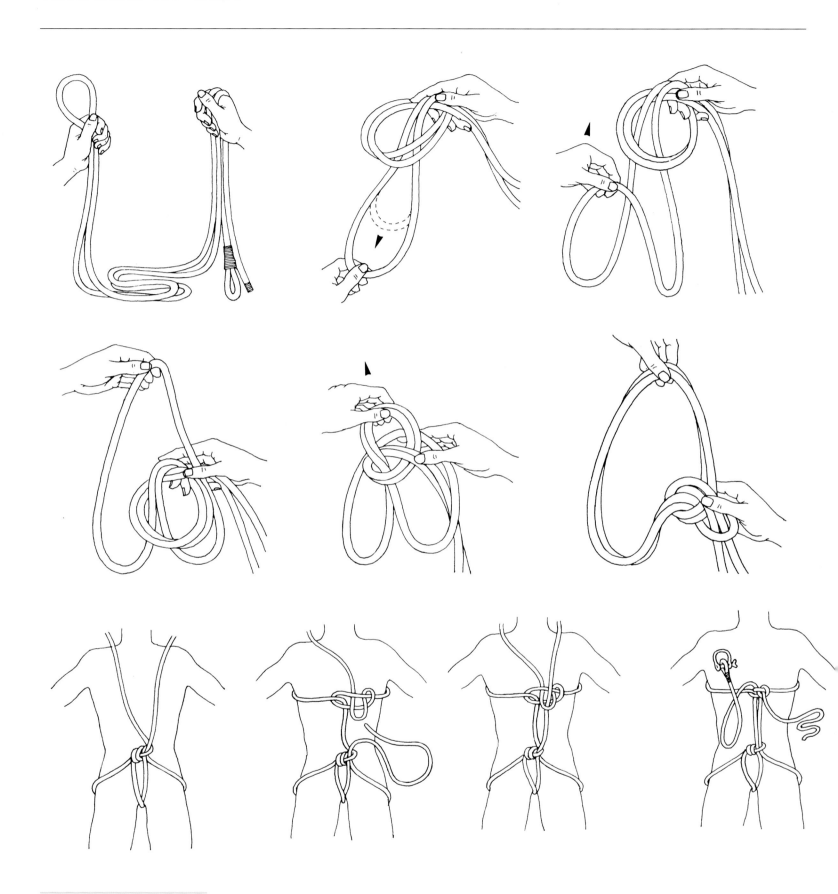

If safety harnesses are not carried in sufficient number for all crew, an reasonable harness can be made from as lone length of high-test line. The diameter of the rope should be sufficient to not cut too much into the clothing or flesh of the wearer.

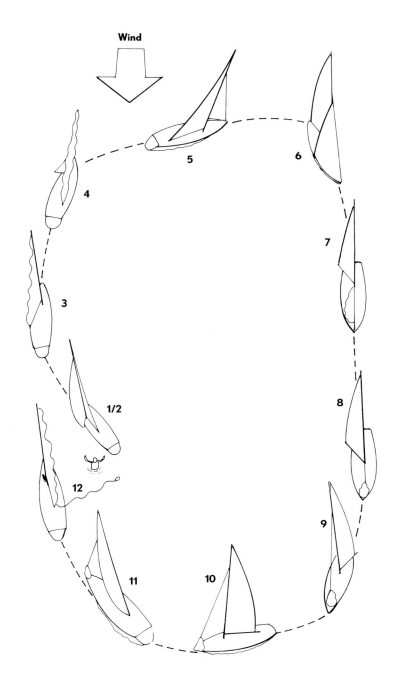

Wind

5 6 4 7 3 1/2 8 12 9 11 10

Left: "Man overboard" is the most terrifying cry aboard any boat at sea. The top drawing demonstrates how a yacht can be sailed around to pick-up a person in the water.=20

Below left: A large bight can be used to help hoist the victim back on board. Below right: Foul weather clothing and boots add enormous weight and drag to the victim. Once spotted, a life ring should be thrown to him or her as soon as possible.

Above: Rescue at sea is always a difficult maneuver. Here a surviving sailor awaits pick-up from his sinking ship by helicopter.

Below left: Helicopter pick-up is tricky no matter what the conditions. The movement of the boat can negate any effort by the pilot to hold steady.

Below right: Deploying a life raft to abandon ship must be done in a relatively clear area, and the raft must be tethered to the mother ship to allow access.

Helicopter rescue arriving at the Cape Decision Lighthouse in Sitka, Alaska.

Above: Rescuing crew members from the *Martela,* which capsized durting the 1990 Whitbread race.

Right: A transfer, also from the *Martela*, using a liferaft to prevent undue immersion and avoid hypothermia.

A line is tossed and secured to allow transfer from the capsized *Martela*.

Frenchman Marc Thiercelin
lowers the mainsail on his 60-foot
yacht *Somewhere* as he arrives in
Cape Town during the Around
Alone race.

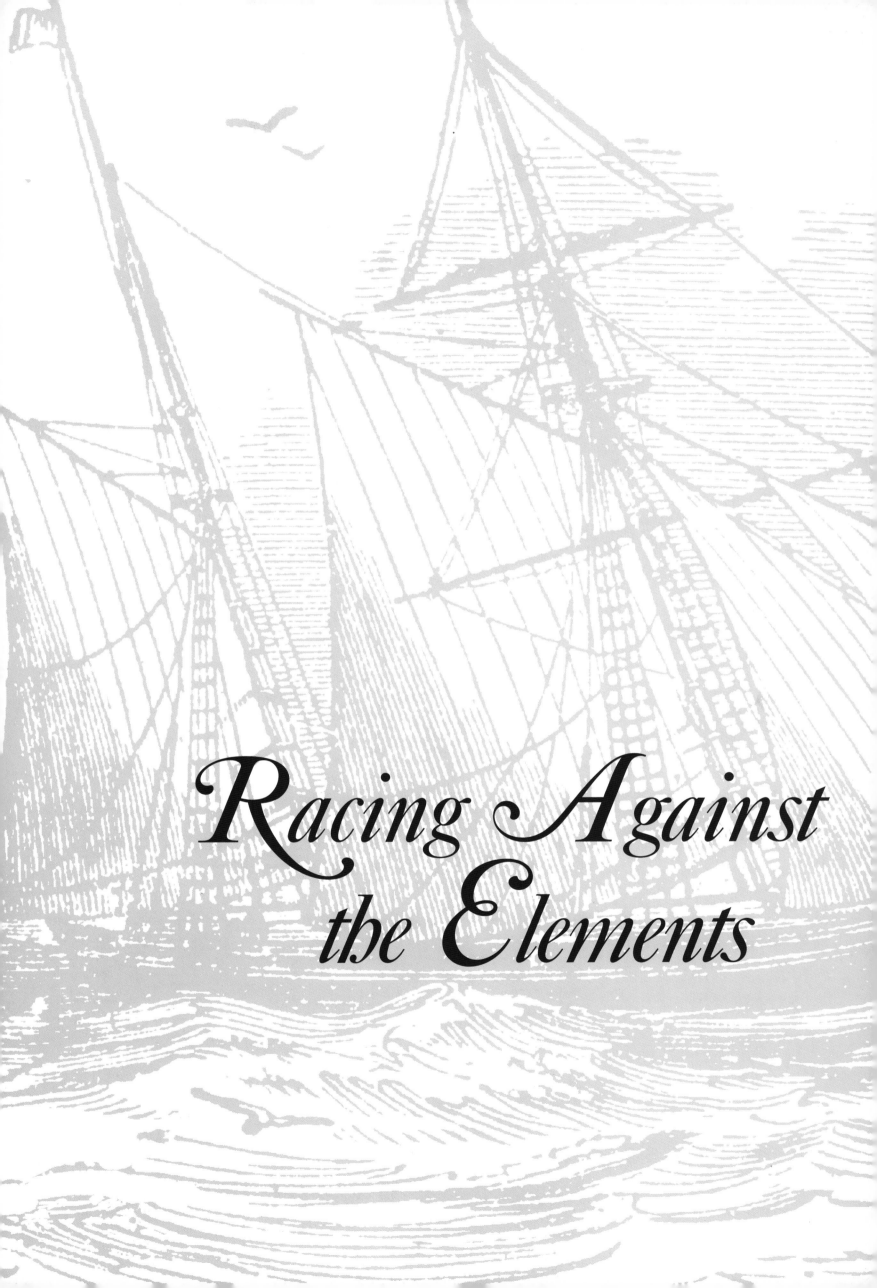

Racing Against the Elements

Dorade sailing to windward in 1932. Olin Stephen's first world-famous yacht, *Dorade* was a radical departure in ocean racing. At 52 feet overall, she was considered pitifully small, but she was fast and as technologically up-to-date as was then possible. Stephens went on to become the greatest American designer of the second half of the 20th century.

Racing as we know it is a comparatively modern sport. For that matter, yachting is a modern sport. The idea that someone would cross a body of water for pleasure was thought distinctly odd at the beginning of the 19ᵗʰ century. The seas were meant to transport men and goods in a reasonably efficient way. Why tempt fate and joust with death?

Certainly, sailors would often times partake of a race in sheltered waters, just for the fun of it, but to spend more than a few hours was certainly folly.

The first great ocean race of this century was the Bermuda Race. Founded by the Cruising Club of America in 1923. Through the efforts of second Commodore Herbert Stone, the Bermuda race has become a classic on the racing calendar, attracting entries from around the world. Held alternate years, participants in the Bermuda Race have experienced everything from calms to raging hurricanes.

The British were the second to venture offshore in a race. The first great ocean race took place in 1926, run by the recently founded Ocean Racing Club.

It included a dash from the south coast of England around the Fastnet Rock to the southwest of Land's End and back. At the time this was considered daring, and the yachts partaking in the race were of the workboats, big, heavy cruisers with gaff rigs. At the time, these were the only boats considered suitable for ocean sailing. They were slow, inefficient, and cumbersome. But

Hauling in lines during the Gloucester Races of 1922. The number of men pictured and the relative size of the mast gives some notion of the size of these ships. Note the thickness of the ropes in the foreground. Sheer human muscle was needed to raise and trim the sails aboard these fishing schooners.

Two racers rounding a buoy in hot pursuit.

NOVEMBER
—•

NO.

Two J-boats racing in the 1937 America's Cup. These behemoths (140 feet) were the great class racers of the interwar years. From America's Cup to match racing, they were the queens of the sea. After World War II, the cost to build and maintain them became prohibitive, though some have been restored by wealthy individuals and used for charter.

it was a great challenge. Naval architect Uffa Fox's gives a history of yacht design and inherent conservatism of yachtsmen of the time in his 1930s-era books. Sailors have always gone with the tried and proven advances in technology. Experimental designers and builders have managed to move the sport toward faster and leaner machines, expressly designed for particular racing conditions.

However, the sea always takes its revenge, and progress was slow. When the young American yacht designer Olin Stephens produced *Dorade* in 1930, she was, at 52 feet, considered dangerously small for ocean racing. But, when she won the Transatlantic Race of 1931 by days without calling on her handicap time allowance, opinion

shifted. Ocean racing was not a mass sport. It was, and remains, the province of the rich. And in the Depression years, despite deflated prices, few could indulge in crossing oceans for fun.

But a racers had crossed a threshold. Not brute strength, but guile and finesse was the route to success in ocean racing. A succession of ocean racers, from *Stormy Weather* to *Ticonderoga*, showed that a well-designed boat and a well-trained crew could, with the help of decent weather, race with astonishing speed.

The Testing Grounds: Great Races, Extraordinary Tragedies
Although much of the glamour and hardship goes to ocean racers, comparatively few people actually partake. Most racing is round-the-buoys, a few hours spent in

comradeship and competition. Until the 1920s, this form of racing, sponsored by yacht clubs or as a simple wager within the confines of a harbor, was almost the only form of racing.

The great exception was the America's Cup. The Cup has held many men in thrall for a century and a half, and shows no signs of losing its fascination. Millions of dollars have been spent in defending and challenging for the cup. Different classes of yachts have been sailed for it, from the mighty J-boats of the period before World War II to the 12-meter yachts of the postwar period to the more radical open classes of today.

The cup started when the yacht *America* sailed to England to compete against the best of the Brits. The New York Yacht Club, founded in 1844, and the only club in America at the time, had John Stevens as its commodore. She started a revolution, and also began the longest-running sports competition of all time.

Stevens, from Hoboken, New Jersey was convinced that the United States should show the world her state-of-the-art sailing and commissioned the yacht from George Steers, a New York designer and builder. Unlike the British yachts that had full bows and long runs, *America* was built more like a clipper ship, long and sleek, with a fine entrance and powerful quarters. She sailed to England on her own bottom and after a few skirmishes in which she trounced her opponents, was allowed to sail in a race around the Isle of Wight for a trophy known as the 100 Guinea Cup. Queen Victoria asked who came in second place behind the *America*.

"Alas, Your Majesty, there is no second," she was told.

Sir Thomas Lipton, of the teas, challenged, unsuccessfully, five times. No matter what, America kept the cup. Even after the war, in a string of 12-meter

Those who live by the
sea can hardly form
a single thought of
which the sea would
not be part.

—*Hermann Broc*

boats designed by Olin Stephens, the United States, always in the guise of the New York Yacht Club, won again and again.

America was a superior boat with faster lines and flatter, more efficient sails. That is, until 1983, when the Australians captured the Cup with a radical design. Traditions die hard. Feverish challenges were mounted, especially by Dennis Connor, which brought the Cup back to the USA, this time to San Diego. The past two Cup Series have been won handily by New Zealand in superbly sailed yachts, against world-class designers and sailors. And though the Cup now resides in Auckland, it is still known as the

America's Cup.

Technology, especially that which came out of military work in World War II, changed the face of racing and changed the odds of disaster as well. Artificial and far more stable sailcloth, stainless steel rigging, forged alloy hardware, fin keels and spade rudders vastly improved navigational devices, better foodstuffs and better-trained and fitter crews all made ocean racing a more competitive sport. With keener competition and with the gentleman sailor image on the wane, the same professionalism and management techniques that were permeating business were brought to bear on the sport.

Racing became like a military

Dumptruck **aground and dismasted in heavy seas in the BOC Challenge, 1995. Also known as the Around Alone race, this intense circumnavigation is sometimes called the BOC, after the race's founding sponsor.**

campaign. But as in war, the unforeseen took its toll. Certainly there were mishaps along the way. Harvey Conover and his entire crew, in his yacht *Renovac*, disappeared in the 1956 Bermuda Race, in the Bermuda Triangle no less. And no one was surprised when someone from a small yacht was lost overboard in heavy weather.

However, during the 1979 Fastnet Race off the southern coast of England, the most cata-

strophic event in ocean racing history up to that time occurred. The Atlantic and the Irish Sea are notorious in the western approaches to the English Channel. Here nature conspires to bring sea, sea bottom and land together in a prescription for disaster.

The Fastnet was started in 1925, and has since become the standard in ocean racing. Despite longer races such as the Transpac, transatlantic and the grueling round the world, the Fastnet was, and remains, the most esteemed prize in ocean racing. Though it is run in the summer, in alternate years, British weather rarely cooperates. In the 1979 Fastnet this lack

of cooperation had devastating results.

During the the course of the race, yachts leave Cowes in the English Channel, sail west along the southern coast of England, and cross the Irish Sea, heading to the Fastnet Rock. This solitary lighthouse, off the southwest coast of Ireland stands as a lonely sentinel to western approaches after 3,000 miles of Atlantic turmoil. And in August 1979, the weather was predicted as moderate to fresh winds, with perhaps heavier air moving in at the end of the race. But the gods weren't so kind. Just at the point when the majority of the fleet were at the point of no return, equidistant from any land, plunk in the middle of the Irish Sea, a truly ferocious storm swept down on the fleet. The larger maxi yachts were well ahead of

it; the smallest boats were about to be engulfed in it; but the midsize yachts took it on the nose. Storm force winds, gigantic, confused seas pummeled the fleet.

Sailors were washed overboard, mast and rigging crashed down, boats were broached and capsized. Of 303 starting yachts, only 85 finished the race, which was won by Ted Turner and his crew in *Tenacious*. But the race had been a bloodbath. Not only were millions of dollars of high-tech, state-of the-art yachts lost, but 15 lives were smothered out in the cold waves.

Despite heroic efforts by air and sea rescue teams, the great seas, coupled with ever-encroaching hypothermia, swept through the fleet, trapped sailors in their boats and cast them into the frigid waters and to their

A wet sheet and a

flowing sea,

A wind that follows fast,

And fills the white and

rustling sail,

And bends the

gallant mast.

And bends the gallant

mast, my boys,

While like the eagle free

Away the good ship

flies, and leaves

Old England on the lee.

—*Allan Cunningham*

deaths. The results, after the tolls were registered, were surprising to the participants. Many of the yachts were lightly-built racing machines, designed for speed above all. Despite safety equipment, the basic fabric of these boats was just not up to the rigors of the race. Much-needed changes were made in regulations and rules following the race and future yachts were to be built to more rigorous standards.

The most recent racing disaster was the Sidney-Hobart Race of 1998. One of the premier events on the world racing calendar, the Sydney-Hobart is a demanding run from Australia's largest city down the east coast, across the Tasman Sea and down the length of the east coast of the island of Tanzania to its capital, Hobart. It's a straight, rhumb line race. The problem lies in the Bass Strait, the body of water between the mainland and the island. This can be one of the roughest spots of water in the world. The Indian Ocean, driven by the prevailing westerlies, has to squeeze through a very narrow funnel—known to sailors worldwide as "Hell on High Water."

The race is normally a tough one with approximately 735 miles of open water racing. But the 1998 event turned into the greatest tragedy in Australian racing history and triggered the biggest search and rescue operation ever in Australia. Staring out under clear skies, the race conditions once past the southern tip of Gabo Island, on the southeast tip of the Australian Coast quickly deteriorated. Despite weather faxes and radio reports, a front swept in arrived swiftly, and most of the fleet was halfway across Bass Strait when it arrived. These were very experienced sailors in well-prepared yachts, yet the weather calamity that befell them was unprecedented in ocean racing history. Waves reached 90 feet and winds of more than 100 mph were recorded. Even the maxi yachts had an almost impossible task: getting to port in one piece.

Twenty-four yachts were abandoned, six men lost their lives, of whom two were never found. The damage was appalling. In all, 57 sailors were rescued from the heaving waters. Still, a lack of prudence and a grim determination to win at all costs, led to death and destruction. Larry Ellison, the founder of the notable tech firm Oracle was there with his maxi *Sayonara*, which took line honors, but the struggle and fear he later related to reporters was something beyond even this business giant's comprehension. And yet it is exactly this duel with death that so many ocean racers find enticing. There are always some among us who must prove themselves again and again. Whether it is worth the risks is something only these sailors can answer.

OSCAR

MAN OVERBOARD.

The *Van den Heede* swept ashore in the Round Britain race. Once grounded, the race is over for these sailors. If the boats is not salvaged before heavy weather brews up, chances are she will be battered to splinters . . a total wreck.

Ready to face an extraordinary test of physical and
psychological strength, sailors set off on a leg of the
1998-99 Around Alone race. All in all, they would
travel approximately 27,000 miles.

Preparing for the start of the fatal Sydney-Hobart Race of 1998. Six lives were lost when a monster storm swept through the fleet in the Tasman Sea.

There is nothing more enticing, disenchanting, and enslaving than the life at sea.

—*Joseph Conrad*

Crew and Equipment

The pressures put upon ocean racers are extreme. This is a sport for tough and resourceful people. Living in confined spaces, keeping watch hours, sleeping in spartan comfort, eating under sometimes perilous conditions all make life aboard an ocean racer something less than luxurious. Coupled with the hard physical labor including sail changes, acting as live ballast, helming in adverse conditions, making repairs with waves washing over one, this is not a sport for backyard racquetball players.

And the organization required is of military proportions. Food, spares, sails, watch schedules, fuel, water, radio checks, instrument calibration and endless details have to be attended to. It's no different than preparing a Formula One car for a grand prix race. On top of this is the human element, which includes assembling a crew, training them, making sure they are compatible, that each knows his job and has the skills necessary to effect repairs. Ocean racing is not a sport to be taken lightly.

Despite tragedies such as the 1979 Fastnet and the 1998

Sydney-Hobart, most ocean racing is neither dangerous nor frightening, but every few years a storm sweeps across some race in the world and, without warning, can devastate the fleet. With few exceptions, the majority of yacht racers are amateurs, often a group of friends who sail together, or a pick-up crew of young, gung-ho sailors. They may have a multitude of skills among themselves, but modern yachts are hi-tech machines, using exotic materials and sophisticated construction techniques. When something goes wrong will anyone aboard be able to fix it? Are the necessary materials aboard? Can something be improvised?

These are questions every racer must ask him or herself. As

Arriving in Auckland, New Zealand after the second leg of the 1998-99 Around Alone race. This grueling leg covers 6,884 lonely nautical miles, from Cape Town, South Africa to Auckland.

Sailing in a broad reach in very heavy winds during the Around Alone Race. This maxi is facing such powerful wind that one of it's two rudders is out of the water.

Philippe Jeantot in his yacht *Credit Agricole III*. Jeantot won the Around Alone race in this boat in both 1982-83 and 1986-87.

Any fool can carry

on but a wise man

knows how to shorten

sail in time.

—*Joseph Conrad*

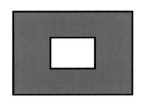

PAPA

• — •

IN HARBOR: ALL
PERSONS SHOULD
REPORT ABOARD FOR
THE VESSEL IS
ABOUT TO PROCEED
TO SEA. AT SEA: MY
NETS HAVE COME
FAST UPON AN
OBSTRUCTION.

we come to rely more and more on state-of-the-art electronics, can someone use a sextant to find the yacht's position? Is there even one on board? If rod rigging breaks, can it be replaced with a wire shroud? There are thousands of parts in every yacht, and all possibilities must be queried.

With the increase in the number of round-the-world races, especially single-handed ones, these problems increase. With modern technology, an experienced solo sailor can handle a 60-foot yacht without much difficulty. But driving these boats at optimum speeds day and night puts enormous strains on both man and boat. And the size and weight of equipment is daunting. With more than 1,000 square feet of sail, just replacing sails can be a gargantuan chore. What can take minutes in a fully-crewed yacht will stretch to hours worth of work for a solo sailor.

A prime example of this was the epic voyage of Robin Knox-Johnston in 1968. Despite the fact that he was only 29 at the time, Knox-Johnston set out on what was until then the race of all time: around the world non-stop. With little money and only partial sponsorship, he sailed from Falmouth, England in *Suhaili,* his old-fashioned, double-ended teak ketch. Knox-Johnston prepared his boat with extreme care, knowing he had no chance of refitting or stocking his boat along the way. He wanted to win despite the fact larger, faster boats were in the race. He was by training and profession a merchant seaman and he had sailed *Suhaili* from India with two friends several years prior to the race.

Yet he went through hell. During the course he was knocked down, his boat leaked, sails ripped, the cabin top split, the engine seized up and he suf-

fered from cuts, bruises, cold and fatigue. But he was inventive. When he lost his reefing handle overboard, he was able to fabricate a new one from a turnbuckle, or rigging screw, by heating it over his cooking stove and banging it into shape. It took an entire day, but it enabled him to shorten sail, a vital necessity for any ocean sailor.

Again and again during his ten months at sea, he had to make repair after repair, and it showed. He was not able to sail at peak efficiency, he was tired, depressed, cranky. But he was also resilient, a prime requisite for any ocean-going sailor, and he was able to effect repairs under the most horrible conditions. Unfortunately, Murphy's Law *always* applies at sea.

The most interesting about this race was that there was no official starting or finish line. Yachts left when their skipper deemed them ready and sailed as they could, through doldrums and storms. The front runners were forced to retire from the race, men like Chay Blyth and Bill King, experienced sailors in highly-suitable offshore boats. They suffered technical difficulties that could not be repaired at sea. Once they touched land, they were disqualified. Knox-Johnston, perhaps because of his training in the merchant marine still rigorous in England at that time, was able to cope. And that is perhaps the key to his success

and to the success of bringing any long ocean passage to completion.

Racing into the 21st Century: The Boats

State-of-the-art vessels all suffer from a similar problem. Each separate element may well be the very latest design, but these parts are usually put together in ways that have never been tried before. No one really knows what will work or not in all sea conditions.

A very recent example is Pete Goss's super catamaran, *Team Phillips.* This 120-foot long, high-tech, two-masted speed machine, designed for The Race, a new Round-the-World interna-

tional event, was set to break all records on transocean passages. Designed by Adrian Thompson, using the latest techniques and most exotic materials, it was engineered to fare-thee-well, Goss and his crew were ensconced in a pod resembling a spaceship situated above the crossbeams. It was one of the most publicized attempts at round-the-world record breaking of all time. As Goss and his crew were gearing up for their trip, one of the hulls broke up in moderate conditions off the coast of England on a shakedown cruise. Goss claims he will try again, but one wonders if the cost is worth it. Goss was lucky, because his break-up occurred

Business Post **dismasted in the 1998 Sydney-Hobart Race. Seen from above, the sea is not nearly as treacherous-looking as it was. Waves up to 95 feet were reported.**

close to land. Had it happened in the middle of the Pacific, no one can tell what the final result might have been.

Some of the more extreme modern racers resemble the toy yachts children used to sail in ponds. Their lean, narrow hulls made of exotic combinations of kevlar, carbon fiber, GRP, laminated woods and light alloys. Their keels are often lead bulbs suspended ten or more feet underwater by a slender foil. Their sails are made of composite mylar and specially woven cloth. Their rigs, that would scare the wits out of our forefathers with rotating wing masts, carbon fiber spars, minimal articulated rod rigging, exotic ropes, titanium, and four sets of spreaders, all tend to make for a potential set of disasters. Eventually, these developments will filter down to the average sailor. But any distance sailor might well be advised to think twice about state-of-the-art equipment. Micronesian islands are not the places to replace a bit of equipment that can only be obtained from a specialty manufacturer in Chicago, Toulouse or Burnham-on-Crouch.

The problem with all these boats is their only life is on the racecourse. They are not suitable for cruising, charter or gunkholing. They are absolute machines. Also, they seem to have a tendency due to their minimal scantlings, of breaking easily. You wouldn't buy one for weekending or club racing. These yachts are meant to be used for spectacle, much like a movie superstar or a great fireworks display. And they *are* spectacular and spectacularly expensive.

The traditional races including Fastnet, Bermuda, Sydney-Hobart, are run under some constraints of rules and classes. The big-name development races including Round-the-World, Transatlantic, Singlehanded Round-the World, are designed with looser parameters to encourage new designs and to create no-holds-barred racers. Ever since the development of the International Offshore Rule (IOR) in the 1970s, boats have been designed to exploit a rule rather than for absolute speed. The latest breed of transocean racers, however, have been built to achieve ultimate speed. Sailors may pick and choose those elements destined to provide maximum performance such as stripped-out interiors, masses of electronics and infinite line handling equipment. Designers and competition sailors are looking for the lightest, sleekest, fastest vessel possible to create.

Right: An exhausted Richard Winning, survivor of the disastrous Sydney-Hobart race of 1998. Hypothermia killed six men.

Below: Sailing a course demands attention to wind direction, sea state, tidal range and current. To the experienced sailor, judging these in combination means making a mark or missing out to another boat.

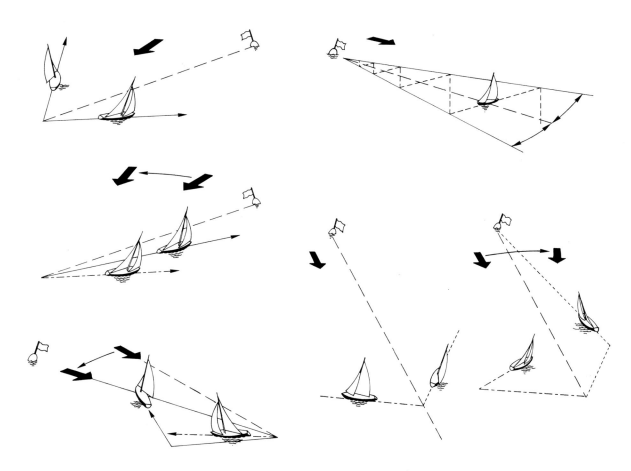

Sayonara, Larry Ellison's superyacht, finishing the 1998 Sydney-Hobart. Ellison reported after that he thought they would all die, so terrible were the seas and winds.

TECHNIQUE IN RAISING A SPINNAKER

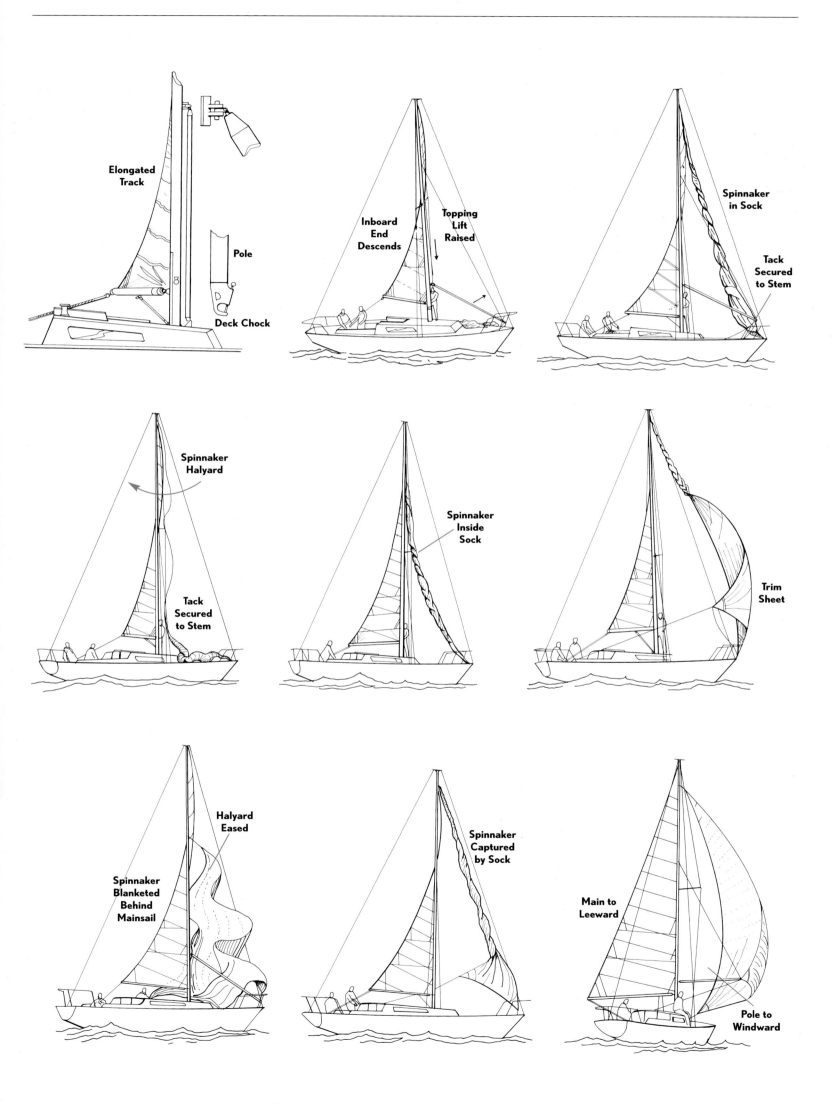

Elongated Track

Pole

Deck Chock

Inboard End Descends

Topping Lift Raised

Spinnaker in Sock

Tack Secured to Stem

Spinnaker Halyard

Tack Secured to Stem

Spinnaker Inside Sock

Trim Sheet

Spinnaker Blanketed Behind Mainsail

Halyard Eased

Spinnaker Captured by Sock

Main to Leeward

Pole to Windward

ISABELLE AUTISSIER

1957–

QUOTATION ▪ *"If I had waited to be invited to join a team, I would still be waiting. We are not far from the times when it was believed that women brought bad luck on boats. Even today the skipper will put together a crew of men rather than women, even though women are very good sailors.... So we see women who sail alone, because at least that way they don't ask anything of anybody."*

HOME BASE ▪ *La Rochelle, France*

ACHIEVEMENTS UNDER SAIL ▪ *Four around-the-world solo races; broke the New York to San Francisco via Cape Horn record by two weeks, arriving in 62 days, 5 hours and 55 minutes.*

Keel up in the 36-degree Southern Ocean, Isabelle Autissier was asleep when a loud bang on the upside-down hull of her 60-foot yacht awakened her. She was 1,900 miles west of Cape Horn when the autopilot of her boat, the PRB, could not compensate for a radical shift in wind, and the boat capsized, dismasted and rigging torn away. Autissier had barely enough time to close the hatch to seal out the water rushing to fill the cabin as the boat inverted and hung upside down. 24 hours later, she was trying to get some sleep, conserving energy and hoping for rescue.

That Autissier would be calm enough to sleep in a capsized boat in heavy seas in arguably the world's most dangerous ocean

wouldn't surprise many who know her. Autissier's brilliant sailing career has been fraught with near misses and touched with tragedy. She first entered a round-the-world solo race in 1990. In 1994 she and a crew of three men broke the record for sailing from New York to San Francisco via Cape Horn by two weeks, making the journey in a little more than 62 days. Later in 1994, she set off on her second round-the-world-solo race and won the first leg from Charleston to Cape Town with a five-day lead. But less than a week after leaving Cape Town her boat was dismasted in heavy seas. She repaired it and pressed on. Less than two weeks later, still in the Indian Ocean, a storm flipped her boat end over end, ripping a hole in the hull and destroying her mast and steering. She was rescued four days later by helicopter. The next year she set out on another solo circumnavigation race and helped lead the search for Canadian Gerry Roufs, a former crew member from the record New York to San Francisco run. Roufs vanished only 150 miles from Autissier, and despite her efforts, was not rescued. Carrying on after the tragedy, she finished the race second across the line, despite being disqualified for going to port to fix a broken rudder.

More people have walked on the moon than have sailed around the world alone. Isabelle Autissier was the first woman to compete in a solo circumnavigation race when she entered the BOC in 1990. She doesn't like to be called a "woman sailor" because she is among the elite of the world's sailors, men and women.

The hammer clanked loudly on the hull. Giovanni Soldini, her rival turned rescuer in the 1999 Around Alone race, was above wondering if Autissier was still alive. She stuck her head out of the escape hatch in the stern. "Super!" she said. Soldini took her aboard and the two sailed on to Punta Del Este, Uruguay. Seemingly unfazed by her dramatic accident, Autissier wrote to her fans by email, "I'm on an Italian cruise now and not unhappy about that."

Autissier has sworn off round-the-world solo racing, but she still sails in a wide range of regattas. "We race boats but we're not out to flirt with death," Autissier said in a 1999 interview. "If one of us doesn't come back, we've all lost."

From A World of My Own

by Robin Knox-Johnston

"as things seemed safe I dropped off to sleep with the wind howling a lullaby in the rigging, and the sound of the water rushing past the hull coming through the planking quite clearly where I lay"

The Roaring Forties
September 11th, 1968 (Day 89)–
November 8th, 1968 (Day 147)

We sailed into the Southern Ocean on September 3rd with three weeks of winter left. That night, perhaps a portent, the spinnaker split. There was, of course, no reason why I should suddenly feel that the weather would get more violent just because we had crossed the parallel of 40° South, but just the same it had a psychological effect on me, and I found myself half wanting the first storm to break so that I could see what I might expect during the next four months.

For two days we had very good weather, but there were obvious signs in the sky that a cold front was coming and the barometer's falling needle confirmed this. I had intended sailing along the 40° parallel right the way to Australia, but, naturally enough, the course zigzagged a good deal, depending upon the prevailing winds. To start with we went south and were about 42° South when the cold front arrived. This was my first experience of a Southern Ocean depression and it was quite

an experience. As the cold front passed, the barometer suddenly jumped up two millibars, and the wind backed in minutes from north to west-south-west and rose to gale force. I reefed right down on the mainsail and mizzen and replaced the jib with the storm jib. These last jobs were done in a vicious hailstorm and I was glad to get below to examine the level in the brandy bottle.

Suhaili was sailing along quite fast, and the Admiral seemed to like the stronger winds and was reacting well. The wind soon built up the sea, and as the old sea, left after the wind backed and coming from the north, was still quite large, we soon had a confused cross sea which was uncomfortable and potentially dangerous. I stayed in my wet weather gear that evening, lying on a piece of canvas on my bunk so that I could rush up immediately if anything went wrong. For an hour or so I made a tape of my feelings and tried to describe the scene, intending to send the tape home from Australia, but then as things seemed safe I dropped off to sleep with the wind howling a lullaby in the rigging, and the sound of the water rushing past the hull coming through the planking quite clearly where I lay. The next thing I remember is being jerked awake by a combination of a mass of heavy objects falling on me and the knowledge that my world had turned on its side. I lay for a moment trying to gather my wits to see what was wrong, but as it was pitch black outside and the lantern I kept hanging in the cabin had gone out, I had to rely on my sense to tell me what had happened. I started to try to climb out of my bunk, but the canvas which I had pulled over me for warmth was so weighted down that this was far from easy.

As I got clear *Suhaili* lurched upright and I was thrown off balance and cannoned over to the other side of the cabin, accompanied by a

mass of boxes, tools, tins and clothing which seemed to think it was their duty to stay close to me. I got up again and climbed through the debris and out onto the deck, half expecting that the masts would be missing and that I should have to spend the rest of the night fighting to keep the boat afloat. So convinced was I that this would be the case that I had to look twice before I could believe that the masts were still in place. It was then that I came across the first serious damage. The Admiral's port vane had been forced right over, so far in fact that when I tried to move it I found that the stanchion was completely buckled and the marine plywood of the vane had been split down about 10 inches on the mizzen cap shroud. The whole thing was completely jammed. Fortunately I was using the starboard vane at the time, because I could not hope to try and effect repairs until I could see, and the time was 2.50 a.m. It would not be light for another four hours. *Suhaili* was back on course and seemed to be comfortable and I could not make out anything else wrong; however, I worked my way carefully forward, feeling for each piece of rigging and checking it was still there and tight. I had almost gone completely round the boat when another wave came smashing in and I had to hang on for my life whilst the water boiled over me. This is what must have happened before. Although the whole surface of the sea was confused as a result of the cross-sea, now and again a larger than ordinary wave would break through and knock my poor little boat right over. I decided to alter course slightly so that the seas would be coming from each quarter and we would no longer have one coming in from the side, and went aft to adjust the Admiral accordingly.

Having checked round the deck and rigging, and set *Suhaili* steering more comfortably, I went below and lit the lantern again.

The cabin was in an indescribable mess. Almost the entire contents of the two starboard bunks had been thrown across onto the port side and the deck was hidden by stores that had fallen back when the boat came upright. Water seemed to be everywhere. I was sloshing around in it between the galley and the radio as I surveyed the mess and I could hear it crashing around in the engine-room each time *Suhaili* rolled. That seemed to give me my first job and I rigged up the pump and pumped out the bilges. Over forty gallons had found its way into the engine-room and about fifteen more were in the main bilge, although how it had all got in I did not know at the time. Doing a familiar and necessary job helped to settle me again. Ever since I had got up I had been in that nervous state when you never know if in the next minute you are going to be hit hard for a second time. I could not really believe that the boat was still in one piece and, as far as I could see, undamaged.

"Almost the entire contents of the two starboard bunks had been thrown across onto the port side and the deck was hidden by stores that had fallen back when the boat came upright. Water seemed to be everywhere."

It's rather similar to when you uncover an ant nest. The exposed ants immediately wash their faces and this familiar task reassures them and prevents them panicking. Pumping the bilges was a familiar task to me and when it was completed I felt that I had the situation under control and set about tidying up quite calmly. The only real decision I had to make was where to start. I couldn't shift everything out of the cabin as there was nowhere else to put things, so I had to search for some large object amongst the mess, stow it away and then use the space vacated as a base. It was

two hours before my bunk was cleared. I found books, films, stationery, clothes, fruit and tools all expertly mixed with my medical stores, and for days afterwards odd items kept appearing in the most out of the way places.

Working aft I started on the galley and put that straight, finding the pliers, which I had last seen on the radio shelf, tucked away behind a pile of saucers in their rack. It must have missed them by millimetres. The radio seemed all right, although it had got very wet. I mopped up what I could see, intending to do the job properly after daylight.

Whilst doing this I noticed a lot of water dripping down from the chart table immediately above the radio, and on following this up I discovered that water was pouring into the cabin round the edge each time a wave broke aboard. Tracing this back, I discovered that there were ominous cracks all round the edge of the cabin, and that the interior bulkheads had been shifted slightly by the force of the wave breaking over the boat. The sight of this, and the realization that if we took many more waves over the boat the weakened cabin top might be washed away, gave me a sick feeling in the pit of my stomach. If the cabin top went it would leave a gaping hole 6 feet by 12 in the deck; I was 700 miles southwest of Cape Town and the Southern Ocean is no place for what would virtually be an open boat. Just then another wave hit and I could feel the whole structure wince at the blow, but it did not appear to shift. Well, there would not be time to put extra fastenings in if it was going. I would just have to put lashings over it if things got worse and hope that the weather would ease and allow repairs to be made the next day.

The cabin was now clear so I found the torch and checked the engine-room for sources of leaks as water was already sloshing about in the bilges again. The fist thing I noticed was that all the batteries were at a crazy angle and were fetched up against the port fuel tank. The side of the battery shelf had been knocked out by the weight of the batteries when the boat lurched and only the fact that the port fuel tank was in the way stopped the batteries from falling and being

ruined. This would have meant no more radio and an end to getting the engine going. My two spare batteries were old, and could only be relied upon to work the Aldis signalling lamp and my tape recorder. I pushed the batteries back onto their shelf and lashed them in place, so that even if the other side of the shelf carried away they would not move again.

There was nothing else I could do until daylight, so I took a tot, folded the jib on the cabin deck, wrapped myself in a piece of canvas and fell asleep. Canvas may seem an odd covering, but it does keep the water out to a certain extent and once my own whisky induced heat had spread, the canvas kept me quite warm.

When I awoke three hours later and poked my head outside, the waves seemed less ferocious, but occasional squalls, usually accompanied by hail, were whipping across the surface and turning the dull grey sea into a milky white. After quickly checking that all was well on deck, I dived below again and started cooking up some porridge. By the time I had put this inside me and followed it with a mug of coffee and a cigarette, I was feeling quite happy. I obviously could not repair the Admiral in the present wind, as the vane would be blown away the moment I tried to unfasten it, so I decided to try and strengthen the cabin.

I got out my box of odd nuts and screws and selected the longest bolts and heaviest screws in order to try to reinforce the cabin top fastenings. The job kept me busy all day, but I slept a lot better knowing it was done.

That evening one of those infuriating little accidents occurred which, although it did not affect my ability to go on, nevertheless left me feeling rankled because it was so unnecessary. I had just opened a new bottle of brandy for my evening drink, and having poured out a good measure I put the bottle on the spare bunk, jammed by the sextant box. About an hour later a strong smell of brandy began to invade the cabin and I eventually traced it to the newly opened bottle. The bottle was sealed by one of these metal screw caps, and as the boat rolled in the sea, the movement had slowly loosened the top until the contents could escape. I was furious about this. As my allowance was half a bottle of spirits a week I had lost two weeks' supply, but I consoled myself with the thought that I had a least taken that day's ration from it!

On September 7th, two days after the knock down, the seas had eased sufficiently to allow me to tackle the Admiral. I had to do the job anyway as the direction had changed and I now needed to gybe round and use the port vane. The whole job was easier than I expected. I had two spare stanchions for the self-steering vanes so I decided to take the plywood fin out of the buckled stanchion and rebolt it into a new one. The job was complicated by the heavy rolls *Suhaili* was making and more than once I found myself completely immersed in the sea, which was most uncomfortable as no wet weather gear is completely waterproof and none is designed for swimming.

Until we reached the Southern Ocean we had met only one gale. The average had now changed dramatically, and five gales passed us in ten days. It was no good taking all sail in and letting *Suhaili* ride them out quietly, as we lost too much distance like that. The winds were from the west and I wanted to go east, and I was racing against time anyway. If I wanted to win I had to keep pushing the boat as much as I dared, but the frequency of the gales appalled me and I began to appreciate what Alec Rose had meant in his message.

Keeping the boat pressed left me on tenterhooks all day in case I was overdoing things, and it was even harder to stop myself from reducing sail at night when the wind always appeared stronger. I slept fully clothed, usually rolled up in the canvas on top of the polythene containers in the cabin. As I would quickly get cramp in that position, I would then try sleeping sitting up. This would be all right for a bit, but sooner or later the boat would give a lurch and I would be picked up and thrown across the cabin. If I tried wedging myself in the bunk I could not get out so quickly in an emergency, and if the boat received a really big bang I would get thrown out of the bunk and across the cabin anyway.

I became rather tired and irritable through lack of proper sleep; an idea of my feelings at this time can be seen in my diary for September 9th.

September 9th, 1968

I finally awoke at 1100 having had three hours uninterrupted sleep in the bunk. The wind was down so I got up and set more sail. We were rolling very heavily and it was difficult to stand inside the cabin, but I managed to hear up some soup and in the afternoon, a superhuman effort, I made a prune duff, which was a great treat. I also made a new drink. Brandy, honey, hot water, sugar and a lemon, which tasted wonderful and bucked me up. I needed it. I felt very depressed on getting up. I cannot do anything in these conditions. (I am writing this late at night and the rolling has eased a bit.) The real trouble is I am so far from achieving anything at the moment. I used up a lot of nervous energy last night by leaving the jib up, for what—maybe an extra 20 miles if we're lucky—and what difference does 20 miles make when I have about 20,000 to go?

The future does not look particularly bright, but sitting here being thrown about for the next 150 days, at least with constant soakings as I have to take in or let out sail, is not an exciting prospect. After four gales my hands are worn and cut about badly and I am aware of my fingers on account of the pain from skin tears and broken fingernails. I have bruises all over from being thrown about. My skin itches from constant chafing with wet clothes, and I forget when I last had a proper wash so I feel dirty. I feel altogether mentally and physically exhausted and I've been in the Southern Ocean only a week. It seems years since I gybed to turn east and yet it was only last Tuesday night, not six days, and I have another 150 days of it yet. I shall be a Zombie in that time. I feel that I have had enough of sailing for the time being; it's about time I made a port, had a long hot bath, a steak with eggs, peas and new potatoes, followed by lemon meringue pie, coffee, Drambuie and a cigar and then a nice long uninterrupted sleep, although, come to think of it, to round it off properly...Here, in a nutshell, is my problem; I have all this to look forward to, but it's so far ahead. I really want something in the more immediate future to look forward to. Australia possibly, and yet that

is eight weeks ahead at least and will only be a brief contact with a boat, not something special I can look forward to, and even then I am only halfway; I still have a slightly greater distance to go. It's all a great prospect; why couldn't I be satisfied with big ships?

The life may be monotonous but at least one gets into port occasionally which provides some variety. A prisoner at Dartmoor doesn't get hard labour like this; the public wouldn't stand for it and he has company, however

"The future does not look particularly bright, but sitting here being thrown about for the next 150 days, at least with constant soakings as I have to take in or let out sail, is not an exciting prospect."

uncongenial. In addition he gets dry clothing and undisturbed sleep. I wonder how the crime rate would be affected if people were sentenced to sail round the world alone, instead of going to prison. It's ten months solitary confinement with hard labour.

Rather an interesting sight this evening. I was adjusting the Admiral at 2000 so that we would run better when I thought I saw a light ahead. I went forward and saw it again quite clearly low down on the surface. It rapidly drew close dividing into two as it did so and we passed between it. It, or rather they, were two wedge shaped lumps of luminescence, about 2 ft. 6 ins. long and about 8 ins. square at the thick end, narrowing down to about 4 ins. square at the other end. Possibly a leptocephalus but if so an unusual shape.

It's quiet just now, although I have one foot on the galley to hold myself steady, as we are rolling heavily. Note that the pressure has remained steady for over twenty-four hours. The wind seems to be veering which is good news.

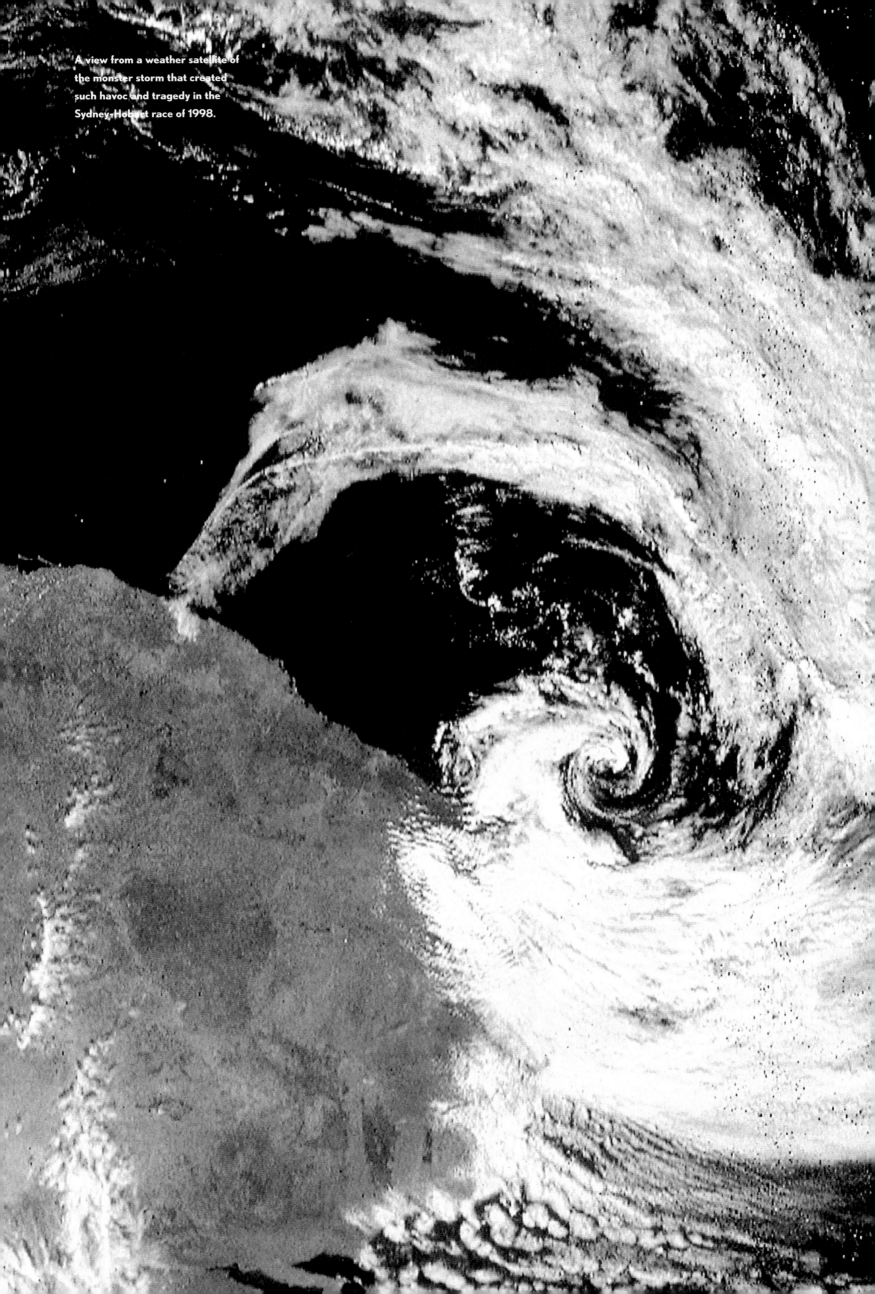

A view from a weather satellite of the monster storm that created such havoc and tragedy in the Sydney-Hobart race of 1998.

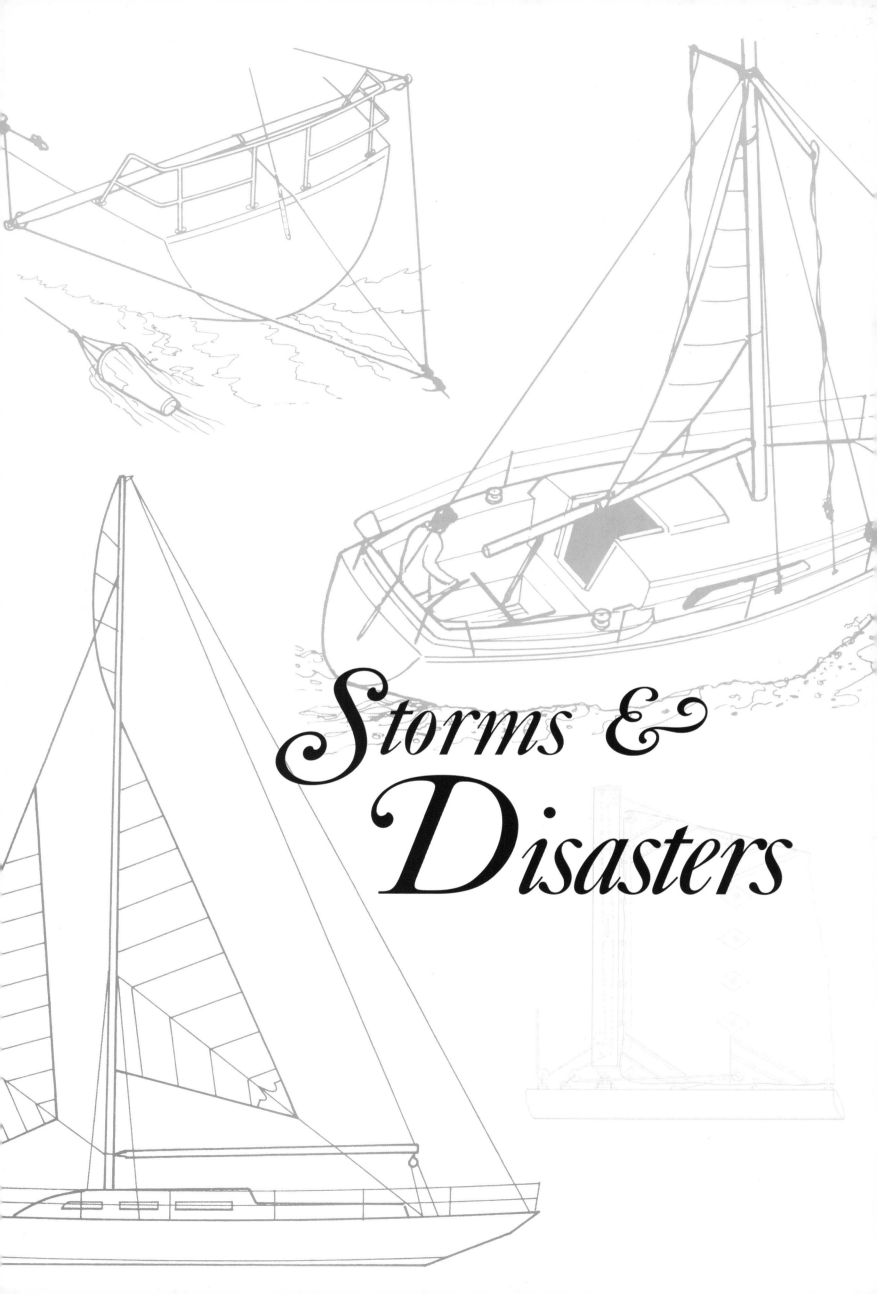

Storms & Disasters

A fierce approaching squall. Squalls can move at frightening speed, the wind rising from virtually nothing to almost hurricane force.

QUEBEC

—— • ——

MY VESSEL IS HEALTHY, AND I REQUEST FREE PRATIQUE.

Nothing is as satisfying to an armchair sailor as tales of storms and disasters. Despite all the science available to man, meteorological forecasting is a chancy affair. Storms seem to roll out of nowhere, leaving paths of devastation that are difficult to fathom if you haven't experienced them.

The average storm is nothing very scary, but in recent years storms of great magnitude and ferocity seem to be appearing with greater frequency. A number of recent bestsellers have celebrated these weather catastrophes: *The Perfect Storm, Knockdown, Isaac's Storm.*

These catastrophic events have resulted in millions, even billions of dollars of damage and loss of life. Scientists increasingly tell us that global warming will make the future even more

prone to storms, and if warming is accompanied by a rise in the sea level, the potential for flooding, surge damage and death can increase exponentially. This is not good news. All around the world, the desire to live by the sea has shifted from commercial activity involving fishing and trade to leisure pursuits. As a result, millions of people have moved to coastal areas, motivating developers to build endless apartment buildings and single homes, often just feet from the beach. The coastline from Florida to Maryland is a disaster waiting to happen. If sea levels rise enough, the protective barrier islands will be covered and the seas will show no mercy. Likewise, much of Micronesia— only a few feet above sea level— could well disappear forever.

Whether or not governments will do anything to slow this

process is open to debate. It's a question of balancing resources and of commitment, and the costs are enormous either way. The hundreds of millions of dollars in damage caused by hurricanes Gloria or Andrew will be repeated again and again

What all these major storms have in common is the loss of life. Throughout history, men and women have been lost at sea and on shore due to the vagaries of weather, but with modern telecommunications, these incidents have assumed a much greater magnitude. If we assume that the biblical flood was the ultimate storm, then what has followed has been a mere shadow of its monstrousness. But now we are able to participate vicariously through television, the internet and radio. Seeing devastation on a screen has a curious effect. It minimizes the

> The wonder is always
>
> new that any sane man
>
> can be a sailor.
>
> —*Ralph Waldo Emerson*

SAFFIR-SIMPSON SCALE FOR HURRICANE CLASSIFICATION

Strength (kt)	Wind Speed (mph)	Wind Speed (millibars)	Pressure (inches Hg)	Pressure (ft.)	Storm Surge
Category 1	65–82 kt	74–95 mph	>980 mb	>28.94 in.	4–5 ft.
Category 2	83–95 kt	96–110 mph	965–979 mb	28.50–28.91 in.	6–8 ft.
Category 3	96–113 kt	111–130 mph	945–964 mb	27.91–28.47 in.	9–12 ft.
Category 4	114–135 kt	131–155 mph	920–944 mb	27.17–27.88 in.	13–18 ft.
Category 5	>135 kt	>155 mph	<919 mb	<27.16 in.	>18 ft.

Tropical Depression 20–34 kt or 23–39 mph

Tropical Storm 35–64 kt or 40–73 mph

Hurricane 65+ kt or 74+ mph

actuality and tends to make us secure. We are not. Technology desensitizes people to nature and we more often experience nature in a carefully groomed and safe form. Visits to nature preserves and national parks or to protected seashores rarely impart an understanding of the potential ferocity of the elements.

Hurricanes

When conditions are right, that is, when colder air passes over warm waters, a hurricane or a cyclonic storm can develop. Depending on the speed at which it moves, the storm can suck up great quantities of energy, increasing in velocity and magnitude. When such a storm approaches land, all hell can break loose. Since hurricanes revolve in a counterclockwise direction, the eastern edge is the most devastating side of the storm. In its movement, a hurricane can be most erratic. Often, a forecast path or a computer model will prove totally unreliable, as the variations in winds, water and land temperatures, and pressure systems will play nasty tricks. Two of the prime examples of this phenomenon are the great hurricanes of 1908 and 1938. The havoc wrecked by these storms is legendary, and unfortunately it is the damage done that makes a storm immortal.

Until fairly recently, forecasting such storms was very much a hit or miss affair. Little was understood about the nature of hurricanes and less was known on how to predict and warn coastal populations of their coming. Only with the advent of satellite scrutiny have we been

able to see these storms generate, often off the coast of West Africa and travel across the Atlantic. The ocean currents and prevailing winds push them along somewhat predictable routes, culminating in either the Atlantic seaboard of the United States or in the Gulf of Mexico

An 1896 engraving of a ship under shortened sail fighting for her life in an Arctic storm.

along the Gulf Coast of the United States and Central America.

The most devastating hurricane of the old days was the one that hit Galveston, Texas in 1908. At that time it was believed by the United States Weather Bureau that no storm could come ashore on the Gulf Coast. This barren region had been settled only a couple of decades earlier, mainly through advertising that promised land, riches and a wonderful Southern lifestyle. Galveston developed quickly, and became a major port. But, the city was only a few feet above sea level. With the exception of a few buildings in downtown, the entire town was covered with frame houses and warehouses. The trestle that connected Galveston Island to the mainland was wooden, and there was no sea wall to protect the waterfront on Galveston Bay, which was wide open to the South.

On a September morning in1908, a monster hurricane, probably a category 5, hit Galveston Bay. Fierce winds, driving rain, pounding surf and flooding were bad enough. People were swimming in the street, clinging to wreckage. But the worst was yet to happen. As the storm moved over the city, the waters of the bay were sucked out, returning as a surge. Water roared back in, swamping the city, leveling houses and wharves, warehouses and office buildings. Thousands were swept to their deaths. More than 4,000 people lost their lives and the city was reduced to splinters. The railroad trestle was carried a half mile from its foundations, beaches disappeared, families wrought asunder. It was the worst marine disaster in United States history. Nothing approached it until the infamous hurricane of 1938.

Though far more people died in 1908, the property damage from the hurricane of 1938 was astounding. On September 21 of that year the New York *Times* editorialized:"Every year an average of three such whirlwinds sweep the tropical North Atlantic between June and November. In 1933, there was an all-time record of twenty. If New York and the rest of the world have been so well informed about the cyclone, it is because of an admirable, organized meteorological service." Little did they know how wrong they were.

Though only a category 3 storm, this was to be one of the most devastating storms in history.

Remember, weather forecasting, though superior to that in 1908, was still in its infancy. Despite knowledge of the storm

Nokia in severe conditions during
the disastrous Sydney-Hobart race
of 1998.

New London, Connecticut Harbor after the Hurricane of 1938. Even large ships were swept ashore, and entire buildings were swept into oblivion.

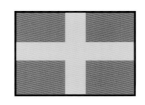

ROMEO

· — ·

NO MEANING IN INTERNATIONAL CODE. USED BY VESSELS AT ANCHOR TO WARN OF COLLISION IN FOG.

and its general path, early meteorologists believed that the storm would speed out to sea.

But Charlie Pierce, a junior meteorologist, thought differently. He was overruled by his superiors and the official forecast was for cloudy skies and gusty winds. Instead of moving out over the Atlantic, the storm moved due north at a rate of 70 mph, a truly astonishing rate of travel, the fastest ever recorded. This forward motion helped to increase the speed of the hurricane winds and 180 mph gusts were recorded on Long Island and New England at the height of the storm.

The blast hit the shores of Long Island, New York in mid-afternoon, just prior to the expected high tide. The tide, combined with a new moon and the tremendous winds, created waves of from 30 to 50 feet high, which pounded the shoreline of Eastern Long Island, creating inlets, sweeping homes and people away, inundating everything. Tides rose to 14 to 25 feet all along the Long Island and Connecticut coastlines. Providence, Rhode Island was submerged under 20 feet of water, and stories are told of people in office buildings seeing automobiles, with their headlights on, eerily glowing under the rising waters. The greatest devastation was along the coasts, of course, but even in the Connecticut River valley, up to 17 inches of rain produced the worst flooding in memory. In all, more than 8,900 homes were

destroyed, 15,000 were damaged. 2,600 boats were reduced to splinters and 3,300 others damaged. 564 people died.

Typhoons and Monsoons

In the Pacific and Indian Oceans, cyclonic storms are known as typhoons. Along the coasts of China, Japan, Korea and west to the Indian subcontinent, these storms sweep in with a ferocity even greater than Atlantic hurricanes. The vast expanses of the Pacific, a comparatively warm ocean, allow for the development of typhoons. Perhaps the best known are those that hit Hong Kong, partially because it is such a major city and partially because of its situation, exposed to the seas in all weathers. Hong Kong is first and foremost a port. Such

Above: The ship *Tulja* aground after the cyclone of 5 October 1864. Refloating a ship of this size is a massive undertaking, dependent of favorable tides and sheer horsepower.

Below: Waterspouts are tornadoes at sea. Though quite common, they are smaller than land-based tornadoes, and rarely cause the same kind of damage. They are, however, extremely erratic in course, and a prudent sailor will be alert, especially in southern waters, where the water temperature can aid their formation.

Devastation wrought by a cyclone in Bangladesh in 1991. The Bay of Bengal is a natural funnel for these storms, and the very low-lying coastal regions are repeatedly hit by these tropical hurricanes. Death tolls range in the tens of thousands.

destructive elements as a storm are felt far more deeply than in isolated coastal areas.

But the greatest devastation is caused by the monsoon storms that sweep up the Bay of Bengal yearly. For those of us who live in temperate climates, the sheer amount of rainfall here is astonishing. An umbrella doesn't help. The coasts of Pakistan, to the east of the Indian Subcontinent are particularly prone to receive these storms. Not only is the Bay of Bengal a natural funnel for pushing wind and water inland, but the land itself is barely above sea level, sometimes for hundreds of miles inland. Thus, when a typhoon sweeps inland, the results are deadly. It is not uncommon, in this area of abject poverty and little in the way of emergency readiness or medical treatment, for tens of thousands to die in a remarkably short time. Storm surges and tidal waves plunder land and life with impunity.

Tsunamis

Tsunamis, or tidal waves, are transocean waves generated usually by undersea earthquakes, but also by landslides and cosmic collisions. The word tsunami comes from the Japanese word for "harbor wave." Tsunamis, however, are not caused by tides, though their impact can be increased or decreased, depending on the state of tide. And though not generated in harbors, this is where their destructive impact is most apparent.

When any large volume of water is displaced from its normal position in the sea, a tsunami can result. During an undersea earthquake or volcano, a very large volume of water can be forced out of equilibrium and travel great distances, causing extraordinary damage *when it comes in contact with land.*

On the open ocean, a tsunami can travel thousands of miles, appearing as a smooth roller a few feet high and causing no problems for mariners. However, when this massive volume of water approaches a shoreline, with its rising sea bottom, the water is pushed up onto land with astonishing speed and force.

Unlike waves generated and pushed by winds—normal waves coming into a California beach might have wave lengths of perhaps 300 feet and a period of 10 seconds—a tsunami can have a wavelength of more than *350 miles* and a period of an hour.

Above: The Japanese character for "tsunami"

Below: A waterspout in formation.

Because tsunamis travel at a terrific speed—sometimes at more than 500 miles per hour—and lose very little energy in the process, their impact, when they reach land, can be shattering.

As a tsunami approaches a shore, it starts to slow down and grow in height. And though some of its energy is dissipated from bottom friction, turbulence and reflection offshore, it can still pack a devastating blow. Tsunamis have been calculated to have reached heights above sea level of as much as 150 feet. Everything in their path is destroyed, including trees, buildings, walls, road, utilities.

Most of the most damaging tsunamis have occurred in the Pacific. A combination of plate techtonics and underwater volcanic activity make for these tsunamis. One of the most dramatic occurred on April 1, 1946 in the northern Pacific, off the Aleutian Islands. Sparked by an earthquake off the Aleutians, this tsunami had ocean-wide effects and caused more than $26,000,000 (1946 dollars) in damages and took the lives of 165 people.

On Unimak Island, Alaska, a newly built lighthouse was struck by a wave that reached a height of more than 100 feet. Five lives were lost and the structure, built to withstand heavy seas and 40 feet above sea level, was totally demolished. As far away as the Hawaiian Islands

Above: The finish of a race in a powerful rainsquall. Visibility can be diminished to mere yards in such storms.

Below: Margaret Roth at the helm in the Strait of LeMaire under bare poles in a southwest gale. Often running under bare poles can keep the ship=B9s speed low enough to prevent pitchpoling (flipping end over end).

The yacht *Doortje* sinks.

Thierry Dubois, in the Vendee Globe Race, capsized. Due to the extreme nature of his yacht, he was unable to right the boat and was rescued by another competitor. Extreme beam, light displacement yachts like this are often lacking in dynamic stability and demand precision sailing in heavy weather.

waves of 40 feet were recorded.

Another major tsunami reached shore May 22, 1960, generated by an earthquake measuring 8.6 on the Richter Scale off the coast of Chile. This was also a Pacific-wide event, with waves of more than 30 feet causing major damage along the coasts of Chile, Hawaii and even parts of Southern California. The Chilean shore experienced the wave for more than 300 miles of shoreline. Off Isla Chiloe, Chile, inhabitants, fearing the earthquake took to boats, all of which were destroyed in the thundering wave.

Despite sophisticated warning systems, many of the areas where tsunamis come ashore are sparsely populated and never receive any forewarning. Thus deaths and damage will continue to occur.

Shipwrecks
Throughout the ages, ships have been lost on rocks, against leeward shores, at sea, in storm and calm. So many factors are involved, including unknown currents and freak storms, rogue waves and faulty navigation. The fact that sailors continue to go to sea is either an affirmation of courage or a confirmation of madness.

One of the most tragic shipwrecks occurred in October 1998, when the cruise ship *Fantome* was lost in Hurricane Mitch. More than 11,000 people

When men come to like
a sea-life, they are not
fit to live on land.

– *Samuel Johnson*

lost their lives in this vicious storm, but the plight of the *Fantome,* one of the largest charter vessels in the Caribbean is instructive. Despite all precautions and evasive tactics, this old ship was caught in the very midst of the storm at its height and was literally obliterated.

This 282-foot, 4-masted schooner was one of the largest sailing ships in existence. She had been built for the Italian Navy in the 1920s, then turned into a pleasure palace by the Duke of Westminster. She passed through various very rich owners, inccluding the Guiness family and Aristotle Onassis before she was bought by Captain Michael Burke, the owner of Windjammer Cruises.

While Mitch was developing from a tropical storm to a hurricane, the barometer plunged more than 50 millibars, signaling a storm of unusually severe strength and the fate of 93 passengers was decided. The storm reached force 4, and just before setting sail on October 25, the captain of the *Fantome,* a Cornishman named Guyan March, decided to get the passengers off and flown to Miami. It was a wise decision, but not wise enough. The options of hiding a ship of *Fantome's* size safely were not great, and it was decided, in conference with the home office, to move her more than 100 miles south to the Island of Roatán. The captain the management of Windjammer cruises though the island was large enough to break the worst winds and seas.

But by the morning of October 26, Mitch had been upgraded to a category 5, and by the next day the storm had turned unexpectedly, heading directly for Roatán. The storm kept changing course, and no matter where she went, *Fantome* seemed to be the cho-

sen one, unable to dodge the ultimate fury. She was directly in the path of the worst storm to hit Central America in a hundred years, with winds of more than 200 miles per hour, and waves up to 50-feet high.

Contact with the ship was lost at four that afternoon. Other than some splinters of wood and lifejackets, nothing was ever found. Neither ship nor crew surfaced. Her emergency beacon was never activated. She simply disappeared. No one knows to this day exactly what happened, but it seems likely that the ship sank suddenly with all the crew strapped in below. There is no denying that modern man has as yet been unable to stand up to the ultimate forces of nature.

Another shipwreck, of more modest dimensions, perhaps, but still horrifying, was the loss of the schooner *Integrity* while it was towed in 1975. *Integrity* was one of the most famous sailing ships on the East Coast of America. Built by Waldo Howland, the creator of the

famous Concordia Company in New England, she had cruised extensively along the coast and across the Atlantic. Abandoned by her crew in a gale and dismasted, she drifted around the ocean, being repeatedly boarded and stripped by scavengers. Finally taken in tow by a trawler, she was towed into the Turks Islands in the Caribbean. She became the object of a great legal battle for salvage, sunk at her mooring, was refloated and finally sold for a pittance. At that point, the great English sailor Frank Mulville entered the story, offering to tow her north to Cat Island. Mulville, sailed out to the Caribbean in the autumn of 1974, where he came upon *Integrity* and offered to tow her to her new home. What he was towing, of course, was a hulk, devoid of spars,engine, steering gear, or any other necessary equipment. Muliville's boat, *Iskra,* is small, about 30 feet on deck, and moved rather slowly.

But fate was to continue to batter the once proud, now

unlucky, *Integrity*. With a friend, he bridled the two boats together and began the tow. As always seems the case, weather intervened. A gale came up, and *Integrity's* motion became more and more erratic, especially because her rudder had jammed. Attempting to move her into a more manageable position, she was overtaken by a rogue wave—one of those monsters that appear from the deep without warning—her towing bridle snapped and she disappeared beneath the seas.

So many ships have disappeared from the surface of the seas without a trace. The ocean's bottom is littered with the gear and bodies of explorers, merchant seamen, warriors, and pleasure seekers. The sea extracts a high price, simply for daring to cross it. But then crossing the street is more dangerous.

TECHNIQUES IN A STORM

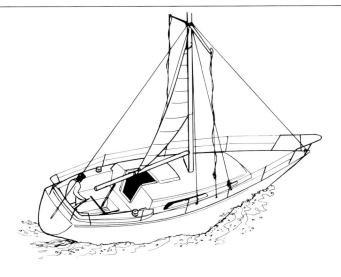

Above: When dismasted at sea without hope of immediate rescue, some sort of jury rig must be devised to propel the boat to port. When the lower part of the mast remains standing, the storm trysail can be rigged to allow sailing.

When the mast is totally lost overboard, the jib can be rigged, using the spinnaker pole as a support. Not efficient, these makeshift rigs can still sail the boat downwind or on a reach.

Deploying a parachute drogue. The drag created by the drogue causes the bows of the yacht to point into the wind, providing some stability and presenting the least vulnerable part of the yacht to advancing seas.

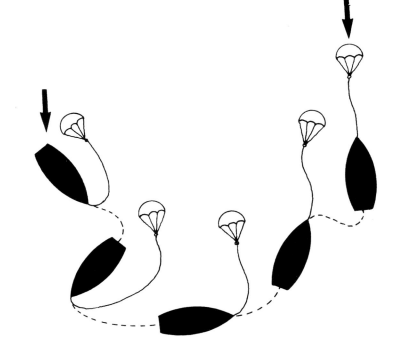

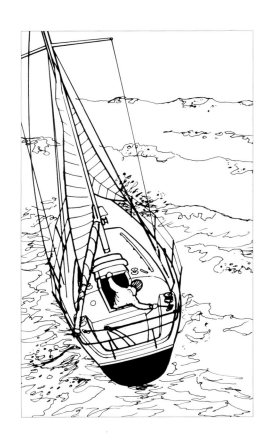

Left: Heaving to allows the boat to fore reach at a slow pace. The jib is backed and the tiller thrust hard to leeward. This maneuver settles the motion of the boat in a seaway and keeps the bows into the wind.

Right: Lying ahull, with all sail doused and the tiller lashed, allows the ship to look after herself. However, the hull will be abeam the wind, motion will be greater, and leeward drift can be excessive. Experience has shown that lighter displacement hulls with fin keels behave better in harsh conditions when lying ahull.

A storm trisail must be heavily reinforced. The top detail shows tape reinforcement, the bottom shows a knot used to tighten the foot and leach.

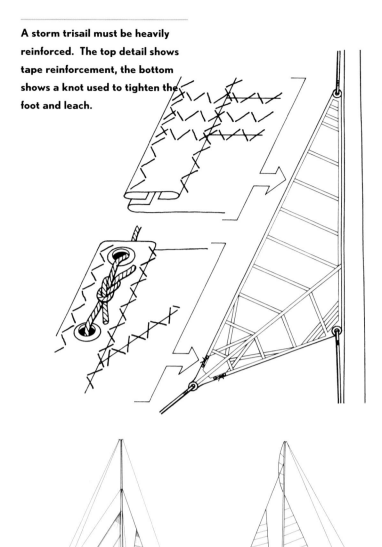

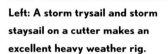

Left: A storm trysail and storm staysail on a cutter makes an excellent heavy weather rig.

Right: The same combination on a sloop, The sloop will not be as well balanced, however, as the storm jib shifts the center of effo

Above: In truly heavy downwind conditions, survival conditions, only running is possible, and a long bight of heavy rope can slow the boat enough to prevent pitchpoling and maintain some steerage.

Below: Sailing to windward in heavy seas demands intense concentration and a good eye. Dropping off is often necessary to avoid burying the bows, and speed must be adjusted to move over the waves, not through them.

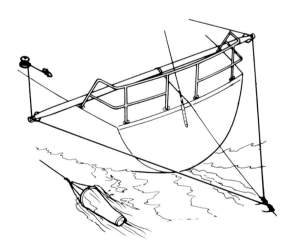

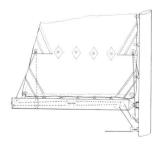

A simple and strong reefing arrangement is a must on all sailing yachts. Sail area can be reduced quickly by means of a slab reefing system.

When the rudder is jammed or lost, a steering device such as this can be deployed to steer the boat. By using lines to pull the drogue from side to side, some semblance of course correction can be achieved.

From The Perfect Storm: A True Story of Men Against the Sea

The Zero-Moment Point

In the 1950's and 1960's, the U.S. Government decided to detonate a series of nuclear devices in the Pacific Ocean. The thinking was that deep water would absorb the shock wave and minimize the effect on the environment, while still allowing scientists to gauge the strength of the explosions. But an oceanographer named William Van Dorn, associated with the Scripps Institute in La Jolla, California, warned them that a nuclear explosion in the wrong place "could convert the entire continental shelf into a surf zone."

Concerned, the Navy ran a series of wave tank tests to see what kind of stresses their fleet could take. (They'd already lost three destroyers to a typhoon in 1944. Before going down the ships had radioed that they were rolling through arcs of 140 degrees. They downflooded through their stacks and sank.) The Navy subjected model destroyers and aircraft carriers to various kinds of waves and found that a single nonbreaking wave—no matter how big it was—was incapable of sinking a ship. A single *breaking* wave, though, would flip a ship end over end if it was higher than the ship was long. Typically, the ship would climb the wave at an angle of forty-five degrees, fail to gain the top, and then slide back down the face. Her stern would bury itself into

the trough, and the crest of the wave would catch her bow and flip her over. This is called pitch-poling; Ernie Hazard was pitch-poled on Georges Bank. It's one of the few motions that can end ship-to-shore communication instantly.

Another is a succession of waves that simply drives the boat under—"founders," as mariners say. The dictionary defines founder as "to cave in, sink, fail utterly, collapse." On a steel boat the windows implode, the hatches fail, and the boat starts to downflood. The crew is prevented from escaping by the sheer force of the water pouring into the cabin—it's like walking into the blast of a firehose. In that sense, pitch-poling is better than foundering because an overturned boat traps air in the hold and can stay afloat for an hour or more. That might allow members of the crew to swim out a doorway and climb into a life raft. The rafts are designed to inflate automatically and release from the boat when she goes down. In theory the EPIRB floats free as well, and begins signalling to shore. All the crew has to do is stay alive.

By the late hours of October 28th the sea state is easily high enough to either pitch-pole the *Andrea Gail* or drive her under. And if she loses power—a clogged fuel filter, a fouled prop—she could slew to the side and roll. The same rule applies to capsizing

as to pitch-poling: the wave must be higher than the boat is wide. The *Andrea Gail* is twenty feet across her beam. But even if the boat doesn't get hit by a non-negotiable wave, the rising sea state allows Billy less and less leeway to maneuver. If he maintains enough speed to steer, he beats the boat to pierces; if he slows down, he loses rudder control. This is the end result of two days of narrowing options; now the only choice left is whether to go upsea or down, and the only outcome is whether they sink or float. There's not much in between.

If the conditions don't subside, the most Billy can realistically hope for is to survive until dawn. Then at least they'll have a chance of being rescued—now it's unthinkable. "In violent storms there is so much water in the air, and so much air in the water, that it becomes impossible to tell where the atmosphere stops and the sea begins," writes Van Dorn. "That may literally make it impossible to distinguish up from down." In such conditions a helicopter pilot could never pluck six people off the deck of a boat. So, for the next eight hours, the crew of the *Andrea Gail* must keep the pumps and engine running and just hope they don't encounter any rogue waves. Seventy-footers are roaming around the sea state like surly giants and there's not much Billy can do but take them head-on and try to get over the top before they break. If his floodlights are out he wouldn't even have that option—he'd just feel a drop into the trough, a lurch, and the boat starting up a slope way too steep to survive.

"Seventy foot seas—I'd be puttin' on my diapers at that point," says Charlie Reed. "I'd be quite nervous. That's higher than the highest point on the *Andrea Gail*. I once came home from the Grand Banks in thirty-five foot seas. It was a scary fuckin' thought—straight up, straight down, for six days. My guess is that Billy turned side-to and rolled. You come off one of those seas cocked, the next one comes at a different angle, it pushes the boat around and then you roll. If the boat flips over—even with everything dogged down—water's gonna get in. The boat's upside-down, the plywood's buckling, that's the end."

When Ernie Hazard went over on Georges Bank in 1982, the motion wasn't a violent one so much as a huge, slow somersault that laid the boat over on her back. Hazard remembers one wave spinning them around and another lifting them end over end. It wasn't like rolling a car at high speeds, it was more like rolling a house. Hazard was thirty-three at the time; three years earlier he'd answered a newspaper ad and got a job on the *Fair Wind*, a lobster boat out of Newport, Rhode Island. The storm hit on their last trip of the year, late November. The crew were all good friends; they celebrated the end of their season at a steakhouse and then left for Georges Bank late the next morning. The winds were light and the forecast called for several more days of fair weather. By dawn it was blowing a hundred:

We were driving the boat well. You

point the boat into the sea and try to hold your own until it blows out—stay there, take your pounding. You balance the boat, flood the tanks, try to save what you have on deck. There was the typical howling of wind in the wires and there was a lot of foam because of the wind, yellow foam, spindrift. We'd lose power on the waves because they were more foam than water, the propeller just couldn't bite.

It happened quick. We were close to the edge of the continental shelf and the seas were getting large, starting to break. Cresting. I remember looking out the pilothouse and this monster wave came and broke over the bow and forced us backwards. There was nothing to hold us there and we must have dug the stern in and then spun around. Now we're in a full following sea. We never went more than one more wave when we buried our bow in the trough and flipped over. There was the wave breaking and then a sensation of the boat turning, and the next thing I knew we were upside-down. Floating inside the boat.

I happened to surface in a small air pocket and I didn't know if I was upside-down or standing on the walls or what. I made a dive into the pilothouse and I could see some light—it could have been a window or a porthole, I don't know—and when I got back up into the wheelhouse there was no more air. It was all gone. I was thinking, "This is it. Just take a mouthful of water and it's over." It was very matter-of-fact. I was at a fork in the road and there was work to do—swim or die. It didn't scare me, I didn't think about my family or anything. It was more businesslike. People think you always have to go for life, but you

don't. You can quit.

For reasons that he still doesn't understand, Hazard didn't quit. He made a guess and swam. The entire port side of the cabin was welded steel and he knew if he picked that direction, he was finished. He felt himself slide through a narrow opening—the door? a window?—and suddenly he was back in the world. The boat was hull-up, sliding away fast, and the life raft was convulsing at the end of its tether. It was his only hope; he wriggled out of his clothes and started to swim.

Whether the *Andrea Gail* rolls, pitch-poles, or gets driven down, she winds up, one way or another, in a position from which she cannot recover. Among marine architects this is known as the zero-moment point—the point of no return. The transition from crisis to catastrophe is fast, probably under a minute, or someone would've tripped the EPIRB. (In fact the EPIRB doesn't even signal when it hits the water, which means it has somehow malfunctioned. In the vast majority of cases, the Coast Guard knows when men are dying offshore.) There's no time to put on survival suits or grab a life vest; the boat's moving through the most extreme motion of her life and there isn't even time to shout. The refrigerator comes out of the wall and crashes across the galley. Dirty dishes cascade out of the sink. The TV, the washing machine, the VCR tapes, the men, all go flying. And, seconds later, the water moves in.

When a boat floods, the first thing that happens is that her electrical system shorts out. The lights go off, and for a few moments the only illumination is the frenetic blue of sparks arcing down into the water. It's said that people in extreme situations perceive things in distorted, almost surreal ways, and when the wires start to crackle and burn, perhaps one of the crew thinks of fireworks—of the last Fourth of July, walking around Gloucester with his girlfriend and watching colors blossom over the inner harbor. There'd be tourists shuffling down Rogers Street and fishermen hooting from bars and the smell of gunpowder and fried clams drifting through town. He'd have his whole life ahead of him, that July evening; he'd have every choice in the world.

And he wound up swordfishing. He wound up, by one route or another, on this trip, in this storm, with this boat filling up with water and one or two minutes left to live. There's no going back now, no rescue helicopter that could possibly save him. All that's left is to hope it's over fast.

When the water first hits the trapped men, it's cold but not paralyzing, around fifty-two degrees. A man can survive up to four hours in that temperature if something holds him up. If the boat rolls or flips over, the men in the wheelhouse are the first to drown. Their experience is exactly like Hazard's except that they don't make it out of the wheelhouse to a life raft; they inhale and that's it. After that the water rises up the companionway, flooding the galley and berths, and then starts up the inverted engine room hatch. It may well be pouring in the aft door and the fish hatch, too, if either failed during the sinking. If the boat is hull-up and there are men in the engine room, they are the last to die. They're in absolute darkness, under a landslide of tools and gear, the water rising up the companionway and the roar of the waves probably very muted through the hull. If the water takes long enough, they might attempt to escape on a lungful of air—down the companionway, along the hall, through the aft door and out from under the boat—but they don't make it. It's too

James Mitchell's painting "A Winter's Gale on the George's Bank" depicting fisherman much like those aboard the Andrea Gail.

far, they die trying. Or the water comes up so hard and fast that they can't even think. They're up to their waists and then their chests and then their chins and then there's no air at all. Just what's in their lungs, a minute's worth or so.

The instinct not to breathe underwater is so strong that it overcomes the agony of running out of air. No matter how desperate the drowning person is, he doesn't inhale until he's on the verge of losing consciousness. At that point there's so much carbon dioxide in the blood, and so little oxygen, that chemical sensors in the brain trigger an involuntary breath whether he's underwater or not. That is called the "break point"; laboratory experiments have shown the break point to come after eighty-seven seconds. It's a sort of neurological optimism, as if the body were saying, *Holding our breath is killing us, and breathing in might not kill us, so we might as well breathe in.* If the person hyperventilates first—as free divers do, and as a frantic person might— the break point comes as late as 140 seconds. Hyperventilation initially flushes carbon dioxide out of the system, so it takes that much longer to climb back up to critical levels.

Until the break point, a drowning person is said to be undergoing "voluntary apnea," choosing not to breathe. Lack of oxygen to the brain causes a sensation of darkness closing in from all sides, as in a camera aperture stopping down. The panic of a drowning person is mixed with an odd incredulity that this is actually happening. Having never done it before, the body—and the mind—do not know how to die gracefully. The process is filled with desperation and awkwardness. "So *this* is drowning," a drowning person might think. "So *this* is how my life finally ends."

Along with the disbelief is an overwhelming sense of being wrenched from life at the most banal, inopportune moment imaginable. "I can't die, I have tickets to next week's game," is not an impossible thought for someone who is drowning. The drowning person may even feel embarrassed, as if he's squandered a great fortune. He has an image of people shaking their heads over his dying so senselessly. The drowning person may feel as if it's the last, greatest act of stupidity of his life.

These thoughts shriek through the mind during the minute or so that it takes a panicked person to run out of air. When the first involuntary breath occurs most people are still conscious, which is unfortunate, because the only thing more unpleasant than running out of air is breathing in water. At that point the person goes from voluntary to involuntary apnea, and the drowning begins in earnest. A spasmodic breath drags water into the mouth and windpipe, and then one of two things happen. In about ten percent of people, water—anything— touching the vocal cords triggers an immediate contraction in the muscles around the larynx. In effect, the central nervous system judges something in the voice box to be more of a threat than low oxygen levels in the blood, and acts accordingly. This is called a laryngospasm. It's so powerful that it overcomes the breathing reflex and eventually suffocates the person. A person with laryngospasm drowns without any water in his lungs.

In the other ninety percent of people, water floods the lungs and ends any waning transfer of oxygen to the blood. The clock is running down now; half-conscious and enfeebled by oxygen depletion, the person is in no position to fight his way back up to the surface. The very process of drowning makes it harder and harder not to drown, an exponential disaster curve similar to that of a sinking boat.

WEBB CHILES

1900–

HOME BASE ▪ *New York, New York*

ACHIEVEMENTS UNDER SAIL ▪ *accomplished solo sailor and author of many books*

Webb Chiles is undoubtably one of the most remarkable sailors of the 20th century. Beginning in the 1970's, Chiles commenced a series of solo voyages around the world that is without parallel in history. He has written extensively about these passages and completes some spectacular voyages in a variety of boats and under extraordinary conditions.

His first trip began when he left San Diego in 1974 aboard his sloop *Egregious*. Thirty-seven feet in length and fast, *Egregious* was to be his home for two years; two of the most strenuous years ever spent by a human being. Although the yacht had been designed to the then current IOR racing rule, Chiles had it extensively modified in the building. He set sail heading south in an attempt to round Cape Horn, yet 20 days later both rigging and rudder were damaged, and he reluctantly headed downwind toward Tahiti for repairs. Again he set off, this time sailing east. Again, he sustained rigging damage. It was becoming evident that a stock boat, no matter how modified, had to be engineered with brute strength. Even more reluctantly, Chiles headed north, returning to San Diego for what he thought would be permanent repairs.

Finally, in October 1975, he headed south once again. In the 1970's very few sailors had voyaged past Cape Horn solo. Yet Chiles was not a publicity seeker. He was that rare breed that sets out to accomplish something for its own sake, to prove himself to himself alone. Three years earlier, Chichester's heroic venture had proven to the world that such a journey could be done and Chiles had a far faster and better balanced boat in which to try. But he lacked good luck.

On the third attempt he did round the Horn, in execrable weather, Force 12, hand steering the entire day that it took to pass the famous rock. After he rounded the Horn, the horrors of the sea befell him.

The hulk of *Egregious* had cracked. Near the keel, a crack appeared in the fiberglass, necessitating constant bailing. Very few sailors would have continued bailing literally tons of water every day, but Chiles was no ordinary sailor. He bailed for days on end, scooping up and dumping overboard about 7 tons of water each day. He battled on for weeks, ever in danger of sinking, until he finally reached Australia and safety. Then he slept.

Chiles' adventures didn't end there. He was, and is, a driven man. Some might call him crazy, but he has proved again and again that he is able to overcome the most monumental obstacles and carry on.

From 1978 until 1983, he attempted a circumnavigation in *Chidiock Tichborne*, a Drascombe Lugger. Eighteen feet long and open—that is with no deck or cabin—the Lugger is a seaworthy and well-built little boat, but hardly designed to cross oceans. Yet Chiles attempted just that. Luggers are surprisingly fast. Leaving from San Diego once again, he made it to the Marquesas in just over a month, and a month later was in Tahiti. His approach to

Tahiti made clear the problems of sailing an open boat, however. Just prior to reaching the passage through the reefs into the harbor at Papeete, a storm came up. *Chidiock* was swamped repeatedly by waves, even with just a scrap of sail up. Running off before 50 knot winds, she sped on but not before some scary moments. Soaked through, with little sleep, grabbing handfuls of cold food, Chiles was so exhausted that his navigation was off. He kept looking for the passage between Tahiti and Morea, but eventually found himself mistaking the two high parts of Tahiti for the desired open passage.

And then he was becalmed, just short of the harbor mouth. Avoiding a tow by inches, the wind finally picked up and Chiles thought he had it made. Unfortunately, a series of squalls descended upon him and his little ship, and for 35 hours he remained at the helm. Things were so bad that he realized that in 4 days sailing, he had sailed only 6 miles. Finally, he anchored in Papeete harbor, where he was greeted by a kind soul in a dinghy, who had rowed over to bring him a bowl of hot chili.

The hulk of Egregious *had cracked. Near the keel, a crack appeared in the fiberglass, necessitating constant bailing. Very few sailors would have continued bailing literally tons of water every day, but Chiles was no ordinary sailor. He bailed for days on end, scooping up and dumping overboard about 7 tons of water each day. He battled on for weeks, ever in danger of sinking, until he finally reached Australia and safety. Then he slept.*

From A Descent into the Maelstrom

BY EDGAR ALLEN POE

"Such a hurricane as then blew it is folly to attempt describing. The oldest seaman in Norway never experienced any thing like it. We had let our sails go by the run before it cleverly took us; but, at the first puff, both our masts went by the board if they had been sawed off—the mainmast taking with it my youngest brother, who had lashed himself to it for safety.

"Our boat was the lightest feather of a thing that ever sat upon water. It had a complete flush deck, with only a small hatch near the bow, and this hatch it had always been our custom to batten down when about to cross the Strom, by way of precaution against the chopping seas. But for this circumstance we should have foundered at once—for we lay entirely buried for some moments. How my elder brother escaped destruction I cannot say, for I never had an opportunity of ascertaining. For my part, as soon as I had let the foresail run, I threw myself flat on deck, with my feet against the narrow gunwale of the bow, and with my hands grasping a ring-bolt near the foot of the foremast. It was mere instinct that prompted me to do this—which was undoubtedly the very best thing I could have done—for I was too much flurried to think.

"For some moments we were completely deluged, as I say, and all this time I held my breath, and clung to the bolt. When I could stand it no longer I raised myself upon my knees, still keeping hold with my hands, and thus got my head clear. Presently our little boat gave herself a shake, just as a dog does in coming out of the water, and thus rid herself, in some measure, of the seas. I was now trying to get the better of the stupor that had come over me, and to collect my senses so as to see what was to be done, when I felt somebody grasp my arm. It was my elder brother, and my heart leaped for joy, for I had made sure that he was overboard—but the next moment all this joy was turned into horror—for he put his mouth close to my ear, and screamed out the word 'Moskoe-strom!'

"No one ever will know what my feelings were at that moment. I shook from head to foot as if I had had the most violent fit of the ague. I knew what he meant by that one word well enough—I knew what he wished to make me understand. With the wind that now drove us on, we were bound for the whirl of the Strom, and nothing could save us!

"You perceive that in crossing the Strom channel, we always went a long way up above the whirl, even in the calmest weather, and then had to wait and watch carefully for the slack—but now we were driving right upon the pool itself, and in such a hurricane as this! ...

"By this time the first fury of the tempest had spent itself, or perhaps we did not feel it so much, as we scudded before it, but at all events the seas, which at first had been kept down by the wind, and lay flat and frothing, now got up into absolute mountains. A singular change, too, had come over the heavens. Around in every direction it was still as black as pitch, but nearly overhead there burst out, all at once, a circular rift of clear sky—as clear as I ever saw—and of a deep bright blue—and through it there blazed forth the full moon with a lustre that I never before knew her to wear. She lit up every thing about us with the greatest distinctness—but, oh God, what a scene it was to light up! ...

"When a boat is well built, properly trimmed, and not deep laden, the waves in a strong gale, when she is going large, seem always to slip from beneath her—which appears very strange to a landsman—and this is what is called riding, in sea phrase.

"Well, so far we had ridden the swells very cleverly; but presently a gigantic sea happened to take us right under the counter, and bore us with it as it rose—up—up—as if into the sky. I would not have believed that any wave could rise so high. And then down we came with a sweep, a slide, and a plunge, that made me feel sick and dizzy, as if I was falling from some lofty mountain-top in a dream. But while we were up I had thrown a quick glance around—and that one glance was all sufficient. I saw our exact position in an instant. The Moskoe-strom whirlpool was about a quarter of a mile dead ahead—but no more like the every-day Moskoe-strom, than the whirl as you now see it, is like a mill-race. If I had not known where we were, and what we had to expect, I should not have recognised the place at all. As it was, I involuntarily closed my eyes in horror. The lids clenched themselves together as if in a spasm.

"It could not have been more than two minutes afterwards until we suddenly felt the waves subside, and were enveloped in foam. The boat made a sharp half turn to larboard, and then shot off in its new direction like a thunderbolt. At the same moment the roaring noise of the water was completely drowned in a kind of shrill shriek—such a sound as you might imagine given out by the water-pipes of many thousand steam-vessels, letting off their steam all together. We were now in the belt of surf that always surrounds the whirl; and I thought, of course, that another moment would plunge us into the abyss—down which we could only see indistinctly on account of the amazing velocity with which we were borne along. The boat did not seem to sink into the water at all, but to skim like an air-bubble upon the surface of the surge. Her starboard side was next the whirl, and on the larboard arose the world of ocean we had left. It stood like a huge writhing wall between us and the horizon.

"It may appear strange, but now, when we were in the very jaws of the gulf, I felt more composed than when we were only approaching it. Having made up my mind to hope no more, I got rid of a great deal of that terror

243

which unmanned me at first. I suppose it was despair that strung my nerves.

"It may look like boasting—but what I tell you is truth— I began to reflect how magnificent a thing it was to die in such a manner, and how foolish it was in me to think of so paltry a consideration as my own individual life, in view of so wonderful a manifestation of God's power. I do believe that I blushed with shame when this idea crossed my mind. After a little while I became possessed with the keenest curiosity about the whirl itself. I positively felt a wish to explore its depths, even at the sacrifice

"…I perceived that our boat was not the only object in the embrace of the whirl. Both above and below us were visible fragments of vessels, large masses of building timber and trunks of trees, with many smaller articles, such as pieces of house furniture, broken boxes, barrels and staves."

I was going to make; and my principal grief was that I should never be able to tell my old companions on shore about the mysteries I should see. These, no doubt, were singular fancies to occupy a man's mind in such extremity—and I have often thought since, that the revolutions of the boat around the pool might have rendered me a little light-headed.

"There was another circumstance which tended to restore my self-possession; and this was the cessation of the wind, which could not reach us in our present situation—for, as you saw yourself, the belt of surf is considerably lower than the general bed of the ocean, and this latter now towered above us, a high, black, mountainous ridge. If you have never been at sea in a heavy gale, you can form no idea of the confusion of mind occasioned by the wind and the spray together. They blind, deafen and strangle you,

and take away all power of action or reflection. But we were now, in a great measure, rid of these annoyances—just as death-condemned felons in prison are allowed petty indulgences, forbidden them while their doom is yet uncertain.

"How often we made the circuit of the belt it is impossible to say. We careered round and round for perhaps an hour, flying rather than floating, getting gradually more and more into the middle of the surge, and then nearer and nearer to its horrible inner edge. All this time I had never let go of the ring-bolt. My brother was at the stern, holding on to a large empty water-cask which had been securely lashed under the coop of the counter, and was the only thing on deck that had not been swept overboard when the gale first took us. As we approached the brink of the pit he let go his hold upon this, and made for the ring, from which, in the agony of his terror, he endeavored to force my hands, as it was not large enough to afford us both a secure grasp. I never felt deeper grief than when I saw him attempt this act—although I knew he was a madman when he did it—a raving maniac through sheer fright. I did not care, however, to contest the point with him. I thought it could make no difference whether either of us held on at all; so I let him have the bolt, and went astern to the cask. This there was no great difficulty in doing; for the smack flew round steadily enough, and upon an even keel—only swaying to and fro, with the immense sweeps and swelters of the whirl. Scarcely had I secured myself in my new position, when we gave a wild lurch to starboard, and rushed headlong into the abyss. I muttered a hurried prayer to God, and thought all was over.

"As I felt the sickening sweep of the descent, I had instinctively tightened my hold upon the barrel, and closed my eyes. For some seconds I dared not open them—while I expected instant destruction, and wondered that I was not already in my death-struggles with the water. But moment after moment elapsed. I still lived. The sense of falling had ceased; and the motion of the vessel seemed much as it had been before while in the belt of foam, with the exception that she now lay more along. I took courage and looked once again upon the scene.

"Never shall I forget the sensations of awe, horror, and admiration with which I gazed about me. The boat appeared to be hanging,

as if by magic, midway down, upon the interior surface of a funnel vast in circumference, prodigious in depth, and whose perfectly smooth sides might have been mistaken for ebony, but for the bewildering rapidity with which they spun around, and for the gleaming and ghastly radiance they shot forth, as the rays of the full moon, from that circular rift amid the clouds which I have already described, streamed in a flood of golden glory along the black walls, and far away down into the inmost recesses of the abyss.

"At first I was too much confused to observe anything accurately. The general burst of terrific grandeur was all that I beheld. When I recovered myself a little, however, my gaze fell instinctively downward. In this direction I was able to obtain an unobstructed view, from the manner in which the smack hung on the inclined surface of the pool. She was quite upon an even keel—that is to say, her deck lay in a plane parallel with that of the water—but this latter sloped at an angle of more than forty-five degrees, so that we seemed to be lying upon our beam-ends. I could not help observing, nevertheless, that I had scarcely more difficulty in maintaining my hold and footing in this situation, than if we had been upon a dead level; and this, I suppose, was owing to the speed at which we revolved.

"The rays of the moon seemed to search the very bottom of the profound gulf; but still I could make out nothing distinctly, on account of a thick mist in which everything there was enveloped, and over which there hung a magnificent rainbow, like that narrow and tottering bridge which Mussulmen say is the only pathway between Time and Eternity. This mist, or spray, was no doubt occasioned by the clashing of the great walls of the funnel, as they all met together at the bottom—but the yell that went up to the Heavens from out of mist, I dare not attempt to describe.

"Our first slide into the abyss itself, from the belt of foam above, had carried us to a great distance down the slope; but our farther descent was by no means proportionate. Round and round we swept—not with any uniform movement—but in dizzying swings and jerks, that sent us sometimes only a few hundred feet—sometimes nearly the complete circuit of the whirl. Our progress downward, at each revolution, was slow, but very perceptible.

"Looking about me upon the wide waste of liquid ebony on which we were thus borne, I perceived that our boat was not the only object in the embrace of the whirl. Both above and below us were visible fragments of vessels, large masses of building timber and trunks of trees, with many smaller articles, such as pieces of house furniture, broken boxes, barrels and staves. I have already described the unnatural curiosity which had taken the place of my original terrors. It appeared to grow upon me as I drew nearer and nearer to my dreadful doom. I now began to watch, with a strange interest, the numerous things that floated in our company. I must have been delirious—for I even sought amusement in speculating upon the relative velocities of their several descents toward the foam below. 'This fir tree,' I found myself at one time saying, 'will certainly be the next thing that takes the awful plunge and disappears,'—and then I was disappointed to find that the wreck of a Dutch merchant ship overtook it and went down before. At length, after making several guesses of this nature, and being deceived in all—this fact—the fact of my invariable miscalculation, set me upon a train of reflection that made my limbs again tremble, and my heart beat heavily once more.

"It was not a new terror that thus affected me, but the dawn of a more exciting hope. This hope arose partly from memory, and partly from present observation. I called to mind the great variety of buoyant matter that strewed the coast of Lofoden, having been absorbed and then thrown forth by the Moskoe-strom. By far the greater number of the articles were shattered in the most extraordinary way—so chafed and roughened as to have the appearance of being stuck full of splinters—but then I distinctly recollected that there were some of them which were not disfigured at all. Now I could not account for this difference except by supposing that the roughened fragments were the only ones which had been completely absorbed—that the others had entered the whirl at so late a period of the tide, or, from some reason, had descended so slowly after entering, that they did not reach the bottom before the turn of the flood came, or of the ebb,

as the case might be. I conceived it possible, in either instance, that they might thus be whirled up again to the level of the ocean, without undergoing the fate of those which had been drawn in more early or absorbed more rapidly. I made, also, three important observations. The first was, that as a general rule, the larger the bodies were, the more rapid their descent;—the second, that, between two masses of equal extent, the one spherical, and the other of any other shape, the superiority in speed of descent was with the sphere;—the third, that, between two masses of equal size, the one cylindrical, and the other of any other shape, the cylinder was absorbed the more slowly.

Since my escape, I have had several conversations on this subject with an old school-master of the district; and it was from him that I learned the use of the words 'cylinder' and 'sphere.' He explained to me—although I have forgotten the explanation—how what I observed was, in fact, the natural consequence of the forms of the floating fragments—and showed me how it happened that a cylinder, swimming in a vortex, offered more resistance to its suction, and was drawn in with greater difficulty than an equally bulky body, of any form whatever. *

"There was one startling circumstance which went a great way in enforcing these observations, and rendering me anxious to turn them to account, and this was that, at every revolution, we passed something like a barrel, or else the broken yard or the mast of a vessel, while many of these things, which had been on our level when I first opened my eyes upon the wonders of the whirlpool, were now high up above us, and seemed to have moved but little from their original station.

"I no longer hesitated what to do. I resolved to lash myself securely to the water cask upon which I now held, to cut it loose from the counter, and to throw myself with it into the that came near us, and did everything in my power to make him understand what I was about to do. I thought at length that he comprehended my design— but, whether this was the case or not, he shook his head despairingly, and refused to move from his station by the ring-bolt. It was impossible to force him; the emergency admitted no delay; and so, with a bitter struggle, I resigned him to his fate, fastened myself to the cask by means of

the lashings which secured it to the counter, and precipitated myself with it into the sea, without another moment's hesitation.

"The result was precisely what I had hoped it might be. As it is myself who now tell you this tale—as you see that I did escape—and as you are already in possession of the mode in which this escape was effected, and must therefore anticipate all that I have farther to say—I will bring my story quickly to conclusion. It might have been an hour, or thereabout, after my quitting the smack, when, having descended to a vast distance beneath me, it made three or four wild gyrations in rapid succession, and, bearing my loved brother with it, plunged headlong, at once and forever, into the chaos of foam below. The barrel to which I was attached sunk very little farther than half the distance between the bottom of the gulf and the spot at which I leaped overboard, before a great change took place in the character of the whirlpool. The slope of the sides of the vast funnel became momently less and less steep. The gyrations of the whirl grew, gradually, less and less violent. By degrees, the froth and the rainbow disappeared, and the bottom of the gulf seemed slowly to uprise. The sky was clear, the winds had gone down, and the full moon was setting radiantly in the west, when I found myself on the surface of the ocean, in full view of the shores of Lofoden, and above the spot where the pool of the Moskoe-strom had been. It was the hour of the slack—but the sea still heaved in mountainous waves from the effects of the hurricane. I was borne violently into the channel of the Strom and in a few minutes, was hurried down the coast into the 'grounds' of the fishermen. A boat picked me up— exhausted from fatigue—and (now that the danger was removed) speechless from the memory of its horror. Those who drew me on board were my old mates and dally companions—but they knew me no more than they would have known a traveller from the spirit-land. My hair, which had been raven-black the day before, was as white as you see it now. They say too that the whole expression of my countenance had changed. I told them my story— they did not believe it. I now tell it to you—and I can scarcely expect you to put more faith in it than did the merry fishermen of Lofoden.

Sirens & Serpents

Jonah and the Whale in a 1577 painting by Adam Willaerts.

Since humans first looked upon the waters, sprites and serpents, mermaids and great sea creatures, gods and angels have visited the imagination. In literature, art, and music, these phenomena and myths have shaped much thought about the seas. The seas have been the most uncharted area of the earth for the longest period—a fact that has helped retain their mysterious legends. Even today, with oceanographers, geologists, marine biologists, and ecologists working around the clock to unravel the mysteries of the deep, the seas are the least explored part of the planet and the most difficult to explore.

For centuries, people thought the depths of the oceans dead, devoid of recognizable life. After all, we tend to extrapolate from our own experience, and even with the advent of modern science in the seventeenth century, observation was only possible in the thinnest top layer of the oceans. Tales of sea serpents, mermaids, giant squid, ghost ships and areas of the ocean where strange navigational anomalies abounded were passed on by seamen to a largely credulous world.

The lost continent of Atlantis has fascinated for centuries. First described by Plato in Timaeus and Critias as having been destroyed 10,000 years earlier, it supposedly lay west of the Straits of Gibraltar in the Atlantic. This great civilization had, according to the Greek philosopher, conquered parts of the West as far as Libya and Egypt. But when the Atlanteans attempted to invade Greece, they were beat back by superior Greek military might.

Shortly thereafter, "there occurred violent earthquakes and floods; in a single day and night of misfortune all your warlike men in a body sank into the earth, and the island of Atlantis in a like manner disappeared in the depths of the sea" (Timaeus).

The legend Plato related was not original; Egyptian antecedents were similar. A more contemporary event (only 1,000 years before Plato wrote), the eruption of a gigantic volcano on the island of Santorini, may have been another basis for the legend. These stories and others assumed that oral tales are historically accurate. Some, like Homer's epics were indeed true, and have been proven so by archaeological research. Others, such as the fantastical tales Herodotus told, were repetition of hearsay and tall tales.

Atlantis was the loadstone for centuries. Men were always claiming to have discovered its whereabouts, or finding bits of columns and vessels from Atlantis, and thousands believed.

Lost worlds of great wealth have a long history…witness the searches for Eldorado and King Solomon's mines. Hundreds of books, plays, films and expeditions have been succored by dreams of gold and wealth. They all remained dreams.

The Flying Dutchman is one of Richard Wagner's earlier great operas. It is also an enduring romantic legend. Many versions

Above: A Greek krater depicts the sirens luring a ship to its doom.

Below: Artists could, of course, represent the most fantastical of fantasies. Here we see a ship being seized by a giant squid. Although giant squid have been proved to exist, they reside in very deep waters and rarely are seen by mariners.

We are as near to heaven

by sea as by land.

—*Sir Humphrey Gilbert*

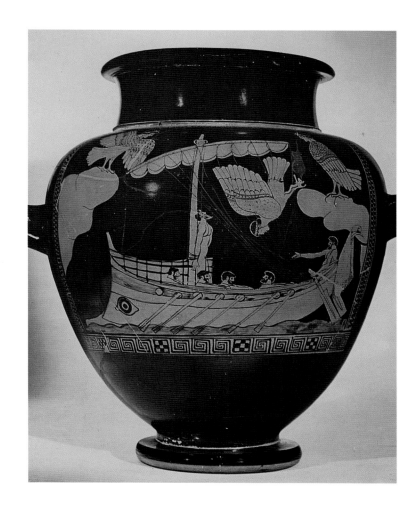

exist, but all have a ghost ship sailing forever, usually off the Cape of Good Hope at the southern tip of Africa. Supposedly declaring an oath against God, the captain, a Dutch mariner, was forever condemned to sail into a ruthless wind. Another version has the captain sailing aimlessly in the North Sea, forever throwing dice with the Devil in a contest for his soul.

The Bermuda Triangle, or Devil's Triangle, is more modern in concept. Columbus noted that his compass went wild in this area‹and it is one of the few places on earth where a magnetic compass points to true north, not magnetic north. The variation between the two must be compensated for, and this difference, if unknown, can cause grave danger to the mariner. The Gulf Stream current runs through the area as well. Interestingly, a similar area is located off the east coast of Japan, called the Devil's Sea by Japanese and Filipino fishermen.

Nevertheless, the Bermuda Triangle, by all scientific standards, is a myth. Between the often violent turbulence of the Gulf Stream and the generally unstable weather patterns of the area, sudden thunderstorms and water spouts can pose serious threats to mariners and airmen. The popular conception of the Bermuda Triangle stems from an article in Argosy magazine in 1968, "The Spreading Mystery of the Bermuda Triangle."

Certainly, unexplained disappearances have occurred. In 1945, a squadron of five Navy planes vanished in a severe storm while on a training mission. Authors Vincent Gaddis and Charles Berlitz went to great pains to inflate this incident into a cult of believers in inherent

Above: Sea serpent and the topsail schooner La Sally off the coast of Long Island, New York. Monsters like this were often spotted but never found. It makes one pause.

Below: A mermaid and other "interesting" fishes. Mermaids probably derived from the legend of the sirens in Greek mythology. They could be both dangerous and benign, tempting ships to disaster on rocks, or rescuing men from shipwreck.

Above: Sea monsters off the coast of Sweden, from a 1592 print. The facility and imagination show scant attention to biology but provide a colorful and scarifying taste of the unknown.

Below: Mermaid and manatee cavort under water.

Dolphins appear throughout literature as friends to man. Stories abound of life saving feats by these mammals. We now know that dolphins and porpoises are voracious hunters, but they show remarkable intelligence, and have aided mariners in distress, leading them to safety when lost or in a storm.

evil, extraterrestrials, sea monsters, and other highly dubious phenomena. Some started to believe that some mysterious force was at work, despite perfectly natural explanations, and the fact that the majority of these "unexplained" disasters were actually outside the so-called "Bermuda Triangle."

A lot of storms do take place within the area of the Bermuda Triangle. This can be explained by a combination of factors: the

Above: The strait of Messina, from which the myth of Scylla and Charybdis sprang forth.

Below: Headfish of approximately 500 pounds, spotted east of Hokkaido, Japan. Such fish could easily inflame the imagination of early mariners.

prevailing winds, the passage of hurricanes from West Africa west to the Caribbean and the East Coast of the United States, and the turbulence wrought by the Gulf Stream. Anyone who has ever gone from Florida to the Bahamas in a small boat knows the jolt experienced when entering the Stream. All currents move around, and the sheer unpredictability of the Gulf Stream has caused plenty of trouble. Water temperatures rise by several degrees. The water can be very rough (after all the Stream moves at a good clip) and in wind against current situations, it can be downright dangerous.

Mermaids and mermen, women and men with the tails of fish from their waists down are derived from ancient water sprites and minor deities.

Mermaids—more prevalent in lore than mermen—were believed by many to be enchanted. The Sirens of the Odyssey are precedents. Their strange and irresistible song from rock perches caused ships to sail toward them to their deaths. Supposedly, in 1403 a mermaid was found stranded on the foreshore of West Friesland. She was, as legend tells us, unable to speak, but was taught to kneel before the crucifix and to spin wool. In fact, the mermaid became a metaphor used by Chaucer and Shakespeare for a beautiful but dangerous woman. Later, Hans Christian Anderson immortalized the creature in The Little Mermaid. Operas, films and novels (especially those written by men) have used the symbol of femininity with glee.

In the eighteenth and nineteenth centuries, sailors came to believe in these sea creatures. Mermaids appear everywhere in the lore of the sea. They have saved sailors lost overboard (as have dolphins), toyed with the imagination and caused madness. The modern legend has been amusingly continued through films such as Splash, in which a mermaid comes to shore with legs, a gift from her gods, and finds a mate after all sorts of travails at the hands of an obnoxious and somewhat nutty scientist.

Sea serpents are another wonder of the deep, and have some basis in fact. Giant squid, which in tradition have risen from the deep and crushed ships in mid-ocean are not such a fantasy anymore. Specimens ranging up to fifty feet and more have been brought up in deep sea nets. When the oceans were unknown, these creatures and others were often spotted by sea-

The Sea

BY LEWIS CARROLL (CHARLES LUTWIDGE DODGSON)

There are certain things -a spider, a ghost,
The income-tax, gout, an umbrella for three -
That I hate, but the thing that I hate the most
Is a thing they call the SEA.

Pour some salt water over the floor -
Ugly I'm sure you'll allow it to be:
Suppose it extended a mile or more,
That's very like the SEA.

Beat a dog till it howls outright -
Cruel, but all very well for a spree;
Suppose that one did so day and night,
That would be like the SEA.

I had a vision of nursery-maids;
Tens of thousands passed by me -
All leading children with wooden spades,
And this was by the SEA.

Who invented those spades of wood?
Who was it cut them out of the tree?
None, I think, but an idiot could -
Or one that loved the SEA.

It is pleasant and dreamy, no doubt, to float
With `thoughts as boundless, and souls as free';
But suppose you are very unwell in a boat,
How do you like the SEA.

There is an insect that people avoid
(Whence is derived the verb `to flee')
Where have you been by it most annoyed?
In lodgings by the SEA.

If you like coffee with sand for dregs,
A decided hint of salt in your tea,
And a fishy taste in the very eggs -
By all means choose the SEA.

And if, with these dainties to drink and eat,
You prefer not a vestige of grass or tree,
And a chronic state of wet in your feet,
Then I recommend the SEA.

For I have friends who dwell by the coast,
Pleasant friends they are to me!
It is when I'm with them I wonder most
That anyone likes the SEA.

They take me a walk: though tired and stiff,
To climb the heights I madly agree:
And, after a tumble or so from the cliff,
They kindly suggest the SEA.

I try the rocks, and I think it cool
That they laugh with such an excess of glee,
As I heavily slip into every pool,
That skirts the cold, cold SEA.

men. In their ignorance, the seamen of those distant days conjured up a bevy of serpents, all probably based on the dragons of earthbound myth and saga—serpents that swallowed ships, devoured crews and disappeared back into the murky deep. Going back to the story of Jonah and the whale, the sheer enormity of these beasts was enough to cause wool-gathering. Despite the relatively benign nature of sea life, size tends to beget horror.

Melville's Moby Dick, the great white whale, was the personification of evil, and of the strength and mysteries of nature. The short history of whaling, spanning only a few centuries, reinforced this concept. What was man, after all, compared to the might of these giants?

Even today, expeditions set forth to discover the Loch Ness monster, that wonderful creature supposedly from the oceans, now landlocked in a deep, fresh water

lake in the north of Scotland. Over the years, dozens of people have claimed to see this multi-humped, snake-like creature swimming across the loch. Even several pictures of the monster exist—all blurry, in bad light conditions, or in terrible weather. Despite soundings, sonar scans and all the myriad devices of modern science, no one has ever found the monster. It is a creature for true believers, and myth dies hard.

From The Little Mermaid

BY HANS CHRISTIAN ANDERSEN

Far out in the ocean, where the water is as blue as the prettiest cornflower, and as clear as crystal, it is very, very deep; so deep, indeed, that no cable could fathom it: many church steeples, piled one upon another, would not reach from the ground beneath to the surface of the water above.

There dwell the Sea King and his subjects. We must not imagine that there is nothing at the bottom of the sea but bare yellow sand. No, indeed; the most singular flowers and plants grow there; the leaves and stems of which are so pliant, that the slightest agitation of the water causes them to stir as if they had life. Fishes, both large and small, glide between the branches, as birds fly among the trees here upon land. In the deepest spot of all, stands the castle of the Sea King. Its walls are built of coral, and the long, gothic windows are of the clearest amber. The roof is formed of shells, that open and close as the water flows over them. Their appearance is very beautiful, for in each lies a glittering pearl, which would be fit for the diadem of a queen.

The Sea King had been a widower for many years, and his aged mother kept house for him. She was a very wise woman, and exceedingly proud of her high birth; on that account she wore twelve oysters on her tail; while others, also of high rank, were only allowed to wear six. She was, however, deserving of very great praise, especially for her care of the little sea-princesses, her grand-daughters. They were six beautiful children; but the youngest was the prettiest of them all; her skin was as clear and delicate as a rose-leaf, and her eyes as blue as the deepest sea; but, like all the others, she had no feet, and her body ended in a fish's tail...

The little mermaid sang more sweetly than them all. The whole court applauded her with hands and tails; and for a moment her heart felt quite gay, for she knew she had the loveliest voice of any on earth or in the sea. But she soon thought again of the world above her, for she could not forget the charming prince, nor her sorrow that she had not an immortal soul like his; therefore she crept away silently out of her father's palace, and while everything within was gladness and song, she sat in her own little garden sorrowful and alone. Then she heard the bugle sounding through the water, and thought— "He is certainly sailing above, he on whom my wishes depend, and in whose hands I should like to place the happiness of my life. I will venture all for him, and to win an immortal soul, while my sisters are dancing in my father's palace, I will go to the sea witch, of whom I have always been so much afraid, but she can give me counsel and help."

And then the little mermaid went out from her garden, and took the road to the foaming whirlpools, behind which the sorceress lived. She had never been that way before: neither flowers nor grass grew there; nothing but bare, gray, sandy ground stretched out to the whirlpool, where the water, like foaming mill-wheels, whirled round everything that it seized, and cast it into the fathomless deep. Through the midst of these crushing whirlpools the little mermaid was obliged to pass, to reach the dominions of the sea witch; and also for a long distance the only road lay right across a quantity of warm, bubbling mire, called by the witch her turfmoor. Beyond this stood her house, in the centre of a strange forest, in which all the trees and flowers were polypi, half animals and half plants; they looked like serpents with a hundred heads growing out of the ground. The branches were long slimy arms, with fingers like flexible worms, moving limb after limb from the root to the top. All that could be reached in the sea they seized upon, and held fast, so that it never escaped from their clutches. The little mermaid was so alarmed at what she saw, that she stood still, and her heart beat with fear, and she was very nearly turning back; but she thought of the prince, and of the human soul for which she longed, and her courage returned. She fastened her long flowing hair round her head, so that the polypi might not seize hold of it. She laid her hands together across her bosom, and then she darted forward as a fish shoots through the water, between the supple arms and fingers of the ugly polypi, which were stretched out on each side of her. She saw that each held in its grasp something it had seized with its numerous little arms, as if they were iron bands. The white skeletons of human beings who had perished at sea, and had sunk down into the deep waters, skeletons of land animals, oars, rudders, and chests of ships were lying tightly grasped by their clinging arms; even a little mermaid, whom they had caught and strangled; and this seemed the most shocking of all to the little princess.

She now came to a space of marshy ground in the wood, where large, fat water-snakes were rolling in the mire, and showing their ugly, drab-colored bodies. In the midst of this spot stood a house, built with the bones of shipwrecked human beings. There sat the sea witch, allowing a toad to eat from her mouth, just as people sometimes feed a canary with a piece of sugar. She called the ugly water-snakes her little chickens, and allowed them to crawl all over her bosom.

"I know what you want," said the sea witch; "it is very stupid of you, but you shall have your way, and it will bring you to sorrow, my pretty princess. You want to get rid of your fish's tail, and to have two supports instead of it, like human beings on earth, so that the young prince may fall in love with you, and that you may have an immortal soul." And then the witch laughed so loud and disgustingly, that the toad and the snakes fell to the ground, and lay there wriggling about. "You are but just in time," said the witch; "for after sunrise tomorrow I should not be able to help you till the end of another year. I will prepare a draught for you, with which you must swim to land tomorrow before sunrise, and sit down on the shore and drink it. Your tail will then disappear, and shrink up into what mankind calls legs, and you will feel great pain, as if a sword were passing through you. But all who see you will say that you are the prettiest little human being they ever saw. You will still have the same floating gracefulness of movement, and no dancer will ever tread so lightly; but at every step you take it will feel as if you were treading upon sharp knives, and that the blood must flow. If you will bear all this, I will help you."

``Yes, I will," said the little princess in a trembling voice, as she thought of the prince and the immortal soul.

"But think again," said the witch; "for when once your shape has become like a human being, you can no more be a mermaid. You will never return through the water to your sisters, or to your father's palace again; and if you do not win the love of the prince, so that he is willing to forget his father and mother for your sake, and to love you with his whole soul, and allow the priest to join your hands that you may be man and wife, then you will never have an immortal soul. The first morning after he marries another your heart will break, and you will become foam on the crest of the waves."

"I will do it," said the little mermaid, and she became pale as death.

"But I must be paid also," said the witch, "and it is not a trifle that I ask. You have the sweetest voice of any who dwell here in the depths of the sea, and you believe that you will be able to charm the prince with it also, but

this voice you must give to me; the best thing you possess will I have for the price of my draught. My own blood must be mixed with it, that it may be as sharp as a two-edged sword."

"But if you take away my voice," said the little mermaid, "what is left for me?"

"Your beautiful form, your graceful walk, and your expressive eyes; surely with these you can enchain a man's heart. Well, have you lost your courage? Put out your little tongue that I may cut it off as my payment; then you shall have the powerful draught."

"It shall be," said the little mermaid.

Then the witch placed her cauldron on the fire, to prepare the magic draught.

"Cleanliness is a good thing," said she, scouring the vessel with snakes, which she had tied together in a large knot; then she pricked herself in the breast, and let the black blood drop into it. The steam that rose formed itself into such horrible shapes that no one could look at them without fear. Every moment the witch threw something else into the vessel, and when it began to boil, the sound was like the weeping of a crocodile. When at last the magic draught was ready, it looked like the clearest water.

"There it is for you," said the witch. Then she cut off the mermaid's tongue, so that she became dumb, and would never again speak or sing. "If the polypi should seize hold of you as you return through the wood," said the witch, "throw over them a few drops of the potion, and their fingers will be torn into a thousand pieces." But the little mermaid had no occasion to do this, for the polypi sprang back in terror when they caught sight of the glittering draught, which shone in her hand like a twinkling star.

So she passed quickly through the wood and the marsh, and between the rushing whirlpools. She saw that in her father's palace the torches in the ballroom were extinguished, and all within asleep; but she did not venture to go in to them, for now she was dumb and going to leave them forever, she felt as if her heart would break. She stole into the garden, took a flower from the flower-beds of each of her sisters, kissed her hand a thousand times towards the palace, and then rose up

This famous statue by Edvard Eriksen of Denmark's national symbol, The Little Mermaid, looks to the sea from her perch in Copenhagen.

through the dark blue waters. The sun had not risen when she came in sight of the prince's palace, and approached the beautiful marble steps, but the moon shone clear and bright. Then the little mermaid drank the magic draught, and it seemed as if a two-edged sword went through her delicate body: she fell into a swoon, and lay like one dead. When the sun arose and shone over the sea, she recovered, and felt a sharp pain; but just before her stood the handsome young prince.

He fixed his coal-black eyes upon her so earnestly that she cast down her own, and then became aware that her fish's tail was gone, and that she had as pretty a pair of white legs and tiny feet as any little maiden could have; but she had no clothes, so she wrapped herself in her long, thick hair.

The prince asked her who she was, and where she came from, and she looked at him mildly and sorrowfully with her deep blue eyes; but she could not speak. Every step she took was as the witch had said it would be, she felt as if treading upon the points of needles or sharp knives; but she bore it willingly, and stepped as lightly by the prince's side as a soap-bubble, so that he and all who saw her wondered at her graceful-swaying movements.

She was very soon arrayed in costly robes of silk and muslin, and was the most beautiful creature in the palace; but she was dumb, and could neither speak nor sing.

Aweigh, Santy Ano

These shanties were probably of West Indian origin. This probably started out as a pump shanty, but was also used as windlass shanties. As iron ships with pumps took the place of wooden ships it were adapted for capstan work. The refrain varies widely. There are patterns of the tune for the Gold Rush, Leaving Liverpool, Leaving New York, The Fishes and The Mail.

From Boston Town we're bound away,
Heave aweigh (Heave aweigh!) Santy Ano.
Around Cape Horn to Frisco Bay,
We're bound for Californi-o.

Refrain:
So Heave her up and away we'll go,
Heave aweigh (Heave aweigh!) Santy Ano.
Heave her up and away we'll go,
We're bound for Californi-o.

She's a fast clipper ship and a bully crew,
Heave aweigh (Heave aweigh!) Santy Ano.
A down-east Yankee for her captain, too.
We're bound for Californi-o.

Refrain

Back in the days of Forty-nine,
Heave aweigh (Heave aweigh!) Santy Ano.
Those were the days of the good old times,
Way out in Californi-o.

Refrain

When I leave ship I'll settle down
Heave aweigh (Heave aweigh!) Santy Ano
I'll marry a girl named Sally Brown
Way out in Californi-o

Refrain

There's plenty of gold, so I've been told,
Heave aweigh (Heave aweigh!) Santy Ano.
Plenty of gold so I've been told
Way out in Californi-o

Refrain

Storm Along

This shanty was originally sung around the pumps and later used as a capstan shanty. According to Hugill there is no doubt it is of African-American origin. It dates to at least the 1830s and 40s.

Hugill lists several shanties of the "Stormalong family;" *Mister Stormalong, Stormy Along, John, Stormalong, Boys, Stormy, Way Stormalong John, Walk Me Along, Johnny (Storm and Blow)* and *Yankee John, Stormalong.* Most of these were halyard shanties, but *Mister Stormalong* and *Storm Along, John* were also sung at the pumps. In most of the Stormalong songs there was a pattern of praising the dead seaman or praising the son of the dead seaman.

Stormie's gone, the good old man,
To my aye storm a-long!
Oh, Stormie's gone, that good old man;
Aye, aye, aye, Mister Storm a-long.

They dug his grave with a silver spade,
To my aye storm a-long!
The shroud of finest silk was made;
Aye, aye, aye, Mister Storm a-long.

They lowered him with a golden chain,
To my aye storm a-long!
Their eyes all dim with more than rain;
Aye, aye, aye, Mister Storm a-long.

He was a sailor bold and true,
To my aye storm a-long!
A good old skipper to his crew;
Aye, aye, aye, Mister Storm a-long.

Of captain brave, he was the best,
To my aye storm a-long!
But now he's gone and is at rest;
Aye, aye, aye, Mister Storm a-long.

He lies low in an earthen bed,
To my aye storm a-long!
Our hearts are sore our eyes are red;
Aye, aye, aye, Mister Storm a-long.

He's moored at least and furled his sail,
To my aye storm a-long!
No danger now from wreck or gale;
Aye, aye, aye, Mister Storm a-long.

Old Storm has heard the angel call,
To my aye storm a-long!
So sing his dirge, now one and all;
Aye, aye, aye, Mister Storm a-long.

Homeward Bound

This shanty was one of the most popular homeward-bound shanties. It was sung at the windlass or at the capstan. There are numerous versions of the shanty. It is also known as *Goodbye, Fare-ye-well* or *Goodbye and Farewell*.

Our anchor we'll weigh,
And our sails we will set.
Goodbye, fare-ye-well,
Goodbye, fare-ye-well.
The friends we are leaving,
We leave with regret,
Hurrah, my boys, we're homeward bound.

We're homeward bound,
Oh joyful sound!
Goodbye, fare-ye-well,
Goodbye, fare-ye-well.
Come rally the capstan,
And run quick around.
Hurrah, my boys, we're homeward bound.

We're homeward bound
We'd have you know
Goodbye, fare-ye-well,
Goodbye, fare-ye-well.
And over the water
To England must go,
Hurrah, my boys, we're homeward bound.

Heave with a will,
And heave long and strong,
Goodbye, fare-ye-well,
Goodbye, fare-ye-well.
Sing a good chorus
For 'tis a good song.
Hurrah, my boys, we're homeward bound.

Hurrah! that good run
Brought the anchor a-weigh,
Goodbye, fare-ye-well,
Goodbye, fare-ye-well.
She's up to the hawse,
Sing before we belay.
Hurrah, my boys, we're homeward bound.

'We're homeward bound,'
You've heard us say,
Goodbye, fare-ye-well,

Goodbye, fare-ye-well.
Hook on the cat fall then,
And rut her away.
Hurrah, my boys, we're homeward bound.

The Bay of Biscay

There are two different tunes named *The Bay of Biscay*, though interestingly, both concern shipwrecks. This, the better known version, was written by Irishman Andrew Cherry (1762-1812).

The other "Bay of Biscay" tune is also known as Ye Gentlemen of England and concerns a ship caught in a storm in the Bay of Biscay. Though the ship was heavily damaged, it made its way to Gibraltar.

The Bay of Biscay is an inlet of the Atlantic Ocean in southeastern Europe, bounded by France and Spain. The coastline varies from rocky cliffs to sandy beaches. Winds and currents make navigation difficult.

Loud roars the dreadful thunder,
The rain a deluge show'rs;
The clouds are rent asunder
By lightning's vivid pow'rs;
The night was drear and dark;
Our poor devoted bark
Till next day, there she lay,
In the Bay of Biscay, O!

Now dash'd upon the billow
Her op'ning timbers creak;
Each fears a wat'ry pillow,
None stop the dreadful leak:
To cling to slipp'ry shrouds
Each breathless seaman crowds,
As she lay, till next day,
In the Bay of Biscay, O!

At length the wished for tomorrow
Breaks thro' the hazy sky;
Absorb'd in silent sorrow,
Each heaves a bitter sigh:
The dismal wreck to view
Strikes horror to the crew,
As she lay, on that day,
In the Bay of Biscay, O!

Her yielding timbers sever,
Her pitchy seams are rent;
When heav'n, all bounteous ever,
Its boundless mercy sent:
A sail in sight appears,
We hail her with three cheer!
Now we sail, with the gale,
From the Bay of Biscay, O!

The Bay of Biscay, O!

There are two different tunes named The Bay of Biscay, though interestingly, both concern shipwrecks. This tune is the older of the two. It is based on a tune by John Phillips, circa 1660 *Neptune's Raging Fury*. This tune is also known as *Ye Gentlemen of England*.

The Bay of Biscay is an inlet of the Atlantic Ocean in southeastern Europe, bounded by France and Spain. The coastline varies from rocky cliffs to sandy beaches. Winds and currents make navigation difficult.

Ye gentlemen of England who live home at your ease,
It's little do you think of the dangers of the seas;
When we receive our orders we are obliged to go
On the main to proud Spain where
    the stormy winds do blow.

Was on the fourth of August from Spithead we set sail
With *Ramely* and Company blest with a pleasant gale;
We sailed along together in the Bay of Biscay, Oh,
Where a dreadful storm it did arise and
    the stormy wind did blow.

The *Ramely* she left us, she could no longer stay
And by distress of weather from us she bore away;
When she arrived at Gibraltar they told the people so
How they thought we were all lost at the Bay of Biscay, Oh.

Kind heaven did protect her, it was not quite so bad,
First we lost our foremast, and then we lost our flag.
And then we lost our mainmast, one of our guns also
And the men, we lost ten on the Bay of Biscay, Oh.

When the mainmast started, it gave a dreadful stroke,
In our starboard quarter, a large hole did it broke.
Then the seas came battering in, our guns soon overflow
So boldly she plowed it on the Bay of Biscay, Oh.

The night being dark and dreary, at twelve o'clock that night
Our captain in the forecastle he was killed then outright.
The ring upon his finger in pieces burst in two
There he laid until next day when we overboard him threw.

The storm it being abated, we rigged up jury mast
And steered it for Gibraltar, where we arrived at last
They said it was a dismal sight as ever they did know
We forced to drink wine and drowned all our woe.

Blow the Man Down

Blow the Man Down originated in the Western Ocean sailing ships. The tune could have originated with German emigrants, but it is more likely derived from an African-American song *Knock a Man Down*. *Blow the Man Down* was originally a halyard shanty. A variant of this is The Black Ball Line (with a more positive view of the Blackball Line as well).

Western Ocean Law was Rule with a Fist. "Blow" refers to knocking a man down with fist, belaying pin or capstan bar. Chief Mates in Western Ocean ships were known as "blowers", second mates as "strikers" and third mates as "greasers".

The ships were famous for their fast passage and excellent seamanship. However, they were also famed for their fighting mates and the brutal treatment of seamen. (Western Ocean seamen were called "Packet Rats"). Many ships bore the name "bloodboat". Most of the seamen hailed from New York or were Liverpool-Irish.

Come all ye young fellows that follow the sea,
to my way haye, blow the man down,
And pray pay attention and listen to me,
Give me some time to blow the man down.

I'm a deep water sailor just in from Hong Kong,
to my way haye, blow the man down,
if you'll give me some grog, I'll sing you a song,
Give me some time to blow the man down.

'Twas on a Black Baller I first served my time,
to my way haye, blow the man down,
And on that Black Baller I wasted my prime,
Give me some time to blow the man down.

'Tis when a Black Baller's preparing for sea
to my way haye, blow the man down,
You'd split your sides laughing at the sites that you see.
Give me some time to blow the man down.

With the tinkers and tailors and soljers and all
to my way haye, blow the man down,
That ship for prime seaman on board a Black Ball.
Give me some time to blow the man down.

'Tis when a Black Baller is clear of the land,
to my way haye, blow the man down,
Our Boatswain then gives us the word of command
Give me some time to blow the man down.

"Lay aft," is the cry,"to the break of the Poop!
to my way haye, blow the man down,
Or I'll help you along with the toe of my boot!"
Give me some time to blow the man down.

'Tis larboard and starboard on the deck you will sprawl,
to my way haye, blow the man down,
For "Kicking Jack" Williams commands the Black Ball.
Give me some time to blow the man down.

Pay attention to order, now you one and all,
to my way haye, blow the man down,
For right there above you flies the Black Ball.
Give me some time to blow the man down.

Nancy Lee

The words to *Nancy Lee* were written by Michael Maybrick, who published under the name Stephen Adams. He was born in Liverpool in 1844. He completed his music studies there and moved to Leipzig and Milan to study further. He became a well known baritone singer. His first appearance was in the New Philharmonic Concerts in London in 1870. His tunes were popular in both England and America.

Nancy Lee was one of Maybrick's first compositions. It was so popular that within two years over one hundred thousand copies had been sold.

The music was written by Frederick E. Weatherly. Weatherly was born in Somersetshire in 1848 and graduated from Oxford in 1871. He practiced law thereafter, but also wrote more that fifty children's books and wrote several tunes with Maybrick.

Of all the wives as e'er you know,
Yeo ho! lads, ho! Yeo ho! Yeo ho!
There's none like Nancy Lee, I trow,
Yeo ho! Yeo ho! Yeo ho!
See there she stands and waves her hands
Upon the quay, and every day
When I'm away she'll watch for me,
And whisper low when tempests blow,
For Jack at sea,
Yeo ho! lads, ho! Yeo ho!

Chorus
The sailor's wife the sailor's star shall be,
Yeo ho! We go across the sea;
The sailor's wife the sailor's star shall be,
The sailor's wife his star shall be!

The harbor's past, the breezes blow,
Yeo ho! lads, ho! Yeo ho! Yeo ho!
'Tis long ere we come back, I know,
Yeo ho! Yeo ho! Yeo ho!
But true and bright from morn till night
My home will be, and all so neat,
And snug and sweet, for Jack at sea;
And Nancy's face to bless the place,
And welcome me;
Yeo ho! lads, ho! Yeo ho!

Chorus

The bosun pipes the watch below,
Yeo ho! lads, ho! Yeo ho! Yeo ho!
Then here's a health afore we go,
Yeo ho! Yeo ho! Yeo ho!
A long, long life to my sweet wife,
And mates at sea, and keep our bones
From Davy Jones, where-e'er we be,
And may you meet a mate as sweet
As Nancy Lee.
Yeo ho! lads, ho! Yeo ho!

Chorus

Red Right Returning

Meeting steamers do not dread.
When you see three lights ahead,
Starboard wheel and show your red.
Green to green or red to red,
Perfect safety, go ahead.
When to starboard red is near,
'Tis your duty to keep clear;
Act as judgment says is proper,
Port or starboard back or stop her.

But when upon your port is seen
A steamer's starboard light of green,
There's not so much for you to do,
For green to port gives way to you.

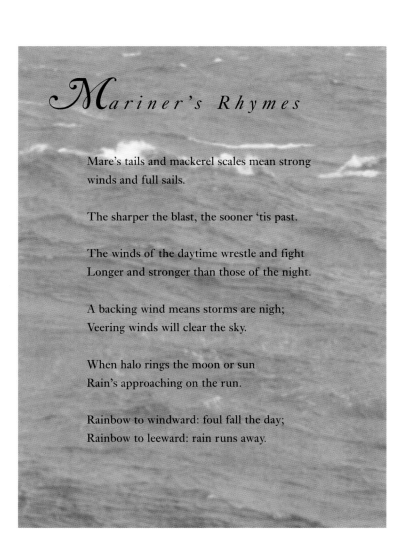

Mariner's Rhymes

Mare's tails and mackerel scales mean strong winds and full sails.

The sharper the blast, the sooner 'tis past.

The winds of the daytime wrestle and fight
Longer and stronger than those of the night.

A backing wind means storms are nigh;
Veering winds will clear the sky.

When halo rings the moon or sun
Rain's approaching on the run.

Rainbow to windward: foul fall the day;
Rainbow to leeward: rain runs away.

From Moby Dick

BY HERMAN MELVILLE

Chapter xli - MOBY DICK

I, Ishmael, was one of that crew; my shouts had gone up with the rest; my oath had been welded with theirs; and stronger I shouted, and more did I hammer and clinch my oath, because of the dread in my soul. A wild, mystical, sympathetical feeling was in me; Ahab's quenchless feud seemed mine. With greedy ears I learned the history of that murderous monster against whom I and all the others had taken our oaths of violence and revenge.

For some time past, though at intervals only, the unaccompanied, secluded White Whale had haunted those uncivilized seas mostly frequented by the Sperm Whale fishermen. But not all of them knew of his existence; only a few of them, comparatively, had knowingly seen him; while the number who as yet had actually and knowingly given battle to him, was small indeed. For, owing to the large number of whale-cruisers; the disorderly way they were sprinkled over the entire watery circumference, many of them adventurously pushing their quest along solitary latitudes, so as seldom or never for a whole twelvemonth or more on a stretch, to encounter a single news-telling sail of any sort; the inordinate length of each separate voyage; the irregularity of the times of sailing from home; all these, with other circumstances, direct and indirect, long obstructed the spread through the whole world-wide whaling-fleet of the special individualizing tidings concerning Moby Dick. It was hardly to be doubted, that several vessels reported to have encountered, at such or such a time, or on such or such a meridian, a Sperm Whale of uncommon magnitude and malignity, which whale, after doing great mischief to his assailants, had completely escaped them; to some minds it was not an unfair presumption, I say, that the whale in question must have been no other than moby Dick. Yet as of late the Sperm Whale fishery had been marked by various and not unfrequent instances of great ferocity, cunning, and malice in the monster attacked; therefore it was, that those who by accident ignorantly gave battle to Moby Dick; such hunters, perhaps, for the most part, were content to ascribe the peculiar terror he bred, more, as it were, to the perils of the Sperm Whale fishery at large, than to the individual cause. In that way, mostly, the disastrous encounter between Ahab and the whale had hitherto been popularly regarded.

And as for those who, previously hearing of the White Whale, by chance caught sight of him; in the beginning of the thing they had every one of them, almost, as boldly and fearlessly lowered for him, as for any other whale of that species. But at length, such calamities did ensue in these assaults - not restricted to sprained wrists and ancles, broken limbs, or devouring amputations - but fatal to the last degree of fatality; those repeated disastrous repulses, all accumulating and piling their terrors upon Moby Dick; those things had gone far to shake the fortitude of many brave hunters, to whom the story of the White Whale had eventually come.

Nor did wild rumors of all sorts fail to exaggerate, and still the more horrify the true histories of these deadly encounters. For not only do fabulous rumors naturally grow out of the very body of all surprising terrible events, - as the smitten tree gives birth to its fungi; but, in maritime life, far more than in that of terra firma, wild rumors abound, wherever there is any adequate reality for them to cling to. And

"It was hardly to be doubted, that several vessels reported to have encountered, at such or such a time, or on such or such a meridian, a Sperm Whale of uncommon magnitude and malignity, which whale, after doing great mischief to his assailants, had completely escaped them; to some minds it was not an unfair presumption, I say, that the whale in question must have been no other than Moby Dick."

as the sea surpasses the land in this matter, so the whale fishery surpasses every other sort of maritime life, in the wonderfulness and fearfulness of the rumors which sometimes circulate there. For not only are whalemen as a body unexempt from that ignorance and superstitiousness hereditary to all sailors; but of all sailors, they are by all odds the most directly brought into contact with whatever is appallingly astonishing in the sea; face to face they not only eye its greatest marvels, but, hand to jaw, give battle to them. Alone, in such remotest waters, that though you sailed a thousand miles, and passed a thousand shores, you would not come to any chiselled hearth-stone, or aught hospitable beneath that part of the sun; in such latitudes and longitudes, pursuing too such a calling as he does, the whaleman is wrapped by influences all tending to make his fancy pregnant with many a mighty birth.

No wonder, then, that ever gathering volume from the mere transit over the widest watery spaces, the outblown rumors of the White Whale did in the end incorporate with themselves all manner of morbid hints, and half-formed foetal suggestions of supernatural agencies, which eventually invested Moby Dick with new terrors unborrowed from anything that visibly appears. So that in many cases such a panic did he finally strike, that few who by those rumors, at least, had heard of the White Whale, few of those hunters were willing to encounter the perils of his jaw.

But there were still other and more vital practical influences at work. Not even at the present day has the original prestige of the Sperm Whale, as fearfully distinguished from all other species of the leviathan, died out of the minds of the whalemen as a body. There are those this day among them, who, though intelligent and courageous enough in offering battle to the Greenland or Right Whale, would perhaps - either from professional inexperience, or incompetency, or timidity, decline a contest with the Sperm Whale; at any rate, there are plenty of whalemen, especially among those whaling nations not sailing under the American flag, who have never hostilely encountered the Sperm Whale, but whose sole knowledge of the leviathan is restricted to the ignoble monster primitively pursued in the North; seated on their hatches, these men will hearken with a childish fireside interest and awe, to the wild, strange tales of Southern whaling. Nor is the pre-eminent tremendousness of the great Sperm Whale anywhere more feelingly comprehended, than on board of those prows which stem him.

And as if the now tested reality of his might had in former legendary times thrown its shadow before it; we find some book naturalists - Olassen and Povelson - declaring the Sperm Whale not only to be a consternation to every other creature in the sea, but also to be so incredibly ferocious as continually to be athirst for human blood. Nor even down to so late a time as Cuvier's, were these or almost similar impressions effaced. For in his Natural History, the Baron himself affirms that at sight of the Sperm Whale, all fish (sharks included) are "struck with the most lively terrors", and "often in the precipitancy of their flight dash themselves against the rocks with such violence as to cause instantaneous death". And however the general experiences in the fishery may amend such reports as these; yet in their full terribleness, even to the bloodthirsty item of Povelson, the superstitious belief in them is, in some vicissitudes of their vocation, revived in the minds of the hunters.

So that overawed by the rumors and portents concerning him, not a few of the fishermen recalled, in reference to Moby Dick, the earlier days of the Sperm Whale fishery, when it was oftentimes hard to induce long practised Right whalemen to embark in the perils of this new and daring warfare; such men protesting that although other leviathans might be hopefully pursued, yet to chase and point lance at such an apparition as the Sperm Whale was not for mortal man. That to attempt it, would be inevitably to be torn into a quick eternity. on this head, there are some remarkable documents that may be consulted.

Nevertheless, some there were, who even in the face of these things were ready to give chase to Moby Dick; and a still greater number who, chancing only to hear of him distantly and vaguely, without the specific details of any certain calamity, and without superstitious accompaniments, were sufficiently hardy not to flee from the battle if offered.

One of the wild suggestings referred to, as at last coming to be linked with the White Whale in the minds of the superstitiously inclined, was the unearthly conceit that Moby Dick was ubiquitous; that he had actually been encountered in opposite latitudes at one and the same instant of time.

Nor, credulous as such minds must have been, was this conceit altogether without some faint show of superstitious probability. For as the secrets of the currents in the seas have never yet been divulged, even to the most erudite research; so the hidden ways of the Sperm Whale when beneath the surface remain, in great part, unaccountable to his pursuers; and from time to time have originated the most curious and contradictory speculations regarding them, especially concerning the mystic modes whereby, after sounding to a great depth, he transports himself with such vast swiftness to the most widely distant points.

It is a thing well known to both American and English whale-ships, and as well a thing placed upon authoritative record years ago by Scoresby, that some whales have been captured far north in the Pacific, in whose bodies have been found the barbs of harpoons darted in the Greenland seas. Nor is it to be gainsaid, that in some of these instances it has been

"Nevertheless, some there were, who even in the face of these things were ready to give chase to Moby Dick; and a still greater number who, chancing only to hear of him distantly and vaguely, without the specific details of any certain calamity, and without superstitious accompaniments, were sufficiently hardy not to flee from the battle if offered."

declared that the interval of time between the two assaults could not have exceeded very many days. Hence, by inference, it has been believed by some whalemen, that the nor' west passage, so long a problem to man, was never a problem to the whale. So that here, in the real living experience of living men, the prodigies related in old times of the inland Strello mountain in Portugal (near whose top there was said to be a lake in which the wrecks of ships floated up to the surface); and that still more wonderful story of the Arethusa fountain near Syracuse (whose waters were believed to have come from the Holy Land by an underground passage); these fabulous nar-

> "The rest of his body was so streaked, and spotted, and marbled with the same shrouded hue, that, in the end, he had gained his distinctive appellation of the White Whale; a name, indeed, literally justified by his vivid aspect, when seen gliding at high noon through a dark blue sea, leaving a milky-way wake of creamy foam, all spangled with golden gleamings."

rations are almost fully equalled by the realities of the whaleman.

Forced into familiarity, then, with such prodigies as these; and knowing that after repeated, intrepid assaults, the White Whale had escaped alive; it cannot be much matter of surprise that some whalemen should go still further in their superstitions; declaring Moby Dick not only ubiquitous, but immortal (for immortality is but ubiquity in time); that though groves of spears should be planted in his flanks, he would still swim away unharmed; or if indeed he should ever be made to spout thick blood, such a sight would be but a ghastly deception; for again in unensanguined billows hundreds of leagues away, his unsullied jet would once more be seen.

But even stripped of these supernatural surmisings, there was enough in the earthly make and incontestable character of the monster to strike the imagination with unwonted power. For, it was not so much his uncommon bulk that so much distinguished him from other Sperm Whales, but, as was elsewhere thrown out - a peculiar snow-white wrinkled forehead, and a high, pyramidical white hump. These were his prominent features; the tokens whereby, even in the limitless, uncharted seas, he revealed his identity, at a long distance, to those who knew him.

The rest of his body was so streaked, and spotted, and marbled with the same shrouded hue, that, in the end, he had gained his distinctive appellation of the White Whale; a name, indeed, literally justified by his vivid aspect, when seen gliding at high noon through a dark blue sea, leaving a milky-way wake of creamy foam, all spangled with golden gleamings.

Nor was it his unwonted magnitude, nor his remarkable hue, nor yet his deformed lower jaw, that so much invested the whale with natural terror, as that unexampled, intelligent malignity which, according to specific accounts, he had over and over again evinced in his assaults. More than all, his treacherous retreats struck more of dismay than perhaps aught else. For, when swimming before his exulting pursuers, with every apparent symptom of alarm, he had several times been known to turn around suddenly, and, bearing down upon them, either stave their boats to splinters, or drive them back in consternation to their ship.

Already several fatalities had attended his chase. But though similar disasters, however little bruited ashore, were by no means unusual in the fishery; yet, in most instances, such seemed the White Whale's infernal aforethought of ferocity, that every dismembering or death that he caused, was not wholly regarded as having been inflicted by an unintelligent agent.

Judge, then, to what pitches of inflamed, distracted fury the minds of his more desperate hunters were impelled, when amid the chips of chewed boats, and the sinking limbs of torn comrades, they swam out of the white curds of the whale's direful wrath into the serene, exasperating sunlight, that smiled on, as if at a birth or a bridal.

His three boats stove around him, and oars and men both whirling in the eddies; one captain, seizing the line-knife from his broken prow, had dashed at the whale, as an Arkansas duellist at his foe, blindly seeking with a six inch blade to reach the fathom-deep life of the whale. That captain was Ahab. And then it was, that suddenly sweeping his sickle-shaped lower jaw beneath him, Moby Dick had reaped away Ahab's leg, as a mower a blade of grass in the field. No turbaned Turk, no hired Venetian or Malay, could have smote him with more seeming malice. Small reason was there to doubt, then, that ever since that almost fatal encounter, Ahab had cherished a wild vindictiveness against the whale, all the more fell for that in his frantic morbidness he at last came to identify with him, not only all his bodily woes, but all his intellectual and spiritual exasperations. The White Whale swam before him as the monomaniac incarnation of all those malicious agencies which some deep men feel eating in them, till they are left living on with half a heart and half a lung. That intangible malignity which has been from the beginning; to whose dominion even the modern Christians ascribe one-half of the worlds; which the ancient Ophites of the east reverenced in their statue devil; - Ahab did not fall down and worship it like them; but deliriously transferring its idea to the abhorred White Whale, he pitted himself, all mutilated, against it. All that most maddens and torments; all that stirs up the lees of things; all truth with malice in it; all that cracks the sinews and cakes the brain; all the subtle demonisms of life and thought; all evil, to crazy Ahab, were visibly personified, and made practically assailable in Moby Dick. He piled upon the whale's white hump the sum of all the general rage and hate felt by his whole race from Adam down; and then, as if his chest had been a mortar, he burst his hot heart's shell upon it.

It is not probable that this monomania in him took its instant rise at the precise time of his bodily dismemberment. Then, in darting at the monster, knife in hand, he had but given loose to a sudden, passionate, corporal animosity; and when he received the stroke that tore him, he probably but felt the agonizing bodily laceration, but nothing more. Yet, when by this collision forced to turn towards home, and for long months of days and weeks, Ahab and anguish lay stretched together in one hammock, rounding in mid winter that dreary, howling Patagonian Cape; then it was, that his torn body and gashed soul bled into one another; and so interfusing, made him mad. That it was only then, on the homeward voyage, after the encounter, that the final monomania seized him, seems all but certain from the fact that, at intervals during the passage, he was a raving lunatic; and, though unlimbed of a leg, yet such vital strength yet lurked in his Egyptian chest, and was moreover intensified by his delirium, that his mates were forced to lace him fast, even there, as he sailed, raving in his hammock. In a strait-jacket, he swung to the mad rockings of the gales. And, when running into more sufferable latitudes, the ship, with mild stun'sails spread, floated across the tranquil tropics, and, to all appearances, the old man's delirium seemed left behind him with the Cape Horn swells, and he came forth from his dark den into the blessed light and air; even then, when he bore that firm, collected front, however pale, and issued his calm orders once again; and his mates thanked God the direful madness was now gone; even then, Ahab, in his hidden self, raved on. Human madness is oftentimes a cunning and most feline thing. When you think it fled, it may have but become transfigured into some still subtler form. Ahab's full lunacy subsided not, but deepeningly contracted; like the unabated Hudson, when that noble Northman flows narrowly, but unfathomably through the Highland gorge. But, as in his narrow-flowing monomania, not one jot of Ahab's broad madness had been left behind; so in that broad madness, not one jot of his great natural intellect had perished. That before living agent, now became the living instrument. If such a furious trope may stand, his special lunacy stormed his general sanity, and carried it, and turned all its concentred cannon upon its own mad mark; so that far from having lost his strength, Ahab, to that one end, did now possess a thousand fold more potency than ever he had sanely brought to bear upon any one reasonable object.

This is much; yet Ahab's larger, darker, deeper part remains unhinted. But vain to popularize profundities, and all truth is profound. Winding far down from within the very heart of this spiked Hotel de Cluny where we here stand - however grand and wonderful, now quit it; - and take your way, ye nobler, sadder souls, to those vast Roman halls of Thermes; where far beneath the fantastic towers of man's upper earth, his root of grandeur, his whole awful essence sits in bearded state; an antique buried beneath antiquities, and throned on torsoes! So with a broken throne, the great gods mock that captive king; so like a Caryatid, he patient sits, upholding on his frozen brow the piled entablatures of ages. Wind ye down there, ye prouder, sadder souls! question that proud, sad king! A family likeness! aye, he did beget ye, ye young exiled royalties; and from your grim sire only will the old State-secret come.

Now, in his heart, Ahab had some glimpse of this, namely: all my means are sane, my motive and my object mad. Yet without power to kill, or change, or shun the fact; he likewise knew that to mankind he did now long dissemble; in some sort, did still. But that thing of his dissembling was only subject to his perceptibility, not to his will determinate. Nevertheless, so well did he succeed in that dissembling, that when with ivory leg he stepped ashore at last, no Nantucketer thought him otherwise than but naturally grieved, and that to the quick, with the terrible casualty which had overtaken him.

The report of his undeniable delirium at sea was likewise popularly ascribed to a kindred cause. And so too, all the added moodiness which always afterwards, to the very day of sailing in the pequod on the present voyage, sat brooding on his brow. Nor is it so very unlikely, that far from distrusting his fitness for another whaling voyage, on account of such dark symptoms, the calculating people of that prudent isle were inclined to harbor the conceit, that for those very reasons he was all the better qualified and set on edge, for a pursuit so full of rage and wildness as the bloody hunt of whales. Gnawed within and scorched without, with the infixed, unrelenting fangs of some incurable idea; such an one, could he be found, would seem the very man to dart his iron and lift his lance against the most appalling of all brutes. Or, if for any reason thought to be corporeally incapacitated for that, yet such an one would seem superlatively competent to cheer and howl on his underlings to the attack. But be all this as it may, certain it is, that with the mad secret of his unabated rage bolted up and keyed in him, Ahab had purposely sailed upon the present voyage with the one only and all-engrossing object of hunting the White Whale. Had any one of his old acquaintances on shore but half dreamed of what was lurking in him then, how soon would their aghast and righteous souls have wrenched the ship from such a fiendish man! They were bent on profitable cruises, the profit to be counted down in dollars from the mint. He was intent on an audacious, immitigable, and supernatural revenge.

Here, then, was this grey- headed, ungodly old man, chasing with curses a Job's whale round the world, at the head of a crew, too, chiefly made up of mongrel renegades, and castaways, and cannibals - morally enfeebled also, by the incompetence of mere unaided virtue or right- mindedness in Starbuck, the invulnerable jollity of indifference and recklessness in Stubb, and the pervading mediocrity in Flask. Such a crew, so officered, seemed specially picked and packed by some infernal fatality to help him to his monomaniac revenge. How it was that they so aboundingly responded to the old man's ire - by what evil magic their souls were possessed, that at times his hate seemed almost theirs; the White Whale as much their insufferable foe as his; how all this came to be - what the White Whale was to them, or how to their unconscious understandings, also, in some dim, unsuspected way, he might have seemed the gliding great demon of the seas of life, - all this to explain, would be to dive deeper than Ishmael can go. The subterranean miner that works in us all, how can one tell whither leads his shaft by the ever shifting, muffled sound of his pick? Who does not feel the irresistible arm drag? What skiff in tow of a seventy-four can stand still? For one, I gave myself up to the abandonment of the time and the place; but while yet all a-rush to encounter the whale, could see naught in that brute but the deadliest ill.

SIGNALS

ALPHA

·—

I have a diver down. Keep well clear at a slow speed

ECHO

·

I am altering my course to starboard.

INDIA

··

I am altering my course to port.

MIKE

——

My vessel is stopped, and making no way through the water.

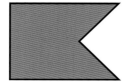

BRAVO

——·

I am taking in or discharging or carrying dangerous goods.

FOXTROT

··—·

I am disabled, communicate with me.

JULIETT

·———

I am on fire, and have dangerous cargo on board. Keep well clear of me.

NOVEMBER

—·

No.

CHARLIE

—·—·

Yes.

GOLF

——·

I require a pilot.

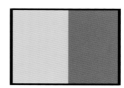

KILO

—·—

I wish to communicate with you.

OSCAR

———

Man overboard.

DELTA

——

Keep well clear of me, I am maneuvering with difficulty.

HOTEL

····

I have a pilot on board.

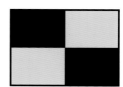

LIMA

·—··

You should stop your vessel instantly.

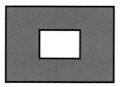

PAPA

·——·

In harbor: All persons should report aboard for the vessel is about to proceed to sea.
At sea: My nets have come fast upon an obstruction.

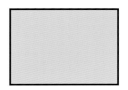

QUEBEC

— — · —

My vessel is healthy, and I request free pratique.

VICTOR

· · · —

I require assistance.

UNA-ONE

· — — — —

(wun)

SOXI-SIX

— · · · ·

(six)

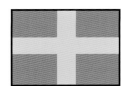

ROMEO

· — ·

No meaning in international code. Used by vessels at anchor to warn of collision in fog.

WHISKEY

· — —

I require medical assistance.

BISSO-TWO

· · — — —

(too)

SETTE-SEVEN

— — · · ·

(seven)

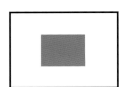

SIERRA

· · ·

I am operating a stern propulsion.

X-RAY

— · · —

Stop carrying out your intentions, and watch for my signals.

TERRA-THREE

· · · — —

(tree)

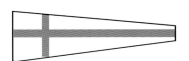

OKTO-EIGHT

— — — · ·

(ait)

TANGO

—

Keep clear of me. I am engaged pair trawling.

YANKEE

— · — —

I am dragging my anchor.

KARTE-FOUR

· · · · —

(fower)

NOVA-NINE

— — — — ·

(niner)

UNIFORM

· · —

You are running into danger.

ZULU

— — · ·

I require a tug.

PENTA-FIVE

· · · · ·

(fife)

NADA-ZERO

— — — — —

(zayroh)

Glossary

ABAFT ▪ Toward the rear (stern) of the boat. Behind.

ABEAM ▪ At right angles to the keel of the boat, but not on the boat.

ABOARD ▪ On or within the boat.

ABOVE DECK ▪ On the deck (not over it - see ALOFT)

ABREAST ▪ Side by side; by the side of.

ADRIFT ▪ Loose, not on moorings or towline.

AFT ▪ Toward the stern of the boat.

AGROUND ▪ Touching or fast to the bottom.

AHEAD ▪ In a forward direction.

AIDS TO NAVIGATION ▪ Artificial objects to supplement natural landmarks indicating safe and unsafe waters.

ALEE ▪ Away from the direction of the wind. Opposite of windward.

ALOFT ▪ Above the deck of the boat.

AMIDSHIPS ▪ In or toward the center of the boat.

ANCHORAGE ▪ A place suitable for anchoring in relation to the wind, seas and bottom.

ASTERN ▪ In back of the boat, opposite of ahead.

ATHWARTSHIPS ▪ At right angles to the centerline of the boat; rowboat seats are generally athwart ships.

AWEIGH ▪ The position of anchor as it is raised clear of the bottom.

BACKSTAY ▪ A wire support for the mast, usually running from the stern to the head of the mast.

BALE ▪ A fitting on the end of a spar, such as the boom, to which a line may be led.

BALLAST WEIGHT ▪ usually metal, placed low in a boat to provide stability.

BARBER HAULER ▪ A line attached to the jib or jib sheet, used to adjust the angle of sheeting by pulling the sheet toward the centerline of the boat.

BATTEN DOWN ▪ Secure hatches and loose objects both within the hull and on deck.

BEAM ▪ The greatest width of the boat.

BEARING ▪ The direction of an object expressed either as a true bearing as shown on the chart, or as a bearing relative to the heading of the boat.

BELOW ▪ Beneath the deck.

BIGHT ▪ The part of the rope or line, between the end and the standing part, on which a knot is formed.

BILGE ▪ The interior of the hull below the floor boards.

BILGEBOARDS ▪ Similar to centerboards, and used to prevent lee way. Bilgeboards are located on either side of the centerline at the bilges.

BINNACLE ▪ A support for the compass, raising it to a convenient position.

BITTER END ▪ The last part of a rope or chain. The inboard end of the anchor rode.

BOARD BOAT ▪ A small boat, usually mono rig. May have a shallow cockpit well. Typically has almost no freeboard.

BOAT ▪ A fairly indefinite term. A waterborne vehicle smaller than a ship. One definition is a small craft carried aboard a ship.

BOAT HOOK ▪ A short shaft with a fitting at one end shaped to facilitate use in putting a line over a piling, recovering an object dropped overboard, or in pushing or fending off.

BOBSTAY ▪ Wire stay underneath the bowsprit; helps to counteract the upward pull exerted by the forestay.

BOOM VANG ▪ A system used to hold the boom down, particularly when boat is sailing downwind, so that the mainsail area facing the wind is kept to a maximum. Frequently extends from the boom to a location near the base of the mast. Usually tackle- or lever-operated.

BOOM CRUTCH ▪ Support for the boom, holding it up and out of the way when the boat is anchored or moored. Unlike a gallows frame, a crutch is stowed when boat is sailing.

BOOMKIN ▪ (bumpkin) Short spar extending aft from the transom. Used to anchor the backstay or the sheets from the mizzen on a yawl or ketch.

BOOT TOP ▪ A painted line that indicates the designed waterline.

BOW ▪ The forward part of a boat.

BOW LINE ▪ A docking line leading from the bow.

BOWSPRIT ▪ A short spar extending forward from the bow. Normally used to anchor the forestay.

BOWLINE ▪ A knot used to form a temporary loop in the end of a line.

BRIDGE ▪ The location from which a vessel is steered and its speed controlled. "Control Station" is really a more appropriate term for small craft.

BRIDGE DECK ▪ The transverse partition between the cockpit and the cabin.

BRIDLE ▪ A line or wire secured at both ends in order to distribute a strain between two points.

BRIGHTWORK ▪ Varnished woodwork and/or polished metal.

BULKHEAD ▪ A vertical partition separating compartments.

BULLSEYE ▪ A round eye through which a line is led, usually in order to change the direction of pull.

BULWARK ▪ A vertical extension above the deck designed to keep water out and to assist in keeping people in.

BUOY ▪ An anchored float used for marking a position on the water or a hazard or a shoal and for mooring.

BURDENED VESSEL ▪ That vessel which, according to the applicable Navigation Rules, must give way to the privileged vessel. The term has been superseded by the term "give-way".

C

CABIN ▪ A compartment for passengers or crew.

CAP ▪ A piece of trim, usually wood, used to cover and often decorate a portion of the boat, i.e., caprail.

CAPSIZE ▪ To turn over.

CAST OFF ▪ To let go.

CATAMARAN ▪ A twin-hulled boat, with hulls side by side.

CENTERBOARD ▪ A board lowered through a slot in the centerline of he hull to reduce sideways skidding or leeway. Unlike a daggerboard, which lifts vertically, a centerboard pivots around a pin, usually located in the forward top corner, and swings up and aft.

CHAFING GEAR ▪ Tubing or cloth wrapping used to protect a line from chafing on a rough surface.

CHAIN PLATE ▪ The fitting used to attach stays to the hull. Chine A line, running along the side of the boat, where the bottom forms an angle to the side. Not found on round-bottom boats.

CHART ▪ A map for use by navigators.

CHINE ▪ The intersection of the bottom and sides of a flat or v-bottomed boat.

CHOCK ▪ A fitting through which anchor or mooring lines are led. Usually U-shaped to reduce chafe.

CLEAT ▪ A fitting to which lines are made fast. The classic cleat to which lines are belayed is approximately anvil-shaped.

CLEW ▪ For a triangular sail, the aftmost cornet.

CLOVE HITCH ▪ A knot for temporarily fastening a line to a spar or piling.

COACH ROOF ▪ Also trunk. The cabin roof, raised above the deck to provide headroom in the cabin.

COAMING ▪ A vertical piece around the edge of a cockpit, hatch, etc. to prevent water on deck from running below.

COCKPIT ▪ An opening in the deck from which the boat is handled.

COIL ▪ To lay a line down in circular turns.

COMPANIONWAY ▪ The main entrance to the cabin, usually including the steps down into the cabin.

COUNTER ▪ At the stern of the boat, that portion of the hull emerging from below the water, and extending to the transom. Apr to be long in older designs, and short in more recent boats.

COURSE ▪ The direction in which a boat is steered.

CUDDY ▪ A small shelter cabin in a boat.

CUNNINGHAM ▪ A mainsail control device, using a line to pull down the mainsail a short distance from the luff to the tack. Flattens the sail.

CURRENT ▪ The horizontal movement of water.

D

DAGGERBOARD ▪ A board dropped vertically through the hull to prevent leeway. May be completely removed for beaching or for sailing downwind.

DANGER ZONE ▪ The area encompassed from dead ahead of your boat to just abaft your starboard beam. You must stand clear of any boat in the "danger zone".

DEAD AHEAD ▪ Directly ahead.

DEAD ASTERN ▪ Directly aft.

DEADLIGHT ▪ Either a cover clamped over a porthole to protect it in heavy weather or a fixed light set into the deck or cabin roof to provide light below.

DECK ▪ A permanent covering over a compartment, hull or any part thereof.

DINGHY ▪ A small open boat. A dinghy is often used as a tender for a larger craft.

DISPLACEMENT ▪ The weight of water displaced by a floating vessel, thus, a boat's weight.

DISPLACEMENT HULL ▪ A type of hull that plows through the water, displacing a weight of water equal to its own weight, even when more power is added.

DOCK ▪ A protected water area in which vessels are moored. The term is often used to denote a pier or a wharf.

DODGER ▪ A screen, usually fabric, erected to protect the cockpit from spray and wind.

DOLPHIN ▪ A group of piles driven close together and bound with wire cables into a single structure.

DOWNHAUL ▪ A line used to pull a spar, such as the spinnaker pole, or a sail, particularly the mainsail, down.

DRAFT ▪ The depth of water a boat draws.

DRY SAILING ▪ When boats, especially smaller racers, are kept on shore instead of being left anchored or moored, they are dry sailed. The practice prevents marine growth on the hull and the absorption of moisture into it.

E

EBB ▪ A receding current.

F

FAIRLEAD ▪ A fitting used to alter the direction of a working line, such as a bullseye, turning block, or anchor chock.

FATHOM ▪ Six feet.

FENDER ▪ A cushion, placed between boats, or between a boat and a pier, to prevent damage.

FIGURE EIGHT KNOT ▪ A knot in the form of a figure eight, placed in the end of a line to prevent the line from passing through a grommet or a block.

FLARE ▪ The outward curve of a vessel's sides near the bow. A distress signal.

FLOOD ▪ A incoming current.

FLOORBOARDS ▪ The surface of the cockpit on which the crew stand.

FLUKE ▪ The palm of an anchor.

FO'C'SLE ▪ An abbreviation of forecastle. Refers to that portion of the cabin which is farthest forward. In square-riggers often used as quarters for the crew.

FOLLOWING SEA ▪ An overtaking sea that comes from astern.

FOOT ▪ For a triangular sail, the bottom edge.

FORE-AND-AFT ▪ In a line parallel to the keel.

FOREPEAK ▪ A compartment in the bow of a small boat.

FORESTAY ▪ Wire, sometimes rod, support for the mast, running from the bowsprit or foredeck to a point at or near the top of the mast.

FORETRIANGLE ▪ The triangle formed by the forestay, mast, and fore deck.

FORWARD ▪ Toward the bow of the boat.

FOULED ▪ Any piece of equipment that is jammed or entangled, or dirtied.

FRACTIONAL RIG ▪ A design in which the forestay does not go to the very top of the mast, but instead to a point 3/4~ 7s, etc., of the way up the mast.

FREEBOARD ▪ The minimum vertical distance from the surface of the water to the gunwale.

G

GALLEY ▪ The kitchen area of a boat.

GANGWAY ▪ The area of a ship's side where people board and disembark.

GARBOARD ▪ Used in conjunction with strake. Refers to the planks, or strakes, on either side of and adjacent to the keel.

GEAR ▪ A general term for ropes, blocks, tackle and other equipment.

GIVE-WAY VESSEL ▪ A term used to describe the vessel which must yield in meeting, crossing, or overtaking situations.

GOLLYWOBBLER ▪ A full, quadrilateral sail used in light air on schooners. It is flown high, between the fore and main mast, and is also known as a fisherman's staysail.

GOOSENECK ▪ The fitting that connects the boom to the mast.

GRAB RAILS ▪ Hand-hold fittings mounted on cabin tops and sides for personal safety when moving around the boat.

GROUND TACKLE ▪ A collective term for the anchor and its associated gear.

GUNTER RIG ▪ Similar to a gaff rig, except that the spar forming the "gaff" is hoisted to an almost vertical position, extending well above the mast.

GUNWALE ▪ The upper edge of a boat's sides.

GUY ▪ A line used to control the end of a spar. A spinnaker pole, for example, has one end attached to the mast, while the free end is moved back and forth with a guy.

H

HALYARD LINE ▪ usually of wire, that is used to pull up or hoist a sail.

HARD CHINE ▪ An abrupt intersection between the hull side and the hull bottom of a boat so constructed.

HATCH ▪ An opening in a boat's deck fitted with a watertight cover.

HEAD ▪ A marine toilet. Also the upper corner of a triangular sail.

HEADFOIL ▪ A grooved, streamline rod, often aluminum, fitted over the forestay. The primary purpose is to provide continuous support of the luff of the sail, but it may also help support the forestay.

HEADING ▪ The direction in which a vessel's bow points at any given time.

HEADWAY ▪ The forward motion of a boat. Opposite of sternway.

HELM ▪ The wheel or tiller controlling the rudder.

HELMSPERSON ▪ The person who steers the boat.

HIKING STICK ▪ An extension of the tiller that enables the helms man to sir at a distance from it.

HITCH ▪ A knot used to secure a rope to another object or to another rope, or to form a loop or a noose in a rope.

HOLD ▪ A compartment below deck in a large vessel, used solely for carrying cargo.

HULL ▪ The main body of a vessel.

I

INBOARD ▪ More toward the center of a vessel; inside; a motor fitted inside a boat.

INSPECTION PORT ▪ A watertight covering, usually small, that may be removed so the interior of the hull can be inspected or water removed.

INTRACOASTAL WATERWAY ▪ ICW: bays, rivers, and canals along the coasts (such as the Atlantic and Gulf of Mexico coasts), connected so that vessels may travel without going into the sea.

IOR ▪ International Offshore Rating

J

JACOBS LADDER ▪ A rope ladder, lowered from the deck, as when pilots or passengers come aboard.

JETTY ▪ A structure, usually masonry, projecting out from the shore; a jetty may protect a harbor entrance.

JIFFY REEFING ▪ A fast method of reefing. Lines pull down the luff and the leech of the sail, reducing its area.

JUMPER STAY ▪ A short stay supporting the top forward portion of the mast. The stay runs from the top of the mast forward over a short jumper strut, then down to the mast, usually at the level of the spreaders.

K

KEEL ▪ The centerline of a boat running fore and aft; the backbone of a vessel.

KEELSON ▪ A structural member above and parallel to the keel. Kick-up Describes a rudder or centerboard that rotates back and up when an obstacle is encountered. Useful when a boat is to be beached.

KNOT ▪ A measure of speed equal to one nautical mile (6076 feet) per hour.

KNOT ▪ A fastening made by interweaving rope to form a stopper, to enclose or bind an object, to form a loop or a noose, to tie a small rope to an object, or to tie the ends of two small ropes together.

L

LATITUDE ▪ The distance north or south of the equator measured and expressed in degrees.

LAZARETTE ▪ A storage space in a boat's stern area.

LEE ▪ The side sheltered from the wind.

LEEWARD ▪ The direction away from the wind. Opposite of windward.

LEEWAY ▪ The sideways movement of the boat caused by either wind or current.

LINE ▪ Rope and cordage used aboard a vessel.

LOG ▪ A record of courses or operation. Also, a device to measure speed.

LONGITUDE ▪ The distance in degrees east or west of the meridian at Greenwich, England.

LUBBER'S LINE ▪ A mark or permanent line on a compass

indicating the direction forward parallel to the keel when properly installed.

M

MARLINSPIKE ▪ A tool for opening the strands of a rope while splicing.

MIDSHIP ▪ Approximately in the location equally distant from the bow and stern.

MOORING - An arrangement for securing a boat to a mooring buoy or a pier.

N

NAUTICAL MILE ▪ One minute of latitude; approximately 6076 feet - about 1/8 longer than the statute mile of 5280 feet.

NAVIGATION ▪ The art and science of conducting a boat safely from one point to another.

NAVIGATION RULES ▪ The regulations governing the movement of vessels in relation to each other, generally called steering and sailing rules.

O

OUTBOARD ▪ Toward or beyond the boat's sides. A detachable engine mounted on a boat's stern.

OVERBOARD ▪ Over the side or out of the boat.

P

PIER ▪ A loading platform extending at an angle from the shore.

PILE ▪ A wood, metal or concrete pole driven into the bottom. Craft may be made fast to a pile; it may be used to support a pier (see PILING) or a float.

PILING ▪ Support, protection for wharves, piers etc.; constructed of piles (see PILE)

PILOTING ▪ Navigation by use of visible references, the depth of the water, etc.

PLANING ▪ A boat is said to be planing when it is essentially moving over the top of the water rather than through the water.

PLANING HULL ▪ A type of hull shaped to glide easily across the water at high speed.

PORT ▪ The left side of a boat looking forward. A harbor.

PRIVELEGED VESSEL ▪ A vessel which, according to the applicable Navigation Rule, has right-of-way (this term has been superseded by the term "stand-on").

Q

QUARTER ▪ The sides of a boat aft of amidships.

QUARTERING SEA ▪ Sea coming on a boat's quarter.

R

RODE ▪ The anchor line and/or chain.

ROPE ▪ In general, cordage as it is purchased at the store. When it comes aboard a vessel and is put to use it becomes line.

RUDDER ▪ A vertical plate or board for steering a boat.

RUN ▪ To allow a line to feed freely.

RUNNING LIGHTS ▪ Lights required to be shown on boats underway between sundown and sunup.

S

SATELLITE NAVIGATION ▪ A form of position finding using radio transmissions from satellites with sophisticated on-board automatic equipment.

SCOPE ▪ Technically, the ratio of length of anchor rode in use to the vertical distance from the bow of the vessel to the bottom of the water. Usually six to seven to one for calm weather and more scope in storm conditions.

SCREW ▪ A boat's propeller.

SCUPPERS ▪ Drain holes on deck, in the toe rail, or in bulwarks or (with drain pipes) in the deck itself.

SEA COCK ▪ A through hull valve, a shut off on a plumbing or drain pipe between the vessel's interior and the sea.

SEAMANSHIP ▪ All the arts and skills of boat handling, ranging from maintenance and repairs to piloting, sail handling, marlinespike work, and rigging.

SEA ROOM ▪ A safe distance from the shore or other hazards.

SEAWORTHY ▪ A boat or a boat's gear able to meet the usual sea conditions.

SECURE ▪ To make fast.

SET ▪ Direction toward which the current is flowing.

SHIP ▪ A larger vessel usually thought of as being used for ocean travel. A vessel able to carry a "boat" on board.

SLACK ▪ Not fastened; loose. Also, to loosen.

SOLE ▪ Cabin or saloon floor. Timber extensions on the bottom of the rudder. Also the molded fiberglass deck of a cockpit.

SOUNDING ▪ A measurement of the depth of water.

SPRING LINE ▪ A pivot line used in docking, undocking, or to prevent the boat from moving forward or astern while made fast to a dock.

SQUALL ▪ A sudden, violent wind often accompanied by rain.

SQUARE KNOT ▪ A knot used to join two lines of similar size. Also called a reef knot.

STANDING PART ▪ That part of a line which is made fast. The main part of a line as distinguished from the bight and the end.

STAND-ON VESSEL ▪ That vessel which has right-of-way during a meeting, crossing, or overtaking situation.

STARBOARD ▪ The right side of a boat when looking forward.

STEM ▪ The forward most part of the bow.

STERN ▪ The after part of the boat.

STERN LINE ▪ A docking line leading from the stern.

STOW ▪ To put an item in its proper place.

SWAMP ▪ To fill with water, but not settle to the bottom.

T

THWARTSHIPS ▪ At right angles to the centerline of the boat.

TIDE ▪ The periodic rise and fall of water level in the oceans.

TILLER ▪ A bar or handle for turning a boat's rudder or an outboard motor.

TOPSIDES ▪ The sides of a vessel between the waterline and the deck; sometimes referring to onto or above the deck.

TRANSOM ▪ The stern cross-section of a square sterned boat.

TRIM ▪ Fore and aft balance of a boat.

U

UNDERWAY ▪ Vessel in motion, i.e., when not moored, at anchor, or aground.

V

V BOTTOM ▪ A hull with the bottom section in the shape of a "V".

W

WAKE ▪ Moving waves, track or path that a boat leaves behind it, when moving across the waters.

WATERLINE ▪ A line painted on a hull which shows the point to which a boat sinks when it is properly trimmed (see BOOT TOP).

WAY ▪ Movement of a vessel through the water such as headway, sternway or leeway.

WINDWARD ▪ Toward the direction from which the wind is coming.

Y

YACHT ▪ A pleasure vessel, a pleasure boat; in American usage the idea of size and luxury is conveyed, either sail or power.

YAW ▪ To swing or steer off course, as when running with a quartering sea.

Bibliography

Abdy, William C.F.
Amateur Sailing, Reminiscences, 1914
Mostly yachting experiences along the south coast of England from Solent to Cornwall beginning in 1871. Also a voyage to New Zealand aboard a square rigger in 1879.

Acton, Shane
Shrimpy, A Record Round-the-World Voyage in an 18-foot Yacht
Acton's 1972 voyage which he began with little experience and less money and set the record for smallest boat to circumnavigate.
Shrimpy Sails Again
This is his second voyage in which he realizes that he cannot handle normal life in England, and sets off again in Shrimpy across the French Canals to the Med. He then crosses the Atlantic again, hangs around in the Barbados Islands region and then crosses to the Pacific.

Adamson, Hans Christian
Admiral Thunderbolt, 1959
The spectacular career of Peter Wessel, Norway's greatest naval hero, who rose from cadet to Vice Admiral in 8 years, 1711-1718.

Aebi, Tania
Maiden Voyage, 1989
Aebi was a troubled teenaged girl when her father offered her a challenge—a college education or a 26-foot sloop which she would sail around the world—alone. This is the story of Aebi's 27,000 mile circumnavigation. Remarkable in that she left New York with little sailing experience and even less navigation experience. That she survived the first part of the trip is testament to higher powers who watch over

fools. To her credit, she became an accomplished sailor and navigator by the end of the 2 1/2 year circumnavigation.

Allcard, Edward C.
Singlehanded Passage, 1950
A transatlantic passage aboard a 34 ft. gaff-rigged yawl from England to Bermuda and New York. *Temptress Returns,* 1953
A single-handed passage across the Atlantic, fighting gales and hurricanes.

Alsar, Vital
La Balsa, 1973
The longest raft voyage in history, 8,600 miles across the Pacific from Guayaquil to Australia on a balsawood raft.

Anderson, Cmdr. William R.
Nautilus 90 North, 1959
Author skippers nuclear sub under the ice to the north pole.

Anderson, Tom
Shiyak!: Misadventures of the Schooner Lottie Bennet
The last windjammer voyage to Alaskan salmon waters.

Anderson, W.H.
The Adventures of Owen Evans, 1863
An unusual story of 5 men abandoned by their ship on a desolate island in 1739.

Andrews, Roy Chapman
Ends of the Earth, 1929
Adventures of an explorer and naturalist on whaling cruises in the Pacific.

Anthony, Irvin
Decatur, 1931
A biography of naval officer Steven Decatur, 1779-1820. He

distinguished himself against the Barbary pirates and in the war of 1812.
Voyagers Unafraid, 1930
Men who dared to cross the Atlantic single-handed in small craft. Johnson, Crapo, Andrews, Slocum, Gerbault, and others.

Arther, Stanley Clisby
Jean Laffite, Gentleman Rover, 1952
From Barataria pirate to his death at age 72 in Alton, Illinois, along with the history of his family including brothers Pierre and Capitaine Dominique. This book challenges all legend about the birth and death of Laffite.

Aymer, Brandt, ed.
Men at Sea
Anthology of sea adventures. Adventure, battles, piracy, storms and shipwrecks.

Ashley, Clifford 1881-1947
(artist and author of the famous Book of Knots)
The Yankee Whaler, 1926
Mostly a history of New England whaling, the adventure part is an account of Ashley's voyage in the whaling bark Sunbeam in 1904, it was previously published as The Blubber-Hunters in Harper's Magazine in about 1906. Illustrated by the author

Attiwell, Ken
Windjammer, 1931
Aboard the four masted barque Archibald Russell, flying the Finnish flag and bound to Queenstown from Melbourne with a cargo of grain.

Babson, Roger W.
The Sea Made Men, 1937

The story of a Gloucester lad, Gorham P. Low, who went to sea at age 16, voyaging around the world in New England merchant ships until a dismasting in the Indian Ocean.

Bailey, Maurice & Maralyn
Second Chance: Voyage to Patagonia, 1977
In 1973, after whales had sunk their first boat, the Bailey's survived 117 days on a raft. This is the story of their second voyage under sail around Patagonia to England via the Panama Canal.
Staying Alive, 1974
Adrift for 117 days in the Pacific after their boat was sunk by a whale.

Barbour, Capt. Job
Forty-eight Days Adrift; The Voyage of the Neptune, 1929
From Newfoundland to Scotland; a three masted schooner caught in a gale at sea.

Barra, E.I.
A Tale of Two Oceans, 1893
An account of a voyage from Philadelphia to San Francisco, via Cape Horn, calling at Rio de Janerio, 1849-1850.

Barras, Leonard
Up the Tyne in a Flummox
A rowing trip up the river Tyne in a small boat.

Barton, Humphrey
Atlantic Adventurers, 1953 (revised 1962)
The book covers tales of many sailors (including the author) who have sailed across the Atlantic in small yatchs.
Vertue XXXV, 1955
The smallest boat at the time, 25 ft., to make a westward crossing of the Atlantic.

Beach, Capt. Edward L. 1918-
Around the World Submerged, 1962
Author commands the nuclear submarine Triton on a history making voyage. Also wrote the novel Run Silent, Run Deep.
The Wreck Of the Memphis,1966.
In August 1916, the Memphis, one of the largest battle cruisers in the US Navy, and commanded by Beach's father, was destroyed in Santo Domingo Harbor, on a sunny day, by a series of freak waves (caused by an offshore volcano/earthquake) which broke over her bridge, slammed her against the bottom, etc. Captain Beach was subsequently court martialed.

Beattie, John
The Breath of Angels, 1995
Beattie's account of his attempt to fulfill his boyhood dream of a circumnavigation. Although unable to complete the circumnavigation, he still manages a series of adventures such as sur-

viving storms inthe N. Atlantic, crossing the Atlantic single-handed and cruising the Caribbean with a series of interesting crew. In a poignant ending, Beattie encounters and saves the life of a man adrift at sea and they develop a deep friendship as they struggle to return the man to his country.

Berry, Don
Magic Harbor, 1995
The online book MAGIC HARBOR is a memoir of people and events from six years on the Puget Sound waters. Every word is true. Only one person's name and one boat name have been changed. Very good reading.

Bestic, Capt. A.A.
Kicking Canvas, 1958
A 1908 voyage aboard a 3-masted schooner, the Denbigh Castle. 253 days at sea with a near shipwreck and mutiny.

Binning, Arthur J.
Survivors, 1994
Online book. The saga of the WW2 U-Boat U-188. This is a remarkable true account of survival at sea against all the odds.

Birtles, Dora
North-West by North, 1935
Personal account of a voyage from Australia to Singapore in 1932 on a 34 ft cutter with a group of friends. Much involved with tensions and inter-personal discord involved with a long voyage on a small boat.

Bishop, *Nathaniel Holmes*, 1837-1902.
Voyage of the Paper Canoe Microform, 1878
A geographical journey of 2500 miles, from Quebec to the Gulf of Mexico, during the years 1874-5.
Four Months in a Sneak Box, 1879
A voyage from Pittsburgh to Florida down the Ohio and Mississippi rivers in a 12 foot duck hunting boat.

Blair, Clay
Hitler's U-boat War: The Silent Hunters, 1939-1942, pub. 1996
An epic sea story, the most arduous and prolonged naval battle in all history. For a period of nearly six years, the German U-boat force attempted to blockade and isolate the British Isles, in hopes of forcing the British out of the war, thereby thwarting the Allied strategic air assault on German cities as well as Overlord, the Allied invasion of Occupied France.

Blake, *Peter & Sefton, Alan*
Blake's Odyssey, 1982
The 1981/82 Whitbread Round the World Race in Ceramco New Zealand.

Blanchet, M. Whylie
The Curve of Time, 1973.
This is an excellent story of a woman who, with her children- spend their summers cruising the waters between Vancouver Island and the mainland of British Columbia.

Bligh, William
The Mutiny on Board H.M.S. Bounty, 1792
William Bligh's account of the fatal voyage of the Bounty, and his subsequent 3,600 mile trip to Timor in an open boat. Bligh was not the tyrant of legend in fiction (in fact, evidence exists that he was the most lenient commander of a Pacific exploration ship of that period). Several modern editions of this book exist, including one by Airmont (1965) and one by Signet (1988).

Blyth, Chay
The Impossible Voyage
Alone in a small yacht, Chay Blyth was the first to sail non- stop around the world uphill against tides and current. In this remarkable saga of 20th century courage and fortitude, he tells the story of his ten month voyage in which he pitted his skill and endurance against the elements of the world.

Bok, Curtis
Maria, 1962
A tale of the Northeast coast of the U.S. and of the North Atlantic. Life aboard a 40' ketch and in port of a small North American town.

Bombard, Alain
The Bombard Story, 1953
65 days crossing the Atlantic in a tiny boat and living on fish juice.

Bradfield, S. E.
Road to the Sea. 1964
After building the 30 foot ketch D'Vara, Bradfield and his wif sail her 18,000 miles from Australia to England , via the Mediterranean.

Bradford, Ernle
Drake, England's Greatest Seafarer, 1965
Biography of Sir Francis Drake, who rose from common origins to become England's foremost fighting sailor of his age.

Bradlee, Francis B.C.
Piracy in the West Indies and Its Suppression, 1923
Accounts from 1820-1860 of piratical boardings, murders, hangings from the yardarm. Taken from logs of merchantmen contempary writings and newspapers.

Brassey, Mrs. Anna
Around the World in the Yacht Sunbeam, 1878
Around Cape Horn to the South Seas, the Orient and back to England via the Suez Canal.

Brenton, Francis
Long Sail to Haiti, 1965
A journey from England to Haiti via the French canals and the crossing of the Atlantic in the yacht Nengo.

Briggs, L. Vernon
Around Cape Horn to Honolulu on the Nark "Amy Turner" in 1880, 1974
To Hawaii, San Francisco and the Orient facing shipwreck, mutiny, a waterspout and a race against another Cape Horner.

Brown, Alexander Crosby
Horizon's Rim, 1935
A voyage around the world aboard a 76 FT. Nova Scotian fishing schooner from Sydney to the Dutch East Indies, the Suez Canal and back to New York.

Bruce, Erroll
When the Crew Matters Most, 1961
An ocean racing story. A British crew aboard the 36' sloop Belmore wins the 1960 Bermuda race.

Buckley, William F.
Airborne:a sentimental journey, 1976
Buckley, with his son and five friends, cross the Atlantic aboard the schooner Cyrano.
Atlantic High, 1982
As in Airborne, Buckley describes sailing across the Atlantic, this time aboard the 71 ft. ketch Sealestial.
Racing Through Paradise: A Pacific Passage, 1987
This is a very interesting account of Buckley's passage across the Pacific. The passage is from the Azores to the Galapagos to the South Seas aboard a 71 foot ketch.

Buckley, Christopher (son of WFB, above)
Steaming to Bamboola : the world of a tramp freighter, 1982
Columbianna (Steamship), seafaring life.

Buenzle, Fred
Bluejacket: An Autobiography
Memoir of the enlisted man's life in the US Navy in 1890's. This period marks the transition from sail to power.

Burgess, Robert H.
The Sea Serpent Journal: Hugh McCulloch Gregory's Voyage aroundthe World in a Clipper Ship, 1854-55, 1975
Two stories exist side by side in this book: both begin in the middle and end in the middle. Hugh tells a story of a cruise around the world and the editor tells about the Sea Serpent, a clipper ship contemporary of The Flying Cloud and Ariel. Routine days, hardship days, adventure, and the "stuff of life" flow from this 19 year old's pen page after page.

Busch, Briton C.
Master of Desolation—The Reminiscences of Capt. J.J. Fuller
An edited manuscript of the memoirs of a whaling and sealing captain active in the late 19th century. Most of the story takes place in the South Indian Ocean near the Kerguelen Island group, aka "Desolation Islands". Relates a brutal and sometimes frustrating occupation of great hardship.

Caldwell, John
Desperate Voyage
It's the end of WWII and the author is stranded in the States, wants to return to his wife in Australia—some merchant marine experience, but no sailing. So he buys a 29 foot boat, teaches himself to sail & navigate and sets off across the Pacific. He sailed 8,500 miles of variable seas, reefs, tropic islands—across the equator, through the doldrums and into hurricane seas singlehanded.

Callanhan, Steven
Adrift:Seventy-six Days Lost at Sea, 1986
Wreck of the yacht Napoleon Solo and the subsequent survival in a raft in the North Atlantic.

Cameron, Silver Donald Wind,
Whales and Whiskey: A Cape Breton Voyage, 1991
Sailing Nova Scotia including Cape Breton Island.

Campbell, Archibald
The Restless Voyage, 1948 (edited by Stanley Porteus D. Sc.)
Scots seaman's adventures around the world in the early 19th century. Expanded version of *A Voyage Round the World* From1806 to 1812, first published in 1816.
A Voyage Around the World, 1969
A voyage from 1806 to 1812 visiting Japan, Kamchatka, The Aleutian Islands and the Sandwich Islands. The author's shipwreck on the island of Sannack, and the subsequent wreck in the ship's boat.

Campbell, Neil
Shadow and Sun, 1947
Irish Ship's Captain's autobiography.

Canot, Theodore (1807- ca 1860)
Memoirs of a Slave Trader, 1854 (republished Jonathan Cape 1929)
Mainly true account of slave trading between West Africa and the Americas. Went to sea in 1819, traded slaves from 1826 until the Royal Navy suppressed the trade in the 1840s.

Carter, Robert
Carter's Coast of New England (also published as "A Summer Cruise on the Coast of New England"),1969
A classic yachting voyage from

Provincetown to Bar Harbor in the summer of 1858.

Carter, Ronald
A Yachtsman's Memories of Long Ago, 1980
A collection of stories of yachting and sailing in and around New Zealand and dating back to 1850s.

Chappell, Edward, Lieut. R. N.
Narrative of a Voyage to Hudson's Bay in His Majesty's Ship Rosamond, 1970
This is a facsimile reprint. This book was originally printed in 1817 for J. Mawman, Ludgate Street, London, England by R. Watts,

Chiles, Webb
Storm Passage, 1977
Alone around Cape Horn. At sea for 310 days aboard a 37' cutter, covering 38,000 miles in 5 difficult passages.
Open Boat, 1982
Across the Pacific in the wake of Capt. Bligh ending with a shipwreck in the New Hebrides.

Chippendale, Capt. Harry Allen, 1879-?
Sails and Whales, 1951
The author, 16, sails as boy in a whaling bark and then follows 8 more whaling voyages.

Chichester, Sir Francis, 1901-1972
Atlantic Adventure, 1962
After failing to fulfill his prediction to cross the Atlantic in less than a month in a single-handed race, Chichester tries again and crosses in 33 days.
Gipsy Moth Circles the World, 1967
Sir Francis' famous circumnavigation in Gipsy Moth IV. Begun at age 64 Chichester set the solo speed record and made only one port of call.
The Lonely Sea and the Sky, 1964
Excellent autobiography. Includes transatlantic voyages and his pioneering first flight across the Tasman Sea in his airplane Gypsy Moth, from which he named his boats.

Clark, D.H.
An Evolution of Singlehanders, 1975 (hardbound edition)
The Singlehanders: The Evolution of a Lonely Art, 1976 (softcover)
A history of singlehanded voyages beginning with Brendan in 545 AD. Clark covers all of the famous and many not so famous voyages made by single handers throughout history. Includes 8 appendices listing eight categories of records and all of the records in these categories at the time.

Clark, Miles
High Endeavors
Biography of Miles & Beryl Smeeton, who at age 50

embarked on a life at sea in their yacht Tzu Hang, and travelled over 130,000 miles; dismasted twice near Cape Horn.

Clements, Rex
A Gypsy of the Horn, 1951
The narrative of a voyage around the world in a square-rigged ship.

Clifford, Brian & Illingworth, Neil
The Voyage of the Golden Lotus, 1962
The building and voyage of a junk from Hong Kong to Auckland, New Zealand.

Cloud, Enoch Center
Enoch's Voyage, 1974
Life on a whale ship, 1851-1854. A greenhorn aboard the New Bedford whaler the Henry Kneeland.

Clough, S.
Cruises and Curses, 1926
A tale of buying a 22 ft. cruising sailboat and sailing on the Thames River. One mishap after another, written in a humorous vein.

Cochran, Hamilton
Pirates of the Spanish Main, 1961
An overview of piracy from the 16th to the 18th century including Drake, Morgan, Kidd, Blackbeard, and the female pirates.

Cochrane, Admiral Lord Thomas (10th Earl of Dundonald)
Autobiography of a Seaman, 1859 (reprinted 1995)
The memoirs of the most colorful captain of the Nelsonian era. Among other exploits, the capture of the Spanish 32-gun frigate Gamo by the 14-gun sloop (!) Speedy (fictionalized by P O'Brian in _Master and Commander_) and formation and command of the Chilean, Brazilian and Greek navies. As O'Brian notes, the exploits would be unbelievable, if they were not true.

Cogill, Burgess
When God was an atheist sailor
Memories of a childhood at sea, 1902,1990

Colas, Alain
Around the World Alone, 1978
Single handed around Cape Horn in a 70 ft. trimaran, an attempt to match Chichester's record.

Cole, Guy
Sailing in Irons, 1954
Cole, handicapped, crosses the Atlantic in the 31 ft. yacht "Galway Blazer" with Bill King.

Cole, Jean (1917–)
Trimaran Against the Trades, A H & A W Reed, Wellington NZ, 1968
The Cole family, including 90-year-old Granny Cole, sail the tri-

maran Galinule against the trade winds: 11,700 miles from Mombasa (Kenya)—Seychelles—Diego Garcia—Cocos I—Christmas I—Darwin—Great Barrier Reef—New Zealand.

Coles, Adlard
Sailing Days, 1939?
A cruising narrative on the south coast of England in boats ranging from 8 ft. dinghies to cruising and racing yachts.

Cooper, James Fenimore
Ned Myers: A Life Before the Mast
A memoir of Meyers' 36 years at sea in the US Navy during the age of sail.

Cottee, Kay
First Lady, 1989
After 189 days at sea and over 22,000 nautical miles Kay Cottee became the first woman in history to complete a solo, non-stop and unassisted voyage around the globe.

Course, Capt. A. G.
Pirates of the Eastern Seas, 1966
Pirate exploits from the Gulf of Arden to the Sea of Japan.

Crapo, Thomas
Strange But True, 1893
Life and adventures of Captain Thomas Crapo and wife. A voyage in the 19 ft dory, New Bedford, from New Bedford, MA, to Penzance, England in 1877. (In 1899, Crapo was lost at sea attempting a passage from Newport to Cuba in the 9 ft Volunteer.)

Crealock, W.I.B.
Vagabonding Under Sail, 1951
Aboard a 40' cutter in 1948, sailing from Falmouth to Gibraltar and on to the Canaries, British Guiana, the Caribbean and New York.

Creighton, Margaret
Dogwatch and Liberty Days, 1982
Seafaring life in the 19th century. Based on journals and daires kept aboard ship as well as sketches by the sailors.

Crighton, Tom
Caribbean Vagabond, 1968
A 10 month leisurely cruise to the West Indies aboard a Colin Archer designed 50 ft. ketch-rigged pilot boat.

Crocker, Templeton
The Cruise of the Zaca, 1933
A 27,000 mile voyage around the world in a tops'l schooner via the Suez Canal to the South Pacific and back to California.

Cultra, Quen
Queequeg's Odyssey, 1977
Sailing around the world with no previous ocean cruising experience, aboard a home built 35' Piver design trimaran.

Daggett, Kendrick P.
Fifty Years of Fortitude—The maritime career of Capt J Blaisdell 1810-1860, 1988
Compiled and edited letters of the Capt. during the course of trading at various ports in Europe, North and South America. Realistic impressions of life at sea and how trade was conducted during the nineteenth century.

Dana, Richard Henry, 1815-1882
Two Years Before The Mast, 1841, 1909, 1948
A personal narrative of the seaman's life in the age of sail. A classic of nautical literature.

Dann, John C., Editor
The Nagle Journal, 1988
A diary of the life of Jacob Nagle, sailor, from the year 1775 to 1841. Nagle served in the Revolutionary army with Washington, on an American privateer, in the Royal Navy, and with the British East India Company. While in the Royal Navy he went to Australia with the First Fleet, and served with Howe and Nelson in the First French War. A truly valuable work, it is one of the few accounts of these events by a common seaman.

Darwin, Charles 1809-1882
The Voyage of the Beagle, first published 1839, revised in 1860
Darwin's account of the voyage around the world in 1831-1836 that was a major inspiration for his theories of evolution has been called "the greatest scientific travel adventure ever written"

Daunt, Achilles
Our Sea Coast Heros, 1887
Stories of wreck and rescue by the Lifeboat and Rocket. Stories from the Royal National Lifeboat Institution.

Davison, Ann
*My Ship Is So Small,*1956
Neophyte sailor Ann Davison got the notion to sail across the Atlantic from England to the US, then bought the 23 foot sloop "Felicity Ann", in February 1952, had her surveyed by Humphrey Barton, and made the trip.

Day, Thomas Fleming
Across the Atlantic in Sea Bird, 1927
From New York to Gibraltar in a 26 ft. yawl-rigged sharpie, with a 3 h.p. engine.

de Hartog, Jan
The Lost Sea, 1951
Memoirs of de Hartog's life as a ship's boy on the fleet of fishing boats that plied the Zuider Zee in the years before the sea was dyked off from the ocean.

A Sailor's Life, 1955
A collection of anecdotes about life as a merchant seaman prior to W.W.II. The book started out as a book of hints for young sailors, but ended up being written as the memoirs of a middle aged mariner.

De Meiss-Teuffen
Wanderlust, 1953
An adventurer who has sailed small boats all over the globe tells of his exploits.

D'Esque, Count Jean Loui ("Chips")
A Count in the Fo'cs'le, 1932
The incidents of his 30 odd years at sea, beginning with his being shanghaied out of a Baltimore bar.

Doubleday, Russell
A Year in a Yawl, 1902
A true tale of the adventures of 4 boys in a 30 ft. yawl on a 7,000 mile cruise down the mississippi and up the Atlantic seaboard.

Dow G.F. & Edmonds J.H.
Pirates of the New England Coast
Based on original documents from Massachusetts and Vice-Admiralty courts.

Downey, Joseph T.
Cruise of the Portsmouth: 1845-1847, 1963
This was Downey's journal written aboard the U.S. Sloop Portsmouth in California during the Mexican War. It is written in a light hearted manner but gives info on events of the time. Really a pleasure to read!

du Baty, Capt. Raymond
15,000 Miles in a Ketch, 1948
Voyaging from 1907-1909 in a small French fishing ketch, the J.B. Charcot, from Boulogne to Melbourne, Australia.

Duxbury, Ken
Lugworm Homeward Bound, 1975
Sailing a Drascombe Lugger from Greece to England.

Dye, Frank & Margaret
Ocean-Crossing Wayfarer
Fantastic adventures of North Atlantic crossings to Norway and Iceland in a Wayfarer Class dinghy. Survival and boat handling.

Elkington, Patrick & Mudie, Colin
Sopranino, 1953
10,000 miles over the ocean in a midget sailboat, less than 20 ft.
The authors were out to prove that you could go anywhere in a small sailing craft.

Endicott, William and Jenkins, L.W.
Wrecked Among the Cannibals in the Fiji's, 1923
A narrative of shipwreck and adventure in the South Seas in 1829.

Exquemelin, Alexander O.
The Buccaneers of America
Chronicles the lives of America's most famous pirates.

Fairfax, John and Cook, Sylvia
Oars Across the Pacific, 1972
An account taken from the diaries of the authors of a rowed journey from San Francisco to Australia. Good account of beauty and danger in the Pacific.

Fanning, Edmond
Voyages to the South Seas, Indian, and Pacific Oceans, China Sea Northwest Coast, Feejee (sic) Islands, South Shetlands..., 1970
Originally published in 1838 describing his voyages in the Southern Hemisphere, 1830-1837

Farson, Negley
Sailing Across Europe, 1926
Aboard a 26 ft. yawl on the rivers and canals of Europe from Holland to the Black Sea.

Fermor, Patrick Leigh
Traveller's Tree, 1950
Tooling around the Caribbean in the 40's.

Forester, C. S.
The Adventures of John Wetherall, 1954 (editor)
Memoirs of shipboard life in the Royal Navy during the Napoleonic Wars by a man who served as a common seaman on the HMS Hussar. Covers the period from 1803 through 1815. Includes a streach as a prisoner of war in France.

Francis, Clare
Come Wind or Weather, ADC
Accutra Races Round the World, 1978
Clare Francis tells the story of her entry in the 1977/78 Whitbread Round the World race.

Gaby, James
Mate in Sail
Chronicle of a lifetime in square-rigged sail by an Australian shipmaster.

Gann, Ernest K., 1910-1991
Song of the Sirens, 1968
Nautical adventures of the author, who loved the sea almost as much as he loved flying.

Gardner, G. Peabody
E 1/2 S, 1953
Cruising experiences in the Maritime provinces.
Ready About, 1959
Sailing Adventures Down East, off Nova Scotia and New Foundland.

Garland, Joseph E.
Lone Voyager, 1963
The story of Howard Blackburn. This giant Nova Scotian rowed sixty miles into Newfoundland

with the frozen body of his dory-mate, five days without food or water, after they were separated in a gale from the Gloucester schooner "Grace L. Fears" in the winter of1883. Blackburn survived but lost all his fingers by frostbite; he returned to Gloucester to keep a saloon. In 1899 he sailed the sloop "Great Western" singlehanded, in spite of his disability, from Gloucester to England. The following year, in 1901, he repeated his astounding feat in the twenty-five-foot sloop "Great Republic," this time sailing to Portugal

Gerbault, Alain
In Quest of the Sun, 1927, 6th ed 1937
Firecrest sails round the world.
The Flight of the Firecrest, 1955
The account of a single-handed cruise from east to west across the Atlantic in 1922 aboard the 39 ft. cutter Firecrest.

Glennie, John
The Spirit of Rose-Noelle, 119 days adrift, 1990
Four men in an upturned trimaran for 119 days before they werewashed ashore.

Goldsmith, John
Voyage in the Beagle, 1978
Voyage from England to Terra del Fuego, Juan Fernandez, Galapagos Islands, etc. in a wooden bark to film a BBC TV film about the famous 1830s voyage of the original HMS Beagle.

Gosnell, Harpur Allen
Before the Mast in the Clippers, 1937
The diaries of Charles A Abbey 1856-60. Recomposed diary of an educated young man serving as ordinary seaman. He served on several of the clippers in the Far East trade during this time.

Gowlland, Gladys
Master of the Moving Sea
The memoirs of Peter Mathieson, ship's captain, compiled by his daughter-in-law.

Graham, R.D.
Rough Passage, 1936
Account of Single-handed voyage from England to Labrador and Bermuda in a 30 ft cutter. Many suggestions for safe single-handed sailing and some interesting accounts of life in the Canadian Maritimes.

Graham, Robin Lee
Dove
Graham set off at age 16 to sail around the world in a 24' Ranger sloop. He returned several years later as a married man in a Luders 33. He and his wife then dropped out, built a lean-to in the mountains and raised a son named Quimby. In the late 60's National Geographic chronicled his story.

Green, Alfred J.
Jottings from a Cruise, 1944, 1947
The captain's diary of an ill-fated voyage aboard the four masted barque Mertola from Wales to the Cape of Good Hope, across to South America and shipwrecked in the North Atlantic.

Griffin, Bob
Blue Water, 1979
A guide to self-reliant sailboat cruising , written by Griffin after he and his family sailed two "Awahnee"'s 200,000 miles over 20 years.

Griffiths, Maurice
Little Ships and Shoal Waters, 1985
Although this book discusses designing, building and sailing shoal draft cruising yachts, included are two cruises in both blue and shoal waters.

Groser, John
Atlantic Venture,1968: The Observer Singlehanded Transatlantic Race
This is a chronicle of the third OSTAR race, reasonably well written by an Observer writer

Gullain, Frances and Christian
Call of the Sea, 1976
From Amsterdam to Tahiti via the Panama Canal aboard a 33 ft. sloop.

Gunn, John
Barrier Reef by Trimaran, 1966
Gunn built a 35 foot trimaran, then sailed it to the Great Barrier Reef and back to Sydney a total of 3000 miles.

Guttridge, Leonard
Icebound, 1987
A new account of the disasterous 1879 voyage of the Jeanrette attempting to find a northwest passage from Alaska to Scandinavia. Takes a different perspective than an earlier recounting of the expedition.

Guzzwell, John
Trekka Round the World, 1963
Sailing Trekka round the world. John took time off when reaching New Zealand to help sail Tzu Hang with the Smeetons to South America where they were pitch-poled. Later the yacht was repaired and rolled when trying to round Cape Horn and the book describing that is "Once is Enough" by Miles Smeeton.

Hall, Captain Basil (1788–1844)
Fragments of Voyages and Travels,
Nine volumes 1831–1840
Hall served in the Royal Navy from 1802 till 1825. He saw action in the Atlantic and the East Indies, and later visited Korea and China, and was involved in the liberation of Chile, Peru, and Mexico in the 1820s. This is a miscellany of

descriptions of life at sea, written for younger readers.

Hamilton, Donald
Cruises with Kathleen, 1980
Cruising from Vancouver to the Bahamas under sail by the author of the Matt Helm detective series.

Hayden, Sterling
Wanderer, 1963
Autobiography of a sailor reluctantly turned movie star. Much better than the author's novel, Voyage.

Hays, David and Hays, Daniel
My Old Man and the Sea: A Father and Son Sail around Cape Horn, *1995*
Some fathers and sons go fishing together. Some play ball. David and Daniel decide to sail 17,000 miles to a dangerous at the bottom of the world and back. On this voyage the father relinquishes control, the son becomes the captain, and before long they are utterly alone,with only the huge waves of Cape Horn, the unceasing wind, a compass, a sextant, a pet cat, and the tiny boat they've built together.

Hayter, Adrian
The Long Voyage, 1959
A six year solo voyage from England to New Zealand on a 32' yawl.
Sheila in the Wind, 1959
From England to New Zealand. Hayter "circumnavigated" by doing the voyage in two directions via the Mediterranean, Red Sea and the Indian Ocean. His boat was a 31 ft. gaff-rigged yawl designed by Albert Strange.

Heaps, Leo
The Log of the Centurion, 1973
Based on the original papers of Captain Philip Saumarez on board HMS Centurion, Lord Anson's flagship during his circumnavigation, this book is a factual account of the events described in the novels Manilla Galleon and Golden Ocean (among others).

Helm, Thomas
The Sea Lark, 1955
Some unusual sailing adventures in a 47 ft. sailing schooner while voyaging 5,000 miles in the Caribbean.

Hemingway-Douglass, Reanne
Cape Horn: One Man's Dream, One Woman's Nightmare, 1995
His Dream—to round Cape Horn and circumnavigate the Southern Hemisphere in their sailboat. Her Nightmare—coping wtih a driven captain and the frightening seas of the Great Southern Ocean. 800 miles WNW of Cape Horn they encountered the ultimate wave.

Heyerdahl, Thor
Kon-Tiki, 1950, 1966
Ill-advised pseudo-scientific raft journey by men accustomed to the thrills of war. Across the Pacific in a balsa raft!
The Ra Expeditions, 1971
Yet another transoceanic voyage—this time from the mouth of the Nile to the Caribbean in a papyrus boat. The first one sinks, so our intrepid hero builds another one and tries again. That a crew with modern navigation, medicine, and food supplies, with a captain that knows where he is bound can sail the Atlantic in two tries is proof (according to the author) that the pre-Columbian civilizations received all of their knowledge from the Egyptians!
The Tigris Expedition: In Search of Our Beginnings, 1980
Following his adventurous investigations of the possibility of long-distance South American and Egyptian seafaring, Heyerdahl undertakes a voyage on a reed raft from Iraq to Pakistan, to illustrate the possibility of sea contact between Sumer and the ancient culture of the Indus Valley. A further leg into the Red Sea is prevented by political unrest in the area.

Hiscock, Eric
Sou'west in Wanderer IV, 1973
From England to the West Indies, a year in California, Hawaii and the South Pacific and heavy weather in the Tasman sea.
Cruising in Wanderer II
(The trip to the Azores plus early experiences.)
Come Aboard, 1978
His third circumnavigation completed in 1976 from New Zealand to England aboard his jib-headed ketch, Wanderer IV.
Around the World in Wanderer III.
Atlantic Cruise in Wanderer III, 1968
Cruising Under Sail, 1981
(Describing yachts and rigging.)
Voyaging Under Sail, 1970 (Updated. These two last have been combined into one in at least one printing.)
Wandering Under Sail, 1939, 2nd ed. 1977
Singlehanded cruises in Wander II.
Two Yachts, Two Voyages, 1984
Last Boat to Folly Bridge, 1970

Holm, Donald
The Circumnavigators, 1974
Small boat voyagers of modern times: Slocum, Voss, Gerbault, and many others up to Robin Graham.

Hitz-Holman, Betsy
Sitting Ducks A True Adventure, 1983
A young couple sets sail for Curacao in their 38 foot sloop "Cheers", and arrive, but not before being robbed, stabbed

and running aground upon a reef where they sit for two weeks.

Hofvendahl, Russ 1921-
Hard on the Wind
The author goes fishing for cod in the Bering Sea in a four masted schooner during the 30's.

Holmes, Capt. James William
Voyaging: 50 Years on the Seven Seas in Sail, 1972
Reminiscences of one of the famous sea-captains of Victorian England covering the years 1869-1921.

Horie, Kenichi
Kodoku, 1964
Sailing alone across the pacific in a 19 ft. boat from Osake to San Francisco, facing 5 major storms in 3 months. Horie's boat is on display at the San Francisco Maritime Museum.

Horr, A. R.
The Log of the Schooner Bowdoin, 1947
A voyage along the Labrador coast and a cruise in the Arctic regions under Capt. Macmillan.

Hough, Richard
Captain Bligh and Mr. Christian, 1973
The men and the mutiny.

Houghton, Philip
Land From the Masthead, 1968
A circumnavigation of New Zealand in the wake of and 200 years after Capt. Cook aboard a 40 ft Bermudian cutter.

Howarth, David
Trafalgar, The Nelson Touch, 1969.
The battle of Trafalgar as told with an emphasis on the officers and men fighting the battle.

Hoyt, Edwin Palmer
The Amistad Affair, 1970
Mutiny aboard the Cuban schooner Amistad in 1839, when the African slaves took command of the ship and tried to sail back to Africa.

Hughes, John Scott, editor
Macpherson's Voyages, 1946
In the closing years of his life, 1932-38, Macpherson logged 45,000 miles in small yacht cruising aboard the 25' cutter, Driac II. This is the Macpherson who gave his collections to the National Maritime Museum.

Hume, David
Blueberry: A Boat of the Connecticut Shoreline, 1994
Hume designed his boat Blueberry with the help of Phil Bolger and then built it over 7 summer vacations while headmaster of a private school in New York City. This book is the story of the building and sailing of Blueberry along the southeastern Connecticut coast. A

very good read about boatbuilding and sailing.

Illingworth, John 1903-
The Malham Story, 1972
  The account of his life in the world of off-shore racing and the yachts he owned and sailed including the Malhams, Maid of, Myth of, Merle of, Mouse of, etc. He designed one of the first yachts expressly designed for ocean racing in 1936, Maid of Malham. He created the Sydney Hobart race just after the war and returned to England and Myth of Malham a yacht that monopolized the ocean racing prize list including several Fastnets.

Irving, Laurence
Bligh and the Mutiny, 1936 (edited by Laurence)
  His narrative of the voyage to Otaheite, with an account of the mutiny and of the open boat journey to Timor.
Windmills and Waterways, 1927
  The log of a summer cruise throughout Holland aboard his cutter, the Pamela Mary.

James, Naomi
Alone Around the World, 1979
At One with the Sea, 1978
  First woman to sail single handed around the world via Cape Horn, from September '77 to June '78, 272 days.

James, Thomas
The Dangerous Voyage of Captain Thomas James, 1973
  This is a facsimile edition. This book was originally published in 1740 in London, England by O. Payne, Cornhill

Jameson, W.M.
Sunfinders, 1937
  Yachting aboard a 36 ft. and then a 42 ft. cruiser for 7 years from England through the canals and rivers of France to the Mediterranean.

Jerome, Jerome K.
Three Men in a Boat; To say nothing of the dog, 1889
  A classic in British humor about travel on the Thames River.

Johnson, Irving
The Peking Battles Cape Horn, 1932 (1977)
  A voyage around Cape Horn in one of the last square riggers to sail the seas, the Peking, now preserved at the South Street Seaport Museum in New York City. Great narriative from Johnson's early days at sea.
Westard Bound in the Schooner Yankee, 1936
  Captain, wife and crew spent 18 months in the early 1930's sailing a 92 foot schooner around the world. Sailing to See Yankee's People and Places Yankee Sails Across Europe

Johnson, Irving & Electa
Yankee Sails the Nile, 1966
  The ketch Yankee was one of the last boats to sail the Nile from the Med to Abu Simbel and back. Navigation is now closed by the Aswan High Dam. The journey is recounted, mostly by Electa Johnson, in a pleasant style.

Jones, Ted
The Dogwatch, 1981
  A collection from this well known yachting writer's yarns and commentaries.

Jones, Tristan, 1924-
Adrift, 1980
  A personal saga of being ice-bound in Arctic seas. He also describes all his 22 years of adventure in small ocean craft.
A Steady Trade: A Boyhood at Sea, 1982
  Jones' early adventures, sailing in Thames barges, etc.
Heart of Oak, 1984
Ice, 1978
  Jones tries to take his converted lifeboat Cresswell further north than any other sailing vessel, adventuring in Greenland on the way and then getting trapped in the ice off of Spitzbergen, finally drifting to 79 deg. 40' north.
Improbable Voyage, 1986
  Across Europe in an ocean-going trimaran from the North Sea to the Black Sea.
Incredible Voyage, 1977
  Jones sails ocean-going yachts in the lowest (Dead Sea) and highest (L. Titicaca) bodies of water that will float them. After Titicaca he takes his boat down the Parana and Paraguay rivers to the Atlantic. Truly an incredible voyage.
One Hand for Yourself, One For the Ship, 1982
  The essentials of single-handed sailing. He sailed the Atlantic 18 times (9 times alone), the Arctic Seas and around the world.
Outward Leg, 1985
  Jones loses a leg to amputation and while recovering decides to acquire a boat, the trimaran Outward Leg, and crew and sail the seas as an example to the handicapped. He and his crew sail from San Diego, through the Panama Canal, along the northern coast of So. America against the winter trades in some of the roughest sailing in the world. Eventually ends up in Falmouth, England.
Saga of a Wayward Sailor
Somewhere's East of Suez, 1988
  Jones takes the trimaran Outward Leg to Asian waters.
To Venture Further
  Disabled Jones, 3 disabled Thai nationals and a German, in a small Thai seagoing fishing boat, encounter sea adventures off the Kra Peninsula of Thailand.

Jones, William H. S.
The Cape Horn Breed, 1956
  The author sails as an apprentice in the full-rigged steel ship British Isles from 1905-1909, on voyages the west coast of North and South America and Australia, encountering fire, storms, bucko mate, etc.

Junger, Sebastian
The Perfect Storm, 1997
  The story of the Oct. 1991 storm that meterologists called "the perfect storm". The book concentrates on the fate of the off-shore fishing boat, Andrea Gail, off the coast of Nova Scotia.In recreating the final moments of the crew of the Andrea Gail, Junger paints a harrowing picture of life at sea in a major storm. Excellent book.

Kalrsson, Elis
Cruising Off Mozambique, 1969
  Coasting along the east coast of Africa aboard an 18' Caprice class sloop.
Mother Sea, 1964
  The author's days sailing square riggers of the Erikson Aland fleet as first mate aboard the Herzogin Cecilie.

Kauffman, Ray
Hurricane's Wake, 1940
  Around the world on a 45 ft. ketch, which the author built along the Mississippi River and then sailed to the South Seas.

Kent, Rockwell 1882-1971
N by E, 1930
  Voyage to Greenland in a 36' cutter, shipwreck there and further adventures. Illustrated with the author's own woodcuts. Voyaging southward from the Strait of Magellan, 1924 Kent bought a lifeboat from a ship he was travelling in and set off in it to explore Terra del Fuego and vicinity. Illustrated by the author.
Voyaging Southward from the Strait of Magellan, 1924
  Kent and his companions sailed southward along the bleak coasts of Terra del Fuego and to the Horn.

King, Dean & Hattendorf, John B., editors
Every Man Will Do His Duty, 1997
  This is an anthology of firsthand accounts (1793-1815) that cover the French Revolutionary War, The Napoleonic War and the War of 1812, but also provide a vivid insight into life at sea, with its deprivation, monotony, pleasure, pain, justice and injustice.

Klein, David and King, Mary Louise
Great Adventures in Small Boats, 1948
  An anthology of accounts of individuals who sailed the open seas in small boats. Includes chapters by Joshua Slocum, Jack London, Richard Maury, Marin-Marie, and others.

Klein, David and Johnson, Mary
They Took to the Sea, 1948
  Personal accounts of the small boat voyages of Joshua Slocum, Jack London, Rockwell Kent, Gerbault, Kaufmann, Maury, Robinson, O'Brien and others.

Knox-Johnston, Robin
A World of My Own, 1969
  Knox-Johnson relates his win in the Golden Globe round the world race that was so disastrous for so many others. Knox-Johnson was the only entrant to finish and won the trophy for first finish and the 5,000 pound prize for fastest finish. His voyage was an incredible adventure, a feat of endeavor and seamanship which will be unsurpassed and unforgotten. Sheer determination helped him survive every imaginable difficulty.
Last But Not Least, 1978
  His own story of the 1978 round the world race in Heath's Condor. (Sir Peter Blake was one of the crew, since then, winning the Americas Cup).

Landery, Charles
Whistling for a Wind, 1953
  Adventures sailing a ketch from England to the Aegean Sea.

Lansing, Alfred
Endurance; Shackleton's incredible voyage, 1959
  Ernest Shackleton's 1914 expedition to cross Antarctica fails when their ship is crushed in the ice.

LeGolif, Louis
The Memoirs of a Buccaneer, 1954
  Being a wondrous and unrepentant account of the prodigious adventures and amours of King Louis XIV's loyal servant, Louis LeGolif, known for his singular wound as Borgnefesse, Captain of the Buccaneers.

le Guay, Laurence
Sailing Free Around the World, 1975
  In 1970 Le Guay and crew left Sydney for a two year voyage around the world in a 12.8 metre steel yawl "Eclipse".

Leigh, Randolf
Forgotten Waters, 1941
  Adventure in the Gulf of California. A cruising and exploring sailing adventure aboard the schooner, Lascar II.

Leslie, Edward E.
Desperate Journey's Abandoned Souls: True Stories of Castaways and other Survivors, 1988
  Alexander Selkirk, Boon Island, etc.

LeSueur, Gavin
The Line, 1997
  The story of the Bicentennial Around Australia Yacht Race. On the first night of this 8000 mile adventure one man died, a

trimaran capsized, a monohull was rescued adrift and a police rescue launch sunk and all had to be rescued. The story is through the perspective of Gavin and Catherine LeSueur, the two crew on 'John West', a Crowther 40ft racing catamaran. Encompasses high sea drama, romance, rescues and controveresy.

Le Toumelin, Jacques Yves
Kurun in the Caribbean, 1963
His second cruise in his gaff-rigged cutter to Madeira, the Canaries, and across the Atlantic to Grenada covering 3,200 miles in 27 days.

Lewis, David
*The Ship Would Not Travel Due West,*1961.
Lewis sailed "Cardinal Virtue" in the first OSTAR race in 1960 and chronicles the trip.

Lewis, David
Ice Bird, 1976
The first single-handed voyage in Antarctica. 3500 miles in a 32 ft. steel sloop circumnavigating Antarctica.
The Ship Would Not Travel Due West, 1963
A 1957 single-handed trans-atlantic race with Chischester as thewinner and Lewis in 3rd place despite a dismasting.

Lipscomb, James
Cutting Loose, 1974
5 young men sail a 60 ft schooner to the South Seas and on to Singapore.

London, Jack
1876-1916
The Cruise of the Snark, 1911
From S. F. through the South Seas to Australia in a 45' WL schooner yacht 1907-1908.

Long, Dwight
Seven Seas on a Shoe String, 1938
Sailing all seven major oceans in the Idle Hour, a 32' ketch. The voyage lasts 3 years and covers 30,000 miles around the world.

Loomis, Alfred
The Cruise of the Hippocampus, 1922
Sailing a 28 ft. auxiliary yawl from New York to Balboa through the Caribbean.

Lormand, Ed
How to Sail the Atlantic Alone, 1980
A 44 day transatlantic voyage in 1977 aboard his 28 ft sloop.

Lyon, Captain G. F., R. N.
An Attempt to Reach Repulse Bay in His Majesty's Ship 'Gripper', 1971
This is a facsimile edition. This book was originally published in 1825 by John Murray, London.

Lubbock, Basil
The Romance of the Clipper Ships, 1958

Selections of Basil's articles from Sail magazine.

MacGregor, John
A Thousand Miles in the Rob Roy Canoe on Rivers and Lakes of Europe, [1866,] 1892
With Numerous Illustrations and a Map
The Voyage Alone in the Yawl Rob Roy, 1867, 1954
This is the story of a 1867 bit of showmanship — MacGregor sailing alone "a 21-foot sailing-boat from Limehouse to Dover, thence to Boulogne and along the north coast of France to the Seine, up the Seine to Paris, down again to Havre, and from Havre across the Channel to Littlehampton, the Solent; and thence back to the Thames. The 1954 edition with an introduc-tion by Arthur Ransome.

MacLean, Alistair
Captain Cook, 1972
Biography of England's greatest explorer by one of England's best known adventure novelists. Not terribly scholarly, but fun to read, and well illustrated.

Marin-Marie
Wind Aloft, Wind Alow, 1947
Two single-handed Atlantic crossings, under sail and under power. One of the classic solo voyage stories.

Maury, Richard
The Saga of Cimba, 1939
From New York to Fiji in a 35' Nova Scotian schooner. Discovers a group of Scandinavians who went to Galapogos Is. to start a Utopia, but ended up as feuding families, with the unexplained deaths of some members.

McCall, Paul Howard Fiona
All in the Same Boat,
(need description)
Still in the Same Boat, 1990
Family of four sails around the world in homemade sloop. Synopsis of previous account of beginning of voyage, then takes up narrative for the major part of the continuing voyage. A cautionary tale, showing considerable resource on part of a determined family.

McConnell, Carol & Malcolm
Middle Sea Autum, 1985
A 2500 mile passage through the Mediterranean aboard their 30 ft. sloop.

McCormick, Donald
Blood on the Sea, 1962
In 1884 the yawl Mignonette sank resulting in a 1500 mile dinghy voyage before the crew was rescued.

McKinney, Sam
Bligh, 1989
A true account of mutiny aboard His Majesty's Ship

Bounty. Extracts taken from the logs kept by Bligh, James Morrison, and Capt. Edwards of the Pandora.

McMullen, R.T.
Down Channel
Small boat sailing in British waters in the late 19th century. Now a yachting classic. Forward by Arthur Ransome.

Merrian, Jean
Lonely Voyagers, 1954
Chronicles of solo voyages beginning with Johnson in 1876, to Slocum, Gerbault, Blackburn, Voss, Rebell, Tambs and others.

Middleton, Empson Edward
The Cruise of "The Kate", 1953
A single-handed voyage in a small yacht around England and through Scotland in 1869.

Mitchell, Carleton
Passage East, 1953
1952 trans-Atlantic yacht race from Newport R. I. to Bermuda in a 57 ft yawl. 2870 miles in 21 days.

Moitessier, Bernard,
19??-1994
The First Voyage of the Joshua
1966 honeymoon voyage from Europe to the South Pacific and around Cape Horn. The longest non-stop voyage in a small boat at the time.
The Long Way, 1971
The 'hippy' sailor's account of his participation in the 1968 nonstop circumnavigation race and his decision not to finish but to continue on a 2nd circumnavi-gation.

Moore, Jim
By Way of the Wind, 1991
A circumnavigation aboard a 36' sloop by 2 novice sailors.

Manry, Robert
Tinkerbelle, 1965
The story of how a middle-aged, married copy editor of a major newspaper gets the idea of sailing across the Atlantic in a small boat. It is the story of the 13 1/2 foot 'Tinkerbelle', believed to be the smallest boat to ever cross the Atlantic non-stop. Manry wrote a good book describing his adventures during the 78 day voyage. He was washed overboard, was awak-ened by a submarine, suffered from strange hallucinations, was given a feast by a Belgian ship captain, and had numerous other adventures.

Mowat, Farley
The Boat Who Wouldn't Float, 1969, 1989
The author's adventure in his Newfoundland schooner Happy Adventure. Very funny and a good sailing story.

Muhlhauser, G. H. P.
The Cruise of the Amaryllis
Around the world, starting in England, 1920-23 in an 1882 built yawl.

Murphy, Robert Cushman
Logbook For Grace, 1947
A soon to be renown naturalist joins one of the last sailing whal-ing brigs in 1912, on a trip to the Antarctic seas. Besides meticu-lously executing his commission as a naturalist, he keeps a beauti-fully written personal journal for his newlywed wife Grace. A wonderful book.

Nalepka, James & Callahan, Steven
Capsized
Story of the 1989 capsize of a yacht and the 4 months the crew spent in a life boat in the wintry South Pacific waters. An "aston-ishing account of how they sur-vived an ordeal unsurpassed in the annals of survival".

Newby, Eric
The Last Grain Race, 1956
Newby sails to Australia and back around Cape Horn aboard the four masted bark Moshulu in 1938.

Newhall, Charles L.
The Adventures of Jack, 1981
A reprint of Newhall's adven-tures in the whaling fleet in the 1850's.

Nichols, Peter.
Sea Change: Alone across the Altlantic in a wooden boat.
Nichols and his wife bought and restored an old wooden sailboat, Toad, and lived aboard it for five years, sailing through the Caribbean and across the Alantic to Europe, where their marriage broke up. Sea Change is the story of Nichols's return to the sea alone. In the middle of the ocean, the twenty seven foot engineless Toad springs a leak, and Nichols struggles to keep his boat afloat. As he tests the limits of his courage and the depths of his fear, he discovers more than he knew about his marriage, his boat, and himself.

Nicolson, Ian
The Log of "The Maken", 1961
The voyage of Maken from England to Vancouver, Canada.

Nielke, Otto
Disaster at Sea, 1958
Stories of history's greatest mar-itime tragedies: lost at sea, rammed, battered by storms and sunk by fire and explosion.

Nilsen, Capt. J.
Leaves from the Log of the Homeward Bound: 11 Months at Sea in anOpen Boat, 1887
From Durban, South Africa to England aboard a 20 ft. gaff-rigged sailboat.

Novak, Skip
One Watch at a Time
Novak was the skipper of Drum during the '86 Whitbread. He tells the story from the purchase of Drum by rock star Simon Le Bon, to the fitting out, the Fastnet disaster in which Drum lost her keel and capsized, the Whitbread where she began to fall to pieces in a storm and her 3rd overall finish. A good read with lots of color photos.

O'Brian, Conor
From Three Yachts: A Cruiser's Outlook, 1928
Sailing adventures from 1910-1927 aboard a 26' cutter, Kelpie, a 42' ketch, Saoirse, and a 56' ketch, Llen.

Oxenhorn, Harvey
Tuning the Rig, A Journey to the Arctic, 1990
A poet joins the crew of a tall ship for a summer of whale research in the far North Atlantic.

Page, Frank
Solo to America, 1972
The 1972 Observer Singlehanded Race which Frank entered and including stories of the previous races.

Palmer, David
The Atlantic Challenge, The Story of Trimaran FT, 1977
FT was the first British boat to finish in the 1976 Observer Singlehanded Transatlantic Race. This is the story of FT's conception and racing history.

Pardey, Lin & Larry
The Capable Cruiser
How to choose the right boat for extended cruising. Then they talk about choosing the right gear and taking care of it and yourself as you cruise. There is a section on working with the crew. The final section talks about the sailors best relaxation pill, the anchor.
The Care and Feeding of the Offshore Crew
A diary of their trip across the Pacific. A list of what they ate each day and how to preserve food for a long trip. There are many simple tasty recipes they used while cruising.
Crusing in Seraffyn, 1976
Their first cruise in Seraffyn. Details the construction, as well as the justification of the 24' Seraffyn. The Pardeys sail from Newport Beach, California to England over 3 years with adventures in the Sea of Cortez, Mexico, Central America, the Caribbean, Virginia, Bermuda, and the Azores.
Well written and a source of inspiration to those who wish to just go cruising the world.
The Self-Sufficient Sailor
A compilation of the skills

learned by building and sailing a boat for many years. Larry shows many of the maintenance techniques used to preserve the materials and looks of a boat. Some tips on where to cruise and where to avoid. They also talk about how to make the cruising boat economical to have, use and maintain.
Seraffyn's European Adventure
Two and a half years of cruising from England through the Baltic Sea. They met a very different culture and many interesting adventures. They even dipped the mast in the Baltic. The story ends in Gibraltar where they spend the winter.
Seraffyn's Mediterranean Adventure
Covers the two and a half years they spent around Spain, Africa, Greece and Turkey. The best part about sailing is the people they meet and their adventures with them.
Seraffyn's Oriental Adventure, 1983
From the Red Sea through the Indian Ocean, The China Sea and the North Pacific and then home to Vancouver.

Payne, G.C.L.
Out of Poole, 1951
A 10,000 mile ocean voyage aboard a 40 ft. yacht from England to New York, then in the Newport to Bermuda race, and then back to Plymouth.

Pears, Charles
From the Thames to the Netherlands, 1914
A voyage in the waterways of Zealand and down the Belgian coast aboard the 25' cutter, Itchen Ferry.

Pidgeon, Harry
Around the World Single-Handed
The author's 1st circumnavigation in the 1920's in the 34 ft. yawl Islander, a boat he built. West out of LA, to the South Seas, across the Indian Ocean to South Africa, across the Atlantic, through the Panama Canal to home.

Pinchot, Gifford B.
Loki and Loon, 1985
Memorable moments aboard the 38' yawl Loki along the Atlantic coast, in Europe and in the Fastnet. Also aboard the 45' aluminum yawl Loon to Galapagos and the South Seas.
To the South Seas, 1930
The cruise of the schooner Mary Pinchot to the Galapagos, the Marquesas and Tuamotu Islands and Tahiti with the Pinchot Children aboard.

Plummer, Henry
The Boy, Me and the Cat
Author's Oct. 1912- Jun 1913 cruise with his son and cat aboard a catboat from Mass. to Fla. and back. Ship's log account

of the cruise. These were different times. Stray cows were fair game and the author provisioned his boat often by shooting a stray and hauling the carcass aboard. He also owned a 22 rifle with silencer nicknamed 'Helen Keller' with which he poaches ducks. Interesting reading.

Pope, Dudley
The Black Ship, (1963) 1998 (Owl Books)
A remarkably in-depth account of the bloodiest mutiny in Royal Naval history. Pope writes his account of the 1797 mutiny on the HMS Hermoine with insight into the personalities involved, a seaman's knowledge of ships and sailing and a novelist's skills at narrative and plot. If Pope's account is correct, Capt. Hugh Pigot of the Hermoine was a most despicable master and probably deserved becoming the victim of the bloodiest mutiny in British naval history. Pigot's uncontrollable temper with his crew, his extreme punishments for the most innocent crimes and his penchant for blaming his own mistakes on subordinates finally drove his men to the final act of mutiny and murder. Pope gives a detailed and exciting account of the events leading up to the mutiny, the mutiny itself and its aftermath.

Popham, Hugh & Robin
A Thirst For the Sea, 1979
The sailing adventures of Erskine Childers, the author of "Riddle of the Sands" and gun runner into Ireland.

Porter, Capt. David
Journal of a Cruise
The story of a cruise of the US frigate Essex to the Pacific, 1812-1814.

Pye, E. A.
Red Mails'l, 1952
A cruise from England through the West Indies aboard a 29', 52 year old sloop by the author and his wife.

Raban, Jonathan
Coasting, A Private Voyage, 1987
A circumnavigation of the British Isles in 1982.

Raigersfeld, Rear Admiral Jeffrey Baron de (1771-1844)
The Life of a Sea Officer, ca 1830 (published in Cassell's Seafarers' Library 1929)
Autobiography of an officer who entered the Royal Navy in 1785, was promoted to lieutenant in 1793 while serving at Toulon, was posted Captain in 1802, and had a not very distinguished career afloat and ashore until 1814.

Ransome, Arthur
Racundra's First Cruise, 1928, 1958
Ransome himself wrote a jolly

good account of his own sailings: "An account of very modest messing about in boats in the Eastern Baltic" (from the dust jacket)...... also (from a review of the book in Yachting Year)...."one of the finest of all cruising tales...."

Rebell, Fred (pseud.)
Escape to the Sea
Voyage from Sydney, Australia to Los Angeles in an 18' open racing dinghy, 1931-33 by an expatriate Latvian ("His name and his passport, like everything else, were homemade", from the introduction).

Ridgeway, John and Blyth, Chay
A Fighting Chance, 1967
Rowing a 22' dory across the Atlantic in 22 days.

Riding, John
The Voyage of the Sea Egg, 1968
An east to west passage of the Atlantic from Plymouth, England to Bermuda in a boat less than 12 ft.

Robertson, Robert Blackwood, 1913-
Of Whales and Men, 1954
Author, a British psychiatrist, sails as surgeon in a whaling factory ship full of Scots and Norwegian whalers to South Georgia and the "Zuther Notion" for the 1950-51 season.

Robertson, Dougal
Survive the Savage Sea, 1973
A British family struggle to survive a shipwreck in a leaky raft and tiny dingy.

Robinson, Charles E.
The Cruise of the Widgeon, 1876
700 miles in a 10 ton yawl from Swanage to Hamburg, through the Dutch canals and the Zuyder Zee, German Ocean and River Elbe.

Rockford, T.Jay and Daniel Parr, Daniel
T.Jay's Log: The Last Voyage of the Frisco Felucca II, 1995
An engagingly narrated account of an epic voyage that he and his companion, Ann Von Ramhorst, made from San Francisco to Mexico and, ultimately, Hawaii, in a converted $150 surplus lifeboat.

Rogers, Woodes d. 1732
A Cruising Voyage Round the World, 1712
Author commanded a privateer expedition around the world in 1708-1711. They captured a Spanish galleon and rescued the inspiration for Robinson Crusoe, Alexander Selkirk, from Juan Fernandez island.

de Roos, Willy
North-West Passage, 1979
Voyage through the NW passage in a 13 meter steel ketch in 1977.

Rose, Sir Alec
My Lively Lady, 1968
   After competing in a single handed race across the Atlantic, Rose sets out on a solo circum- navigation of the world. Having sailed for a total of 318 days he returns to London and is knighted by the Queen.

Roth, Hal
After 50,000 Miles, 1977
   Experiences of 11 years at sea, living aboard a 35 ft. yacht for extended passages.
Always a Distant Anchorage, 1988
   An account of a 46 month, 30,786 mile voyage around the world in a 10.7 meter cutter yacht built in Vancouver.
Chasing the Long Rainbow, 1990
   The story of Hal Roth's unspon- sored participation in the 1986- 87 BOC Challenge Race, sailing single-handed around the world in American Flag. Reissued in 1997 by seaworthy.com
Chasing the Wind, 1994
   The story of Hal Roth's second BOC Challenge Race 1990-91, sailing single-handed around the world in Sebago. Reissued in 1997 by seaworthy.com
The Longest Race, 1983.
   An account of the 1968 Golden Globe race, describing each of the 9 contestants' backgrounds and voyages, including Robin Knox-Johnson, the only one to finish, and Donald Crowhurst, who tried to fake his circumnavi- gation(see The Strange Voyage of Donald Crowhurst).
Two on a Big Ocean, 1972
   Personal account of a man and woman who circumnavigate the Pacific in a 35 ft. sailboat.

Ruhen, Olaf 1911-
Minerva Reef, 1962
   Sailing cutter full of Tongans on their way to New Zealand in the 1950s wrecks on remote barren reef, submerged at high tide except for the hulk of a wrecked Japanese fishing boat, where they survive months of hardship while awaiting rescue and finally build a small boat to send for help.

Samuels, Capt. Samuel
From the Forecastle to the Cabin, 1924, 1926
   The memoirs of Capt. Samuel Samuels of the famous packet ship Dreadnought. Samuels spent 50 years at sea beginning in 1836.

Sargent, Henry Jackson
The Captain of the Phantom, 1967
   The story of Henry Jackson Sargent, Jr., 1834-1862, as revealed in family letters. The clipper ship master lost his ship Phantom on the Pratas Shoals, 200 miles southeast of Hong Kong.

Schildt, Goran
In the Wake of Odysseus, (translated by Alan Blair) 1953
   With his wife, sailing "Daphne" through Geek waters and a 3000 mile journey.
In the Wake of a Wish, 1954
   Sailing aboard a 34 ft. ketch from Finland through the French canals to the Mediterranean.

Schmitt, Lou A.
All Hands Aloft!, 1965
   An account of the voyage of the square-rigger Arapahoe to Manila in 1918. The author, a 16 yr. old Oregon farmboy, sails as a U.S. merchant marine cadet in the big Clyde built full rigged ship Arapahoe from San Francisco to the Philippines with a load of dynamite and gasoline during WWI.

Sculley, Vince, 1985
Poles Apart With Northanger, 1991
   Sailing in Antarctic and Arctic waters. Vince was on Northanger for the first season of her voyage through the Northwest Passage.

Seligman, Adrian
The Voyage of the Cap Pilar, 1939
   A group of impecunious friends buy a delapidated 3 masted square rigger during depression years and head to the south seas to find adventure and fortune.

Severin, Tim, 1940
The Brendan Voyage, 1978
   Sailing a leather boat across the Atlantic, recreating the voyage of St Brendan who sailed to America before the Vikings and 1000 years before Colombus.
The Sinbad Voyage, 1982
   Building an Arab dhow and sail- ing it to China.
The Jason Voyage: the quest for the golden fleece, 1985
   Building and sailing a greek ship to the Black Sea, folowing the route of Jason in search of the golden fleece.
The China Voyage, 1994
   Crossing the Pacific on a bamboo raft.
The Ulysses Voyage, 1987
   Retracing the voyage home by Ulysses after the Trojan war.

Seymout, John
'Willynilly' to the Baltic, 1965
   The author and a crew of one sail a 21' Northumberland coble, rigged with a dipping lugsail from Northumberland, England, to Copenhagen, via Belgium, the Netherlands, Germany and Sweden.

Shackleton, Sir Ernest
South! 1920
   The story of Shackleton's last expedition (1914-1917), by the expedition's leader.

Shairer, Gerda and Jameson, Egon
Heroes of British Lifeboats, 1938
   Exciting rescues along the British coasts as told by the life- boatmen themselves.

Sharp, Andrew
Ancient Voyagers in the Pacific, 1956
   The Polynesian exploration of the Pacific, written for the gen- eral reader by a scholar in the field. Fascinating account of how these barbarian sea kings settled the Pacific.

Shaw, Frank Hubert
White Sails and Spindrift, 1947
   Literally awesome...57 days try- ing to make the horn rounding the hard way as Shaw relates his early days on the England-Pacific routes.

Shelvocke, Captain George (1675–1742)
A Voyage Round the World, 1726 (published in Cassell's Seafarers' Library 1928)
   Account of a cruise, under Letters of Marque, against the Spaniards in the Pacific, 1719- 1722. It started with 2 ships and 286 men, ended with1 ship car- rying Shelvocke, 32 men, and considerable gold and other booty. An incident on the voyage in which an albatross was shot inspired Coleridge to write "The Ancient Mariner".

Sherwood, Martyn
The Voyage of the Tai-Mo-Shan, 1957
   The story of a 54 ft. ketch built in a Hong Kong shipyard and sailed back to England via Japan, Alaska and the Panama Canal.

Slocum, Joshua
Sailing Alone Around the World, 1900
   Slocum's solo circumnavigation aboard the 37' Spray.
Voyage of the Liberdade, 1894
   After Slocum is wrecked in Brazil (1886), he builds a 35' cross between a dory and a canoe with Chinese lugsails and sails it back to NY with his wife and two sons.
The Voyage of the Destroyer from New York to Brazil, 1894
   Slocum skippers a monitor being towed from NY to Brazil, Dec. '93 to Jan. '94.

Slocum, Victor
Capt. Joshua Slocum: The Life and Voyages of America's Best Known Sailor, 1950
   Bio of Slocum by his son, who accompanied him in the Liberdade. This book details some of Slocum's adventures the Capt. never wrote about and gives a different view of those he did write about.

Smeeton, Miles
Once Is Enough, 1959
   While sailing from Australia to the Atlantic, via the Horn, in a 46' ketch, their boat is pitch poled and his wife is thrown 30 yds. from the boat.
Because the Horn is There, 1971
   Their third attempt to round the Horn in a voyage from England to British Columbia. (Apparently once was NOT enough)

Snaith, William
Across the Western Ocean, 1966
   From the log of the 'Figaro' on a Transatlantic cruise and a Transatlantic Race, with some sea-borne meditations of her Skipper.
On the Wind's Way, 1973
   The account of the transatlantic race from Bermuda to Sweden on board the 46 foot yawl Figaro III.

Snow, Edward Rowe
Great Sea Rescues; and tales of survival, 1958

Snow, Capt. Elliot, ed.
Adventures at Sea in the Great Age of Sail
   5 true stories on high adventure on the high seas aboard tall ships.

Spiess, Gerry
Alone Against the Atlantic, 1981
   A 54 day voyage aboard the small- est sailboat the author could build and still survive the open sea. Spiess was a beginning school teacher when he decided to build a 10 foot plywood sail- boat and sail alone across the Atlantic. His problems and frustrations as he builds the boat named "Yankee Girl", as well as his Atlantic cross- ing are described in detail.

Steel, David J.
Yachtman in Red China, 1970
   While on assignment overseas, Steele built 4 boats and experi- enced some hair-raising adven- tures during his sailing ventures in the East.

Tabarly, Eric
Lonely Victory, 1967
   The 1964 OSTAR from Plymouth to Newport. The author beats Chichester's 1960 record by completing the cross- ing in 27 days.

Tambs, Erling
The Cruise of the Teddy, 1934
   A three year cruise around the world with 2 small children aboard a 40' cutter, ending in a dramatic shipwreck near Auckland.

Tangvald, Peter
At Any Cost: Love, Life and Death at Sea
   Autobiography of a man who built his own 49' wooden gaff rigged cutter and sail with his wife around the world. In 1991, while sailing with his son and daughter, the boat smashed into a coral reef killing Peter and his daughter.

Thomas, Stephen D.
The Last Navigator, 1987
   The author attempts to preserve

the secrets of Polynesian navigation by seeking out and becoming the student of a venerated polynesian navigator.

Thompson, Harold W., editor
The Last of the Logan, 1941
True adventures of Robert Coffin, Mariner, in the years 1854-1859. Pursuit of whales, shipwreck on Rapid Reef, life among the cannibals of Fiji and search for gold in Australia.

Thompson, Keith A.
HMS Beagle, The Story of Darwin's Ship, 1995
History of the ship in which Darwin made his epic voyage. The book focus's on the mystery of the ship' appearance, the history of 10-gun "coffin brigs" class to which the ship belongs, the Beagle's three expeditions of exploration and vessels ultimate fate. Much of the book reads like an adventure novel, but the story is true.

Tilman, H. W.
In Mischief's Wake, 1971
After Mischief met her end, the next summer found the author off the coast of Greenland with a new crew and a new boat, Sea Breeze, a pilot cutter.
Mischief Goes South, 1968
Mostly Mischief, 1966
Mischief in Greenland, 1964
Mischief Among the Penguins
Ice with Everything, 1974
Triumph and Tribulation, 1977
Tilman and crew sail 'baroque' a 50 foot cutter on three voyages to Greenland, Iceland and Spitzbergen

Tomalin, T. & Hall R.
The Strange Voyage of Donald Crowhurst
Account of Crowhurst's faked circumnavigation in the 1968 Golden Globe race and his subsequent suicide when he couldn't face the consequences.

Tompkins, John Barr (editor)
A Voyage of Pleasure, 1956
The log of Bernard Gilboy's singlehanded trans-pacific cruise in 1882-83 aboard a 19 ft. boat. The voyage originated in San Francisco and terminated in Australia.

Uring, Captain Nathaniel
(ca 1682–1742)
Voyages and Travels, 1726
(published in Cassell's Seafarers' Library 1928)
Was at sea during the first 20 years of the 18th century, in both the Royal and the Merchant Navy. Travelled to West Indies, West Africa, Angola, New England, Mediterranean.

Veedam, Voldemar and Wall, Carl
Sailing to Freedom.
Extended family of Estonian refugees sail through Sweden and across the Atlantic.

Vihlen, Hugo
April Fool, 1971
The author sails a six foot boat, "the size of a bathtub", from Casablanca to Florida using sails and a 3-hp outboard.

Villiers, Alan 1903-
Sons of Sinbad, 1940
An account of sailing with the Arabs in their dhows, in the Red Sea, around the coasts of Arabia, and to Zanzibar and Tanganyika; pearling in the Persian Gulf; and the life of the ship masters, the mariners, and merchants of Kuwait. Author sails in a Kuwaiti dhow to Africa in the late 30's.
Cruise of the Conrad
A journal of a voyage round the world, undertaken and carried out in the ship Joseph Conrad, 212 tons, in the years 1934, 1935 and 1936 by way of Good Hope, the East Indies, the South Seas and Cape Horn.
The Quest of the Schooner Argus: A Voyage to the Banks of Greenland, 1951
A codfishing trip with Portuguese dorymen in 1950.
By Way of Cape Horn
A tragic voyage from Australia to England in the fully-rigged ship Grace Harwar in 1929.
The Set of Sails
Villiers autobiography.
The Voyage of the Parma, 1933
The Great Grain Race of 1932, aboard the four masted barque Parma, from Australia to England in 103 days, racing around the Horn.
Falmouth for Orders, 1929
Young newspaper reporter Villiers ships out as sailor in the 4 masted steel bark Herzogin Cecilie when she races the bark Beatrice from Australia around Cape Horn to Falmouth England in 1927 loaded with grain. The last clipper ship race around Cape Horn.
Vanished Fleets, 1931
Account of trade and sailing anecdotes around Tasmania and Australia in the late 1800's and early part of this century. An early work of this well regarded and prolific maritime author.

The War with Cape Horn, 1971
Recorded from logs and diaries of able seamen and captains. The achievements and disasters of the past 100 years rounding Cape Horn in square riggers.

Violet, Charles
Solitary Journey, 1954
The author sails his 20' yawl from Britain to France and transits the French canal system to the Mediterranean. He then visits Sicily, Corsica, Italy, northern Africa and winters over in France before returning to England via the canals of France. A well written account of an enviable adventure with an enphasis on places visited and people met.

Vogel, Karl
Aloha Around the World, 1922
A windjammer voyage in 1921-1922 aboard a 218 ft. steel bark, Aloha. Through the Suez and Panama canals.

Voss, John Claus 1854-1922
The Venturesome Voyages of Captain Voss, 1913
A treasure hunt to Cocos Island from British Columbia in a 30' sloop, a voyage from Victoria to London in a modified 38' indian dugout war canoe in 1901-190?, and riding out a typhoon off Japan in a 19' Sea Bird style yawl. A classic.

Vogt, Richard J.
Altering Course, 1978

Walter, Richard
Anson's Voyage Around the World, 1748
Author was chaplain aboard the British ship HNS Centurion when she was sent to the west coast of Spanish America in 1740, and then the rest of the way around the world. They managed to capture a Manila Galleon and some of them, not very many, survived many hardships. It is interesting to compare this book with Woodes Roger's account of his similar voyage.

Whipple, A.B.C.
The Challenge, 1987
A well organized history of the story of the clippers with an account of a "race" between two of the last and best ships in the mid 1850's.

Wharram, James
Two Girls, Two Catamarans, 1969
Two trans-Atlantic voyages aboard a 23 ft. and then a 40 ft. home made catamaran.

Wightman, Frank
The Wind is Free, 1955
Two men aboard a 34 ft. yawl, Wylo, sailing from Cape Town to the Caribbean in 1947.

Williams, James H.
Blow the Man Down: A Yankee Seaman's Adventures Under Sail, 1959
An autobiography of a black man's adventures at sea, surviving two shipwrecks.

Willimas, Neville
The Sea Dogs, 1975
Privateers, plunder and piracy in the Elizabethan Age. Includes Drake, Hawkins, Grenville, Raleigh, Willoughby, Chancellor, Humphrey Gilbert, John Davys and Cavendish.

Wilmore, C. Ray
Square Rigger Around the Horn, 1972
The making of a sailor. Life aboard the steel 4-masted bark, John Ena, in 1911.

Wilson, Derek
The Circumnavigators, 1989
Global circumnavigations from Magellan through Dodge Morgan in 1985. Emphasis on the seamanship required and difficulties encountered in each era.

Woolass, Peter
Stelda, George, & I, 1971
A single handed sailing adventure from England to the Caribbean.

Worsley, Frank Arthur 1872-1943
First Voyage in a Square-Rigged Ship, 1947
His Autobiography, with day-to-day detail of life in a windjammer and other seafaring adventures. Later in life he captained the Endurance, sailing with Shackleton to Antarctica (see title below).
Shackleton's Boat Journey, 1977
1914 Antarctic expedition is trapped when their ship is crushed by ice. The expedition leader sails to South Georgia in a lifeboat to get help. Worsley was the ship's captain and went on the small boat voyage. A most remarkable small boat journey.

Zantzinger, Richard
Log of the Molly Brown, 1973
Sailing a 35' sloop 31,000 miles around the world in 14 months.

Zweig, Stefan
Magellan, 1948
The Pioneer of the Pacific. His voyage to the Pacific and circumnavigation with only 1 returning ship in 1522.

Index

Photo Credits

Hal Roth: p. 2, 17, 59, 78, 139, 118, 124, 200, 218, 229b, 249t, 252, 254 (both), 268

Jacques Vapillon: p. 8, 42, 43, 61, 81, 91b, 92 (both), 93, 187, 196, 198, 201, 202, 210, 211t, 274

PPL: p. 12, 46 (Tom Benn), 48 (Alastair Black), 49 (Tom Benn), 51t (Alastair Black), 51b, 60, 93, 105 (Raaf), 108 (Nigel Bennetts), 181bl (Philippe Schiller), 181br (Philippe Schiller), 182 (Philippe Schiller), 183, 189 (Jon Nash), 195 (Barry Pickthall), 197 (David Tease), 206 (Jay Town), 207 (Ian

Mainsbridge), 211b, 212 (both), 220 (Ian Mainsbridge), 226 (Ian Mainsbridge), 230 (Roel Engels), 232 (

Corbis: p. 14t, 18, 19, 20, 25, 27, 31, 32, 62, 74, 80, 82, 135, 110, 115, 116, 194, 204, 205, 208, 226, 228, 251b, 257

National Maritime Museum: 14b, 15t, 15b, 16, 24, 64 (both), 65, 83, 84 (both), 86 (both), 87, 91t, 120, 225 (both), 246, 248

© Rosenfeld Collection, Mystic Seaport Museum, Inc.: p. 22, 30, 50, 52, 53, 54, 57, 58, 88, 190, 191, 221b, 229t

The Mariner's Museum: p. 23, 26, 56, 113, 219, 221t, 240, 242, 249b, 250b, 251t

Peabody Esssex Museum: p. 250t

James Mitchell: p. 69, 98, 238

AP/World Wide Photos: p. 90, 130, 224

Carlos Calderon: p. 106, 233

United States Coast Guard Historical Office: p. 126, 127 (DM Schaefer), 128, 181t

Reprint Credits

Excerpt from The Armada by Garrett Mattingly copyright © 1959 Garrett Mattingly. Copyright renewed © 1987 by Leonard H. Mattingly. Reprinted by premission of Houghton Mifflin Co. All rights reserved.

Excerpt from My Old Man and the Sea by David Hays and Daniel Hays copyright © 1995 by the author. Reprinted by permission of Algonquin Books of Chapel Hill, a division of Workman Publishing.

Excerpt from Ice Bird by David Lewis copyright © 1975 by the author. Reprinted by permission of W. W. Norton & Company.

Excerpt from A World of My Own by Robin Knox-Johnston copyright © 1969 by the author. Reprinted by permission of W. W. Norton & Company.

Excerpt from The Perfect Storm by Sebastian Junger copyright © 1997 by the author. Reprinted by permission of W. W. Norton & Company.

Excerpt from Survive the Savage Sea by Dougal Robertson reprinted by permission with Sheridan House, Inc.

Excerpt from The Long Way by Bernard Moitessier reprinted by permission with Sheridan House, Inc.

Maiden Voyage by Tania Aebi with Bernadette Brennan reprinted with the permission of Simon & Schuster. Copyright © 1989 by Tania Aebi.